THE COLOR OF WORK

THE STRUGGLE FOR CIVIL RIGHTS IN THE SOUTHERN PAPER INDUSTRY, 1945-1980

TIMOTHY J. MINCHIN

THE UNIVERSITY OF NORTH CAROLINA PRESS   CHAPEL HILL & LONDON

Portions of Chapter 3 previously appeared in Timothy J. Minchin, "Federal Policy and the Racial Integration of Southern Industry, 1961–1980," *Journal of Policy History* 11, no. 2 (1999): 147–78 (© 1999 by The Pennsylvania State University Press; reproduced by permission of the publisher). An earlier version of Chapter 9 was published as Timothy J. Minchin, " 'There Were Two Job in St. Joe Paper Company, White Job and Black Job': The Struggle for Civil Rights in a North Florida Paper Mill Community, 1938–1990," *Florida Historical Quarterly* 78, no. 3 (Winter 2000): 331–59 (reproduced by permission of the Florida Historical Society).

Manufactured in the United States of America
Designed by April Leidig-Higgins
Set in Minion by Keystone Typesetting, Inc.

The paper in this book meets the guidelines for permanence and durability of the Committee on Production Guidelines for Book Longevity of the Council on Library Resources.

Library of Congress Cataloging-in-Publication Data
Minchin, Timothy J.
The color of work : the struggle for civil rights in the Southern paper industry, 1945–1980 / Timothy J. Minchin.
p. cm.
Includes bibliographical references and index.
ISBN 0-8078-2618-9 (cloth: alk. paper)
ISBN 0-8078-4933-2 (pbk.: alk. paper)
1. Discrimination in employment—Southern States—History—20th century. 2. Paper industry workers—Southern States—History—20th century. 3. Race discrimination—Southern States—History—20th century. 4. African-American labor union members—Southern States—History—20th century. I. Title.
HD4903.3.P332 U66 2001
331.13′3—dc21   00-068312

05 04 03 02 01 5 4 3 2 1

CONTENTS

ILLUSTRATIONS AND TABLES

ACKNOWLEDGMENTS

This project began in 1996 when I came across the records of several large civil rights lawsuits involving southern paper mills at the Federal Records Center in East Point, Georgia. I decided to look into the struggle for civil rights in the South's paper mills and was only able to do so because of the expertise of the staff at the Federal Records Center. They helped me a great deal during my prolonged visits, especially in locating cases that often proved difficult to track down.

This manuscript also owes a great debt to the staff of the United Paperworkers' International Union, who helped me locate large numbers of both whites and blacks who worked in the industry between the 1930s and the 1970s. Many valuable interviews resulted from these contacts. At the union's headquarters in Nashville, Leeann Anderson showed a immense interest in this topic from the start and assisted me a great deal in arranging interviews. I am also grateful to several other union officers and staff members in Nashville, particularly Boyd Young. My chief debt, however, is to Chuck Spence, a former paper worker who served as an international representative for the UPIU in the South between 1972 and 2000. Chuck's knowledge of the southern paper industry is unsurpassed, and he was instrumental in arranging interviews across the region. He also welcomed me into his home while I was staying in Alabama. Various members of his family, particularly Vonnie, Kyle, Kimberly, D. J., Jennifer, and Elizabeth, brightened up my research trips.

Many other people helped me a great deal in arranging interviews in various towns across the South. I am very grateful to Ben Montgomery, who helped me set up several valuable interviews in Savannah, Georgia, and Charleston, South Carolina. In Mobile, Alabama, Donald Langham and Ima Jean Bounds provided much assistance. Elvin King helped me in Moss Point, Mississippi, and in Port St. Joe, Florida, Lamar Speights arranged and rode with me to several interviews. Several retired company executives, particularly John VanDillon and Ed Bartlett, were also very helpful.

I am grateful to both the Mellon Research Fund at Cambridge University and the School of History at the University of St. Andrews for financial assistance. A grant from the Carnegie Trust for the Universities of Scotland also enabled me to carry out some follow-up research. Some of the early writing was carried out while I was a fellow at Sidney Sussex College, Cambridge, and I would like to thank the college for providing such a supportive research environment. I am especially grateful to the late Graham Smith, with whom I had many enjoyable and productive lunches at Sidney Sussex. I miss his sound advice and friendship. A great deal of writing was also carried out in St. Andrews, and I am very grateful to my colleagues in Scotland for the consistent encouragement that they have given to my research. I especially wish to thank Keith Brown, Steve Spackman, Richard Saville, Michael Bentley, and Jerry DeGroot for all their support and encouragement.

I am very grateful to Bob Zieger, who read an early draft of this manuscript and consistently provided me with friendship and advice. Tom Terrill and Jim Hodges also read drafts of the manuscript and provided helpful support and advice. Tony Badger has continued to provide encouragement and guidance, as have Jim Leloudis and Howell Harris. I would also like to thank the staff of the University of North Carolina Press for all their help in seeing this project to publication. Finally, I owe a great debt to my family for all their help and love, especially to my parents and to my wife, Olga.

June 2000
Cupar, Scotland

ABBREVIATIONS

BVL	Bogalusa Voters' League
DSA	Defense Supply Agency
EEOC	Equal Employment Opportunity Commission
GSA	General Services Administration
IBPSPMW	International Brotherhood of Pulp, Sulphite, and Paper Mill Workers
IP	International Paper Company
LDF	Legal Defense Fund
NAACP	National Association for the Advancement of Colored People
OFCC	Office of Federal Contract Compliance
SNCC	Student Non-Violent Co-Ordinating Committee
UPIU	United Paperworkers' International Union
UPP	United Papermakers and Paperworkers
Westvaco	West Virginia Pulp and Paper Company

THE COLOR OF WORK

INTRODUCTION

Shortly after 4 o'clock on the afternoon of May 19, 1977, Henry Armistead Jr. rose to take the stand at Washington County courthouse in Plymouth, North Carolina. A fifty-one-year-old black worker, Armistead had come to testify about the racial discrimination he had experienced in the twenty-five years he had worked at the Weyerhauser Company, the paper mill that dominated Plymouth's economy. Armistead related that jobs at the mill had been strictly segregated, with blacks forbidden from operating positions: "They had a black and white job, that's just the way it was. . . . Very definitely back in the years when I was a crane helper there was very much discrimination—There was discrimination on the parts that we couldn't go up for operators . . . you very definitely couldn't go up for an operator." Armistead remembered that he trained whites for the crane even though he was not allowed to become an operator: "I trained several white operators out there myself. I could train them and teach them to run the cranes, but I very definitely couldn't run them myself." He asserted that his experience was typical of the problems faced by black workers at the mill: "Well, it's not only the way I've been discriminated against, it's against every black that's ever worked out there. Every black that's ever worked on that yard can tell you there is discrimination there. You don't have to look for it to see it. It was all right in front of you. You just didn't get it because they didn't let you have it."[1]

Armistead's testimony epitomized that given by many other black paper workers in lawsuits brought under Title VII of the 1964 Civil Rights Act. He highlighted the extent of discrimination that prevailed across the southern paper industry in the 1940s and 1950s. Jobs were assigned as "white" or "black," with white jobs invariably being well-paid operating positions and black jobs, lower-paid laboring jobs. These jobs were represented by segregated unions, a system that existed across the southern paper industry until the mid-1960s.[2] Thus, it was agreed by both sides in a major case against one of the largest paper companies that "racial segregation of jobs and local unions was characteristic of the pulp and paper industry throughout the South." This system of strict segregation produced a rash of lawsuits when the 1964 Civil Rights Act prohibited racial discrimination in employment.[3]

Thousands of African Americans worked in paper mills under the strict system of segregation that Armistead outlined. Many of them gave similar testimony in the scores of lawsuits that took place in the South between 1964 and 1980. In recent years, there has been an upsurge of studies of southern workers, and southern labor history has emerged as an important and growing field. Influential studies have appeared on southern workers in industries as diverse as textiles, coal mining, and longshoring.[4] Despite the growing number of studies being published on southern workers, very little attention has been focused on the paper industry.[5]

One of the most notable trends of the recent scholarship is its concentration upon race. In particular, a number of studies have explored the possibilities for interracial unionism in the South. A "new southern labor history" has argued persuasively that interracial unionism was possible where union leadership confronted the race issue and utilized black militancy.[6] Writers who have explored interracial unionism, however, have paid no attention to the paper industry. It is vital to reverse this neglect, especially given the major role that the paper industry has played in the southern economy.

Focusing on the paper industry offers an excellent opportunity to extend our knowledge of southern workers and to contribute to the interracial unionism debate. Prior to the 1960s, the industry was one of the largest employers of black labor in the South. Unlike leading southern industries such as textiles, the paper industry did not exclude blacks but instead restricted them to a defined number of undesirable jobs. The paper industry was also unusual in that it was solidly unionized. In fact, from the time that paper mills first located in the South in the 1920s and 1930s, companies recognized unions and the industry had an almost 100 percent unionization rate. These two factors meant that the issue of interracial unionism was always of vital importance in the paper industry. The fact that African Americans have always been hired in the paper industry, in particular, ensured that unions were pushed to confront the race issue early on.

The response of unions was to organize on a segregated basis. As the paper industry developed in the South on a large-scale basis, it became the norm to organize segregated local unions. Over sixty separate black locals were in existence by the end of the 1950s, operating alongside an even greater number of all-white locals. Segregated unions were commonplace in the region, especially in unions such as the Tobacco Workers' International Union, the International Longshoremen's Association, and the Brotherhood of Railway Carmen of America. The "new southern labor history," however, has generally concentrated on progressive unions that often were under a significant communist influence.[7] In contrast, very little is known about the large number of unions that failed to confront the black question fully, hence the experience of workers who belonged to segregated locals remains unexamined.

A study of the paper industry also allows us to explore the crucial question of whether black workers tried to use unions to fight racial discrimination. As Alan Draper has noted in a recent study, the question of whether southern black trade unionists saw their unions as a "legitimate or relevant conduit for their civil rights demands" has yet to be explored by historians. The paper industry, with its tradition of black employment and high rate of unionization, offers an excellent opportunity to answer this question.[8]

Study of the paper industry also takes us into an area of the South that has been overlooked by other historiography. Paper mills were generally located in remote, rural areas away from major towns. They were often the largest industrial employer for a large geographical area and thus possessed considerable economic, cultural, and political influence. Yet perhaps because of their remote location, little has been written about the Deep South areas dominated by the paper industry, such as small towns in Panhandle Florida and eastern North Carolina. It was often in small, isolated communities that white resistance to job integration was strongest. The strength of opposition to integration is explored in this book through a case study of Port St. Joe, Florida, a small paper mill community that witnessed one of the largest and longest-lasting Title VII cases in the paper industry.[9]

Armistead's testimony highlights the fact that rich and often neglected sources exist for scholars to explore black employment in the southern paper industry. In the 1960s and 1970s, virtually every southern paper mill was engaged in a class action racial discrimination lawsuit brought under Title VII of the 1964 Civil Rights Act. Title VII of the act outlawed discrimination in employment, making it an unlawful practice "to fail or refuse to hire or to discharge any individual, or otherwise to discriminate against any individual with respect to his compensation, terms, conditions, or privileges of employment, because of such individual's race, color, religion, sex, or national origin." The Civil Rights Act created the Equal Employment Opportunity Commission (EEOC) to monitor and enforce compliance with the act. The commission was authorized to solve job discrimination complaints through "conference, conciliation, and persuasion." If the EEOC failed to achieve voluntary compliance within sixty days, however, it was required to notify the complainants that they were permitted, within the next thirty days, to bring civil action.[10]

The records of lawsuits brought under Title VII are voluminous and valuable. The depositions and trial testimony of African American plaintiffs, in particular, give voice to blue-collar workers, allowing them to describe in detail the conditions that they faced in their working lives. Claim forms and letters written by black workers also highlight their motives for protesting against the industry's racial practices. Legal records allow us to examine closely the efforts that black workers often made to tackle discrimination through their unions before they turned to federal agencies. These records are also valuable because they contain a great deal of information that might otherwise be shielded from the historian, including material reproduced directly from company records. In particular, court testimony often pushed company officials to explain the reasons for the industry's historic practices of racial segregation.

These legal records are supplemented by a large body of oral history interviews, including many with African Americans who were members of segregated unions. Their memories offer valuable insights into the black experience in the paper industry, calling attention to the way that separate black locals pushed repeatedly to end racially discriminatory job assignments. The paper industry, however, was characterized by determined white resistance to integration, and interviews with retired white workers offer valuable insights into the strength of this resistance. These interviews highlight a hidden history of integration that was characterized by harassment, violence, and boycotts of integrated facilities. Job integration represented only part of the major adjustment that white workers were forced to make as segregation was broken down simultaneously in schools, in public accommodation, and at the ballot box. In the paper mill community of Bogalusa, Louisiana, for example, major civil rights protests occurred in the town at the same time that these rapid changes were taking place, exacerbating white resistance and anger.

The struggle for civil rights in the southern paper industry uncovers a number of other important untold stories. As in the textile industry, federal intervention was key in pushing companies to curtail discrimination. The Office of Federal Contract Compliance (OFCC) was especially influential because it negotiated an agreement with International Paper Company in 1968 that was copied by paper mills across the South. The Jackson Memorandum, so called because the negotiations were conducted in the Mississippi state capitol, is well known in the paper industry and widely acknowledged as a vital part of the struggle for civil rights in the industry. Despite its importance, this landmark agreement has yet to be explored in detail.

The federal government also had a considerable impact on southern paper workers themselves. Its Civil Rights Act of 1964 was critical in stimulating protest among black paper workers. Recognizing that nondiscrimination was now a federal law, black paper workers were encouraged to protest against segregation and were determined to make the act's mandate a reality. Since historians usually view the act as a culmination of civil rights protest rather than the cause of it, the fact that the act stimulated a new round of black protest is significant.[11]

The Civil Rights Act, however, was far more effective as a weapon of protest than as a weapon of change. It provided the machinery for African American workers to fight discrimination, but because of resistance from companies and white workers, the battle to secure integrated jobs and facilities was long and difficult. Efforts to integrate the industry were hampered by lingering ideas of segregated job assignments and white resistance to blacks gaining access to white jobs. The color of work was the central theme of the struggle for civil rights in the paper industry between World War II through to the 1980s. Thus, in the late 1960s and 1970s, the EEOC and federal courts repeatedly found that historic patterns of job segregation remained intact in many mills. In a typical decision in 1968, for example, the EEOC found that black workers at International Paper Company in Moss Point, Mississippi, were still frozen in "all-Negro and low-paid job classifications in all-Negro lines of progression" that had changed little since the early 1950s.[12]

Many of those who worked in the pulp and paper industry during the era of segregated locals are conscious of the fact that the story of the industry's integration has been left untold. This feeling is shared by white union leaders who now acknowledge that unions failed to confront the race issue. "This is a story that needs to be told," declared United Paperworkers' International Union (UPIU) president Boyd Young in 1997. "This is part of our history, whether its uncomfortable or not, it happened, we've got to talk about it."[13]

CHAPTER 1
IRRETRIEVABLY MIRED
IN UNDESIRABLE JOBS
THE COLOR OF WORK
BEFORE THE 1960S

Across the South, African American men helped build many of the first paper mills in the region in the 1930s and 1940s, going to work in them when they were completed. These workers, testifying in court cases in the 1970s, often had had a lifetime of experience in the southern paper industry, yet they usually had held laboring jobs all their lives and the positions they filled at the end of their working lives were often less skilled than those they had performed as young men when they first helped build the mills. In Plymouth, North Carolina, many black men left farming to help build the huge paper mill that was established in the town in 1937. Samuel H. Moore, for example, quit farming and helped clear the land that the paper mill was built on. Once the plant opened, he got a laboring job "pulling" wood in the woodyard, a position that he still held forty-one years later.[1] In 1937, Alphonse Gaillard helped build the West Virginia Pulp and Paper Company (Westvaco) plant in Charleston, and he was still working for the company when he took part in *Gantlin v. Westvaco* thirty-five years later. Despite Gaillard's long record of service, the official complaint in the case described how his job was one of the lowest paid at the plant, adding, "No white employee has been so grossly mistreated."[2]

The life stories of these workers typified the problems faced by African Americans who worked in the South's paper mills between the 1930s and the 1960s. As the industry became established in the South, it operated on a strictly segregated basis that restricted blacks to a small number of laboring positions. Black workers found that the industry offered no outlet for their skills; regardless of their abilities, they were limited to menial, laboring work with few opportunities for promotion. In Savannah, Georgia, veteran black worker James Tyson summed up the limited opportunities available to blacks at the Union Camp paper mill, where he started working in 1945: "The conditions was that all labor, all blacks were given the menial task jobs, clean-up, they was doing a lot of log work, they would do all this kind of work, clean-up behind the whites. They wasn't any progression jobs at Union Camp for blacks. The jobs in progression was all white. . . . The company gave certain jobs with no progression, nonprogression jobs, to blacks." In the paper industry, Tyson added, "the black stayed back."[3]

As Tyson related, the crux of the problem for black workers concerned promotional opportunities. In the paper industry, jobs were organized into lines of progression, collections of related jobs that were theoretically ranked according to the skill and experience necessary to perform each job. As workers became skilled and experienced in the lowest job in the line of progression, they built seniority. When a vacancy occurred in the next highest job in the line of progression, then the worker with the most seniority in that line of progression theoretically received the job.[4]

Most southern mills, however, had segregated lines of progression, with separate local unions having jurisdiction over particular jobs. Black lines of progression usually covered a small number of undesirable jobs, whereas white lines were invariably longer and led to the best jobs. On some occasions, black "lines of progression" covered only one job. As seniority in one line of progression could not be transferred to another, black workers were locked into a single job or the small number of jobs in their line. Any workers wishing to change lines of progression had to forfeit their seniority and start at the bottom of the new line of progression, a sacrifice that few were willing to make. The court's decision in one of the major Title VII cases summed up the situation: "For a white employee, seniority on the job could be used to advance into jobs with more opportunity and higher pay. To most black employees, however, seniority meant nothing. A black employee often reached the pinnacle of his one-job 'line of progression' on the first day he started work. . . . Because transfers into white lines of progression were made impossible by the jurisdictional seniority system, black workers were irretrievably mired in undesirable jobs, no matter how much seniority they accumulated."[5]

Separate lines of progression thus limited blacks to a small number of laboring jobs. The vast majority of jobs in paper mills were under the jurisdiction of white unions and were not available to blacks. At International Paper Company (IP) in Mobile, the limited opportunities available to black workers were summed up well by Alphonse Williams, who started working at the company in 1942: "Our line of progression was like a short ladder up the side of a tall building. If you stayed on that ladder, it would never get you to the top jobs because you see the top jobs was represented, ranked into the jurisdictions of the other locals, and of course they never consented to merge the lines of progression."[6]

Employment Discrimination: The South before 1964

The discrimination that blacks faced in the paper industry was part of a wider pattern of employment discrimination that existed across the United States prior to the mid-1960s. In 1960, for example, 45 percent of nonwhite males worked in low-wage, dead-end jobs as laborers, compared to only 13 percent of whites. As a result, the average black family earned only 55 percent of what the average white family earned. In addition, the black unemployment rate was around twice that of whites.[7]

Employment discrimination was especially marked in the South. In the 1960s, civil rights groups active in the region described the South as unyielding in its patterns of job discrimination. The American Friends Service Committee (AFSC), for example, ran a merit employment program in the region that struggled to make any real progress throughout the late 1950s and early 1960s. In 1962, AFSC executive secretary Tartt Bell told a congressional hearing about the severity of employment discrimination in the South: "In industry after industry and company after company, in town after town, across the Southeast, there is the pattern of vicious discrimination on the basis of race and religion."[8] In the same year, Herbert Hill, labor secretary for the National Association for the Advancement of Colored People (NAACP), claimed that employment discrimination in the South was the worst in the United States: "I realize that civil rights represent the great unresolved social problem of the whole American society, but there can be no doubt that in the Southern States there currently exists the most extreme, rigid, and systematic pattern of employment discrimination to be found anywhere in the United States."[9]

There were several distinguishing features of the southern pattern of employment discrimination. As in the paper industry, jobs were usually segregated and racially identifiable, with blacks assigned to the least desirable positions and locked into these jobs by racially separate seniority lines. Leslie Dunbar, the executive director of the Southern Regional Council, claimed in 1963, "[T]here have been some unwritten rules in the southern labor market for a long time: Negroes and whites do not work alongside of each other; Negroes never have a supervisory position over whites, and so forth. There has grown up a system of Negro jobs and white jobs. And this is the toughest job facing the Negro southerner in employment."[10]

Separate seniority lines and segregated unions, two of the central features of employment discrimination in the paper industry, were common in several southern industries, including the chemical, oil, steel, and tobacco industries. In these industries, as in the paper industry, blacks were kept out of operating positions and were hired exclusively for labor-based jobs. Black workers hired into these laboring classifications were denied seniority and promotional rights into the production classifications, where whites worked, thus ensuring that the only "promotion" they could receive was from one menial job to another. Prominent civil rights leaders repeatedly spoke out against these conditions. Herbert Hill, for example, time after time criticized separate seniority lines, referring to them as "a major problem" for black workers in southern manufacturing industries.[11] A. Philip Randolph, the president of the Negro American Labor Council and one of the principal organizers of the 1963 March on Washington, consistently stressed the importance of equal job opportunities throughout his life. In 1962, Randolph attacked segregated locals, calling them "as morally unjustifiable and organizationally indefensible as racially segregated public schools, housing, recreation, or transportation."[12]

Although the paper industry reflected wider patterns of employment discrimination, the extent of segregation that existed in the industry did mark it out for special attention. From the 1950s on, indeed, civil rights leaders again and again pointed to the industry as a classic example of employment segregation. NAACP executive secretary Roy Wilkins, in particular, repeatedly pressed the International Brotherhood of Pulp, Sulphite, and Paper Mill Workers (IBPSPMW) to merge separate locals.[13] In testifying before a congressional hearing in 1962, Herbert Hill devoted a considerable amount of time to the paper industry, citing a long list of mills that operated with segregated locals and racially separate seniority lines. Hill noted that the NAACP had made efforts to eliminate these discriminatory practices "for years."[14] With the passage of the 1964 Civil Rights Act, the pressure on the paper industry intensified. In 1966, for example, the NAACP told the *New York Times* that segregated locals and separate seniority lines were "a very hot issue." The civil rights group claimed that they were facing a "major conflict" with organized labor because unions were not moving fast enough to eliminate segregated locals and seniority lines. By this time, the NAACP had already filed several EEOC complaints against paper mills.[15]

These efforts reflected the priority that civil rights leaders accorded to equal employment opportunity. Although efforts to integrate industry have not always been at the center of civil rights historiography, civil rights leaders repeatedly asserted that real progress in race relations could not be made unless job discrimination was overcome.[16] In 1963, for example, Congress of Racial Equality (CORE) leader James Farmer claimed that "access to public facilities is a token without a pocketful of money to use them." For Farmer, fair employment represented "something extremely basic in the civil rights struggle. . . . It will be a hollow victory, indeed, if we win the important rights to spend our money in places of public accommodation, on buses, or what have you, without also winning the even more vital right to earn money."[17]

The Southern Paper Industry

In the late 1960s, the American paper industry employed nearly 700,000 people, ranking it on a par with the steel industry. The South, moreover, emerged as a key region for this major industry between the 1930s and the 1960s. By the mid-1960s, the South had become the leading paper-producing region in the United States, generating over half of the national output. The industry began to develop in the region on a large scale in the 1930s, partly because the warm climate ensured that it took less time for pine trees to reach maturity than in the Northeast and Midwest, where early mills were located. In the 1920s and early 1930s, refinements in the sulfate process for making kraft paper also aided the expansion of the paper industry into the South. These changes, together with the availability, adaptability, and low cost of southern pine as the basic raw material for this process, enabled the South to produce 80 percent of all kraft paper and board by the late 1960s.[18]

Across the South, paper mills are generally found in isolated locales, often in remote areas where they are the only industrial employer for a large surrounding area. Paper mills require huge sites and large supplies of water, so they are often located on large pieces of property adjacent to rivers. In the South, most mills are located in the Carolinas, Georgia, Alabama, Mississippi, Louisiana, and northern Florida, with large concentrations occurring near the Gulf and Atlantic Coasts. In addition, paper plants emit noxious smells that mitigate against locating in large urban centers. Working in a paper mill is noisy, smelly, and entails exposure to dangerous machinery that has occasionally claimed workers' lives. For both blacks and whites, however, the industry's high wages have traditionally compensated for these drawbacks, especially since mills are often the only manufacturing employer in the area. "Mills are normally in small, rural communities," explained Boyd Young. "They are the dominant employer, and so if the mill dies, the town would die. So practically everyone in town works for the mill either directly or indirectly."[19]

The paper industry in the post–World War II era has been divided into two distinct sectors—a primary pulp and paper industry and converting operations. Primary mills turn raw wood into rolls of paper, and converting plants turn this paper into finished products such as boxes, tissues, copy paper, and bags. In the 1950s and 1960s, the two parts of the industry were very different from each other. Converting operations were far more labor intensive than the production of primary paper, requiring many more employees to complete the manufacturing process. Since the 1960s, however, the converting sector has become increasingly automated, thereby reducing employment opportunities for both blacks and whites.[20]

Prior to the 1960s, most black workers were confined to working at the first stage of the primary manufacturing process—in the woodyard. In today's paper mills, pulpwood logs and chips are still brought to the mill by rail and truck, much as they were in the 1950s and 1960s. But since the 1950s, automation has reduced the physical labor required to process lumber through the woodyard. Today, various pieces of machinery, including cranes and bulldozers, dispatch the logs and chips from the woodyard through various sawing, sorting, and debarking processes, in preparation for chemical treatment in the pulp mill. In the 1940s and 1950s, most of the wood brought to mills was moved by hand, and in southern mills these heavy, labor-intensive jobs were assigned to blacks.[21]

All the logs leave the woodyard in chip form and are treated in the digesters with chemicals and water, the latter drawn from nearby rivers. This process produces pulp, which then flows to the paper machine, where the liquid is squeezed out between huge, continuous rollers. Once the paper is made by the machine, it is shipped either to converting plants or directly to customers who use it in roll form. Paper machines are huge, measuring several hundred feet in length, yet they require only a small number of operators. Paper machine jobs consistently have been some of the best-paying in the industry, and until the 1960s they were occupied exclusively by whites. For African Americans, the battle to gain access to these jobs has indeed been long and difficult.[22]

Because paper-making machinery and the paper machines in particular are complicated and expensive, all mills have traditionally employed a sizable number of maintenance workers, particularly electricians, millwrights, and mechanics. Prior to the 1960s, these skilled craft jobs were held exclusively by whites and gaining access to them was one of the major battles for African Americans in the civil rights era. The larger companies also have sizable research and testing laboratories, and jobs in them also have been traditionally dominated by whites.[23]

Prior to the 1960s, blacks were thus excluded from the central production jobs in the industry. As the only jobs available were labor based, the overwhelming majority of black paper workers were men. In the industry as a whole, the primary production jobs have traditionally been filled by men. As late as February 1998, for example, only 6.5 percent of workers in UPIU Region V, the union's main southern region, were women.[24] In 1960, around 15 percent of paper workers were classified as laborers, and the proportion of black workers in the industry roughly corresponded to this figure. At this time, for example, the southern paper industry employed 144,459 workers, of whom 20,061, or 13.9 percent, were black.[25]

The large number of segregated local unions that existed in the southern paper industry was partly a reflection of the fact that the industry was one of the few southern industries that was solidly organized. The primary sector of the paper and pulp industry has always been one of the most organized industries in the United States. Most mills were organized between the 1930s and the 1950s, and by 1970, 98 percent of production workers in primary pulp and paper mills were unionized. Since the mid-1970s, the proportion of unionized workers in the paper industry has slipped slightly, although the industry has still remained largely unionized. The percentage of organized paper workers fell from 96 percent in 1982 to 85 percent in 1992.[26]

The industry's capital-intensive structure and isolated location are largely responsible for the high rate of unionization. Both executives and union leaders recalled how paper mills traditionally recognized unions as soon as the factories were built. In 1966, John Bryan, director of industrial relations at Albemarle Paper Company, related that plants in the South were usually started "way out in the woods." Management, however, needed skilled labor to start the plants, which they could secure only by recruiting from outside the area. With skilled workers tending to be unionized and with management anxious to avoid costly shutdowns, Bryan claimed, management decided to voluntarily recognize unions in order to get mills running. "Labor is a small part of cost so that it does not pay to fight and close down the mill over labor," he asserted. According to Bryan, management thus recognized unions and "[i]n return for very high wages, unions let management run the plant."[27]

In general, the paper industry has indeed been characterized by a high wage structure, with average weekly and hourly earnings exceeding those in most manufacturing industries. In 1968, hourly paid workers in the industry earned an average of $130.85 a week, compared to $122.51 in all other manufacturing industries and $109.05 in nondurable industries. Since the 1930s, moreover, wages in southern paper mills have been broadly similar to those paid in other regions. The industry's high wages have also ensured that turnover traditionally has been low.[28] High wages also have served partly as compensation for shift work. Because of high start-up costs, paper mills have always sought to minimize shutdowns, usually running twenty-four hours a day all year round. Weekend and night work were thus part of the job, meaning that the occasional weekends that paper workers did receive off were, as one of them put it, "just like Christmas."[29]

In the 1960s, International Paper Company was by far the largest company in the industry. At this time, IP had a significant presence in the South, its Southern Kraft Division comprising eleven mills that employed over 14,000 workers. These mills included a large facility in Mobile, Alabama, and others in South Carolina, Florida, Mississippi, Arkansas, and Louisiana. Within the industry as a whole, IP was a dominant influence. In 1968, the company employed over 53,000 workers and accounted for about 10 percent of the industry's production and sales. The paper-making giant owned vast forest resources that made it the largest landowner in the United States, with the exception of the federal government. Partly because of the company's dominance, IP figured heavily in many of the civil rights lawsuits brought in the paper industry.[30]

Along with IP, a number of other leading companies operated large mills in the South but were based outside the region, including Scott Paper Company, based in Philadelphia, and Weyerhauser, headquartered in Tacoma, Washington. The Union Camp Corporation was based in New York and operated facilities across the United States, including a variety of paper mills and lumber plants in Georgia and Alabama. While generally relying on local plant managers, corporate management often exerted an influence over management policy in these chain companies, and it customarily responded more favorably to integration than the managers of small, locally owned southern mills. Nevertheless, chain companies acceded to the industry's pattern of segregation prior to the 1960s and made few moves to integrate until significant outside pressures were exerted upon them.[31]

Along with IP, the company that figured most prominently in the battle to integrate the paper industry was Crown-Zellerbach, which was based in San Francisco and owned a large mill in Bogalusa, Louisiana. It was the setting for a landmark legal case, *United States v. Local 189*. The decision in the case came to be used as the basis for revising discriminatory seniority systems in paper mills across the South. Bogalusa, an isolated community located near the Mississippi state line, was also reputed to be a stronghold of the Ku Klux

International Paper Company's Georgetown, South Carolina, mill in 1991
(Courtesy PACE International Union)

Klan, which was reflected in the racial violence and tension that accompanied the integration of the paper mill.[32]

Although many paper mills were located in small communities, the industry also dominated some larger southern cities in the civil rights era. The biggest manufacturing employer in Savannah, Georgia, was Union Camp Corporation, which operated a large paper-making complex on the site of a former plantation. In March 1969, the plant employed 4,928 workers, 18.3 percent of whom were black. By the early 1970s the company claimed that the Savannah mill produced more paper than any other mill in the world, with seven paper machines turning out 3,000 tons a day.[33] Mobile, Alabama, has also been dominated by the paper industry since both International Paper Company and Scott Paper Company opened mills in the Gulf Coast city in the 1930s.[34]

"Job Opportunities Were Segregated on the Basis of Race": The Color of Work before 1964

It was the rigid segregation of the paper industry before the 1960s that made the battle to integrate the industry so difficult and lengthy. Court decisions give good insights into the way that southern paper mills were run on a completely segregated basis before 1964. In the Title VII case of *Stevenson v. International Paper* (1971), for example, the court outlined the history of segregation at IP's plant in Mobile: "There is no dispute that prior to 1962, IP operated on a segregated basis, pursuant to the policy of IP and the unions. All black employees had the lowest paid and the most menial jobs in the

Bag machine operator, ca. 1960s (Courtesy PACE International Union)

production department." All the best-paid jobs were "reserved for whites."[35] Government reviews of paper mills also often highlighted the discriminatory nature of job assignments in the industry. At the Union Camp mill in Savannah, for example, the Defense Supply Agency (DSA) noted that until the company announced an equal employment opportunity policy on January 1, 1963, "Negroes were engaged solely for the performance of labor functions and were restricted from advancement into the better paying classifications which were traditionally held by white employees."[36]

Segregation was an industrywide practice before the 1960s. There were no

Examining the finished product, ca. 1960s (Courtesy PACE International Union)

significant variations between companies; all of them restricted blacks to a small number of jobs and operated separate lines of progression. Scott Paper Company, for example, was a northern-based chain company and was seen as progressive in race relations, yet the company's plant in Mobile operated on the same segregated basis as other southern mills. In *Watkins v. Scott Paper* (1971), a case brought at Scott's Mobile plant, the court found that until 1963, "job opportunities were segregated on the basis of race. Black employees were channeled into lower paying, more physically demanding jobs."[37] James Coil, manager of administrative services, testified that when Scott took over the Mobile mill in 1954, it operated on a segregated basis because of the "resistance of the social structure of the United States." Although Scott, unlike most paper companies, did have an equal employment policy, it failed to push the issue in the South, asserting that "the implementation of this program is going to take some time."[38]

Segregation ensured that there were large pay disparities between black and white workers. At Scott in Mobile, data collected in 1971 indicated that blacks hired between 1940 and 1954 earned over $1.00 an hour less than whites hired at the same time.[39] At Westvaco in Charleston, the EEOC found in 1969 that there were twenty-seven jobs allocated to the black local, paying between $2.39 and $2.72 an hour. Seventy-nine jobs were allocated to the white local, however, and these paid between $2.50 and $3.95 an hour.[40] Significant pay disparities often persisted long after the Civil Rights Act. At the Carolina Paperboard Company in Charlotte, for example, a 1975 case found that black workers were still limited to a small number of jobs in the yard crew and shipping department. As a result, in 1971 black workers at the company earned an average of $7,820, compared to $10,704 for whites.[41] At International Paper Company in Mobile, striking pay disparities were noticeable in data compiled for the *Stevenson* case in 1971. In the whole mill, which employed 1,785 workers, whites earned an average of $4.08 an hour and blacks, an average of $3.47.[42]

In Title VII court cases brought against them in the 1960s and 1970s, company officials acknowledged that the industry operated on a strictly segregated basis before 1964. Elmer Melvin Levitt, the plant superintendent of Weyerhauser's mill in Plymouth, North Carolina, testified in 1978 that separate lines of progression and black and white jobs were standard throughout the paper industry. "It was a generally accepted situation," he conceded, "not only in this mill but in all the mills in the South. They [blacks] went to certain jobs that were reserved for them." Levitt added that in Weyerhauser's woodyard, "the mechanical work was done by whites, the other jobs were all filled by colored."[43] At the Container Corporation in Brewton, Alabama, personnel manager Arthur Larson testified in 1972 that until very recently the company had restricted blacks to a small number of positions in the woodyard. Indeed, prior to 1966, all blacks at Container worked in jobs paying less than what a wood sorter received, while all whites worked in positions paying more than that.[44] The extent of segregation at most mills was such that executives were able to identify the color of every job. Walter Russell Owens, the assistant paper mill superintendent of Weyerhauser's Plymouth plant, illustrated this fact when he testified in *Garrett v. Weyerhauser* in 1977. "Chipper feeder, that's a black job; all of the crane operators were white," Owens commented as he examined a job chart from the mill's woodyard. He added that the whole general yard department "was black jobs," explaining that these jobs were all represented by a separate local union.[45]

IP officials also admitted that all jobs in their mills were racially designated. William J. McCanless, the assistant manager of industrial relations for IP's Southern Kraft Division, testified that at the company's facility in Pine Bluff, Arkansas, "there were white jobs and black jobs in the woodyard."[46] John F. VanDillon, the director of industrial relations for IP's Southern Kraft Division, testified in the same case that until the 1960s, "whites could not go over here, blacks could not go over here . . . the black locals represented certain jobs in certain lines of progression, and that was the way it was."[47]

THE COLOR OF WORK BEFORE THE 1960S

Table 1. Job Distribution at Continental Can Company in Port Wentworth, Georgia, July 2, 1965

Department	No. of White Jobs	No. of Black Jobs	No. of White and Black Jobs	No. of White Employees	No. of Black Employees
Woodyard (black line)	0	8	0	0	52
Woodyard (white line)	5	0	0	23	0
Pulp mill	13	0	0	52	0
Paper mill	18	0	0	76	0
Power	13	0	0	56	0
Laboratory	8	0	0	26	0
Maintenance	35	0	0	131	0

Source: Findings of Fact, August 18, 1976, *Miller v. Continental Can*, p. 8.

The complete segregation that existed in southern paper mills until the mid-1960s is illustrated by Table 1, which depicts the racial composition of jobs at Continental Can in Port Wentworth, Georgia, on July 2, 1965, the day that the Civil Rights Act became effective.

Company officials were reluctant to accept sole responsibility for segregated job assignments. Most claimed that they were merely following "industry practice" in segregating workers. At Pine Bluff, for example, William McCanless claimed in 1972 that IP had merely "followed traditional practices in existence in the pulp and paper industry in the South at that time."[48] Executives often refused to take responsibility for separate lines of progression, arguing that worker preference dictated that employees segregate. At Albemarle Paper Company in Roanoke Rapids, North Carolina, for example, plant manager Kirkwood F. Adams claimed in 1967 that separate lines of progression developed informally and were maintained by worker preference: "These lines of progression became known as colored lines of progression and white lines of progression, and the white people would decline to accept employment in a so-called colored line of progression. We had nothing to do with this. This judgement is made by the people in the area and our employees."[49]

Throughout the 1960s and 1970s, IP was widely acknowledged as a pattern-setter. IP clearly played an important role in setting patterns of segregation. Throughout this period, the giant paper maker had a declared policy that all of its mills would be operated according to the customs of the area in which the mill was located, ensuring that the company effectively sanctioned segregation in its southern mills. IP managers, however, insisted that they were merely following the South's accepted social customs and tried to downplay the company's influence in shaping these customs. Jim Gilliland, IP's current director of employee relations, claimed that before the 1960s, "we were simply following the customs and practices of the communities where we had facilities."[50] In a lengthy interview, John F. VanDillon, who was IP's manager of industrial relations in the 1950s and 1960s, similarly asserted that the company had no direct desire for segregation but acceded to it in order to operate successfully in the South: "Well, I can say this, I never had any sense of the top managers of International Paper Company referring to their black employees as a bunch of damn niggers and stuff like that. . . . They were only after getting the best trained employees that they could get to produce their product in the cheapest possible way so that they could make a profit, and it's always been that way. Either that or they don't stay in business. . . . We didn't want to create a situation whereby we had a physical battle day in and day out in the plants or something like that because people couldn't get along." VanDillon emphasized the constraints under which management operated in the South, faced as they were with white workers' resistance to integration and a segregated social structure. Management was, in his words, "between a rock and a hard place."[51] He claimed, in particular, that the company deferred to the unions' desire to set separate lines of progression: "The company initially, as I recall, would let the matters of the lines of progression, and who was in those lines and so forth, up to the unions. . . . The company, if it really had a say-so, probably would have said, 'Well that's not right,' but, you know, when you start, as the manager of a company interfering with the union's so-called political business, you get yourself into trouble."[52]

While this emphasis on worker preference may seem like an excuse, it is clear that many companies, especially large corporations who also operated plants outside the South, had little direct interest in segregation. Ed Bartlett, Union Camp's manager of industrial relations in the 1960s and 1970s, felt that the company yielded to segregation because that was what was necessary for the company to survive in the South. He recognized that blacks "had to suffer the indignities that that system created" but felt that "the company was sort of caught in the middle. Not by way of an excuse but just a matter of fact, we didn't consider ourselves a leading social institution but a manufacturing for-profit entity that we had to look to the stockholders to make sure that they got their dividends. So that's just the way it worked out in the South." Before the 1960s, Bartlett conceded, Union Camp "just flowed with the tide." Although black paper workers were reasonably well paid, he accepted that this did not justify segregated job assignments: "A lot of accommodations had to be made under the old system, and out of the South we didn't have any of that. It wasn't a problem in California or New York or where we had plants outside the South." Bartlett acknowledged that blacks "weren't equal at all" in the southern paper industry, adding that "they were very limited in the lines of progression and the job opportunities that they had compared to the whites."[53]

Although managers clearly were constrained by the resistance of white workers and social custom, their pleas of powerlessness minimized the important role that company officials themselves played in establishing segregation in the southern paper industry. At International Paper Company's mill in Moss Point, Mississippi, for example, written responses that the company made to a series of charges filed by a group of black workers with the President's Committee on Equal Employment Opportunity in 1962 revealed that company managers had "designated" certain jobs as "for 'colored only'" and had placed strict limits on black promotional opportunities. Although the arrival of the union helped to codify segregation, the company did little to challenge the practice. IP executives even described how their former practice had been to hire black workers primarily for their physical capabilities, noting that "Negro employees were hired in past years without much regard as to mental ability (some could not even read or write) or mechanical comprehension because they were confined to such jobs as could be performed primarily by pure physical exertion."[54]

The reluctance of IP and other large companies to challenge social custom in the South was also important because smaller companies followed the patterns of segregation established by the industry's giants. As one industry executive testified in 1978, separate lines of progression were "a general pattern throughout the South, mostly established by International Paper Company, which was pretty well followed by all of the paper mills."[55] Executives from these smaller companies were also keen to stress that they segregated only in order to operate successfully in the South. John Love, the senior vice president of industrial relations at Gilman Paper Company, explained in 1998 that segregation "was part of the society of the South. That's just the way it was. . . . If we were going to exist in the South as an entity, we had to adopt the mores of the community." Love stressed that if IP had taken a stand against segregation before the 1960s, it would have had "an impact upon Gilman."[56]

In court cases, companies also argued that the paper industry's seniority system was not discriminatory because it was industrywide. Marvin Waters, Weyerhauser's personnel manager in Plymouth, for example, claimed in 1977 that the seniority system "is exactly the same in Pittsburgh as it was in

Plymouth. They are one and the same. . . . [I]t is not the South, it is an industry practice."⁵⁷ The comparison with northern mills was somewhat misleading, however. Outside of the South, the paper industry was located in states with minuscule black populations, such as Maine and Wisconsin. UPIU Region IX, which was one of the UPIU's largest areas in terms of membership, covered the states of Minnesota, Wisconsin, North Dakota, South Dakota, and Michigan. In the 1970s, the union had only 20 black members out of a total of 22,000 members in these states. The lack of a sizable black population allowed most northern mills to sidestep the racial issue. Paper mills in the Northeast and Midwest also tended to be located in small towns, and it was commonplace for there to be a close bond between local management and the white families who had worked in the mill for generations. Thus, blacks found it hard to penetrate the industry in the first place. In these states, white workers did do jobs that were set aside specifically for blacks in the South. The crucial difference, however, was that these jobs were placed in lines of progression that led into operating positions, while in the South, this was not the case. Breaks were created that restricted blacks to a small number of low-paying positions. By placing black jobs in separate lines of progression in the South, companies were able to permanently assign the worst jobs to blacks, whereas in the North, black-assigned duties were integrated with white jobs and led to better-paying positions. White workers were therefore willing to perform these jobs on a temporary basis in order to get a foothold into the industry.⁵⁸

Company officials repeatedly defended the industry's system of job and department seniority as vital for efficiency and safety. According to this argument, jobs within a department were functionally related, so it made sense to group them into long and narrow lines of progression.⁵⁹ Marvin Waters claimed that the production of paper "lends itself to departmentalizing" because it involved processes that were "separate and distinct."⁶⁰ Companies claimed that plantwide seniority could be dangerous because it would lead to the promotion of workers into processes of a particular department with which they were unfamiliar. Both unions and company officials raised the specter that the promotion of workers from outside a department could place unqualified individuals into positions where they might "blow up the plant."⁶¹ Company executives in particular vigorously defended the paper industry's job seniority system. In 1965, for example, the industrial relations director of Albemarle Paper Company said that the company was not "the least bit interested" in introducing plantwide seniority because it "would destroy our whole system."⁶²

In seeking to justify the industry's long history of segregation, paper industry executives were also eager to emphasize the lack of education among the black workers hired in the industry before the 1960s. Although blacks were restricted to laboring jobs, many companies claimed that they had done a good deed in hiring them at all. At Albemarle Paper Company, for example, the company's main brief in *Moody v. Albemarle Paper* expressed annoyance that black workers were claiming that the jobs they had been given constituted discrimination: "Quite a few of the 'affected' class in this case trace their relationship with the Company to the 1920's and 1930's. They were employed to drive mules or stoke boilers; some can neither read nor write. Today, what was a lifesaver to them at the time, is now alleged to be racial discrimination." The company asserted that blacks came from rural backgrounds and lacked the qualifications to occupy skilled jobs: "On account of their rural background, lack of education and lack of industrial experience, many Blacks in the Roanoke Rapids area were, and are, not good prospects for skilled jobs."[63]

This emphasis on illiteracy was a central feature of the *Moody* case; the company claimed that higher-paying jobs required literacy skills that few blacks possessed. Many other paper companies also emphasized black illiteracy, arguing that black workers were restricted to laboring positions because these were the only jobs for which they were qualified. In *Miller v. Continental Can*, for example, plant manager Claude Adams, who had been involved in setting up the Port Wentworth, Georgia, mill when it opened in 1948, testified in 1978 that blacks had been ruled out of most of the skilled jobs because of the need for prior education or industrial experience: "To the extent that it was necessary to hire inexperienced workers for the lowest jobs in the lines of progression, the Company looked for employees who nonetheless had the ability and educational background to advance up the lines of progression to skilled jobs requiring good writing and arithmetic skills and ability, requirements which in 1948 in Georgia disqualified virtually all blacks." Thus, "[t]he only good area in which neither prior experience nor reading, writing and arithmetical skills were required was in certain of the Woodyard jobs which consisted solely of manual labor. Consequently, the Company determined that these jobs could be filled by black employees with little or no education or training, and it proceeded to fill these jobs on that basis. Many of the employees hired for these jobs were farm workers from South Carolina. Most were illiterate and there was no expectation that they would be able to progress to any of the skilled jobs or lines of progression."[64]

At Albemarle Paper Company, management argued that the differing racial assignments in the paper industry simply reflected the differing skills and abilities of the races. In a detailed memorandum written in 1967, Vice President John E. Bryan noted that Albemarle "never had a policy" of excluding blacks from certain jobs, but he accepted that segregation had resulted. He pondered how this had come about, reaching a conclusion that freed the company from any responsibility for racial hiring patterns:

> Why was this so, if the Company did not have a policy against them? I'll answer that this way. I watch football on Sunday afternoons and I notice that most of the running backs are Negroes, but I've never seen a Negro quarterback. I don't think the NFL has a policy against Negro quarterbacks—there just has not been a good Negro quarterback to come along. The same thing is true in our mill. I cannot say we were exactly scientific in our appraisals, but generally speaking the Negroes who historically have applied for work at our mill have been by aptitude and educational standards best suited for certain lines of work.

This argument led the company back to its assertion that most blacks came from farming backgrounds, lacked education, and were not qualified for the higher-paying jobs. The company also argued that the few blacks who were qualified for skilled jobs left Roanoke Rapids to seek better lives, usually in the North.[65]

Another central defense of paper industry executives was that the jobs given to blacks in the industry were better paying than others available to African Americans in the South at the time. Companies thus used the paper industry's high pay structure to argue that they did not discriminate. Albemarle Paper Company, for example, asserted that the black workers it had hired, although working in separate lines of progression that were lower paying than the white lines, still held desirable jobs. As the company's brief declared:

> Albemarle . . . admits that the white lines were higher paying than the Black lines. . . . But, the Black employees at Albemarle earned substantially more than the police and firemen in Roanoke Rapids, more than the teachers in the Roanoke Rapids schools, several times more than the agricultural workers in the area, which was and is a predominantly agricultural area . . . and way above the average earnings for the people in the community. . . . Thus, Albemarle contends that the jobs in the Black lines of progression were, and are, highly desirable jobs, not only to Blacks, but also to the majority of whites in the community.[66]

Many paper industry executives were genuinely proud of the relatively high paying jobs that their industry had traditionally offered to African

American workers. John F. VanDillon remembered with some pride the fact that IP had hired large numbers of blacks when it opened its southern mills: "But I will say this, I was happy to see, and so were my superiors, that in the South we were able to hire a lot of blacks and they got paid good wages and benefits, it helped their communities, no question about that."[67] Union Camp's Ed Bartlett also stressed that the company employed around 900 black workers who were "probably among the highest paid, with benefits, of any black population in the South, they were well paid for what they did." Bartlett recognized that blacks were "limited" in their job opportunities, but he emphasized that they were proud of working at the company, which was called Union Bag in the 1960s: "They were always happy. They always said, 'Where do you work?' 'I work at the Bag.' Boy, they were proud of it. It was a good job and it was a good-paying job, good vacations, holidays, health insurance, life insurance."[68]

The Role of Unions in Establishing Job Segregation

Management's claim that unions pressed them to uphold separate lines of progression raises important questions about the exact role played by organized labor in establishing segregated job patterns. While both sides had a tendency to blame the other for wanting segregation, ultimately they shared the responsibility for the industry's long history of discriminatory job assignments. In many mills, companies initially established informal segregation that was later formalized by union representation.[69]

The first local union in the paper industry was organized as early as 1884, and by the start of the twentieth century two separate international unions represented workers in the United States and Canada. The International Brotherhood of Paper Makers (IBPM), formed in 1902, represented skilled production workers, and the IBPSPMW, chartered in 1906, represented mainly unskilled workers. Both unions were relatively small until the New Deal, when they made big strides in organizing workers. In the 1930s and 1940s, some paper workers were also organized by the fledgling Congress of Industrial Organizations (CIO), which in turn established the United Paperworkers of America (UPA) in 1948, a new union with over 30,000 members. Nine years later, the UPA and the IBPM merged, building on the spirit of unity in organized labor shown by the 1955 merger of the AFL and CIO, which created the modern-day AFL-CIO. The newly created United Papermakers and Paperworkers (UPP) existed alongside the IBPSPMW, but there was little direct competition between the two unions. The IBPSPMW, indeed, continued to represent semiskilled and unskilled workers, while the

UPP was restricted to machine tenders and other skilled workers. Recognizing the strength that unity could bring them, however, the two unions merged in August 1972, creating the UPIU. At the time of the merger, Harry Sayre was president of the UPP and Joseph Tonelli headed the IBPSPMW. Sayre stepped down from the presidency of the smaller union, yielding the leadership of the UPIU to Tonelli. The UPIU existed until 1999, when it merged with the Oil, Chemical, and Atomic Workers' International Union to form the Paper, Allied-Industrial, Chemical, and Energy Workers' International Union (PACE).[70]

Events at International Paper Company highlighted the important role that unions often played in formalizing segregated job assignments that had been initially established by management. In 1939, IP voluntarily recognized five unions, including the IBPSPMW, the International Brotherhood of Electrical Workers, and the International Association of Machinists, to represent all of their plants in the South. There were no clear jurisdictional lines between these unions, which operated with informal lines of progression that placed black workers in the lowest-paying jobs. In 1951, however, the unions called for a National Labor Relations Board (NLRB) election that certified each union to represent different groups of workers. The unions reached a jurisdictional agreement on November 16, 1951, that divided jobs up between them. The agreement placed all "colored employees" under IBPSPMW jurisdiction and placed most of the highest-paying production jobs under the jurisdiction of the UPP. Thus, racial jurisdictions became formalized in the immediate postwar years.[71]

The 1950s saw a further expansion of the paper industry in the South, but mills built in these years continued to follow the standard industry practices. Moreover, unions continued to formalize and codify patterns of segregation that companies had initially established. In 1958, for example, IP constructed a large new paper mill in Pine Bluff, Arkansas. The EEOC, in a 1978 investigation into the racial history of the mill, found that "[a]s a matter of company policy, initial mill staffing was done along strict racial lines," with blacks relegated to lower-paying, physically demanding jobs. As in other mills, the EEOC found that the arrival of the union had the effect of strengthening and formalizing company-established patterns of segregation. A separate black local was set up, and black workers, who all worked in the woodyard, were prohibited from transferring to any other lines of progression. The EEOC concluded that the unions and the company had combined to lock blacks into a small number of low-paying positions, adding, "The first collective bargaining agreement covering the Pine Bluff mill was negotiated in an atmosphere of planned racial discrimination."[72]

Although separate unions allowed black workers to have representation at the local level, black workers complained that the top leadership of paper unions remained all white. Here, UPP Executive Board members are pictured in Miami in February 1965. (Courtesy PACE International Union).

IP apart, a certain amount of mythology surrounds the exact process by which other southern paper plants came to be run on a segregated basis. Some workers and union officials remembered backroom deals being struck between company officials and white leaders that determined segregated job assignments.[73] Companies who moved South followed a "southern pattern" that was widely recognized throughout the industry and involved strict segregation. When the Marathon Corporation decided to build a paper mill near Butler, Alabama, in 1956, for example, James Crowell, a janitor at the County Courthouse, testified that the company struck a deal with county officials to follow the "southern pattern," placing strict limits on the numbers of blacks hired and the types of jobs they could hold. The company had originally wanted to hire a greater number of blacks, but local officials insisted on restricting the numbers in order to adhere rigidly to traditional segregation.[74] Both blacks and whites claimed that at other mills local managers and white workers made covert agreements when mills were first built to reserve all the best-paying jobs for white workers.[75] Black workers claimed that their efforts to secure better-paying jobs in new plants were brushed aside. For example, black local union leader Charles Gordon maintained that, when Union Camp constructed a box plant in 1947, he asked for blacks to be given some operating positions but was asked by the white union representative, "Do you expect me to go against my friends for you?"[76]

The organization of segregated unions clearly helped to lock African American workers into the lowest-paying jobs. At the Crown-Zellerbach mill in Bogalusa, Louisiana, for example, black workers complained that the union "was organized on the basis that certain jobs would be reserved for 'white' employees and certain other jobs would be reserved for 'Negro' employees," with all good-paying jobs placed under the jurisdiction of the white locals.[77] At Gilman Paper Company in St. Marys, Georgia, the court found that a separate black local had been created in 1942 that coexisted with three all-white locals. All locals were given jurisdictions over certain jobs, but white workers were allowed to transfer union jurisdictions, whereas blacks were not. The court concluded that the creation of separate union jurisdictions was therefore a way of locking black workers into the worst jobs: "The black local 616 was given the dead-end jobs while the white locals retained jurisdiction over the more desirable and higher paying jobs. . . . A black worker hired at the mill would be ushered into one of the 'black jobs' (a job over which Local 616 had jurisdiction). No matter how long a black employee worked at Gilman, he could never transfer to, or be promoted to a job over which a white local had jurisdiction. Since black employees could not join a white local, their fate was sealed; they could never obtain one of the 'white jobs' at the mill." Thus, as the plaintiffs' attorney put it, " 'Union jurisdiction' in this instance is a euphemism for race."[78]

Union leaders often admitted that separate lines of progression and segregated locals were desired by white workers as a way of securing control of the best jobs, and they acknowledged that the union had reflected the demands of these workers, who made up a majority of its membership. Wayne Glenn, who was a vice president of the IBPSPMW in the 1960s and served as president of the UPIU between 1978 and 1996, stressed that lines of progression "were set up to deny the blacks promotions, I mean just being honest about it, that's the way they were set up."[79]

World War II and the Establishment of Segregation in the Southern Paper Industry

At IP, the representation election that took place in 1951 showed a desire to formalize lines of progression that reflected the way that whites across the South reacted to World War II. Evidence indicates, indeed, that because lines of progression had not been formalized in many mills, African American workers were able to make some progress onto skilled jobs during the war.

After the war ended, both white workers and management were anxious to regain control of these jobs and to ensure that blacks did not aspire to them again.

As interviews conducted more than fifty years later indicate, some African American workers retained bitter memories of being fired from higher-paying jobs at the end of World War II. Ervin Humes, who was hired at International Paper Company in Georgetown, South Carolina, in 1943, remembered that many blacks were promoted to higher-paying jobs in the Georgetown mill during World War II: "During the height of World War II, most of the older men during that draft age, they went to war, you know, they were drafted . . . they did give us a higher job, what they called dumping the beater." Once the war was over, however, the black workers were returned to the bottom jobs: "But listen, I dumped that beater five years, about five years, until those men started returning back and being discharged from the army and navy, out of the service, and Boom!, they took us off. . . . That Sunday morning when they got enough of those guys, they didn't even tell us nothing . . . they says, 'Don't need you, you can go back downstairs,' just that quick, without any explanation, without any thank you . . . we went back on the same bottom line."[80]

A restrictive racial order was clearly being imposed in the paper industry at the end of the war. At Union Camp's mill in Savannah, for example, Willie Holder recalled that blacks had been demoted from operating positions as whites returned from military service. Holder's testimony also highlighted again how companies claimed that they were merely acceding to unions' desires for complete job segregation: "I was a presser as far as sugar bags, a sugar bag presser. And that was in '47. And I was removed from there because they put just only whites on this job, and I was removed because there were a lot of fellows coming out the service. And I asked why. And they told me that the union saw fit that white only should have that job." As a result, Holder was given a "harder job" as a baler.[81] Holder's testimony was supported by other Union Camp workers. Veteran worker John Bonner, for example, claimed that blacks worked as truck drivers "all over the mill" during the war but were taken off these jobs shortly after the conflict ended: "Soon as the war was over with, they took them off. Said they wasn't qualified. Put white on there."[82]

At other mills, many black workers hired in the late 1940s and early 1950s later described how they were restricted to purely laboring positions, even if they had carried out skilled work during World War II.[83] In Mobile, for example, paper mills refused to assign skilled jobs to blacks who had worked as welders in the city's shipyards during World War II.[84] Louis Robinson found that when he was laid off from his job as a welder at Alabama Ship-building Company he came up against an open color bar at IP: "I asked about welding but I was explained—it was told me in the beginning they didn't use colored welders, so I accepted what they had."[85] Jessie Stevenson testified that IP told black workers immediately after the war that "the company don't hire no damn nigger bosses."[86] This color bar was also in force at neighboring Scott Paper Company. Sykes Bell was hired as a laborer at Scott after the war, having worked for Alabama Shipbuilding as a fireman and as a part-time mechanic. "At that time there wasn't nothing for blacks but labor," he asserted.[87]

The experience of another Scott worker, Horace Crenshaw, typified that of many other black workers across the South. He testified in 1973 that he was taking part in the *Watkins* lawsuit so that he could finally secure the welding job that had been denied him when he was first hired in 1946: "I welded at the shipyard all the time the War was going on, and I had the experience. I was a first class welder at that time. . . . I had a certificate that proved I was a first class welder. And I was going hunting a job and they asked me what kind of job I was looking for and I told them I was looking for a job. And at that time he asked what I had been doing so I give him this certificate that I had welding. And he told me at that time well, he wasn't hiring blacks. They only had labor jobs for blacks at that time." Consequently, Crenshaw worked for many years as a laborer.[88] Other blacks used the GI Bill of 1944 to learn new skills, but these workers were also frustrated by the response of paper mills when they sought skilled jobs immediately after the war. World War II veteran Griffin Williams trained to be a welder and machinist under the GI Bill but claimed that he was told by International Paper Company "that no black person at this time would be able to get a job there in this particular field." As a result, Williams was also hired as a laborer.[89]

World War II would ultimately prove to be very important to the struggle for civil rights in the southern paper industry. Indeed, many of the African American workers who led the fight against discrimination in the 1960s were motivated by their experiences during the war, especially in military service.[90] Yet, although the war was partly responsible for the eventual integration of the paper industry, the way that white workers and management reimposed strict job segregation immediately after it showed that only significant outside pressures could effectively disturb segregation in the industry. Fundamental change would not occur on a voluntary basis. Indeed, all parties—white workers, managers, and black workers alike—recognized after the fact that segregation would have continued if significant outside pressure had not been exerted in the 1960s and 1970s. Julius Gerard, the head of industrial relations at Westvaco in Charleston, South Carolina, in the 1960s and 1970s, for example, acknowledged this in a 1997 interview: "The South was segregated, we were segregated in most of the things that we did, and the mill certainly reflected the society at large. . . . When you talk about an institution, a tradition that was so well embedded, it would have been fairly difficult to change without the Civil Rights Law of '64." Pushed through Congress by President Johnson in the summer of 1964, the Civil Rights Act indeed posed the most obvious challenge to segregation in the paper industry since American entry into World War II some twenty-three years earlier.[91]

CHAPTER 2
THERE WAS NOTHING FOR
US BUT LABOR WORK
BLACK WORKERS IN THE PAPER
INDUSTRY, 1945–1965

One of the most striking features of the legal records produced by Title VII cases was the compelling testimony by African American workers. In case after case, black workers described how they experienced the segregation and limited job opportunities that company officials and court decisions had outlined. This testimony provides compelling insight into black working conditions in the twenty years before the passage of the Civil Rights Act and is supplemented well by oral interviews in which black workers also shared their personal experiences of the color of work.

African Americans who worked in the paper industry before the 1960s usually described the jobs assigned to them as the least desirable positions, the jobs that whites did not want. They also described how the industry operated on a strictly segregated basis until the 1960s. As Sidney Gibson, who started working at International Paper Company in Natchez, Mississippi, in 1951, recalled, "When I first went there, you didn't do anything but whatever a white person didn't want to do. They didn't want to dig no ditches, and didn't want to run no jackhammers, this kind of thing, so that's what we did. . . . The whites get the better jobs, blacks get the lower-paid jobs. . . . They had that thing about white jobs and black jobs and that was the difference."[1] African Americans who worked at other southern mills had very similar memories. State Stallworth, a tall, lean man, vividly recalled starting work at ip's Moss Point mill in 1954: "They had white jobs and black jobs . . . and all of the blacks naturally had the lowest-paying jobs, the hardest jobs, the nastiest jobs. . . . We got all the low-paying jobs and the hard jobs and the back-breaking jobs and the dirty jobs."[2]

As well as being labor based, black jobs were also characterized by their lack of promotional opportunities. "The jobs that we was offered was dead end jobs," commented one Union Camp worker. "They wasn't in the line of progression. You couldn't go any higher. There was no place to go."[3] Even when blacks rose to the top of their limited lines of progression, their jobs were still poorly paid and labor based. In legal testimony, Arthur Kilroy, who started work at the Union Camp mill in 1942, also outlined the lack of opportunities for African Americans at Savannah's largest employer. "The only thing a Negro was hired at Union Bag for was as a laborer, and they gave you a few dignified titles, but they never paid you for them," he noted. In detailed testimony, Kilroy linked the limited opportunities at the plant to the wider segregation facing blacks in Savannah: "Well, it's just like the rental agents in the city. You can go to apply for a dwelling house and they'll hand you a list with houses primarily in Negro districts, or black districts. Although they have a rental list of apartments that you probably would desire, they don't hand you the complete list or a dual list, they hand you one list and you're relegated to choose an apartment in that if you desire one of those. And that's the way the job category—when you were hired out here at Union Camp—or Union Bag at that time, from 1942, at that point, they used to hire at the gate."[4]

The lack of promotional opportunities in the southern paper industry clearly frustrated many black workers, especially those who possessed mechanical or technical qualifications. Edward Cox, who worked in Weyerhauser's woodyard, summed up how many felt in testimony he gave in 1977. A high school graduate who had also attended technical college, Cox began working at the company's mill in eastern North Carolina in 1949. "I know that all of us have been denied promotion," he declared, "because I could see whites who were coming in, and steadily climbing up the ladder, and we were still down in the pit. So we are bound to have been denied promotion on account of the color of our skin. It wasn't nothing but the color of our skins . . . it was just as hard for a black man to get a promotion as it is to get a camel through the eye of a needle."[5]

One of the central complaints of African American paper workers before the 1960s was that inexperienced whites were hired into the mill and placed over veteran blacks. Black workers also complained that they often had to train these whites to run jobs that they were not allowed to hold themselves. Willie Ford, who was hired at Mobile Paperboard in 1947, was one of these African American workers. A tall, slim, dark-skinned man, Ford worked at the small paper mill on the outskirts of Mobile until his retirement in 1984. "The whites had the best jobs," he recalled. "What they would do, they'd hire white, and if he just didn't know nothing, me, I had to train him to do what I was doing, and then he would just move on up. But you see, we had to stay in one spot, we never did move up. . . . Boy got out of service . . . and he come there . . . I had to learn him how to run the beater. Man, he didn't even know how to do nothing. But what I'm saying, I was still a helper and he got to be a foreman, he moved right on up, just like that, that's the way they done, and nothing you could do about it."[6]

Across the South, African American workers had similar complaints. At International Paper Company's mill in Pine Bluff, Arkansas, N. A. Thompson started working as a laborer when the mill first opened in 1958. He testified in 1972 that black workers had trained many newly hired whites who subsequently moved above them: "We have helped to train a lot of fellows, a lot of them would come out and not know what to do and how to do a certain job. I say, for instance, running a jackhammer. A lot of times, they would put him with me, you know, to try to teach him. I would take the biggest load of the work and go ahead and do it and show him the easy way to do certain jobs. Yeah, they subsequently came up and passed by me in the line of progression."[7] Sidney Gibson recalled that at the company's mill in Natchez, he spent most of his twenty-four years in the mill training inexperienced whites to run jobs that he was not permitted to hold himself on a permanent basis, a situation he found deeply frustrating: "See if you were white, and you were hired this morning, this afternoon you'd be a truckdriver, even though I was training you. You had some guys that come in there that couldn't even find the gears on a straight shift, standard shift truck. 'We're going to give you truck drivers' pay for a week, we want you to show this guy how to drive a truck.' "[8]

Prior to the 1960s, paper companies hired black workers primarily for heavy, menial laboring jobs. Physical strength was the main qualification that companies looked for, and the industry had a tendency to hire black men from farming backgrounds with little formal education. These workers were often placed in the woodyard, where they helped load large sticks of lumber onto boxcars. In court cases, company officials often admitted that physical strength was their main requirement in filling black jobs. At Continental Can in Port Wentworth, Georgia, for example, plant manager Claude Adams testified that blacks were hired only into the woodyard. "The requirements for employment in the black line was predominantly interested in the physical capabilities of the personnel employed, whereas in other lines that was not necessarily the limitation," he explained.[9] Leon Moore, who was hired at Scott Paper Company in Mobile in 1960, remembered that black workers even had their strength tested before they were hired at the paper mill: "There was a stick of pulpwood that sat at the main entrance at the guard post. If you were able to muscle that stick of wood, you automatically qualified for a person to fill a slot in the woodyard." Blacks who did not qualify for the woodyard were given lighter menial jobs, and Moore himself, who has a slender build, started working at Scott as a janitor. As he remembered, black jobs fell into two categories: "We used to use an old cliché: if you were an Afro-American, you either pulled something or pushed something."[10]

At the Weyerhauser plant in Plymouth, North Carolina, most blacks hired at the mill before the 1960s worked as laborers in the woodyard, most of them doing the physical work of "pulling wood." Indeed, this job was one of the most common held by blacks in southern paper mills up to the 1960s.[11] Blacks who pulled wood basically loaded raw lumber by hand, a job that today is performed by machine. Dennis Cox, hired in 1941 at Weyerhauser, described the job: "Pulling wood out of boxcars. You know the boxcars are loaded with wood. We'd throw it out of the boxcar into a conveyer." Cox, like other black workers, felt that jobs were clearly racially designated: "In the beginning when they hired me, there were white jobs and black jobs, but I couldn't get a job above pulling wood unless I was cleaning up or something. That's the only job I could get at Weyerhauser."[12]

The job of pulling wood was so physical that many blacks remembered that over time they developed large muscles. At the Crossett Company in Crossett, Arkansas, for example, Nathaniel "Beby" Reed, who was hired in 1940 to pull wood, recalled the physically challenging nature of his work. Reed, who retired from the mill in 1981, was still heavily built in his eighties. "I worked for forty-one cents an hour at that time," he remembered, "and of course they didn't have anything like a crane or anything, everything you handled out there you man-handled. . . . I used to have to work out there, I used to bring wood in in boxcars, told me I had to unload three boxcars in eight hours, you had to do that, and then you were being cursed and everything else while you were doing that. . . . People used to ask me did y'all lift weights, I used to be muscular, that was lifting those big sticks of wood, you had to do it. . . . Now I'm paying for it, arthritis tearing me up, but I don't mind it."[13]

Another traditional area of black work prior to the 1960s was the "bull gang." "Bull gang," a slang term, was used throughout the industry to refer to the workers who performed some of the most physically demanding jobs in the mill. Bull gangs were used to perform a variety of laboring jobs all over the mill, depending on what needed to be repaired. Many of the tasks involved outside labor, such as digging ditches and laying cement, or inside cleaning jobs that were often very dirty. Tarlton Small, who started working at Weyerhauser in 1941, remembered, as did many black workers who performed similar tasks, that his work on the bull gang involved "[d]igging ditches and grading places where they pour the cement, and pour[ing] cement, too, part of the time."[14]

By the early 1960s, many companies were trying to rename these jobs as "general yard maintenance" and the like, but the term "bull gang" persisted among both white and black paper workers.[15] Many white workers indeed used the term "bull gang" because they recognized the physical nature of black jobs. Even in interviews conducted in the 1990s, they often referred to the physical size and muscular physique that blacks had developed by working in their labor-based jobs. Plez Watson, a white worker at IP in Mobile, recalled that black jobs were a "completely different world" from white jobs when he first started at the mill in 1941: "They wasn't allowed to go in on the paper machines. . . . The jobs that the blacks had to do in my local were strictly confined to shipping department, where its hard, menial labor. And that was it really." Watson recalled that some of the blacks that carried out these jobs were referred to as "bulls, they were as strong as hell. . . . Oh boy, they were big."[16]

If there was one word that black workers used most often to describe their experiences in the paper industry before the 1960s, it was "rough." Like Plez Watson, Alphonse Williams started working in IP's Mobile mill at the start of World War II and soon became active in one of the mill's segregated local unions. Looking back on more than forty years in the mill, he recalled that "it was rough and it was tough . . . either we had to fight or succumb to what they were doing, let them continue on doing it."[17] At Scott Paper Company, located adjacent to the IP mill in Mobile, black workers described a similar picture. As was typical, one of them described black work as "just labor— wherever you go you was either going to be on a shovel, a broom, a pick, a wheelbarrow, a jackhammer, whatever was the roughest work there, that's what you got."[18]

Many African American workers understood that paper companies looked to hire them primarily for physical labor. In some mills, black workers described how they even understated their educational qualifications because they had heard that companies favored those with "strong backs and weak minds." At Union Bag in Savannah, for example, James Fields, who was hired as a laborer in the mill in the 1940s, testified that before applying he had been told by a black worker to conceal his high school education: "I know when I first started working to Union Bag, I'll tell you just like it was. I asked a guy, and I said, 'How is the job?' And he told me the job was good, but they didn't want no smart black man. When I filled my application out—you have my records, you look—I put ninth grade instead of twelfth, because I figured they didn't want no black man, no smart black man, in order to get hired. I was hired."[19]

Throughout the paper industry, black workers who were hired in the 1940s and 1950s claimed that companies did not want them to have a good education. These workers indeed generally saw laboring jobs in the wood-yard as the only jobs available. At Continental Can in Port Wentworth, Georgia, Moses Baker, who was hired in 1948, started work as a laborer in the woodyard. "That's where they was hiring," he stated, "that wasn't nothing else to get, but the wood yard that was hiring. . . . Education wasn't a factor then, it didn't take education to use a shovel, and that's what I was going to get, a shovel and a pick, and nobody used to worry about the education then."[20] At St. Regis Paper Company in Jacksonville, Florida, Willie Jernigan, who began work in 1953 as a laborer, also claimed that there were no other jobs available: "At that time there was nothing, no more than this labor, so it wouldn't have made sense for me to ask for nothing I know at that time I wasn't going to get. There was nothing for us but labor work." Jernigan explained that an education could be a disadvantage in the company's eyes because "they didn't want no black who had no education. . . . They didn't want no black help with real good education."[21]

Many paper mills were located in remote areas of the South in which there were large black populations. Companies were thus able to attract young black men from farming backgrounds who had no industrial experience but an abundance of physical energy. Weyerhauser's main plant in the South, for example, was built in an area of eastern North Carolina with little industry. Blacks who were hired usually came off the farm to work in the mill, which was called Keichkefer before Weyerhauser owned it. "Well, the first company I ever worked with was Keichkefer Company," remembered one black worker. "But if you want to know where I first worked, it was on the farm. There wasn't no companies then."[22]

Most black workers were hired straight off the farm without even having filled out an application. Emanuel Small described how he was hired at Weyerhauser in 1947: "I farmed until I went to Weyerhauser Company. . . . I went to Weyerhauser when I was nineteen years old. . . . Along at that time they had to fill out no application."[23] Workers described a hiring process that was very informal and over which they had no control. They simply turned up at the gate each morning and took whatever the company offered, which were usually jobs pulling wood. Gurvies Bryant, hired in 1948, outlined the process well: "I was unloading wood out of boxcars . . . at that time . . . you just apply for a job, and they fill out the form themselves, you know. Well, at that time you didn't have any choice. You asked for a job and they give you where they put the black peoples at the time."[24] A similar hiring process existed at Union Camp's mill in Savannah. Black workers turned up at the gate and were hired solely on the judgment of a white superintendent widely referred to as "Chief Edwards."[25]

After leaving farming, many black men worked as loggers before entering the paper mill, with lumber work serving as a transition between the farm and the mill. Leroy Griffin, who was hired at Weyerhauser in 1944, described how many blacks came to work at the paper mill: "Well, I didn't get no schooling. No black folks didn't get no schooling when I come along. The only thing they got is in the cornfield. . . . I worked on a farm, and from the farm I went to the log woods, and from the log woods I went to Mr. Keichkefer's job, and from that to the Weyerhauser."[26] Charlie Miller, a black worker at Continental Can in Port Wentworth, Georgia, also came to the paper industry from a rural background via the lumber industry. He was raised in Uvalda in the Georgia countryside and worked in lumber for three years, helping deliver wood to paper mills on the Georgia coast, including Continental Can, where he was hired in 1948. "I was in pulpwood for about three years," he explained. "We dealt in logs, pulpwood, blocks, at that time. We used to haul blocks to different plants. And I even hauled some wood out here at the first of the beginning."[27]

In Halifax County, North Carolina, African American laborer Joe P. Moody also came to the paper industry through the farm and lumber route. Moody, who was the lead plaintiff in *Moody v. Albemarle Paper*, testified that he had no schooling because he had been "raised up on the farm." In a 1966 deposition, he related how he ended up working as a laborer at Albemarle: "I farmed some for Mr. Hubert Floyd. He's dead now. After I stopped farming, I went to the pulpwood—cut a little pulpwood for Mr. Biddy Shaw. Then, I left there. . . . Mr. Buster Seay, Personnel Manager at Albemarle Paper Company, he was up on the yard one day and I asked him about a job. He told me to come over next morning—'see about starting you to work.' "[28]

As companies recognized, farm labor was a good preparation for the physical tasks that black workers were assigned in the paper industry. Some African American workers who had worked in the paper industry before the 1960s themselves felt that their experience of farm work prepared them well and helped them survive the physical work in the industry. Sammie J. Hatcher, a small, stocky man, was hired at Mobile Paperboard in 1952 as a laborer. "Me being pretty used to rugged work, so I could hang in there," he recalled. "I used to farm for my grandmother and I tried to go to school and farm and all that at the same time. So, I was used to rugged work. I guess I thought that was a way of life."[29]

Since paper mills were built in the South in remote locations, a few companies sought to attract workers by offering them housing. The Crossett Company, which built a sawmill and paper mill in the late 1930s in the southern Arkansas community of Crossett, for example, constructed houses and a company store near the mill. The company's first workers remembered that housing was also segregated. Nathaniel "Beby" Reed recalled that the company houses along Main Street were strictly divided: "I came in 1940 and Crossett owned everything. . . . Like I said, west side of Main Street was for blacks, east side for white. They had some people, some women doing domestic work over there on the east side, and if you had a girlfriend over there, you had to be away from over there by nine o'clock, they caught you after nine o'clock they'd put you in jail."[30]

Black jobs in the southern paper industry were also characterized by a high degree of danger. Many black workers lost fingers working on the woodyard.[31] Others suffered permanent scarring of the hands and arms carrying out jobs such as broke beater, which involved picking up pieces of hot paper. Ervin Humes, who worked at International Paper Company in Georgetown, South Carolina, bore the scars of working in a paper mill for forty-six years: "Look at that [showing burns on hands], where that paper hot, pulling that, you know, and that burn forever . . . that paper was hot." Like many other black workers, Humes also claimed that companies were more tolerant of white workers who received injuries.[32]

Many African American workers also complained that companies neglected safety requirements on black jobs. In *Gantlin v. Westvaco*, for example, black workers complained in 1972 that they were hired exclusively in "the most menial, physically demanding and hazardous jobs." They added that white workers were given equipment with much better safety features than that provided to blacks.[33] Similarly, in *Moody v. Albemarle Paper*, plaintiffs were keen to ensure that the company improved safety on black jobs.[34] They asked that Albemarle furnish them with rain suits and boots and keep "the tractor seat fixed." They also demanded that the machinery they operated had lights attached, as white workers' machinery did. "They got us out there operating these pieces of equipment with no lights on and we have to see the best we can," complained one black worker. "Sometimes, it's so foggy we can't see; but then if you get hurt, they say you done it on carelessness. . . . Take every piece of equipment most of the white people got down there, they got lights on it. They got cranes that got lights on it. . . . All the trucks got lights on it. We, the—only the colored people have equipment with no lights on it. Bad working conditions, can't hardly get nothing fixed."[35] Black workers at Albemarle also tried to address safety concerns through the grievance procedure.[36]

One of the curious aspects of segregation in the paper industry was that black and white workers were not always segregated physically from one another. Since the labor content of jobs determined whether they were performed by whites or blacks, black workers sometimes performed the labor necessary for a job while a white worker worked on the skilled part of the same job. Thus, black and white workers often worked in close proximity to one another. Willie Ford, for example, worked as an electrician's "helper" at Mobile Paperboard in the 1940s and 1950s. He remembered that his job was to carry the tools of the white electricians and to hold the pipes while they welded: "See, black couldn't be nothing but a helper, pulling a welding machine, or burning torch, whatever he wanted, and hold that pipe until he weld. I've got shocks so many times over there, you know when they stick that rod to that pipe to weld it, sometime it will shock you, but you had to hold it. If you turn it loose, you talk about cussing you, oh Lord." Ford added, "Man, to tell you the truth, if I could write a book, I could write a book about that place over there, that's true, and everything I put in there would be true."[37]

Many other blacks worked in close proximity to the white millwrights, pipefitters, and electricians. These black laborers assisted the white workers but were forbidden from performing any skilled work. "Like I said, blacks was common labor," recalled Collis C. Jordan, a retired Union Camp worker. "If a pipefitter went to a place, maybe a pipe was leaking, that water coming up out of the ground, he didn't touch it, he called for what they called a laborer. Then they sent him a couple of laborers, a couple of blacks, and they'd go there and dig the pipe up or dig down in the ground so he could find the leak or whatever. Whites just didn't put their hand on a shovel, that just didn't happen. That was the black."[38] Leon Moore remembered that white millwrights walked to a job site "with their hands in their pockets chuckling with each other" while black laborers carried their tools. Once at the job site, the black laborers "were not allowed to touch a wrench" but had to wait until the job was finished and then carry the tools back.[39]

Especially frustrating for black workers was that they often developed a close knowledge of skilled jobs by watching whites perform them, yet they were still not allowed to work at these jobs. At Hudson Pulp and Paper Company in Palatka, Florida, black workers related that they had gained a close knowledge of millwright work by working on a daily basis with whites and by carrying out "whatever they needed us to do." Yet "helper" Isiah Griffin described that whenever a new millwright was appointed, "the blacks was moved and the whites took over."[40]

The fact that many blacks and whites worked in close proximity to one another made many whites especially anxious to defend the skilled or "white" part of any job. The clearest example of this occurred in mills where many blacks worked as crane helpers but were forbidden from actually operating the crane. At Weyerhauser's Mill in Plymouth, for example, Leroy Griffin worked for twenty-five years as a crane helper and never was allowed to operate the crane himself: "Just because of my color I couldn't operate and I knew darn well I could operate the crane and I can now. . . . The operator sit on his seat just like he was and then I couldn't pull a lever. That ain't right." Griffin related that he oiled and greased the crane but was not allowed to get in the seat: "They wouldn't let us pull a lever and we were not to get in the seat. We was told that. . . . In the twenty-five years, I couldn't get in the seat unless I was being fired. That was true. . . . They always told us they didn't allow no black men in the seat."[41]

The fact that black jobs were essentially defined by their labor content was illustrated by the way that when these jobs were automated, they often became white jobs. In Westvaco's plant in Charleston, South Carolina, for example, one of the central complaints of a class action lawsuit brought in 1972 was "the transformation of formerly black jobs into white jobs whenever such jobs are automated or made less demanding physically."[42]

"I Needed to Work and I Had a Family"

In the 1940s and 1950s, many black paper workers did try to challenge segregation and often asked about promotions to white jobs, but they made very little progress. Executives responded by rebuffing black workers and often by threatening to fire them.

In legal testimony, African American workers often related that they had fought in vain against segregation from the day they were first hired at the mill. In 1975, veteran Union Camp worker Arthur Kilroy gave typical testimony: "All these years, we've been arguing for that point, to elevate Negroes or blacks, as you're now called, to the position of the line of progression, but each time we would ask for that, we would be told that the time wasn't right. One day it would be."[43] Testimony from other Union Camp workers similarly highlighted the persistence of black protest. Black union leader James Tyson related that when he was hired in 1945, he had asked for a job in the line of progression but was rebuffed by the company. Tyson refused to accept company assertions that he had experienced a "pretty good life" with Union Camp:

I went there trying to get in the line of progression and was denied, for 26 years I just made out. I mean, of course, I was a guy that felt like at that time that I needed it as much as anybody else, so I couldn't say I've had a pretty good life. This is the difference in a man being able to use his ability and go on up or a guy just—he has to recognize the fact that he can't. . . . No sir; pushing bricks—if you've got ambition, pushing bricks and cutting out a hole down there, menial jobs, you wouldn't call that a good job . . . working is one thing, and to satisfy a man's ambition is another.[44]

Workers who had particular educational or vocational qualifications often found it particularly difficult to accept being channeled into unskilled, laboring positions. These workers, too, had little success when they tried to challenge the color of work. At International Paper Company in Pine Bluff, Arkansas, Booker T. Williams worked as a laborer in the 1950s while he was completing a college degree. He tried repeatedly to get a management position so that he could use his qualifications at the company, but he was told that management "were not hiring blacks in that position." After "15 to 20" unsuccessful efforts, Williams left the mill and took a lower-paying job as a teacher.[45]

In many other paper plants, well-qualified African American workers often challenged the paper industry's racial job assignments before the 1960s. A large number of plaintiffs in *Myers v. Gilman Paper* described these efforts in claim forms that they filed as part of the case. Luther Walker, for example, indicated that he tried repeatedly to secure work as a painter but maintained that "they didn't take blacks for those jobs."[46] At Gilman, all blacks in the paint department were classified as trainees but were actually limited purely to laboring jobs that assisted the white painters. Several workers questioned this system. Sam Fuller, for example, did some painting and, as a result, was summoned to the supervisor's office, where he continued to question the bar upon blacks painting: "'Maybe I misread the contract, but will you show me where it says I can't paint?' He says, 'You're a trainee.' I said, 'How can you train but by picking up the tools and doing the work?' He looked down, then looked up and said, 'Sam, you're right. Just don't paint anymore to keep down confusion.'"[47]

Other Gilman workers who challenged racial classifications also found out how fiercely they were maintained. Nathaniel Joseph described his unsuccessful efforts to secure a promotion: "I spok[e] to Mr George Howerly about being a scale clerk, he told me that they don't have any black scale clerk, that was a white man job."[48] Roosevelt Dawson similarly claimed that he was unable to move into the job he wanted "because that was not a black job."[49] Not surprisingly, some workers concluded that there was little point in trying to challenge the color line. As one worker succinctly put it: "Wasn't any need—just be losing wind."[50]

Although the company frequently blamed the union for preventing blacks from getting better-paid jobs at Gilman, the claim forms filed in the *Myers* case show that company officials helped to enforce segregation at the mill.[51] Supervisors indeed often threatened or harassed employees who asked for white jobs. When John Eaddy asked for a job in the machine shop, his supervisor told him that he would be sent "back to the farm" if he did not forget the idea.[52] Rufus Dawson described a similar incident: "I asked my foreman, George Harvey, if I could move to a higher paying job. He said yes, one more—out the gate. These conversations were before the civil rights act."[53] Many supervisors were clearly very annoyed by black workers who asked them for promotions. Harvey Jordan related the reaction of his supervisor when he had asked him for a higher-paid job: "Guy Austin, late 1950's, I asked him if there was any possible chance of my getting into either the painters or carpenters. He cursed and said, 'if you want to work; you stay where you are.'"[54]

It is no surprise that many workers became afraid of losing their jobs if they pushed too hard. Nathaniel McGauley, an outspoken young activist, explained that senior black workers had warned him not to force the issue: "In talking with others who had been working there for some time reminded me it was not a good Idea for fear of loosing [*sic*] my job."[55] Fear indeed played a major role in keeping segregation in place in the paper industry. Many black workers at Gilman described how they knew they were not being afforded equal opportunity but were afraid to ask for a promotion for fear that they would lose their jobs. "I was scared I would lose the job I did have if I ask the official for a set up," wrote Johnny L. Stafford.[56]

Throughout the southern paper industry, many black workers claimed that they had to accept discrimination prior to the 1960s because they needed to keep their jobs in order to support their families. Almost all black paper workers were men, and they were often the sole breadwinner for large families.[57] Many related that they could not afford to protest because companies fired workers easily. "You couldn't raise too much sand, a man say you gone, you just gone," recalled Sammie Hatcher. Hatcher felt that his need to support his large family made it impossible to protest: "There wasn't no promotions for you back then. . . . I didn't like it but just like I said, I

needed to work and I had a family. . . . I had six children at the time. . . .
There was nothing I could do about it and I needed to work so I just hung in
there. . . . I know if I hang in there long enough a change would come."[58]

Other African American workers stressed that they had to accept the
authority of any white worker, no matter how junior or inexperienced that
worker was. As Willie Ford related, "I don't care if he was no more than that
high, you had to say 'Yes, Sir,' to them, white, as long as he was white, sure
did. He could be a little old boy like that." Ford claimed that whites regularly
used racial epithets and had all the "best jobs" at the mill. He explained that
the need to support a large family left him with no choice other than to
tolerate these conditions: "You had to put up with it to stay there. I left many
days saying I wasn't going back but I didn't have no other choice. I had a wife
and five head of children, I had to go back. Sure did."[59]

It was indeed accepted wisdom among many retired black paper workers
that the only way to survive in a paper mill before the 1960s was to "keep
your place." Collis C. Jordan was hired at Union Camp in 1948, working as,
what he termed, a "common laborer." Looking back on his early years in the
mill, he repeatedly stressed the powerlessness of black workers: "You don't
buck your supervisor but so much because see he controls your paycheck,
and there were just certain things that you just didn't do, certain things that
you didn't say, you know to a supervisor. . . . At one time 'Yes sir' and 'No sir'
initially that was the words that you didn't forget. You didn't forget those
words. . . . You had your place in society, and from a family viewpoint, you
just didn't break it."[60]

Apart from fear, ignorance also played an important role in maintaining
segregation in the southern paper industry. Black workers repeatedly complained that companies concealed job opportunities by refusing to post
vacancies. It was very difficult for many workers who labored in all-black
departments to find out about openings in all-white areas.[61] At Gilman
Paper Company, for example, David L. Williams wanted to work in a higher-
paying job but complained that it was impossible to find out about openings. "I believed that I could do those job's," he asserted. "I had the ability to
do the work. But when better jobs were open [I] did not no [sic] about them.
Job's or opening's weren't posted."[62]

Many African American paper workers across the South voiced this complaint. Moses K. Baker, a veteran worker at Continental Can in Port Wentworth, Georgia, for example, gave a graphic description of the way that lack
of job postings had held back black workers: "I wanted to know when a job
was open over there, in the middle, and put me to someplace else, and they
send it to somebody else all the time. And I'm in the woodyard, ain't nobody

telling me they want me to go no place else, and I don't know when the job comes available, I don't run the personnel. And nobody would tell me when it become available and so those jobs, we didn't know about a job being available, just licked to start with."[63]

Many black workers described the toll that job segregation exacted upon them. Ervin Humes, who started working at IP in Georgetown, South Carolina, in 1943, vividly recalled the lack of job opportunities and segregated facilities at the mill: "It grind me to go through that kind of treatment, but I had a family and I had to bear it." Humes felt that the way that whites were promoted over blacks with more seniority was particularly hard to accept because it allowed whites to take better care of their families:

> It was a hurtful thing to see a young white boy come out of high school and he could go on a job and keep advancing, taking care of his family, more money to make because money talks, and I, with the same training, I couldn't do nothing of that sort to take care of my family. . . . Now on the job I was on, pulling the paper from the machine that breaks, you had what we call a white pusher, a foreman, listen now. . . . He would come and they'd put him as a foreman when we'd been down there ten or twelve years. He didn't actually know where the restroom or the water fountain was. He was just a plain rookie, but his face was a different color, and they'd put him over us, and he didn't know actually nothing about the job. That was bitter. If I'd have come in your, you're a professor in Cambridge, I'd have come in as a rookie and they'd put me as a professor with tenure and you'd been there all that time, that's wrong. But that's what they did. And many times the guy has just come out of high school, so they put him right over us.[64]

Retired African American paper workers often remembered specific injustices that illustrated their low status in the industry before the 1960s. Bobby Radcliff, who worked at Scott Paper Company in Mobile, recalled that white truck drivers refused to allow blacks to ride in the cab with them: "They couldn't even ride in the cab with the driver. They had to ride on the back, rain, shine, cold or hot, they had to ride on the back."[65] Sidney Gibson similarly recalled with sadness that black workers were never allowed to touch trucks unless they were assigned to wash them.[66]

White supervisors' and workers' use of demeaning epithets was also a feature of daily working life in many mills. "They called you 'nigger' and there wasn't nothing you could do about it," recalled one retired worker.[67] Many other workers described how they were subjected to racial epithets. In 1972, Lee Jewell Randle testified that racial epithets had often been used during the fourteen years that he had worked at IP's mill in Pine Bluff, Arkansas: "I've been cursed ever since I've been at the mill. . . . I wish I could name some of the things that Mr. Crow have called me and the other blacks. You can just name most anything. I don't want to repeat the word that he have called me."[68] Other black workers, meanwhile, complained that supervisors made them work much harder than whites and enforced disciplinary rules unequally. Union Camp worker James Hardy, for example, claimed in 1975 that supervisors had consistently treated black workers at the mill more harshly than whites: "I wonder why they so hard on the blacks and, you know, like we could be working in an area and we could be doing what the foreman tell us to do, we finish . . . and when you could have fifteen whites over there standing around doing nothing. He just pass by them, but he just see the blacks standing up."[69]

Before the 1960s, the southern paper industry was explicitly segregated, with jobs divided by racial categories that were universally accepted. Most white workers themselves later acknowledged the inequities that black workers faced.[70] As one of them commented, both management and workers "wanted blacks to do the black work and whites to do the white work."[71] This philosophy determined all job assignments, even when students were hired for temporary positions.[72] Donald L. Langham, a white worker, outlined how all work was segregated at IP's Mobile mill when he started working there in 1957:

> I recall many professional baseball players, for example, that have gone on to be professional baseball players out of this Mobile area, would come to work at the paper mill. They would put them down on what they call the broke beater or either in the bull gang, which was the lowest-paid jobs in the mill, and put the white kids on the paper machines, which was a higher-paying job. . . . That's right, temporary workers, summer workers. Even if a black person decided to stay on permanent, or got hired on permanent, they would be put in the menial jobs and the white people would be put up in the more permanent jobs, like in a air-conditioned, controlled finishing and shipping department for example, and the black person would be put on the broke beater or in the bull gang.[73]

Many of the Title VII cases brought in the southern paper industry after the 1964 Civil Rights Act was passed were clearly characterized by the outspoken and vivid testimony given by black workers, testimony that emphasizes the importance of the act to paper mill workers throughout the South. In their own words, African Americans described how they had worked in an industry with few promotional opportunities and little room to protest. Despite their efforts, companies and unions were very successful at maintaining the system of complete job segregation. The 1964 Civil Rights Act, however, enabled these workers to protest effectively against a lifetime of discrimination. Across the South, black paper workers understood the possibilities that the law opened up to them and they acted quickly to ensure that its nondiscrimination mandate became a reality.

BLACK WORKERS

CHAPTER 3
ALL THIS COME THROUGH THE CIVIL RIGHTS ACT
FEDERAL MANDATES AND BLACK ACTIVISM IN THE SOUTHERN PAPER INDUSTRY, 1964–1980

Prior to the 1960s, African Americans had tried in vain to fight against segregation in the southern paper industry, but they lacked the machinery that could sustain this protest. With the passage of the 1964 Civil Rights Act, this situation changed dramatically. Racial discrimination in employment was, for the first time, prohibited by federal law, and black workers could file charges with the federal Equal Employment Opportunity Commission if they felt the law was being broken. More importantly, Title VII of the act gave aggrieved workers the right to bring civil lawsuits if the EEOC was unable to secure voluntary conciliation. Across the South, black workers used these provisions to improve their job opportunities. Between 1964 and 1980, Title VII litigation affected all of the major industries that operated in the American South. A plethora of cases tackled issues as varied as hiring discrimination in the textile industry and employment testing in the power industry. The paper industry, however, was involved in more litigation than possibly any other industry in the South. Between 1964 and 1980, indeed, the paper industry experienced so many Title VII suits that Kent Spriggs, an NAACP Legal Defense Fund (LDF) lawyer, called it "perhaps the most litigated industry in the south."[1]

Written records support Sprigg's comment, showing that almost every major paper company was involved in at least one class action Title VII case between 1965 and 1980. The files of the AFL-CIO Civil Rights Department indicate that within five years of the act's passage, EEOC charges were filed at almost every paper mill in the South, with many of these charges leading to lawsuits. It is no surprise that company and union attorneys complained of being swamped. In 1970 UPP attorney Warren Woods wrote a colleague, "At the moment so many new sets of charges have been filed against paper companies in the South that it is hard to tell exactly where we stand."[2] The paper industry indeed became somewhat notorious for the volume of charges filed. In 1973, for example, Christopher Jenkins, a black worker at Westvaco in Charleston, South Carolina, testified that when he went to file charges, the EEOC's representative told him that the federal agency already "had complaints against several [paper] mills" and had decided to concentrate on the industry as a result: "After they had so much complaining in the paper industry about the discriminatory practices, they were going to work on this first, although they had other companies that have practices too, but not as much as the paper industry."[3]

Paper unions, in particular, felt the impact of black activism, since many EEOC charges and Title VII cases asserted that the union had acquiesced in discriminatory practices. John Defee, the former head of the UPIU's human relations department, remembered that in the 1970s the union "had over 190 charges against our union for discrimination by our members," adding that union officials came to expect lawsuits wherever they worked: "You knew it was coming, you just backed up and waited. Well, you couldn't blame them [black workers], they had been mistreated for a long, long time, and they could see a little bit of a way out."[4]

Clearly, the large number of paper industry cases indicates that African American workers very actively used the 1964 Civil Rights Act to protest against discrimination. Very little is known about such activism, since the Civil Rights Act generally has been seen as the culmination of civil rights protest rather than the cause. Historians have concentrated more upon "classic" activism directed at integrating public facilities and schools rather than on the fight for civil rights in southern industry. In fact, the 1964 Civil Rights Act had a huge impact on black paper workers, stimulating a new phase of protest across the South's paper mill communities. The act, together with other federal pressure, also prodded companies and unions to improve opportunities for African Americans and enabled them to blame the law for integration, thus helping to neutralize potential white opposition.[5]

Black Activism: An Overview

Black activism in the southern paper industry first became noticeable after the creation of the President's Committee on Equal Employment Opportunity in 1961.[6] Many workers filed charges with the committee, complaining chiefly about job segregation. At the Union Camp mill in Savannah, for example, a group of charges were filed with the President's Committee in 1963. The charges were principally about testing and segregated locals. Workers felt that the tests, which involved answering general-knowledge questions, were not job related and ignored their extensive on-the-job experience.[7] It was the creation of the EEOC in 1965, however, that really opened the floodgates in the paper industry. Charges poured into the new agency at an alarming speed, with many being filed by groups of black workers simultaneously.[8] At the Federal Paper Board Company in Richmond, Virginia, for example, a group of African American workers charged in June 1966 that segregated local unions restricted their job opportunities. "I am a member of Local 528, an all-Negro Local," wrote Earnest Smith. "The Negro Local has attempted to merge with the white Local several times in an attempt to comply with Title VII; these attempted mergers have been unsuccessful. We would appreciate the assistance of the Equal Employment Opportunity Commission in effectuating a merger of these Locals because continued segregation will perpetuate dual lines of progression in the Federal Paper Board Company."[9]

As Smith's statement shows, African American workers usually complained about segregated locals because they contributed to the exclusion of blacks from the better-paying jobs. Over and over again, black workers complained that they were placed in low-paying, segregated jobs and prevented from gaining access to better-paying jobs by separate locals and employment tests. At the Continental Can Company in Port Wentworth, Georgia, for example, four workers claimed in 1971 that they had been discriminated against, asserting that they were placed in segregated job classifications and were denied promotions.[10] At Union Camp, twelve black workers filed a "Charge of Discrimination" in January 1969 that detailed how they were restricted to the lowest-paying jobs.[11]

While some southern industries, such as textiles, largely excluded blacks before 1964, there were others that followed the paper industry's example. The steel industry, for instance, was another process industry that had also traditionally restricted black workers to low-paying jobs. Union attorneys who handled a large number of Title VII cases highlighted the similarities between the two industries.[12] "The paper and the steel industry attracted more civil rights litigation because . . . steel and paper are organized similarly," explained UPIU attorney Michael Hamilton. "They are what are called process industries and because they're process industries the way work gets organized is in lines of progression, and so that created again a context where this kind of litigation was just tailor-made. People were locked into by virtue of systems, into lower-paying, less desirable lines of progression."[13] The structured segregation of the paper industry both led black workers to file many charges and produced a considerable amount of support for these charges from the EEOC.[14]

The amount of litigation that occurred in the paper industry also reflected the influence of civil rights groups, particularly the NAACP Legal Defense Fund. The NAACP and the NAACP LDF found that segregated locals provided them with an excellent symbol of the discrimination black workers faced in the union movement, and they set about abolishing these unions well before the Civil Rights Act was passed. In 1958, for example, NAACP members who worked in southern paper mills contacted the association's national office and requested their assistance in eliminating "the rigid pattern of segregation and discrimination" maintained by the IBPSPMW and the UPP. In response to these grievances, the NAACP filed a number of complaints with the AFL-CIO's Civil Rights Department.[15] Throughout the 1960s and 1970s, the NAACP continued to target the paper industry because of its historic practice of chartering segregated unions.[16] In addition, in July 1968, the NAACP LDF asserted that it was giving "heavy emphasis" to fighting job discrimination in the pulp and paper industry because the industry was undergoing a $3 billion expansion and offered well-paid jobs in areas of the South in which there were high incidences of black poverty.[17]

As was the case in other industries, the suits that the NAACP LDF brought in the paper industry played an important role in enforcing Title VII.[18] The LDF's Jack Greenberg indeed declared in 1971 that the civil class action had been "the only truly effective vehicle for affirmative relief under Title VII."[19] By October 1971, the LDF had already brought more than 150 Title VII cases in U.S. district courts, including many in the paper industry. These cases represented a "substantial portion" of all the Title VII cases filed across the country.[20] The fund was principally involved in major cases that became "mileposts in the field," including *United States v. Local 189*.

The *Local 189* case was one of the landmark cases in the paper industry. Seeking an injunction for violations of Title VII, the U.S. Justice Department brought this action against the UPP and Crown-Zellerbach Corporation on January 30, 1968. In June 1968, the district court ruled that both the company and the union had violated Title VII, a decision that was affirmed by the court of appeals a year later. The court ruled that the seniority system should be changed so that seniority was based on time at the plant rather than on time in a particular job, a move that greatly improved job opportunities for senior black workers who had always worked in segregated jobs. This ruling was copied by the Office of Federal Contract Compliance (OFCC) in its monitoring of civil rights compliance and became the basis for the Jackson Memorandum of 1968.[21]

After the Jackson Memorandum came into effect, black workers in two IP plants also sought and gained further relief from alleged racial discrimination in transfers and promotions. Two major cases, *Rogers v. International Paper* and *Stevenson v. International Paper*, were tried in 1972 and 1973, respectively.[22] The *Rogers* case involved workers at IP's mill in Pine Bluff, Arkansas, and the *Stevenson* case was filed by African American workers at the company's plant in Mobile, Alabama. In 1975, both cases were decided by the court of appeals in favor of the plaintiffs after the district courts had refused to grant orders enforcing the provisions of the Jackson Memorandum.[23]

Some of the Title VII cases in the paper industry took many years to settle. One of the earliest cases was filed by African American workers against Albemarle Paper Company in Roanoke Rapids, North Carolina, in August 1966. In *Moody v. Albemarle Paper Company*, the plaintiffs sought permanent injunctive relief for acts at the paper mill in violation of Title VII. After a trial in July and August of 1971, the district court ruled on November 9, 1971, that it had found no evidence of "bad faith non-compliance with the Act." In 1973, the Fourth Circuit Court of Appeals reversed the district court, holding that back pay could not be denied merely because the employer had not acted in bad faith. On certiorari, the Supreme Court vacated the judgment of the court of appeals and remanded the case to the district court, although the case was never decided on remand.[24]

Several major Title VII cases were filed against mills located in coastal Georgia. On May 6, 1971, for example, African American workers at Continental Can Company in Port Wentworth, Georgia, filed suit alleging racial discrimination. The case went to trial in August and September 1973. On August 18, 1976, the district court held that the minuscule representation of blacks in salaried and clerical jobs was sufficient by itself to demonstrate a violation of Title VII and that injunctive relief was a proper remedy.[25] In nearby Savannah, black workers at the Union Camp Corporation also brought a Title VII case in 1971. The plaintiffs sought injunctive, declaratory, and affirmative relief, as well as back pay. The company tried to dismiss the case on the grounds that it had instituted an affirmative action program in 1970 that had eliminated all the claims of racial discrimination. On November 10, 1972, however, the district court held that this program was not a conclusive defense, asserting that it was deficient in several respects.[26]

In many Title VII cases, plaintiffs sued unions and companies together, asserting that both had acquiesced in establishing segregation in the industry. For unions in the paper industry, a particularly important case was *Myers v. Gilman Paper Company*, which was filed in 1972 by a group of black workers at the company's plant in St. Marys, Georgia. Plaintiffs and the company proposed a consent decree, but the union asked the district court to reject it. On January 14, 1975, the district court approved the decree, stating that there had been Title VII violations at the plant and that the union and Gilman were "equally responsible" for the discrimination. The basis of this ruling was that the company had assigned blacks to certain jobs and that job and department seniority systems as provided in the labor agreement had prevented them from transferring to other lines of progression. The union was thus liable for 50 percent of the lost income that black workers had suffered because they were confined to low-paying jobs. The union appealed this decision to the Fifth Circuit Court of Appeals, but the court affirmed that unions were liable for preserving the effects of past discrimination through the collective bargaining agreement.[27] At one stage, the union feared that it might have to pay as much as $850,000 to the large class of plaintiffs, but UPIU attorneys eventually reached a compromise settlement for an undisclosed sum, which was "considerably less than any of us anticipated."[28]

Following the *Myers* case, the UPIU increasingly sought to settle Title VII litigation out of court, usually through consent decrees. One of the largest cases brought in the paper industry, *Garrett v. Weyerhauser Corporation*, was originally filed at the start of 1977 and involved a class of around 3,000 black employees at the company's plant in Plymouth, North Carolina, a small town located in the eastern part of the state. This large case was settled by a consent decree in mid-December 1981, with Weyerhauser contributing $820,000 in back pay and attorney's fees to effectuate the settlement. The union, however, escaped with much smaller damages; they were ordered to contribute $20,000 to help defray plaintiffs' attorney's fees.[29]

"If I Had Been Given the Same Opportunity as White Employees"

EEOC charges document the formal grievances of African American workers in the paper industry, but more personal evidence affords a closer look at black activism: a number of claim forms submitted by workers in several legal cases were accompanied by workers' handwritten letters or other notes relating their experiences and their reasons for supporting particular cases. Over 400 claim forms completed by plaintiffs in *Myers v. Gilman Paper Company*, for example, outline exactly what motivated workers to support this case.

Black workers' activism in *Myers* was especially notable because the case was brought against Gilman's mill in St. Marys, Georgia, a remote company town in the southeastern corner of the state. Gilman Paper Company was based in Vermont and had opened the St. Marys mill in 1941. In 1972, the small Georgia town had a population of only 5,200 and the paper mill was the largest employer. As *Harper's Magazine* noted, "Practically all of the town's breadwinners are employed by the Gilman Paper Company. . . . The worker who does move to St. Marys is drawn into an intricate web of economic and financial relationships, the strands of which all lead back to the mill."[30]

The workers' claim forms in *Myers* show clearly that although black protest came to fruition after 1964, it had begun much earlier. The legacy of World War II was crucial, since many workers who were fighting for equal job opportunities in the 1970s cited their experiences during the war to justify their claim that they could run "white" jobs. Many of these workers had performed skilled work in the service and felt that they could perform similar jobs at the mill. "I was in the Army from 1944 to 1948 (WW. II) and during that time worked as switchboard operator and [did] some electrical work," wrote Robert Edwards. "I was a satisfactory employee and was discharged honorably. I feel that if I had been given the training and opportunities that whites had, I could perform the jobs on the Paper Machine."[31] Albert Lee Price used his experience in World War II to justify his claim to a carpenter's job: "I rigged in Pearl Harbor. Had papers. I am a trained carpenter."[32] Rossie Massey similarly claimed that he was qualified for a skilled job. "From 1941–1945 While serving in the U.S. Army I had training as a Carpenter," he explained. Many other workers, and especially those who had worked as welders in the shipyards of nearby Brunswick during the war, cited their war experience on their claim forms.[33]

Gilman plaintiffs referred not only to their World War II experiences but also to military service in general. Many protested because they were unable to find a jobs in the paper industry comparable to those that they had held in service. Vietnam veteran Lionel Smith related that he had held an engineering job in the navy with "12 men directly under me." Brown found it hard to accept not being able to transfer into maintenance at Gilman after returning from Vietnam. "After haveing [*sic*] advanced that far in four years," he wrote, "I was sure I could come home and get a good job because of my past experience but instead I have found almost total discrimination."[34]

Across the South, many other black paper workers were motivated to protest against discrimination by their experience of military service, especially during World War II. Samuel Roberson, for example, went to work at Weyerhauser's Plymouth mill after leaving the army at the end of the war.

Testifying in 1977, Roberson claimed that he was taking part in *Garrett* so that "me and other blacks would have the same right to move as other people. The same seniority, the same rights as the white have." Roberson used his experience of fighting for his country to justify his plea for equal treatment in the mill: "These jobs that certain ones have to have—Certain ones can get and certain ones you can't, I think that's unfair. I feel like, you serve the country, the war comes and you fight for the country. I think the black man should have the same right as whites. You do the same thing they do."[35]

Military service had often given African Americans leadership experience that prompted them to challenge segregation when they entered the paper mills. At Georgia Kraft Company in Rome, Georgia, for example, Linell Long returned from being a corporal in the medical corps to work in the mill. In the army, he had served as a ward master in charge of twenty-five people. Once he returned to Georgia Kraft, he became president of the black local and led the class action suit of *Long v. Georgia Kraft*, which was filed in 1969. In court testimony, Long cited his army experience to justify his claim that he was qualified to be a supervisor at the mill.[36] Other black workers compared the qualifications they had acquired in the service with those of the whites that were supervisors, often concluding that they would be able to perform a supervisor's job. At Weyerhauser, World War II veteran William D. Gee testified in 1977 why he had joined the *Garrett* suit: "I had some foremans, when I started in the forestry—couldn't read or write and they were in charge of me. They would send the payroll out and I had to pay off. And I didn't think it was right to have a man that's not capable of doing these things. And I was trained in the service for such work."[37]

Some younger workers were moved to protest against discrimination in the paper industry after serving in integrated armed forces.[38] Herman Robinson began working at International Paper Company in Moss Point, Mississippi, in 1954 and then served in the military for six years. Upon returning to the mill, Robinson no longer accepted segregation and he played a leading role in filing EEOC charges against the company. Robinson recalled,

> When I went in the military, you know you meet all kinds of people in the military, and I was stationed in different places overseas and everything, and I come back, what made me, what pushed me into getting it sorted out, when I come back out, I saw how silly that was. I say now here I've been sleeping with white guys, eating with them, taking baths with them and all that, and then you come back into International Paper Company you look there you've got separate water-fountains,

you've got separate toilets. That really opened my eyes. I said, "This is silly, it don't make no sense." I say, "Why you got to live like this here and I lived for four years drinking out of the same coke bottle as white guys." . . . I say, "What's different, it don't make no sense."[39]

World War II also had a radicalizing effect on many African Americans who stayed in the paper mills during the war. Many of these workers ran more responsible jobs during the war, and this experience proved to them that they could perform white work. Gilman worker Roosevelt Dawson used his experience during the war to argue that he should be awarded a maintenance job. "I operated the bulldozer for the company during the war," he explained. "Equipment operator is in the yard line of progression, where I was. If it had not been for the seniority system, I would have moved into the job. I have good mechanical ability."[40] At Westvaco in Charleston, black plaintiffs also argued that they should have been promoted because they had performed white jobs during the Second World War. I. Watson Sr., for example, wrote on his 1973 claim form that he could perform "[e]very job in the Finishing + Shipping Dept. above car bracer. I drive platform truck during World War II but when the war was over they give the job to the white men, and I was put back."[41]

The way that black workers often took advantage of the advances they made during World War II to justify their fight against segregation in the civil rights era was illustrated well by the experience of W. H. Mason. Mason was hired at Albemarle Paper Company in Roanoke Rapids, North Carolina, in 1936 and started working in a laboring job, stoking coal for the company's boilers. During World War II, Mason worked as a welder, although he was still classified as a laborer. Once the war was over, he remembered, he was not allowed to weld anymore: "Well, after the War was over and they could get the mens back to work . . . they stopped me from using the torches, said if I used it, they would have to pay me, and said they couldn't pay me on account of I was a Negro, so they just took the torch away from me."[42]

More than twenty years later, Mason became one of the leading plaintiffs in the *Moody v. Albemarle Paper* class action. Citing his war experience, he repeatedly argued in his 1968 testimony that he could work in the all-white maintenance department. "I can do the same work that they are doing or better, right now. I have did it," he declared. Like many black paper workers, he drew confidence from his close knowledge of a large number of jobs in the mill. "I knowed the Mill just like you know your law book," he told the lawyer who was questioning him.[43]

At Gilman Paper Company, black activists also drew upon other aspects of their experiences outside the mill. Many related how they had built their own houses as proof that they could perform skilled jobs at the paper mill. "I have farmed almost all my life and built the house I live in," wrote Wordie Hubbard, who wanted to secure a white job on the paper machine. "I feel confident that I could learn to do any of the jobs that I mentioned, if given the same training and opportunities as given whites."[44] Similarly, Alfred Bryant described how he had acquired relevant practical experience outside the mill: "Before coming to work at Gilman I was a painter for Mr. George Long, I practically built my own home, and do farming on the side. I feel that I could have worked the towerman job, if I had been given the same opportunity as whites were given."[45] Many other Gilman employees submitted similar claims.[46] The forms reveal, indeed, that many black workers possessed a great variety of practical qualifications that they believed they could utilize in the paper industry.[47]

Regardless of whether they had acquired their skills during military service or in their lives outside the mill, workers with mechanical experience found it especially difficult to accept the laboring positions that blacks were restricted to in the paper industry. Robert L. Jordan, for example, had worked as an auto mechanic before coming to Gilman, where he was frustrated at being placed in a cleaning position. "I was working as a mechanic [at] Grays Auto Service," he wrote. "When they asked me to come to work at Gilman, I thought it was in the machine shop. When I got there, it was clean up in the paper mill. I begged and asked to go on the paper machine." In the early 1970s, Jordan's efforts paid off; he was "the first black to go on the paper machine."[48]

Blacks who had experience within the paper industry also believed that they were capable of running higher-paying jobs. Herbert Myers, for example, wrote: "Have been there 36 years—Know the work."[49] Warren Mitchell, who had always wanted one of the white jobs on the woodyard, wrote that he felt that he could perform them because he had spent over twenty-five years in the woodyard and was familiar with all the jobs. He added that when some white jobs had finally opened up in the 1970s, it was too late for him. "I am 74 years old," he wrote in 1981. "By the time the opportunity came, I was too old to take it. Also arthritis had set in."[50]

Mitchell's problem was a common one. Many other black workers found that opportunities only became available when they were close to retirement. George Edwards, who had retired before the *Myers* case was settled, wanted "any job" in the recovery room, which was part of the powerhouse operation. "I am familiar with the operation, and could learn anything I was asked to do," he declared. "By the time black people were given the opportunity, I was too old. I would have moved up this line if the seniority had been right."[51]

Many other African American workers did not live to see better job opportunities open up in the paper industry. Several claim forms were written by relations of workers who had died before the *Myers* case was finally settled. Relatives described how these workers had attempted to get different jobs and how their efforts had been fruitless. Explained the wife of the late Ferris Everett, "He spoke to me a number of times. He was very active in trying to get better jobs for his people." Nevertheless, Everett worked all his life as a laborer.[52]

The fact that many African American workers had trained whites also fueled their confidence to claim that they were qualified for white jobs. "They told me I didn't know the job and I taught two white men," noted Westvaco plaintiff John B. Neal.[53] Even when they had not had direct experience of running white jobs, black workers had often watched whites carry them out and they used this knowledge to argue that they were qualified. At Scott, for example, Wilbert Brown was denied the painter's helper job because the company claimed he did not have enough education. Brown, however, refuted this: "I felt like it didn't require that much education, not for a Painter's Helper. Not at least when I see what the painter does. Most any ten or fifteen year old child could do what they are doing, with most skills and using an ordinary paint brush."[54]

Many African American paper workers also used their extensive on-the-job experience as a way of protesting against the tests and educational qualifications that companies often introduced when lines of progression were opened up in the 1960s. At this time, many companies instituted testing as a prerequisite for entry into a line of progression, or they began to require that certain jobs required a high school diploma. At Scott Paper Company, a high school requirement was introduced at the same time that the company merged its lines of progression in 1962.[55] African American workers across the South viewed testing as discriminatory because they felt that promotions should be based on actual job experience rather than upon tests, which they viewed as abstract. The 1975 testimony of paper worker Arthur Kilroy captured how many black workers felt: "Then it came up that we had to take a test and it became quite odd that doing the same job for nineteen and a half to twenty years, then having to take a test to determine your mental capability to learn how to do what you already were doing, seemed a little bit ridiculous." He added, "It was just the irony of it all. You do a job for twenty years and then you have to go take a test to determine whether you have the mental capability to learn how to do it."[56]

Family members clearly helped to sustain black workers even when they were repeatedly told by company officials that they were not qualified to perform white jobs.[57] Several Gilman plaintiffs described how they constantly discussed ways of fighting discrimination at the mill with their co-workers and families. "I spoke with relatives, fellow union members and friends, on numerous occasions," wrote one black worker. "Almost everyone I knew then and know now works for the company and we all wanted the same thing—to be able to work in the better-paying, white jobs."[58] The determination of many black workers was summed up by Calvin P. Wilson, who included on his claim form a long list of jobs that he felt blacks could do if they were "given the chance." Wilson related that black workers continually discussed the injustice of segregated jobs and resented having whites promoted over them: "I talked to all of my co workers, I always discuss with them about we having a chance to move up to any jobs in the plant that the whites have, and that it wasn't right for us to be at certain jobs for about 4 years and they would hire a white man and put him over us." Although admitting that he had been afraid to speak out against segregation, Wilson described how he covertly kept his faith alive: "I always had a strong desire to move up in life. When I had a job to do I always try to do a good job, because I knowed that if I did a good job and try to come to work every day, that it might pay off for me someday."[59]

After years of working in southern paper mills, many veteran black paper workers clearly felt cheated. They had entered the industry with hopes of being able to progress to better jobs and were angered by being locked into low-paying, segregated jobs. In testimony typical of many black mill workers, Weyerhauser worker Samuel Moore, who had worked at the mill since it opened in 1937, said in 1978 that he was still working "right where I started. . . . The other guys would come in there and work this job a while, and then they'd move on up. And it wouldn't be long they'd be gone and somebody else would come and they'd move on out. So you wondered, 'Are you going to be here all of your days?'"[60] In *Boles v. Union Camp*, veteran worker John Bonner, who had worked at the mill since 1946, stated in a 1975 deposition that he supported the case because he felt that black workers had not been rewarded for their efforts in building the company: "I feel like that I helped build the company since '46 up until now, because it wasn't like it was out here when I come out here. This part here—this here—wasn't nothing along here. No buildings at all. And I think I should get a run around like that? I think it's wrong."[61]

In bringing Title VII suits, most African American plaintiffs emphasized that they wanted to end collective discrimination rather than secure individual goals.[62] Weyerhauser worker Gurvies L. Bryant, who had worked at the company since 1948, summed up how many felt: "We were not working for one individual; we were working for the entire black race."[63] Plaintiffs were often older workers who were keen to create better opportunities for succeeding generations. Testifying in Plymouth in 1977, senior Weyerhauser worker William D. Gee said that he wanted to make sure that future generations of whites and blacks were not segregated when they went to work in the mill: "I did this for myself and others . . . we played together with one another, but when you come down to the work, some gets jobs and some not. And we live in the same area. I hope that my son, grandchildren won't have . . . to go through what we had to go through. I hope we create a better atmosphere."[64]

Similar collective motives were cited by other African Americans who played a leading role in lawsuits, especially by older workers. At Hudson Pulp and Paper Company in Palatka, Florida, senior black worker George B. Williams testified that he had written to the EEOC shortly after the Civil Rights Act was passed because he wanted to provide more jobs for blacks in the future, and especially women: "Well, the purpose I wrote them about, I wrote them about jobs for black people. There was only 85 blacks at Hudson and 2,200 union employees. I had gone into the company and had a meeting with the company. I told them that I was getting old, and I wanted to see some black men and black women out in the mill before I retired. They told me, George, we didn't hire but six women this year. I said I didn't want them to fire a white woman to hire a black woman, but I wanted to see a black woman out at the mill. I said them six should have been black."[65]

The strength of white resistance to job integration compelled many black workers to point out that they did not wish to take jobs away from whites; like Williams, they argued that all they wanted was equal opportunity for blacks. "I don't feel like you should take a job away from nobody," declared one worker, "but I feel like they should give everybody equal chance on a job." These sentiments were repeated by many other African American plaintiffs.[66]

"When the 1964 Civil Rights Came Out, That Opened the Door": The 1964 Civil Rights Act and Black Activism

Black activism in the paper industry was sustained by workers' long-term experiences, but the passage of the 1964 Civil Rights Act allowed these long-term grievances to be expressed. African American paper workers, moreover, were acutely aware of the act's passage and were determined to enforce its nondiscrimination mandate. At St. Regis Paper Company in Jacksonville, Florida, for example, Tony Neal testified in 1971 that black St. Regis workers had been discussing how to combat discrimination for many years: "We had been talking about that for a long time . . . about doing something about being discriminated." Neal added, however, that the group had been able to file a lawsuit only when they "found there was a law against being discriminated."[67]

The Civil Rights Act clearly raised black workers' expectations of job progression. In 1966, Albemarle Paper Company worker Theodore Daniel testified, "Since the Civil Rights Bill passed, the old guys should have an opportunity to go as far as they could."[68] The act also gave many workers the individual confidence to push for better jobs.[69] Gilman worker Oscar E. Morris, for example, wrote that he had asked for the "top job" on the paper machine "[w]hen Civil Act came into efect [sic]."[70] Union Camp's George Postell, who started working at the company as a laborer in 1947, explained in a 1975 deposition why he was supporting the Boles case. Referring to President Kennedy's introduction of a comprehensive civil rights bill in 1963, he noted, "Well, the reason I'm here and the complaints are is that I put in in '63—'63—when the Job Right becomes approved by the President of the United States, Kennedy, so I put in a temporary transfer for the Automotive Shop." He was refused the job, so he became one of the plaintiffs in Boles.[71]

The leaders of segregated black unions also used the Civil Rights Act to bolster their drive to open up more jobs for black workers. At Gilman Paper Company, for example, Johnnie L. Robinson, the president of the black local at the time of the 1965 contract negotiations, described how he tried to push both the company and union to live up to the Civil Rights Act. "As president of Local 616," he wrote, "I request[ed] that Gilman paper Copany [sic] and UPIU to execute Title VII of the Civil Rights Act of 1964 into the 1965 agreement." Robinson outlined that, despite resistance from both the company and the union, from July 2, 1965, the day the Civil Rights Act became effective, he carried on a sustained campaign to force both parties to open up more jobs to black workers: "From 7-2-65 for the next 31 months I make many request to the Company and union for Jobs for Local 616 members, and for myself I spoke with Mr C. L. Blondheim of process control and Mr E. L. Kerry Sr. At the collective bargaining meeting for the 1966 Agreement I told Mr. Steward of UPIU that Local 616 wouldn't sign or be parties to any agreement that didn't include a non-discrimination clause." Despite these efforts, the company did not begin to make the changes that Robinson desired until 1972, reportedly initially telling him that the act "didn't apply" to Gilman.[72] With the company unwilling to change voluntarily, Gilman workers filed a Title VII suit. As *Myers* plaintiff Thomas McGauley recalled, "They didn't start to change, we were looking for change, the company didn't do anything. What we were saying all the time, we told them that the Civil Rights Act had passed, the company had to do this because this was the law."[73]

In many other locations, the leaders of black locals used the passage of the Civil Rights Act to bolster their efforts to fight discrimination. At Weyerhauser's mill in Plymouth, for example, the president of the black local demanded the merger of segregated lines of progression less than a month after Title VII became effective.[74] Similarly, at the American Can Company in Butler, Alabama, black local president James B. Crowell met with plant management in the summer of 1965 and demanded that Title VII provisions be included in the contract.[75] Many other workers began to file charges soon after the act became effective in July 1965.[76] At the Olin-Mathieson paper plant in West Monroe, Louisiana, a group of workers filed charges on September 17, 1965, and at International Paper Company in Moss Point, Mississippi, a large number of EEOC charges had already been investigated by November 1965.[77]

Throughout the paper industry, indeed, African American activists used the machinery provided by the Civil Rights Act to fight ongoing discrimination. Alphonse Williams, the president of a black local in Mobile, recalled, "We had no choice either to go along with the segregated thing or to fight it, so when the 1964 Civil Rights came out, that opened the door, but even then they didn't wholly cooperate. . . . The Civil Rights law was signed in 1964, went into effect in 1965, and the reason why the Negro was fighting then was because he thought the civil rights law, according to the wording of the law, them things wasn't supposed to have been, so . . . we just went to fight then."[78]

Many activists educated themselves about the provisions of Title VII, becoming familiar with the law from their own reading. George Williams, a senior black worker at Hudson Pulp and Paper Company in Palatka, Florida, testified how he started a major Title VII case: "I seen it in a book. I used to get every law made from Washington. I didn't have to read the paper. It came in the mailbox to my house. . . . When this equal rights thing started, I looked in the book and saw who to write about the equal employment. From that book I started thinking, and so I wrote the letter."[79] Robert Hicks, the black paper worker at Crown-Zellerbach in Bogalusa who was responsible for bringing the major case of *Hicks v. Crown-Zellerbach*, similarly remembered that he learned about Title VII through his own reading at the local library. Hicks thought that the Civil Rights Act was very important in providing groups of black workers with the "structure" that they needed to protest effectively against discrimination in the industry. "I used the law, Title VII," he explained. "I filed a charge of discrimination under Title VII, and I filed the company and the unions as contributors to it."[80]

The militancy that the Civil Rights Act produced was not simply confined to paper mills. In Bogalusa, indeed, the civil rights demonstrations that occurred in 1964–65 were spurred on by the passage of the act and residents' desire to test the law in practice. As Adam Fairclough has noted, "The Civil Rights Act gave blacks a powerful incentive to demonstrate when, as in the case of Bogalusa, whites sought to preserve the racial status quo."[81] Hundreds of local activists, many of them paper mill workers, deliberately sought to test whether the town's businesses and public facilities were obeying the new law. On February 28, 1965, for example, Hicks led a group of blacks to test integration at Redwood Cafe in Bogalusa by going through the white entrance.[82] In May 1965, following a statement by the mayor that public facilities were integrated, Hicks led another group to the city park. When the police ordered the group to leave, local activists sent a telegram to the U.S. attorney general, calling for him to use his authority to make the Civil Rights Act a reality.[83]

That nondiscrimination posters began to be displayed in all paper mills after the Civil Rights Act became law and the executive orders were formalized was an important development that easily can be overlooked. Many African American workers who initiated lawsuits indeed testified that they had started the litigation by writing to the address listed on the posters. Christopher Jenkins, one of the lead plaintiffs in *Gantlin v. Westvaco*, for example, helped initiate the suit by writing to the OFCC: "Why did I file this charge? . . . [T]hey had a white local, and all the labor job and, I would say, the lower pay job was in the—in 620, which was the black local, and I felt like this wasn't right, and I wrote to the Federal *Contract* and Compliance about this because they have notice post all over the plant that if you feel like you discriminated against to contact them, and that what I did."[84] Similarly, Charles Munn, who worked at the Federal Paper Board Company in Riegelwood, North Carolina, explained that he initiated the suit of *Munn v. Federal Paper Board* after seeing "one of these signs they had up saying if you feel you were discriminated against."[85] The importance of these posters is also suggested by black workers' memories of whites repeatedly tearing down the posters from the plant walls.[86]

"Both Sides Needed the Federal Government to Make This Happen"

As well as being important in encouraging black protest, the Civil Rights Act was also instrumental in pushing paper industry executives to abandon many discriminatory practices. Although a great deal of discrimination continued to exist in the industry well after 1965, there is much evidence to support the view that the act, together with other federal pressure, provided the crucial breakthrough that pushed the industry to change.

Company officials themselves often admitted that they gave no thought to integrating any jobs until federal regulations were passed. This was clear from the notes of a 1967 interview that Wharton School researcher Herbert Northrup conducted with the manager of Bowater Paper Company in Calhoun, Tennessee. "The only Negroes they hired at the beginning were about 100 out of 1300, who worked as janitors and wood yard workers," Northrup noted. "They made absolutely no change in this until the passage of the civil rights act."[87]

Leading management executives acknowledged that the industry would not have changed without a federal mandate. Ed Bartlett, the manager of industrial relations at Union Camp throughout the 1960s and 1970s, claimed that white resistance to integration was so strong that it could "never have happened" without the federal government. "Both sides needed the federal government to make this happen," asserted the retired executive. "I think if we'd initiated it on our own, to do that, the mill would have gone down."[88] The records of *Boles v. Union Camp* highlight the importance of the federal government in integrating Union Camp. In a 1972 affidavit, Bartlett described integration as "the product of management efforts in conjunction with federal authorities." The importance of government business was one of the major reasons for changing. As Bartlett admitted, "Union Camp wanted an opportunity to bid on the several millions of dollars yearly spent by the government for paper and paper products." He also added that the company believed in the "essential rightness" of a nondiscriminatory policy.[89]

The federal government was also crucial in facilitating integration because both companies and unions found that they could minimize white resistance by blaming the government for the changes. Companies also often exaggerated the power of the federal government in order to minimize white opposition. Crown-Zellerbach's top managers, for example, emphasized integration as something that was being pushed by the federal government, which, they stressed, could not be resisted, implying that resistance could jeopardize workers' job security. Thus, the outline for a company address to a union meeting on August 24, 1965, indicated to workers that the Civil Rights Act was "the law of the land. It will be enforced by the federal government. Crown-Zellerbach must abide by the provisions of this law." Company officials also stressed that they had to comply with the Civil Rights Act in order to maintain important government business: "Government held up $1.8 million worth of contracts to dramatize the point. . . . We had *no alternative* but to agree to come back to Bogalusa to review our progression lines with union leaders." Government requirements had to be complied with in order "to keep the plant running. . . . We who are here in Bogalusa can sit down and solve this problem for ourselves. We must do so to save the mill, to save your jobs, and to save the entire town of Bogalusa. We need your full support."[90]

In further meetings with workers, the company continued to stress that government regulations had to be obeyed. On December 3, 1965, executives told white workers, "We have no choice [but] to comply with government regulations. Alternative is to face 'blacklisting.'" Being debarred from government contracts in this way, workers were warned, "could affect our ability to provide jobs."[91] Following a meeting with EEOC chairman Franklin D. Roosevelt Jr. to discuss merging lines of progression, the company reported to workers that Roosevelt had "left no doubt about government intentions or ability to enforce its decision."[92]

Union Camp's managers used arguments similar to Crown-Zellerbach's. At a meeting on September 1, 1967, for example, company chairman J. R. Leintz told the union that the paper mill had to comply with Executive Order 11246, maintaining that continuing present practices would only invite "criminal proceedings." As the union's minutes noted, "Mr Leintz opened the meeting by explaining in great details the importance of complying with E.O. 11246, and how it's important that this company comply with this order to stay in business because over half of the company's business is either direct or indirect Government orders, and we would be out of business if we didn't comply."[93]

In oral and written records, both black and white workers repeatedly stressed that the Civil Rights Act was the central cause of racial integration in the paper industry and doubted whether the industry would have changed without it. Given the broad differences in white and black viewpoints over other aspects of job integration, these shared opinions were significant.[94]

Melvin King, a white veteran worker from Moss Point, Mississippi, for example, expressed a typical view: "I don't think the company would have ever changed. . . . The Civil Rights Act is what changed the whole thing. . . . That's when we changed here at Moss Point. . . . They systematically kept the blacks and the whites separate when they went in the mill. .... I don't think the company would have ever changed it until it was mandated."[95]

White workers also argued that the Civil Rights Act was important because it had created what they saw as the main mechanism of integration—the flood of Title VII lawsuits that occurred in the paper industry. "I think they would have continued on until they were forced to change but because of the threat of lawsuits and mandatory change, the unions and the company had no choice but to meet it," declared former IP worker Frank Bragg. "What we have now is the result of legal action, you know the Civil Rights Act of 1964, that's what forced it forward." Bragg added that the law "had a hell of an impact."[96]

African American workers shared this view. Leroy Hamilton, who worked at Gilman Paper Company between 1953 and the 1980s, felt, as many black workers did, that the federal government forced the industry to integrate:

> You see the Civil Rights Act, the reason they had to go by the laws, this was signed, the government was behind it, and they sent people in to see whether they were changing, whether they were operating under the Civil Rights Act, and they put signs up all over the mill, nobody be discriminated against, if they do, a number on that paper for you to call in Washington DC, and the company had to do it you see, and a lot of times the company put them papers up and the whites would tear them down, but the company had to do it in order to keep the government from shutting them down, they had to operate by the rules. .... They didn't have no choice, they was forced into it . . . I tell you all this come through the Civil Rights Act, all this come through the Civil Rights Act.

Hamilton thought that the Civil Rights Act "was a big change for the whole world."[97]

Willie Ford, another black worker, held a similar view: "I don't believe it would ever have changed if the federal government hadn't of stepped in there. You had some fellas that wouldn't give up for nothing but to try and get you away from there. But after the federal government stepped in there and told them what had to be done or else, they'd shut it down, close the gate or something or other, they knows when its time to straighten up."[98] In legal testimony, black workers repeated these views, often pointing to the act as an important watershed.[99] "After the Civil Rights Act was passed," asserted one worker, "the company gave us a chance to come in and try to advance ourselves."[100]

It is incontrovertible that many blacks were able to receive promotions either directly because of the Civil Rights Act or as a result of Title VII litigation. Black workers often related that they had secured a better job after a lawsuit, and they often added proudly that they were performing it competently. For these workers, their satisfactory performance proved that they would have been able to carry out the job much earlier if they had been given the opportunity. Noted Gilman worker Wilbert D. Sidley, "After the lawsuit I recived [sic] A chance to become a scale clerk and I made it *A Good one*."[101] In some cases, black workers related that they were able to get the job they had always wanted once the Civil Rights Act passed. "As soon as the civil rights act passed, I moved to maintenance," N. E. Foreman noted proudly on his claim form, adding that this promotion had allowed him to fulfill a long-term goal.[102]

White union leaders tended to be especially positive about the Civil Rights Act. Chuck Spence, a white local union leader at International Paper Company in Mobile in the 1960s, felt that the Civil Rights Act was "*the* big change. Without the Civil Rights Act of 1964, it wouldn't have changed because there was no contract language to force them to do it." Spence concluded that the Civil Rights Act opened up "every avenue" that had previously been closed to black workers.[103] Wayne Glenn, who was president of the UPIU between 1978 and 1996, admitted that unions had tolerated segregation in the paper industry until the Civil Rights Act had been passed. "They went along with it until the passage of the Civil Rights Act, that's the only thing that stopped it," he acknowledged.[104] Glenn's view was echoed by other union leaders and by labor lawyers.[105] Michael Hamilton, a lawyer with the UPIU since the 1970s, for example, stressed the importance of Title VII litigation, asserting that the industry would never have voluntarily changed without this litigation.[106]

Title VII litigation also induced paper companies to abandon many specific discriminatory practices. The personnel manager of Weyerhauser, for example, admitted in 1977 that court decisions citing the discriminatory impact of job testing had led the company to abandon testing as "an unnecessary risk."[107] Other companies abolished high school education requirements in order to avoid litigation or to achieve compliance with federal agencies.[108] The amount of Title VII litigation that occurred in the paper industry also pushed many companies to introduce equal employment memorandums that allowed black workers to use their mill seniority for promotions. James How, the manager of industrial relations at the Continental Can chain, for example, explained in 1973 how litigation prompted the company to hold a "summit meeting" that led to the introduction of its equal employment memorandum.[109]

Federal agencies such as the Defense Supply Agency, the Office of Federal

Contract Compliance, and the General Services Administration (GSA) were central to reducing discrimination in the paper industry. All of these agencies monitored the companies' civil rights compliance by carrying out regular inspections and compliance reviews. The DSA and GSA paid particular attention to ensuring that facilities were integrated, but they also took the necessary steps to enforce job integration. Although in some of the biggest cases companies complained that agencies worked at cross-purposes, overall it is clear that these agencies secured many positive changes that executives were reluctant to implement voluntarily.[110] In several locations, the EEOC and companies worked out conciliation agreements or consent decrees that afforded African American workers better promotional opportunities. At Stone Container Corporation in Mobile, Alabama, for example, a settlement agreement was drawn up in 1970 that allowed black workers to transfer to white jobs by using their mill seniority.[111] At the Olin Mathieson Company in West Monroe, Louisiana, the EEOC worked out a conciliation agreement in 1966 that abolished testing and merged the separate lines of progression.[112]

Title VII litigation also had a significant impact on unions in the paper industry, forcing them to abandon discriminatory practices. In most Title VII suits, unions were sued with companies and the cost and frequency of suits pushed unions to implement changes in order to avert litigation. From the mid-1960s on, both the IBPSPMW and the UPP continually worried about the "burden" of Title VII litigation. In 1966, for example, the UPP was already expressing concern about the rise in its legal costs since the Civil Rights Act had been passed. Title VII had "further expanded the legal obligations and responsibilities of the Union and the need for employing lawyers."[113] Three years later, the union's attorney was pictured with his head in his hands alongside a report that detailed how "[e]qual employment opportunity problems have continued to multiply. . . . The most disturbing feature of the recent batch of Title VII cases against the International Union is that all of them demand substantial back pay. . . . [M]oney judgements against the Union could be paralyzing."[114] Indeed, a leading union attorney reported that the cost of Title VII litigation threatened "the future solvency and possible continued existence of the union."[115]

The burden of Title VII litigation eventually pushed the union to act. In May 1973, the UPIU set up a human relations department in order to provide some internal machinery to handle discrimination complaints. The union admitted that the move had been made to "help bring to a halt the unjustifiable assessments that have been made against the union."[116] In 1975, the UPIU urged all locals to implement a "supplemental agreement" to ensure that seniority systems were nondiscriminatory. UPIU president Joseph Tonelli noted in a memorandum to union officials that the union had to act in order to avoid being liable for back pay because of its "acquiescing" in discriminatory job assignments. The supplemental agreement brought all contracts in line with the *Local 189* case, substituting plant seniority in place of job or department seniority for the purpose of promotion and layoff. If we do not make this change, Tonelli warned, "the courts have declared [that] women and blacks will be 'locked in' and be unable to reach their 'rightful place.'"[117]

In communicating the change of policy to his international representatives, Tonelli also stressed, as did paper company executives, that change had to be carried out because it was decreed by federal law. Anticipating resistance from local unions, the UPIU leader urged his representatives to make it clear that the union was changing only because it had to; the alternative was further Title VII suits that might lead to possible financial bankruptcy. He explained, "We are forced by the developments in the field of civil rights to make substantial and radical changes in our seniority, progression lines, promotion, and lay-off practices. . . . We must face the fact that unless we do what the law requires we will be bled to death financially."[118]

The Civil Rights Act was also responsible for outlawing segregated unions, since such locals were a clear violation of Title VII. By abolishing separate locals, the act transformed the whole system of labor relations that had governed the paper industry since its establishment in the South. Across the region, after the Civil Rights Act was passed, international union representatives encouraged local unions to merge. As southern UPIU representative Don Walker testified in 1971, "Because of Title 7, 1964 Civil Rights Act, I spoke to all of my Local Unions that I represented, trying to get them to merge Local Unions where there was segregated Local Unions. Not only here, but everywhere else. . . . Since passage of the Civil Rights Law . . . we had been instructed as International Representatives that wherever possible to get a voluntary merger from our Local Unions where there were segregated Locals."[119]

The Civil Rights Act thus had a huge impact on black employment in the southern paper industry. The act gave black workers a mechanism with which to protest against segregation, and they used it. Motivated by their close knowledge of the industry, which had been nurtured over many years, workers seized the opportunity provided by the federal government to secure long-held goals of equal employment opportunity. Not surprisingly, workers who took part in the lawsuits saw the act as crucial, recognizing that it was the watershed that had at last allowed them to mount an effective challenge against the paper industry's racial practices. The Civil Rights Act also undoubtedly had an important impact upon paper industry executives and upon union leadership. As they acknowledged, the act pushed them to start addressing the problem of equal employment opportunity. Companies began to open up traditional white jobs to blacks, and unions abandoned the system of segregated local unions, which they had maintained since they first organized in the South.

Workers tried for many years to address discrimination through their segregated local unions, but it was the federal government's 1964 Civil Rights Act that allowed African American workers to make important strides toward ending racial segregation in the southern paper industry. Discrimination persisted after 1964, however, and new barriers to equal employment opportunity were erected. The color of work proved to be very stubborn, and the road to equal employment opportunity was not easy or quick.

CHAPTER 4
WE WANT OUR PEOPLE TO HAVE AN OPPORTUNITY TO ADVANCE
THE CIVIL RIGHTS ACTIVISM OF SEGREGATED BLACK LOCAL UNIONS, 1945–1970

I n the 1940s and 1950s, the pages of the *Pulp, Sulphite, and Paper Mill Workers' Journal*, the IBPSPMW's main publication, recorded the history of segregated local unions operating across the paper industry. Pictures regularly showed both black and white locals auditing their books, renewing contracts, and swearing in new officers. Most of the news recorded in the *Journal* was routine, but, on one occasion in 1950, Frederick M. Jones, the corresponding secretary of a black local in Panama City, Florida, wrote a remarkable plea for civil rights: "After many years of service, we are now able to say that our union has made progress and we are now facing the dawn of day. But the day is not quite dawning for millions of my people who stand pleading at the bars of justice with no ballots in their hands. So then, as we have opportunity, let us work, that which is good toward all men."[1]

This plea echoed many others made by the leaders of black paper industry locals in the 1950s and 1960s. These leaders repeatedly used the guaranteed representation they gained at contract negotiations to push for civil rights and greater job opportunities. Little is known, however, about these efforts or the wider history of segregated locals highlighted by the *Journal*.[2] In many ways, African American workers found that segregated locals were something of a paradox. As officeholders in segregated locals, many African American workers were able to press for improved job opportunities for their members and to develop their own leadership skills in the process. At the same time, the very system of segregation that was responsible for the locals' existence placed strict limits on the effectiveness of their efforts. Segregated locals helped to entrench and codify segregated jobs, and they rendered black workers powerless and outnumbered, unable to affect any meaningful racial change. As hard as they tried, African American workers found that they were unable to alter the system of segregated job assignments.

The Organization of Segregated Locals, 1933–1958

Although separate locals existed in other southern industries, as long-serving UPIU representative Chuck Spence admitted, paper unions had "more segregated locals than any other industry in the South."[3] In the early 1960s the IBPSPMW had fifty-two separate black locals in the South, thirty-five in its southeastern region and another seventeen in the southwest. A list compiled by the union at the end of 1965, after many mergers had taken place, indicates that the IBPSPMW still had thirty-five black locals and sixty-seven white locals across the southern states. In addition, the UPP had separate locals in some of the same locations as the IBPSPMW did.[4]

Black locals were usually identifiable because their local union numbers began with a "6." White locals usually had numbers beginning with "4" or "3." In some mills, however, black locals were given the same number as the main white local but with an "A" added. Thus, at the Crown-Zellerbach paper mill in Bogalusa, the main white local was UPP local 189 and the main black local was UPP local 189A. This system was also used at St. Joe Paper Company in Port St. Joe, Florida, where the two locals were Locals 379 and 379A.

Most segregated locals were chartered in the 1930s and 1940s, as an increasing number of paper mills opened in the South. It was a time when segregation was firmly established in most areas of southern life, and the pages of the *Pulp, Sulphite, and Paper Mill Workers' Journal* consistently defended segregation in these years. In 1942, for instance, Homer Humble, the southern director of the IBPSPMW, claimed that segregated locals reflected the wishes of both black and white workers: "In my capacity as an International Representative of our union here in the South, I have come to know and understand the problems of the colored. . . . Some may call it discrimination to separate the races under certain conditions. As far as I know, there are no objections either by white or colored. . . . I think the southern colored people enjoy being by themselves as much as do the whites."[5]

The establishment of separate locals in the 1930s and 1940s clearly reflected paper unions' reluctance to challenge this pervasive acceptance of segregation. The IBPSPMW, as Robert Zieger has shown, tried to organize in the South "along the path of least resistance," deferring to white workers' desires for separate locals.[6] Paper unions in general were cautious as far as the race issue was concerned. At International Paper Company's mill in Mobile, for example, the Paper Makers union chartered a local on September 10, 1933, that had around 750 members. The 250 black workers who had taken part in the campaign were given a separate charter. This move was made because the AFL organizer "thought best to play safe in the organization of these Southern men, most of who[m] never before had belonged to a labor union."[7]

Most black unions were formed shortly after a plant was initially organized. Rather than reflecting black preference, separate locals were usually insisted upon by white workers, who were anxious to secure control of the better-paying jobs. At the Weyerhauser mill in Plymouth, North Carolina, the deposition of black worker Joseph Hooker gave a clear insight into how the black local at the mill was set up. Hooker had started working at the mill in 1940 and remembered clearly the chartering of separate black and white locals in 1941. He testified that whites organized their own union first, leaving blacks with no line of progression and confined to laboring jobs. A separate local was then chartered for blacks, with the union's international representative and white local union leaders playing the leading role in its formation. Clearly uneasy about the arrangement, the international representative told black workers that he supported the plans for a separate local because "he had to live down here." Hooker recalled that blacks had little say about the organization of the union but were simply "notified" by the leaders of the white local that "we were going to be organized." He added, however, that black workers were concerned about the fact that their local was given jurisdiction over only a small number of laboring jobs, with few opportunities for advancement: "Most of the time the black boys seemed to worry about there was no advancement with the blacks at that particular time. We just had to stay right there and work, whatever that job was paying." Hooker felt that the establishment of a separate local was a way of formalizing this discrimination.[8]

Segregated locals were similarly established in other mills. In 1948, the white IBPSPMW local at Hudson Pulp and Paper Company in Palatka, Florida, was organized first and quickly secured bargaining rights for production jobs. Immediately after this, white maintenance locals were formed to secure control of the skilled maintenance jobs. The last union to organize was IBPSPMW Local 623, the black local, whose members were left with control of only a small number of laboring jobs. Given the way that black locals were usually organized last, it is not surprising that black workers often felt that they did the jobs in the paper industry that whites did not want to do.[9]

In some mills, blacks formed their own locals because white workers simply barred blacks from joining their union. At Scott Paper Company in Mobile, for example, IBPSPMW local 423 was organized in 1946 and developed as an all-white local union, refusing to represent any of the black workers. As a result, in 1948 black workers at Scott organized their own union, Local 613, which was approved by the international union.[10] The black local at Westvaco in Charleston had similar origins, with whites organizing in 1944 and refusing to allow blacks to join their union. Blacks therefore formed their own union at a later date.[11]

In several mills, only one union was initially established for both black and white workers. African American workers, however, requested separate charters after complaining that white union leaders refused to represent them effectively. At International Paper Company in Natchez, Mississippi, for example, Sidney Gibson, who started working at the mill when it first opened in 1951, remembered that he asked for a separate charter because he felt it was the only way that black workers could receive any representation: "We were getting such a small amount of representation from the white union officials that we asked for a charter. They just wouldn't represent you, if you got fired you were gone, you didn't have anybody to ask why. They had certain foremen down there that would just come and walk up, if he didn't like the way you looked, he'd say, 'Come here, boy, you go home.' After we asked for a charter, we started to represent our own people . . . so they started giving us a little more respect."[12]

In many cases, black workers recognized that a separate local was the only opportunity they had to receive any kind of protection on the job. At the Crossett Company in Crossett, Arkansas, the mill was organized shortly after opening in 1937, with one local union for both white and black workers. Black workers eventually complained that this union failed to represent them and engaged in a wildcat strike in 1941 because the all-white union was not negotiating any wage increases for them. Led by laborer Nathaniel "Beby" Reed, the workers demanded a pay raise before they returned to work. As Reed recalled, the local union president suggested to him that he organize a separate black local: "He said, 'Well, why don't you form your own union?' I said, 'Well, if we can negotiate our own working agreements then we will do that.' He said, 'Well I'll get the international representative round here and he can meet with you.' I says, 'Okay, we'll talk about that.' So then I asked the fellas what they thought about that, they said that would be fine. . . . So then from that we got the international representative in and we formed union 369A, and we did our negotiating." Reed became the first president of Local 369A, securing black workers' first wage increase during negotiations in 1942. "I felt like we could do better by taking care of our own business for a while," he recalled, "and we did . . . having the separate union, we began to get better representation from the international union."[13]

White workers often helped black workers to organize because they recognized the threat that unorganized blacks represented to their own standard of living. At International Paper Company in Moss Point, Mississippi, for example, white workers organized first and then encouraged black workers to set up a separate local. Black workers who joined the fledgling union understood that whites wanted blacks to be in the union fold with them. "The white local started first, and then they encouraged the blacks," recalled Howard Bardwell, who started working at the mill in 1946. "In order for them to work here and get a decent wage, they had to get the blacks organized to join a union, you got me, because then they could always go and negotiate for better working conditions, and then they'd be united when you had a strike, because see the black and the white both walked the picket line when you had a strike. We didn't always walk together but we had a picket line." Bardwell also recalled that most black workers supported the separate union because they recognized that it could negotiate some improved benefits for them: "See we was working there when they [whites] started, but after they started then they went around and circulated with the blacks, said, 'Look, you fellas need to get you a local.' We met with them and they showed us how to organize, and the international would send a person down there to train, so we joined too. It had some good points in it. And see that's the way we started out getting more vacation, the union helped negotiate that."[14]

By the end of the 1950s, civil rights groups were complaining about the number of separate locals existing in the paper industry. The NAACP, in particular, acted on complaints it received from black workers and repeatedly pressed the paper unions to merge segregated locals. In April 1960, for example, NAACP president Roy Wilkins wrote the presidents of both the UPP and the IBPSPMW to protest that both unions maintained "a pattern of segregated affiliated local unions throughout the South."[15] The unions, however, showed few signs of concern. When the UPP's executive board met in June 1960, it brushed aside the NAACP's concerns, claiming that "the colored members participate on a basis of equality in the International Union" and that "no discrimination exists."[16] Both the UPP and IBPSPMW continued to charter new segregated locals at least into the late 1950s, and existing separate locals persisted for much longer. At the American Can Company in Butler, Alabama, for example, a separate IBPSPMW local was organized in 1959, with jurisdiction over traditional black jobs in the woodyard and yard crew.[17] Similarly, at International Paper Company's plant in Pine Bluff, Arkansas, separate white and black locals were chartered shortly after the plant began operations in 1958.[18]

In Title VII cases, union leaders were called upon to justify their history of chartering separate locals. Most argued that the locals had been necessary in order to organize the paper industry in the South. UPIU president Wayne Glenn, for example, sought to justify the union's position. A World War II veteran, Glenn started working at IP's mill in Camden, Arkansas, in 1946, quickly becoming local union president. In 1957, he became an international representative for the IBPSPMW in the South, a job that involved chartering and servicing segregated local unions. In his 1980 affidavit in the case of *Miller v. Continental Can*, Glenn argued that separate locals were the only way of organizing paper workers at a time when every other aspect of southern life was segregated: "Had the UPIU predecessor organizations declared at the outset of its organizing campaigns in the south that it would issue only one local union charter, a situation which would require the mixing of the races . . . it would not have been successful in recruiting the support of the whites and the blacks as members." Glenn argued that the union did not want to exclude blacks from the benefits of union membership, so they decided that separate unions would allow them to be members without challenging segregation. As he put it, separate unions "removed a substantial impediment to organizing, and opened the way for black participation in union activities." The veteran union leader also claimed that all black and all white local unions had "equal rights and privileges."[19]

Most union representatives who were active in the South before the 1960s also saw segregated locals as a necessary organizing tool. Russell Hall, a former southern paper worker who became an international union representative in 1963, felt that the union had to accept segregation in order to organize southern mills: "If you was going to organize when the industry moved South, the international didn't have no other choice, it wasn't that they believed in it. If you said that you was going to have black and whites in the same union, then the whites wouldn't have joined. So the international didn't have no other choice. In order to organize they had to agree to separate locals."[20] Local union leaders also accepted that segregated locals were primarily a reflection of white desire for segregation. This view was expressed well by Chuck Spence, who worked at International Paper Company in Mobile before becoming a representative for the UPIU. "It's the way we were raised," he explained. "The whites didn't like to have to associate with [blacks], so its just something that was carried over from your child-

A native of Arkansas, Wayne Glenn worked as a IBPSPMW southern representative in the 1960s and early 1970s before serving as president of the UPIU from 1978 to 1996. Here, Glenn is pictured visiting UPIU members in Port Wentworth, Georgia, in the late 1980s. (Courtesy PACE International Union)

hood and the way that your parents was raised, it was carried right on into the workplace, and they started them up like that."[21]

Many black workers believed that separate locals were set up because whites did not want blacks in their unions. At St. Regis Paper Company in Jacksonville, Florida, for example, James C. Green testified that he joined the "colored union" when he started at the mill in 1953 because blacks were not allowed in Local 749, the white union: "You won't join 749 at that time . . . they didn't accept any."[22] Similarly, Horace Gill, the former president of a black local in Mobile, felt that separate locals reflected white workers' wishes: "They had separate unions because they didn't want you meeting with them. They didn't want you knowing what they was doing, how they was doing it or whatever. So they had two locals. . . . They didn't want you there."[23]

We've Always Tried to Get Better Jobs, That's the Purpose of Our Union: The Civil Rights Activism of Segregated Unions

Although segregated unions confined African American workers to a limited number of jobs, they also provided them with a forum to protest against discrimination. Across the South, these locals, which pressed both companies and unions to open up more jobs and end segregation, became a focus of civil rights activity. Since both companies and white unions strenuously resisted any merger of racially separate lines of progression, in the 1960s black local union leaders turn to federal agencies to fight discrimination. They understood the importance of federal nondiscrimination mandates and usually played a central role in filing Title VII lawsuits. Indeed, the history of several major Title VII cases highlights that litigation resulted from the long-term efforts of black locals to overcome segregation.

At the West Virginia Pulp and Paper Company in Charleston, South Carolina, the black local was instrumental in black workers' struggle to end segregation. A group of workers in IBPSPMW local 620 formed a committee, which was active for over fifteen years, "to better the racial situation." Its chairman was Willis Gantlin, who was also president of the local.[24] Beginning in the early 1950s, Gantlin and other officers of the local met repeatedly with company officials in order to, as Gantlin put it, "try to work out a system which would enable blacks to move in some of the better jobs." These efforts achieved little, however, since both company and union officials passed the black local's committee between them. When Gantlin met with company officials, he recalled, "The response was negative, they would always tell me that it was the Union, and when I went to the Union the Union would always tell me it's the Company, so they kept me going back and forwards, see-sawing, more or less."[25]

As was the case in other locations, the black local's activism intensified at the beginning of the 1960s. After several years of unsuccessful meetings, the local voted at a meeting in 1963 to write a formal letter seeking "to try to get blacks into the lines of progression." In June 1963 the black local's committee, headed by Gantlin, sent copies of the letter to the two white locals in the mill and called for a meeting to discuss compliance with President Kennedy's nondiscrimination order of 1961. "The members of Local NO. 620," the letter stated, "will like to negotiate in good faith a program to comply with Executive Order NO. 10925 as set forth and approved by our President John P. Burke and Vice-President Lyndon B. Johnson. We would like to have a date for this discussion." Copies of the letter were also sent to company officials and representatives of the international union.[26]

This letter also produced few results. The white locals in the mill ignored it, and the international union told the black local that "the time was not right" for the lines of progression to be merged. After further unsuccessful meetings between the committee and the company's officials, the black local voted to seek outside help for the first time by writing to the President's

ACTIVISM OF BLACK LOCAL UNIONS

Pictures from contract negotiations highlight how representatives from black locals were outnumbered by whites, one of their central complaints. Here, the 1965 union negotiating team at West Virginia Pulp and Paper Company in Charleston, South Carolina, includes Willis Gantlin (back row, third from left), the black local president who led efforts to end job segregation at the mill.
(Courtesy PACE International Union)

Committee on Equal Employment Opportunity, a forerunner of the EEOC. "After exhausting all possible means," Gantlin later explained, "with meeting at every possible time with various members of Management and of Union, I had no other alternative but to seek some other means of trying to relieve. . . . the people of Imperial Local 620 in order to get into lines of progression because we was being seriously discriminated against."[27]

The letter that the black local union wrote to the President's Committee continued the plea for lines of progression to be merged and jobs to be awarded on merit. It complained that whites were hired off the street for skilled jobs that established black employees could perform: "We feel that there was and still is qualified members in Local 620 to staff these jobs if they where given the opportunity. We definetly [sic] feels that the Company use RACIAL DECRIMINATION [sic] in doing this, we request that you send a Representative down to investigate FAIR EMPLOYMENT, AND EQUAL JOB OPPORTUNITY."[28]

In 1967, the black local union agreed that they should file EEOC charges "since we had exhausted all other means." Gantlin filed the first charges on April 25, 1967; other members of the committee followed suit later in the year. Christopher Jenkins, for example, wrote the EEOC in November 1967 to complain about the way that blacks were confined to the worst jobs: "The White employees are given first preference for promotion within a department, regardless of his seniority. The imaginary line for promotion is still in existence as it has been for the past twenty years." These EEOC charges were the basis of the lawsuit that was eventually brought by the black workers at Westvaco.[29]

What is striking about the Westvaco story is that black workers used the separate union as a forum to press for the merger of the local unions and the lines of progression. Although the union was segregated, it was an important organizing tool for African American workers seeking to end segregation. Indeed, plaintiffs' attorney Gail Wright told the court: "[T]he story of the 1960s is the story of Local 620's efforts to overcome the separate structure, led by Mr Gantlin with the participation of other Local 620 officers."[30] Many black workers also testified that their local union had been very active in pressing the company for better job opportunities. "We've always tried to get better jobs, that's the purpose of our union," declared one veteran union member.[31]

In many other locations, African American workers who wanted to end segregation recognized that black local unions could be used as a vehicle for civil rights activism and became active in them as a result. At the Union Camp Corporation in Savannah, Georgia, there were two black IBPSPMW locals—Local 615, in the bag mill and Local 601, in the paper mill. In the 1950s and 1960s, both unions had long-serving presidents who led efforts to integrate the mill.

James Tyson, the president of the black local in Union Camp's paper mill, was active in the civil rights movement in Savannah, serving for many years as state labor chairman of the NAACP. He was also a cofounder of the Crusade for Voters, an organization that led voter registration drives in the Savannah area in the 1960s. As a civil rights activist, Tyson admitted he had initial reservations about taking part in a segregated local union when he first started working at Union Camp shortly after World War II. Like others, however, he came to recognize the union's potential as a tool to fight segregation at a time when there were few alternatives available. "I didn't think I should join the black union when I first went there," he testified in 1971, "but I found out that was the only way I could do a little pushing, so I got in it."[32]

Tyson, indeed, became the president of the union and used his position to press the company to merge the lines of progression. In 1959, he filed a formal complaint with the NAACP about segregated unions and separate seniority lines at Union Bag.[33] "I felt like in the paper industry we should have had one union, we shouldn't have black and white unions," Tyson recalled in 1997. "Immediately after I became president of 601 I proceeded to integrate the unions." With the passage of the Civil Rights Act in 1964, Tyson played a central role in formulating the class action suit that became *Boles v. Union Camp.*[34]

Like many black union activists, Tyson sought to register his protests with as many federal agencies as possible, and records of his charges can be found in a variety of different places. In 1963, Tyson, along with several other members of the black local, protested to the President's Committee on Equal Employment Opportunity about testing and segregated unions. Tyson, moreover, in a complaint to the national AFL-CIO, used his position as president of the black local to speak for black workers as a whole. "I have been employed at the Union Bag–Camp Paper Corporation for 17 and a half years and during this time no Negroes have ever been employed in skilled labor positions or supervisory positions," he asserted. "At present there are approximately 5,300 employees and Negroes are only employed in the menial positions. I am personally aware of the circumstances surrounding the employment of Negroes by virtue of the fact that I am President of the Negroes Union Local 601 which consists of 400 plus members."[35]

The bag mill local president at Union Camp was George Sawyer. Sawyer had grown up in Georgia and started working for the company on September 21, 1942. In May of 1943 he entered the army, where he served until returning to the paper mill in March of 1946. Like many African Americans who led the fight against segregation, Sawyer looked back on his military service as a formative experience: "By being in service it gave me an opportunity to see kind of how things were in other parts of the world. It was a lot different in some of the other parts of the world where I had an opportunity to go while I was in service. And so when I came back and went back out there, I saw a need for a change, a very valuable need for a change." Sawyer remembered that his initial reaction was to consider leaving Georgia for the north. "But then I realized," he continued, "I said you can't solve a problem by running away from it, see you have to stay there and do what you can to change a problem. So a few of us and myself we felt that we needed to start doing something to change the situation at Union Bag. And that was kind of the beginning of some of the changes at Union Bag."

Sawyer turned to the union to help him improve the racial situation at Union Bag, and in 1956 he was elected president of the black local in the bag mill. In a speech written when he retired from the mill in 1987, Sawyer remembered how he used his position in the union to press for the integration of the mill: "As President of this local union my first objective was to integrate the plant, remove all signs that read Colored and White, and have one line of progression for all employees." Both black locals began meeting with company officials in order to make these changes, but they made very little progress. Sawyer recalled that his local came to the conclusion that they had to file a complaint with the federal government in order to force change: "We continued to meet with the company officials, asking for better job opportunities. We finally had to file a complaint with the federal government. Then things began to change. The Jim Crow signs which read White and Colored were removed from the water fountains, restrooms, and cafeterias." The federal complaint filed by the black locals was also the start of meaningful job integration in the mill—the lines of progression were merged and blacks began moving onto better jobs. "It was quite a struggle," Sawyer recalled. "It wasn't easy, but we finally got the door open."[36]

Sawyer's local also carried on a battle with the international union to abolish separate locals, thereby opening up better-paying jobs to blacks. In 1959, Local 615 submitted a resolution to the IBPSPMW convention that called for the union to "take action toward eliminating the segregated local unions in the South" so that "all employees will have the right to promotions according to seniority and ability." In 1962, Sawyer's local submitted another resolution that called for more blacks to be appointed to the international union's staff and asked the union to "represent all Union members in a like manner."[37] The resolutions were defeated, however, and the international union took no immediate steps to merge the local unions.

Other black local union leaders protested against discrimination at international union conventions. At the 1963 UPP convention, for example, a group of black locals from a number of different companies put forward a nondiscrimination resolution.[38] To a certain extent, the fact that black locals were able to speak out at union conventions did demonstrate one of the benefits of self-representation, which white union officials often touted. At the same time, however, black locals often faced hostile opposition at conventions and their resolutions were usually defeated. At the 1956 IBPSPMW convention, for example, a nondiscrimination resolution was soundly defeated. Three years later, Local 601 member Charles A. Gordon expressed the frustration of many black union members when he spoke in support of the resolution that George Sawyer introduced: "I rise to discuss Resolution No. 103. . . . We have introduced it year after year, and we have not gotten any results. All our people are tired of working on the job just like we started, and never having any opportunity to advance. We want our people to have an opportunity to advance, according to their qualifications." Sawyer seconded Gordon, saying, "We are getting tired of doing the same thing for twenty or twenty five years."[39]

The 1959 convention showed clearly the distance between black and white union members, as black pleas for the resolution were matched by white speakers who opposed it. Many black speakers made an appeal to whites by emphasizing the economic damage caused by discrimination. Harry L. Brown, a representative from a black local in Port Wentworth, Georgia, took this approach when he argued for equal job opportunities: "When I go to the store, my groceries cost the same as yours, and what we want is to have opportunities to get a job paying $4.00 an hour." White speakers from the South, however, countered that merging the lines of progression would destroy the union by alienating whites, who were the majority of members. "I could not think of a better way to break this International's back than to try to load something like this on them in the South," stated one white speaker from Mobile.[40]

By the early 1960s, black workers were pleading with the international union to do more to eliminate discrimination so that they would not have to turn to the federal government for help. At the 1962 IBPSPMW convention, for example, a black local from St. Regis Paper Company in Jacksonville, Florida, introduced a resolution calling for the international union to adhere to the nondiscrimination policies of the national AFL-CIO. Local union delegate M. B. Randall spoke in favor of the resolution. "We are protected, as has been said in the said resolution, by the government," he stated. "Brothers and sisters, our contention is that the International Brotherhood of Pulp, Sulphite and Paper Mill Workers should do its part so that we will not have to appeal to the government. We would rather not appeal to the government as that would indicate that we have failed in our Union." Like many other black speakers before and after, Randall called upon the union to live up to its democratic language and posture: "We are interested in helping to carry out the objectives of this Union, which speaks to us about the 'Brotherhood of Man.' . . . We must recognize the fact that we are so closely connected together that none of us can be free until all men are free. . . . We want to help build a stronger America, but this can only be done by removing the wall that divides us."[41]

Across the South, black local unions led efforts to fight discrimination and open up more jobs for their members. A representative from the black local at International Paper Company in Pine Bluff, Arkansas, for example, testified that the union had repeatedly sent delegations to the company's personnel office in an effort to merge the lines of progression.[42] At the Olin Mathieson Corporation in Monroe, Louisiana, black local union president Ray Robinson filed EEOC charges on behalf of black workers at the mill in September 1965, claiming that they were discriminated against "as a daily, continuing grievance." Robinson described the major problem as "Segre-

Although they were usually unable to alter segregated job assignments, African Americans used the guaranteed representation they received at union conventions to voice their concerns, as illustrated by these black speakers (above and opposite) at the 1957 UPP convention. (Courtesy PACE International Union)

gated Jobs," adding, "All of the jobs held by Members of my local have a common characteristic: there is no line of progression or advancement. . . . In short jobs are as thoroughly segregated now as they ever were and Negroes still have the least desireable, lowest paying jobs."[43] At Georgia Kraft Company in Rome, Georgia, black workers related that they had tried to fight discrimination by filing grievances with their separate union, which existed until 1972. Joe L. McElroy testified in 1968 that he felt the company was trying to keep blacks out of the better jobs: "We have been to 'em, we've talked to 'em, we have filed grievances to the effect that they was showing partiality between Negroes and whites, and they would deny them to the last step, you know, just as high as we would carry them, and just keep right on in the act." McElroy and some of his African American coworkers also attempted to make changes by filing grievances collectively: "They was barring Negroes mostly from moving up," McElroy charged. "We filed one to that effect, with a great number of employees' signatures to it."[44]

At IP's mill in Moss Point, Mississippi, a group of black workers who were active in the local NAACP held offices in the segregated union and used them to press the company for greater integration. The civil rights activity of the black local, in turn, encouraged other black workers to become members of the NAACP. "I started being active in the union," recalled State Stallworth.

I ran for President, and I won it. The local union then under my leadership began to work in good relations with the NAACP and with an organization out of Mobile called the Non-Partisan Voters' League. . . . Then I became affiliated with the NAACP Legal Defense, which was under Thurgood Marshall and Jack Greenberg, so I began to work with them. . . . Lots of members in the union, 608, in the black union, because of this activity, joined the NAACP, took out membership and supported them. . . . Most of them joined and supported it because they could see the thing the NAACP was doing and was trying to do on our behalf.

Stallworth used his position as union president to file a number of charges with federal agencies, charges that eventually led to a consent agreement that began the process of integrating the mill.[45]

At Scott Paper Company in Mobile, the black local, IBPSPMW Local 613, was very active in trying to end job segregation. At the 1968 contract negotiations, for example, the local submitted a detailed proposal that called for complete integration of the mill. The proposal demanded that "any department and any job that Local 613 holds jurisdiction over, the job shall become a part of the establish line of progression."[46] The proposal failed, however, chiefly because of opposition from the white local, which Elijah Watkins, the black local's vice president, described as "hung up over jurisdiction." The black local eventually walked out of the negotiations because the white local, IBPSPMW Local 423, refused to even discuss their program for merger. "Every time we got to Item One on our local program," explained Watkins, "the union committee they had to have a coffee break or something would happen. So, we decide we wouldn't go for that. . . . We boycotted it."[47] But the black local persisted. As late as 1970, indeed, the black local appointed a special committee that proposed complete job integration in the mill. The committee conducted a detailed job study aimed at allowing senior black workers the opportunity to move to their rightful place.[48] Black workers, however, remained dissatisfied with the pace of integration at the mill and filed a Title VII lawsuit in 1971.

At International Paper Company in Natchez, Mississippi, black workers were led by Sidney Gibson, a soft-spoken yet determined man. Gibson was a local civil rights activist and served as president of the local union for over fifteen years. Between 1951 and 1974, he filed "numerous complaints" with the Labor Department, the EEOC, and the GSA in an effort to integrate the plant.[49] "Repeated complaints to the EEOC and to the OFCC have produced no significant change in the Company's or Unions' historical practices of job segregation," Gibson wrote in one 1969 EEOC charge.[50]

Unions not only gave outspoken blacks a forum for protest, they also encouraged civil rights activity in the community. In Natchez, the leading officers of the black union were all active in civil rights protests in the community. Sidney Gibson felt that his segregated union, in one of the few organized plants in the area, was important in providing a base for civil rights activity outside of work. "One of the reasons that we took top positions in the civil rights movement was because we were unionized and they couldn't fire us," he recalled. "We participated more openly than a lot of people because of our protection we had on our jobs down there by being union, and I was a union president."[51] In Moss Point, State Stallworth also recalled that his civil rights activism was encouraged by the protection from discharge that the union gave him.[52]

On some occasions, black locals used visits to their mills by federal officials as opportunities to exert outside pressure on the company. In 1967, at the Container Corporation of America in Brewton, Alabama, for example, the officers of IBPSPMW local 943 swore a statement of discrimination to a GSA compliance officer who was inspecting the plant that eventually led to an EEOC-backed lawsuit against the company in 1972. In their statement, the officers of the local highlighted a wide range of discriminatory practices, including segregated facilities, the use of discriminatory tests, and the perpetuation of segregated lines of progression.[53]

Black locals expressed their activism in several other ways. Until the late 1960s, southern paper mills hired very few black women, reflecting the wider problems that black women faced in getting hired in manufacturing industry.[54] A few black locals tried to address this problem. At International Paper Company in Pine Bluff, Arkansas, for example, black worker Lee Jewell Randle remembered that when the black local visited the company's personnel manager to press for better job opportunities, they "asked him why we couldn't get some black females, some of our lady peoples, out there as well as the white."[55]

While the bulk of their efforts concentrated on trying to secure better job opportunities for their members, black local unions also led protests against segregated facilities in some cases.[56] In 1963, the black local at Gilman Paper Company, for example, sent a letter to IBPSPMW president John P. Burke that called for both integration of facilities and merger of the local unions: "We intend to inter two nondiscriminatory clauses into our next contract, Concerning items such as the washrooms, Tolets, Drinking fountains, And so foth, We would like hear from you on this matter as soon as possible, We have wrote a letter to Local 446 asking for a meeting to dicuss the merging of the two unions." The black union at Gilman also used the contract negotiations to promote integration, making proposals at both the 1965 and 1968 negotiations to open up more jobs.[57]

At St. Regis Paper Company in Jacksonville, Florida, surviving minutes from black local union meetings reveal that the union tried to address discrimination on a variety of fronts. The local, for example, took a strong stand against the company's attempts to introduce tests as a qualification for entering the white lines of progression. At a meeting on September 11, 1963, members decided to "let the Company know that Local said they will not take the test," a position that was reiterated in subsequent meetings.[58] Opening up more jobs for black workers was another major concern of the St. Regis local. As black locals did in most mills, the black St. Regis local made attempts to merge the local unions, approaching the all-white IBPSPMW local 749 with their request.[59] "Rev Calhoun said some years ago 757 wanted to merge with 749 and they refuse to do so," noted the minutes of a June 19, 1968, meeting.[60] The black local also complained about the slow pace of integration, claiming that whites were being hired "to block the colored employees" who were trying to enter the lines of progression.[61]

"If I Could Go and Fight for My Country, I Could Die for My Race": Common Characteristics of Black Union Activists

Many of the leaders of the black local unions who were very active in fighting against discrimination cited their experience of military service as an important motivator.[62] Military service exposed young southern blacks to areas of the United States that were not segregated, and they returned to the region after the war with a renewed determination to fight discrimination. James Tyson, George Sawyer, and Sidney Gibson all served in the Second World War, for example, and cited it as a major influence on their postwar activism. In addition, some black activists served in an integrated military during the Korean and Vietnam conflicts, and these experiences highlighted to them that segregation was not necessary. Military service, whether in World War II or subsequent conflicts, was particularly influential in helping black leaders to endure the harassment and intimidation that they often faced. "I didn't mind doing it because I felt it was doing me injustice," explained Korean War veteran Willis Gantlin. "If I had to die for my country for a lot of these things that I didn't know anything about, I felt why couldn't I give my life for my race at injustices being done to me and my fellow man. . . . It got to the point where if I could go and fight for my country, I could die for my race, that's the way I felt."[63]

Many African Americans who worked in the paper industry prior to the 1960s claimed that the need to support their family inhibited them from protesting discrimination. Black union activists, in contrast, were willing to jeopardize their job security in the interest of equal employment opportunity. A quiet, determined man, George Sawyer vividly recalled being threatened by the Ku Klux Klan, who left a bloody cross on the porch of his Savannah home. He recalled that many of his coworkers were afraid for his safety, but he remained steadfast, citing his military service as one of the main reasons: "It took a lot of courage, yes it did, because a lot of people was scared for us. They said, 'Man, you're going to mess around and get fired, y'all had better back off.' I said, 'Uh-uh, I ain't about to back off.' I had four children and a wife, sure did. They depended on me, because I was the breadwinner. . . . My experience in the service caused me to realize that we needed to make a change here so it was very beneficial those few years that I spent in the service. . . . I saw how people were getting along in other areas."[64]

World War II veteran Sidney Gibson recalled that one of his first acts after returning from the war was to register to vote. Because of his activism in the mill, Gibson was also threatened by the Ku Klux Klan, of which, he felt, many white paper workers in Natchez were members. Again, however, he claimed that his experience in the military during World War II helped sustain him: "It wasn't that much bravery. I would be scared but I knew it was something that had to be done. I had just come out of World War II and I had to go over there, so I said, 'Well, this is something that has to be done and somebody's going to have to do it, so I might as well go on and take the lead as much as I can and hope people will follow.' Sometimes they would leave a note, something like, 'Some Niggers are going to get killed.' . . . They was always put them around where I was working so they'd be sure I'd see it."[65]

Another common characteristic of black activists in the paper industry was their belief in self-defense. In general, many leaders of black unions felt that the nonviolent philosophy of the national civil rights movement was unrealistic in paper mill communities. Many mills were located in remote areas of the South with a strong Klan influence, and black union leaders felt that the right to self-defense was essential in these areas. The Deacons for Defense and Justice (DDJ), an armed group originally formed by local blacks in the paper mill town of Jonesboro, Louisiana, in July 1964, was also active in Bogalusa, where members guarded the leaders of the black locals at Crown-Zellerbach. Black local union president Robert Hicks recalled that during much of the 1960s, he was escorted to work at Crown by armed guards who also guarded his house at night: "There was a lot of violent people, shooting, beating up people, running people, breaking the windows out of cars, jumping on people. . . . It was just a lot of violence."[66] The violence that characterized the Bogalusa movement also led Hicks to question nonviolence to some degree.[67]

Other paper mill towns also had active DDJ groups, and many black paper workers saw them as essential. In Natchez, Sidney Gibson remembered that many blacks armed themselves despite the insistence of national civil rights leaders that protesters remain nonviolent at all times. "They tried to stop us from carrying arms," he asserted, "but they couldn't do it because we had a right to carry them if we wanted to, self-defense."[68] In many paper mill communities, gun ownership was so common that to many people, the nonviolence that national civil rights groups insisted upon was unrealistic and even suicidal. Union representative John Defee, for example, recalled that in towns like Bogalusa, white union workers made fun of CORE and refused to take them seriously specifically because they were unarmed: "Everybody had a gun, including myself. Most of the guys in the white locals down there just made fun of CORE. It was a kind of a humorous situation to them. CORE was not mean and tough and belligerent as DDJs and some of those were. . . . Nobody really paid too much attention to CORE. I guarantee you they were aware of that DDJ bunch."[69]

A belief in economic integration was also common to many of the black union activists, causing them to disagree with the national civil rights movement's emphasis upon securing equal access to public facilities such as restaurants and movie theaters. These local union leaders were much more concerned with economic issues, and particularly securing better job opportunities. In Bogalusa, for example, black local vice president David Johnson disagreed with protesters in the town who were concentrating on ending segregated facilities in downtown stores and restaurants. "I didn't think we could win it [economic equality] on those grounds," he recalled, "so I took mine to the real core, I took mine to the paper mill, where our livelihood was, in the paper mill. . . . That was my point. . . . If you've got the dollar, you can go where you want to go."[70]

Sidney Gibson also felt strongly that economic issues were far more important than integrating public spaces. He too argued that equal access to facilities was rendered meaningless if blacks were prevented from using these facilities because of their lower wages: "We were just more or less protesting because there wasn't much integration, you know social integration. I always advised against that. I said, 'Well we can go to the Newark hotel if we want to, can't anybody stop me, but when we get there, who's going to pay the bill?' " Like other black leaders, Gibson's firsthand experience in the paper industry gave him an appreciation of the importance of economic issues that student activists perhaps lacked: "I was more concerned with the economic part of it in the whole movement, with the economic part of it than the social part. I wasn't strung out on socializing too much, because really dollars are social integration. . . . If you can afford to do it you have a right to do it. . . . I say, 'Now let me make the dollar, the dollar will make the rest.' . . . I think the majority of the black people that participated in civil rights were more sold on social integration than economic integration."[71]

Although many of the most famous civil rights protests did concentrate on securing equal access to public facilities, civil rights leaders did increasingly recognize the validity of those who stressed the importance of "the dollar." Rev. Martin Luther King Jr. repeatedly spoke of the importance of economic equality to the civil rights struggle, especially in the later years of his life.[72] Black union activists themselves repeatedly emphasized the way that job discrimination locked black communities into a cycle of poverty.[73]

Segregated Locals and the Bogalusa Story

Segregated unions played a central role in the civil rights demonstrations that occurred in Bogalusa, Louisiana, in 1964–65. The protests were initiated by local blacks who launched a series of protests designed to integrate stores and restaurants. When the militant Bogalusa Voters' League (BVL) joined the demonstrations, however, the protests quickly attracted the attention of CORE, members of which had been working on civil rights projects in Louisiana since 1962. On July 5, 1965, delegates to CORE's twenty-first annual convention voted to make a "major assault" on segregation in Bogalusa, and subsequently, the civil rights organization began to dispatch large numbers of volunteers to the town. From the very beginning, the Crown-Zellerbach paper mill was at the center of CORE's strategy in Bogalusa. A major goal of the campaign was to "win broader opportunities for Negroes in the Crown-Zellerbach plant," and CORE promised to carry out "economic boycotts, if needed," against the company in order to achieve this.[74]

In many ways, Crown-Zellerbach *had* to be at the center of CORE's strategy in Bogalusa because the company completely dominated the economy of the area. The mill's dominance was further emphasized by its location in downtown Bogalusa, literally casting a shadow over surrounding stores and houses. As a preliminary report by the agency discovered, Crown's influence spread into every aspect of life in the town: "Crown dominates Bogalusa physically, financially, politically, and—through example—morally. Crown is the economic foundation of Bogalusa. Its workforce of about 3,000 with its payroll of $19 million annually provides, directly and indirectly, 70 percent of Bogalusa's income." Like most other paper mills in the South, Crown operated on a strictly segregated basis before 1964. Jobs were divided into racially separate lines of progression that were represented by separate local unions. "Job segregation in Crown is real and is a deadend to the Negroes now employed," the report concluded.[75]

But CORE also found that the black local unions—Local 189A of the UPP and Local 624 of the IBPSPMW—had a long history of fighting against segregation. The former local represented black workers in the paper mill and the latter covered the company's large bag plant. When CORE first "scouted" Bogalusa in the spring of 1964, they drew up a list of their most promising contacts in the black community, concluding that many of them were leaders of Local 189A. Of the ten names on the list, CORE noted that "all persons from 3 through 10 can be reached through Local 189A of the United Papermakers and Paper Workers Union." CORE found that many of the local's leaders were already extremely active in civil rights activities in Bogalusa, including Vice President Pedro Mondy, who promised CORE that they could use the union hall for "any meeting we might have." Mondy also impressed the civil rights group when he told them that he was already holding voter registration classes at the hall. CORE concluded that Bogalusa was "ripe for CORE's type of program," calling the town "one of the most exciting and challenging places this summer and for a long time to come." The civil rights agency credited the segregated union with an important role in producing a well-organized black community that was receptive to civil rights: "The union, which is a segregated union, is very well informed about its rights. . . . The existence of the union has also contributed highly to the sophistication of the Negro community. The rest of the parish stands in stark contrast to Bogalusa; the country areas are governed by fear, ignorance, and apathy."[76]

Local 624, the black local in the bag mill, produced two of the central leaders of the civil rights movement in Bogalusa, Robert Hicks and A. Z. Young. In April 1965, Young became president of the BVL and Hicks served as vice president. CORE worker Vera Rony, in a detailed reflection on the Bogalusa movement, noted that their union activity had helped both Hicks and Young when they became active in the Bogalusa civil rights movement: "Both men had developed their skills and reputations in the service of Local 624, the Negro wing of the Pulp, Sulphite Union; Young was the local's president for a decade; Hicks was a trustee for years and is now on the grievance committee. Their union experience, moreover, has equipped them well to voice those fundamental economic grievances that do not surface in every civil rights battle but could hardly be suppressed in Bogalusa."[77]

Robert Hicks remembered that he became active in the segregated paper union specifically because he recognized that it could be a useful forum from which to advance civil rights. "See once I became involved in civil rights we had to control the union so we could change the system," he recalled. Hicks's efforts eventually led to *Hicks v. Crown-Zellerbach*, a Title VII lawsuit filed against the company in 1966. He recalled that both he and Young had realized from their civil rights activity outside the mill that discrimination at Crown had to be tackled if there was going to be progress in other areas: "We found out with integration outside the plant, with the restaurants and the stores and different things, that type of integration, we saw that there was a bigger problem inside the plant, and then we talked with lawyers and attorneys about Title VII under the Equal Employment Act, and then we started coming inside the plant."[78]

The fact that the BVL met at Local 189A's union hall, coordinated its protest strategy, and planned its demonstrations there highlights the pivotal role that the black unions played in the Bogalusa civil rights movement. A large number of marches and other protests literally began from the union hall. On April 9, 1965, for example, CORE's national director, James Farmer, led a march of around 500 protesters from the hall. The marchers intended to picket outside city hall, but finding "inadequate police protection," they returned to the union hall.[79] Another march led by Farmer attracted journalists from the BBC and West German television, who went to the hall to carry out interviews.[80] On July 20, 1965, at the same time that pickets were protesting against segregation in Bogalusa's stores, a march of over 400 people left the union hall and marched in front of the paper mill.[81]

The activity also attracted the ire of the Ku Klux Klan, which was active in Bogalusa and happened to meet in a building less than two blocks from the union hall. On one occasion, in response to the voter registration classes, the Klan burned crosses and placed coffins with the names of local leaders on them in front of the hall. On another occasion, a tear gas bomb was thrown into the union hall shortly after a BVL meeting had taken place.[82]

Both local unions were also very active in pushing for improved opportunities for black workers at Crown itself. In 1961 and 1963, for example, the leadership of Local 189A demanded in contract negotiations that racially separate lines of progression be abolished.[83] Crown-Zellerbach responded by creating an integrated "extra board," allowing blacks to enter white lines of progression. At the same time, however, the company instituted testing as a prerequisite for entry into the white line, a move that most black workers saw as designed to halt their progress up the lines.[84]

In the 1965 negotiations, Local 624 presented a list of seventeen civil rights demands to the company, including complete compliance with Title VII, the abolition of testing, and the merger of separate seniority lines.[85] Despite their best efforts, however, contract negotiations did not prove to be an appropriate forum. Jeremiah S. Gutman, Local 624's attorney, reported that the overwhelming opposition of the white locals to their demands meant that the black local was unable to bargain effectively. Consequently, the BVL decided to meet independently with the company. As Gutman put it, "Since many of the members of the white local are prejudiced against Negroes in general and wish to preserve the repressive social system of which economic discrimination is a vital part, Local 624 is receiving no help from either its brother local or from the white southern Brotherhood negotiators." Black workers felt they could "achieve positive results with C-Z but for obstruction by their white brother workers." As was the case across the South, Local 624 was unable to advance black demands because of opposition from white locals.[86]

On July 15, 1965, the BVL engaged in a four-hour discussion of discrimination complaints with Crown-Zellerbach officials. The civil rights group presented the company with "a detailed list of complaints," arguing that Crown had done little to comply with the Civil Rights Act. They expressed particular frustration with the tiny number of blacks who had been placed in the lines of progression. "Crown has yet to make a good faith attempt to comply with the requirements of Title VII of the Civil Rights Act of 1964," the BVL asserted. "It seems clear that the few Negroes hired represent only 'token' compliance, useful to Crown for public relations purposes, useless to the Bogalusa Negro Community." The BVL asserted that at the box factory there was "outright segregation" and complained that conditions were "patently discriminatory and repugnant to Title VII."[87] The BVL pointed out in particular that both the seniority system and job testing were unfairly blocking black advancement into the better-paying jobs.[88] They demanded that Crown-Zellerbach take concrete action to improve the opportunities for blacks already working at Crown. They also insisted that the company hire more blacks, and particularly women. The BVL asserted that in the bag mill black women should be hired "to the exclusion of whites until equality is reached." In short, the BVL maintained that Crown had to adjust its Bogalusa mills "to the needs and requirements of a new era in race and labor relations."[89]

Crown-Zellerbach's failure to hire black women was a central issue of the civil rights campaign in Bogalusa. In July 1965, Otha Peters, the president of Local 624 and a leading member of CORE, outlined the poor employment prospects for black women in Bogalusa. "We particularly want jobs for Negro women in the Crown-Zellerbach plant," he told *The New York Times*. "Now, Negro women are working as maids for approximately $3 a day for white women who work at Crown-Zellerbach for $15 a day."[90] The BVL took up this issue when it met with Crown in July 1965, claiming that "one of the most glaring inequities at Bogalusa Crown-Zellerbach is the fact that of its many woman employees, not a single one is Negro. For example, there are approximately 125 women working at Bag; there has never been Negro women among them." White women who had previously worked in the mill retained recall rights, which helped to lock black women out of the plant at a time when few new jobs were becoming available. The BVL called for these recall rights to be abolished.[91]

After most CORE workers left Bogalusa in the fall of 1965, black local union leaders continued to fight for civil rights. A. Z. Young's activism became nationally prominent in the summer of 1967 when he led a 106-mile march from Bogalusa to the state capitol in Baton Rouge. As in the wider Bogalusa movement, the issue of job opportunity was at the fore of the BVL-led march. On August 19, 1967, Young told the *New York Times* that the march had been staged to "protest the lack of job opportunities for Negroes in Bogalusa."[92] He reaffirmed this goal when he addressed the marchers in Baton Rouge. "I'm not here to incite a riot or to create a disturbance," he told them from the steps of the state capitol, "but to get jobs for black folks."[93]

The Bogalusa-to-Baton Rouge march attracted national attention, mainly because of the violence from whites with which it was greeted as it passed through parishes with strong Klan influence. In the town of Holden, Louisiana, for example, the marchers were attacked by a group of white men and crosses were burnt. In Satsuma, Louisiana, whites marched directly into the protesters, leading to a "brief but fierce melee" that left several injured. Eventually the march was completed, but only after Governor John McKeithen called up the national guard, which reduced white protests to the hurling of "eggs, epithets and bottles."[94]

As well as spotlighting white violence, the march also pointed to the growing militancy of civil rights groups. Marcher Lincoln Lynch, CORE's associate national director, claimed that the marchers received state protection only after they made it clear they would defend themselves if the authorities failed to do so. "The whites all have rifles," he asserted. "Why can't black people carry guns if that's what they must do to protect themselves?" In addition, the *New York Times* reported that when the marchers reached Baton Rouge, "a predominantly youthful crowd of about 400 Negroes was led in cries of 'Black Power,'" with some adding, "Black Power is supreme" and "Down with the honkies."[95] The march was publicized partly because H. Rap Brown, the national chairman of the Student Non-Violent Co-Ordinating Committee (SNCC), promised to return to his hometown of Baton Rouge to address the group. Known for his inflammatory rhetoric,

Brown had been arrested for inciting a riot in Cambridge, Maryland, after describing recent race riots in Newark and Detroit as "just dress rehearsals for the revolution." In the end, however, Brown's visit to Louisiana did not take place because he was arrested for trying to carry a weapon onto a flight from New York to New Orleans.[96]

In locations such as Bogalusa, segregated locals clearly became strong black community organizations that were used as platforms for advancing civil rights. They played a role similar to that of other segregated institutions, such as black schools and black churches, that historians have recognized as central to the civil rights movement. Indeed, segregated unions must be recognized for the efforts they repeatedly made to combat persistent job discrimination in the southern paper industry.[97]

CHAPTER 5
SEGREGATED LOCALS AND THE TURN TO THE FEDERAL GOVERNMENT

Across the southern paper industry, black local unions tried repeatedly to open up more jobs for black workers and were active in protesting against discrimination. Very few of these efforts, however, were successful. The experiences of black leaders such as Willis Gantlin, George Sawyer, and James Tyson were typical of black union leaders across the South. Segregated unionism did give African American workers a voice to protest against discrimination, but black locals lacked the power to bring about lasting changes in job assignments.

This failure poses intriguing questions about whether black unionists viewed federal agencies as a more effective means of tackling the job discrimination they faced. Clearly, black paper workers did try to use their unions to advance civil rights demands, but at what point did they stop trying to use the union structure and seek help from the federal government?[1]

"We Didn't Have Too Much of a Voice, They Outvote Us": The Limits of Black Union Activism, 1945–1965

Black locals failed to effect significant racial change because they operated in a segregated system and lacked bargaining power. Although union leaders such as Wayne Glenn often claimed that separate black and white locals had "equal rights and privileges," records indicate that this was seldom the case. At contract negotiations, in particular, black union leaders complained that they were at best outnumbered and at worst simply ignored. Black local union leaders came to realize that they were unlikely to secure fundamental change through their union, but this did not stop them from making repeated efforts to do so.[2]

Many black workers were initially optimistic that they could secure positive changes by working through the union. At the Federal Paper Board Company in Riegelwood, North Carolina, for example, Charles Munn testified that when he started work at the mill in 1956, he was eager to join the union: "When I came to the mill in 1956 we had two locals. We had a white local and a black local . . . and I felt that being in the local would give me some voice." When he became active on the local's grievance committee, however, Munn found that the black local lacked the power of its white counterpart: "They had more consideration as a white union than we did as a black. They practiced discrimination against us at that time, because they were pushing the jobs for whites, and we were denied a lot of jobs because they were predominantly more in number." Munn felt that the white union used its greater power and numerical strength to continue segregated job patterns at the mill: "Every job that was at the top in these departments, whites held those jobs, and blacks held the lower jobs in that department. And at that time, the whites would fight that these top jobs stay white."[3]

This problem of being outnumbered was the central cause of black unions' failure to achieve any job integration before 1964. Arnold Brown, a former UPP international representative who serviced many black locals, remembered that these locals "didn't have bargaining power for the simple reason that you had a majority of whites. When a vote was held on the bargaining committees, it was held among all the committees." Brown added, "I felt for them [black locals] and thought it was wrong but it was the procedure and the democratic procedure that we had to go by at that time."[4]

The fate of the black locals' efforts to end job segregation at International Paper Company illustrated this problem. In IP plants, blacks typically comprised between 15 and 20 percent of the workforce in the 1960s. At Mobile, for example, blacks made up 18.6 percent of the workforce in 1968.[5] African American workers in Mobile were represented by two local unions that bargained with four or five white locals. Any change in the contract had to be approved by a majority vote, which black locals could never achieve on their own. Alphonse Williams, president of one of the black locals from 1958 to 1970, remembered that he repeatedly fought for integration even though open voting produced regular defeats: "Voting in big, open voting, where four or five locals was represented and they all was white, most of them was white, everytime we'd be outvoted, you see what I'm saying. So that's the reason why, it wasn't that we didn't make no effort to try, we sure enough tried. . . . We first tried to merge the lines of progression . . . but that was rejected. . . . It was specifically spelled out that the lines of progression cannot be changed except by mutual consent."[6]

The same problem faced black locals across the South. At Gilman Paper Company in St. Marys, Georgia, Leroy Hamilton, who served as a shop steward (a union representative elected by union members) in the black local in the 1950s and 1960s, remembered that the union was confronted with a barrier that could not be penetrated. Efforts to use negotiations to open up more jobs got nowhere because the larger white locals would never allow blacks to "go where the money was." "We fought for it," Hamilton explained, "but we couldn't change it because there wasn't enough of us . . . we didn't have too much of a voice, they outvote us. . . . We were overpowered, it was out of the question. We tried in the negotiations, but we had to draw a line and couldn't cross it."[7] Thomas McGauley, another former officer in the black union, also saw its power as strictly limited by the color line: "Anything that conflicted with the other local unions and the company, you know, that was just a no-no, such as lines of progression, job promotions out of your—you had a black line, you'd go and you'd stop, you couldn't move no further."[8]

Black locals, of course, would not have been outnumbered in this way if some whites had supported their efforts, but such support seldom occurred. Most whites were reluctant to surrender the benefits of segregation voluntarily. As Howard Bardwell, a former black local union officer in Moss Point, Mississippi, recalled, the black local simply "couldn't do it by itself" because whites were "used to eating all the good cake" and would not share it voluntarily.[9] Still, black locals often went to painstaking efforts to solicit white support. At Gilman Paper Company, for example, Thomas McGauley recalled that the black local formed a committee in the early 1960s to "integrate the lines of progression." The committee tried to set up meetings with the white locals, but they refused to even consider discussing job integration. "We were never able to meet with the other local unions," McGauley remembered. "We would set up big meetings with them, they never would show up at meetings. We tried to work it out with the local unions, but they never would meet."[10] This complaint was also voiced elsewhere.[11]

In some locations, black locals were afraid to even raise the topic of job integration, knowing that it could subject them to racist threats and harassment. At Scott Paper Company in Mobile, Alabama, Leon Moore, a former president of the black local, felt that any black worker who proposed to merge the lines of progression before the 1960s might "become a candidate for a lynching." Moore believed that blacks had to exercise "patience" in contract negotiations because black workers were not allowed to go beyond a "given line."[12]

The experience of workers at the Weyerhauser mill in Plymouth, North

Carolina, provides more evidence of the problems many black paper workers faced at the negotiation table. The black local at Weyerhauser repeatedly tried to eliminate discriminatory pay rates but was fobbed off with excuses from both the company and the white locals. "Every year [in] negotiations," related Tarlton Small, "we would send in . . . you know, what we want, try to get the rate up every year when negotiation time, we'd write on some paper and try to get it. And then when they came out, they said they couldn't do nothing for you." Small explained that these repeated failures led to the development of large pay disparities, allowing white workers to get "far ahead" of blacks.[13] Other senior black workers testified how the black union was given excuses by both the company and the white unions. Sylvester Small, for example, remembered that the black local was told by the white union that " 'the cow's gone dry'; can't give no more milk."[14]

Black locals' lack of bargaining power was also illustrated by events at the Olin Mathieson Corporation in Monroe, Louisiana. In 1965, Ray Robinson, the black local's president, exposed the unequal treatment black workers received at contract negotiations. "A representative of Local 654 [the white local] is in charge of the employees['] side at the bargaining table," he wrote to the EEOC. "He bargains very hard and well for proposals made by Local 654 but, when one of our proposals comes up, he gives me the floor and lets me argue for it. Local 654 does not actively support our proposals. The employer adopts far more of the important proposals of Local 654 than of ours." Robinson also alleged that grievances from the black local received less attention than those coming from Local 654. His complaints were upheld by an EEOC investigation in 1966, leading to a conciliation agreement.[15]

Across the South, black locals were often ignored and excluded during contract negotiations. At the Crossett Company in Crossett, Arkansas, for example, the company and white locals repeatedly tried to get black business "out of the way" first, suggesting to black workers that they leave the negotiations after their business was taken care of. It was only by insisting on their right to stay that the black representatives were able to participate on a more equal basis.[16] But even when their representatives were present, black locals often found it difficult to make themselves heard. At St. Regis Paper Company in Monticello, Mississippi, the company's managers reported to Wharton School researcher Herbert Northrup in 1967 that in the first negotiations the company had spent all their time talking to the white local, ignoring the black representatives. This practice continued, Northrup noted, "until finally the Negroes forced their way up to the head of the table after [many] years and demanded that they have a right to be called something but laborers." Although St. Regis was a northern-based company, it had maintained segregated locals because it "didn't interfere with customs."[17]

The former leaders of black locals at Crown-Zellerbach in Bogalusa also vividly recalled their lack of bargaining power, especially during contract negotiations. Former president Robert Hicks remembered that the black local in the box plant had to present its proposals to the white local and was never able to secure positive changes: "What they done, they kind of had a little show. What you done, the black local would have their proposals . . . and they would take those proposals and turn them into the white local . . . that's how they would negotiate . . . through the white local. They would give you an opportunity or a chance to say something at the thing . . . but in total reality it was already cut and dried on what they were going to give you. You really didn't have a chance to vote. The white local voted on whether to accept the proposals of the company."[18] David Johnson, who was the last president of the black local at the Crown-Zellerbach paper mill, remembered a similar scenario. "We didn't have no voice," Johnson asserted. "What happened in the negotiations, when you had the two locals, well the general negotiation was done in here, and we sit back in the back until they finished, and they would just tell us what they had agreed upon. . . . They did not let you participate properly."[19]

Interviews that federal officials conducted in 1966 with the leaders of the main white local at Crown indicated that these union officials expected to be allowed to bargain for black workers and felt hurt when black workers hired a lawyer to help them secure an independent voice. Although blacks often viewed presenting their proposals to white union leaders as discriminatory, white union leaders saw it as a sign of trust and cooperation. Indeed, the OFCC reported that W. D. Walker, the president of Local 189, saw the black local's refusal to work through the white local as "evidence of mistrust." Walker claimed that Local 189A's black attorney was "the cause of the ill feeling between the two unions." But clearly white leaders representing black workers was problematic because, as OFCC interviews demonstrated, white union leaders might hold prejudicial views about blacks. Walker himself proffered his own view that blacks "had difficulty in performing some jobs because of their inability to stand cold weather."[20]

Many African American workers felt that segregated unions encouraged companies and white workers to collude together against them.[21] James Tyson, a worker at the Union Camp mill in Savannah, felt that the black local was powerless in negotiations, since both the company and white unions wanted to maintain the status quo. "When they negotiated," he charged, "we

Taken in 1965, this picture of union and management representatives from Crown-Zellerbach's mill in Bogalusa, Louisiana, also highlights how blacks were outnumbered by whites. Local 189A vice president Pedro Mondy is second from the right in the front row; white local president Jack Gentry is fourth from the left in the back row. (Courtesy James Tyson)

all was in the same union, but they negotiated in the interest of the whites."[22] Many black workers indeed believed that the idea that a separate black union could be equal to a white union was as false as the whole separate but equal doctrine. Westvaco worker Charles Jenkins, who had been active in the black union since joining the company in 1946, summed up how many black workers felt. "Different unions is something like separate but equal," he declared in 1973. "There is no equal in separate; we got the black local here and the white local here, there's no such thing in being separate."[23]

What was most damaging about segregated unions, indeed, was the way that they helped to codify discrimination and lock black workers into a small number of low-paying jobs. Separate unions were especially effective at achieving these objectives because they provided company officials with a perfect excuse to refuse black workers' demands for equality. On a claim form written in 1981, for example, Gilman Paper Company worker George Jones described his unsuccessful efforts to secure a maintenance job at the plant in the 1960s: "Spoke to company official Gerald Bass supervisor, and asked why can't we get the job as shipping clerk. . . . He replied, it is not the company; it is your local unions. Spoke to president of local 958 Robert Woods on same question; He replied, local 616 employees can't merge into local 958 jurisdiction. Result: none."[24] Many other black Gilman workers related similar experiences.[25]

Many black union leaders also remembered indignities that they had to endure when they attended contract negotiations. Union representatives from all Union Camp plants in the South met in Mobile for contract negotiations, and black local union leaders were not allowed to stay in the same hotel with whites. Black locals protested this segregation, but it still continued.[26] At other mills, although the representatives of black locals sat in on contract negotiations, the participants were usually segregated. All of International Paper Company's southern plants bargained together, for example, yet the representatives from black and white locals sat separately.[27]

Overall, the leaders of black locals generally felt that a separate union did give them a voice but that this voice was only heeded when it supported white demands. "If a conflict came up between a white and a black," recalled one black worker, "then you voiced your opinion, but nine times out of ten it didn't work."[28] Similarly, Alphonse Williams remembered that the black local he led was only effective when its demands were for economic benefits that would also profit whites: "The only time that we got some help, was when the same thing was bothering us was bothering them, and to get the contract changed, you had certain language encroached into the contract and you had to go before the company on a united front, so that was the only time. . . . They supported us because they needed our help as well as we needed theirs."[29]

Black Workers, Civil Rights Demands, and the Grievance Procedure

The powerlessness of segregated unions before 1965 ensured that many black leaders would seize upon the opportunity that the 1964 Civil Rights Act presented to them. Prior to the Civil Rights Act, African American workers had little option but to accept their lack of bargaining power; with the implementation of Title VII in July 1965, however, they had an outside agency with which to register their protest, and they used it.

In Bogalusa, where the black locals had failed to secure any positive changes in contract negotiations, local union leaders turned to the federal government to fight discrimination. When leaders of Local 189A filed a class action case in 1966, they noted that they were outnumbered in negotiations by the white locals and thus could never effectively secure integration without the help of an outside agency. "Local 189, the 'white' local, has approximately 1700 members," explained the black workers in their official complaint. "Local 189A, the 'Negro' local, has 350 members. By dealing with the employees as a single unit, known as 'the Union,' there is no possibility of the desires and needs of Negro members being affected. . . . For so long as the bargaining agent for Plaintiff and others similarly situated continues to be 'the Union' . . . no relief will be possible from the very source from which relief should be forthcoming." The 1966 contract negotiations in which members of the black local were outnumbered were cited as an example: despite Local 189A's refusal to accept a contract that it felt did not go far enough to advance equal employment opportunity, the international union signed the agreement and it was put into effect.[30]

In many other plants, those who had tried for many years to fight discrimination led the turn to the federal government after 1965. The many years of futile efforts convinced these union activists that federal litigation was vital. At Union Camp in Savannah, for example, James Tyson filed the EEOC charges that later became the basis of *Boles v. Union Camp* (1969), a class action Title VII case. "It didn't make any difference, you could propose to change it," Tyson recalled. "See you had to do what I did, you had to go to the federal government and say, 'This is wrong, in America, this is wrong.' . . . We were citizens in America. . . . We could go to the wars, we could do whatever was necessary to fight to maintain this country other than reaping the benefits."[31] At Westvaco in Charleston, leaders from the previously separate black union filed the EEOC charges in 1968 that led to the 1972 class action lawsuit *Gantlin v. Westvaco*. Local union president Willis Gantlin related that his members had told him to file the charge as a last resort. "A drowning man will reach out for a straw," he explained. "I had exhausted every means possible of still trying to seek some help out of this situation and still seeking more help as far as the black man is concerned." As was the case in several other mills, the EEOC charges were filed with the help of the local NAACP.[32]

Workers at International Paper Company in Moss Point, Mississippi, epitomized the way that black union activists used Title VII as a vehicle to launch an effective fight against discrimination. State Stallworth, the president of the black local in the early 1960s, remembered that he had tried for many years to achieve results through the contract negotiations but that his efforts just "hit a brick wall." With the passage of the Civil Rights Act, however, Stallworth immediately contacted the NAACP Legal Defense Fund, who assisted him in filing EEOC charges against the company. Stallworth regarded Title VII as the key that allowed black workers to finally dismantle segregation: "The only thing that brought results was when we filed charges under Title VII of the Civil Rights Act, and that's when the improvements began to come. Through the Title VII of the Civil Rights Act and through the courts, and with the legal experts that the NAACP afforded us made the changes, that's what broke it down. . . . Title VII broke down the jobs, it broke down the separate locals . . . it come over like a blanket. It covered from the front gate to the back gate, or from the front gate to the river." Stallworth felt that the company would "never" have changed without Title VII.[33]

This view was shared by other Moss Point workers, including Howard Bardwell, a former recording secretary of the black local. "We couldn't do it by ourselves," he declared. "We had tried everything. We had to go through the government. You heard of the NAACP? Okay, we had to go through the NAACP and they the ones showed us how to get to the federal government." Without the help of the NAACP, Bardwell claimed, "we still have been scuffling, and a whole lot of people in the United States would be scuffling."[34]

Although the difficulty of producing positive change through contract negotiations led black locals to seek other means to fight segregation, lawsuits were not always the result. At the Crossett Company in Crossett, Arkansas, for example, the leaders of the segregated black local engaged in a series of secret nighttime meetings (to avoid antagonizing white workers) with company officials to discuss their strategies for tackling job discrimination. Nathaniel Reed, the black local's president who initiated the meetings, recalled that the fact that the black local was outnumbered by whites in contract negotiations meant that he had to seek another way of discussing desegregation with the company: "In negotiations, we knew we didn't have a chance. There'd be two to three of us in there negotiating with, oh, I'll say, twenty-five to thirty white people, and we knew that they didn't want it and it wasn't no use bringing it up because if we'd to vote on it, they were going to outvote us. Like I say, two of us went out there at night for about three months talking with management about these things." Reed felt that the separate union was important in providing blacks with representation but that the black local could attack segregation effectively only by meeting directly with the company: "By having a separate union, that helped us a lot. . . . We got representation and recognition from the international union by having a separate union. . . . But when it came to desegregation, no, we had to do that on our own and at night." Eventually, the meetings led to a consent agreement between the two parties, which was implemented with the help of federal officials from the GSA. Crossett, in turn, was able to avoid a lawsuit.[35]

The passage of Title VII, moreover, did not mean that African American workers abandoned their efforts to fight discrimination through their unions. Title VII and other federal pressure led to the merger of most segregated unions (as discussed later in this chapter). Although black workers could now turn to the federal government, many tried first to tackle discrimination through the grievance procedure of their merged union, hoping that it might be more effective than the grievance procedure that had existed when local unions were segregated. Grievances were written complaints that shop stewards were supposed to present to the company. If no agreement could be reached with the company, after the appropriate steps had been taken, a grievance could be handled through outside arbitration. At Continental Can in Port Wentworth, Georgia, a large number of African American workers testified that they had repeatedly filed grievances with their merged union in order to protest against discriminatory practices. "I have filed some discrimination grievances all right," declared Harry L. Brown, "but, in fact, I have a couple in the first, second step. . . . In fact, I have one for myself on discrimination down at the woodyard."[36] Shop steward Charlie Miller also testified that many black workers had filed grievances with him about discrimination, including supervisors' unequal treatment of white and black workers.[37]

Many black workers at Continental Can expressed frustration with the grievance procedure, however. "What's the use in filing the grievance?" asked Moses K. Baker in 1971. "You don't get nowhere. As soon as they get in the office, they bog down, don't come out."[38] With the grievance procedure failing to provide results, black union leaders at Continental Can concluded that they had to turn to outside agencies. These active union members often played a leading role in filing suits because they had experienced the inefficacy of the grievance procedure firsthand. Shop steward and local union officer Charlie Miller, who was the lead plaintiff in *Miller v. Continental Can*, informed the president of the merged union that he felt that persistent discrimination left him no choice but to seek help from outside agencies: "I told him we were going to have to turn somewhere to help, because we wasn't getting it from the company or either the local."[39]

Blacks' complaints about the reluctance of white union officials to process grievances increased after union mergers. At the Weyerhauser plant in Plymouth, black workers claimed that white union leaders refused to process their grievances,[40] so they began to consider filing charges with the federal government instead.[41] "We weren't treated fair," charged Morris Garrett, lead plaintiff in *Garrett v. Weyerhauser*. "We kept asking and asking and asking, so we just got tired of waiting. They were not going to do anything about it, so we decided to go to the NAACP. They told us that we would have to do this, and that's why we did it."[42] Some Weyerhauser workers even claimed that the only way the grievance procedure could be made to work was if they threatened to take their complaints to federal agencies. William E. Gibbs, for example, testified, "The union wouldn't represent you; like you could file a grievance. Well, they would keep hemming and hawing until it was finally torn up or filed away. And if you don't keep arguing and fussing, and say, 'Well, if you don't do nothing about it, I'm going to the federal government.' Then they might make a move."[43]

The repeated attempts of a group of African American workers at Albemarle Paper Company in Roanoke Rapids, North Carolina, to have their grievances addressed by first the company and then their integrated union before they initiated *Moody v. Albemarle Paper Company* on August 25, 1966, is indicative of the struggle many black workers endured.[44]

A large group of black workers first sent a letter to the company on January 11, 1966. The letter was essentially a plea for equal promotional opportunities, yet it also addressed white fears of job competition: "We would like for the company to know that we're not trying to take the white man's job, all we're asking is that the company give us, the colored employees, the same opportunity concerning jobs as the white. . . . We're not mad with anyone, all we're asking is to be treated equal." The letter also called for the company to abandon tests as a requirement for entering lines of progression. Like most black workers, the Albemarle group viewed tests as discriminatory and felt that blacks should be promoted on the basis of on-the-job experience. The workers also spoke out against the company's demands that they have a high school education before they enter the lines of progression, maintaining that Albemarle was not making a proper effort to integrate jobs: "We indeed feel that we are held back from these jobs because we do not have a high school education. . . . Our fellow Government said integrate all jobs. They did not say anything about high school education. If they integrated the jobs it wouldn't be any two line of progression."[45]

The Albemarle plaintiffs also made extensive efforts to fight discrimination through the union. But, like most black workers who tried to work through the union, they experienced frustration partly because they faced the continuing problem of being outnumbered. Even when they belonged to integrated unions, blacks were usually a minority and found it very difficult to push whites to take up their claims. Twenty-three black workers signed a letter asking the union to present a long list of discrimination complaints to the company on their behalf: "The reason that we're bring this up before the union is because Pat Greathouse, Vice president of the United Auto Workers Union said, 'in big business today, the individual can't bargain for himself but must have a union to do his bargaining for him.' " As in their previous letter, Albemarle workers expressed their particular concerned about the way that separate lines of progression still existed at the plant: "The employees would like to know what the basic issue in two line progression. Is it because of the color of the man skin? or because they don't want the colored man to make as much money as the white does? or maybe it could be that the white man is reco[g]nized over the color."[46] Both the company and the union refused black workers' demands, however, which prompted the lawsuit.[47]

Black union leaders often used the possibility of turning to federal agencies as a threat, hoping that it might push companies and unions into action. Thus, African American activists adopted a dual strategy. They were aware of their ability to use the courts but were hopeful that the passage of Title VII might push some companies and unions to change voluntarily.[48]

Likewise, some African American workers used the passage of the Civil Rights Act as leverage against the union. They wrote to the AFL-CIO asking them to eliminate separate locals and separate lines of progression. Black workers often suggested in such letters, which can be found in the files of the AFL-CIO Civil Rights Department, that they would turn to the federal government if the labor movement did not act to end discrimination. Thus they were offering an open challenge to the AFL-CIO to live up to its professed support for civil rights. In September 1965, for instance, a member of a black IBPSPMW local in Hodge, Louisiana, wrote to the AFL-CIO Civil Rights Department to complain about the continued segregation that black workers were up against: "The locals at this plant are racially segregated; there are two all-Negro locals and four all-white locals. Separate seniority lists are maintained for white and Negro workers[,] making it impossible for Negro workers to advance in the company as do the white workers." The letter noted that this situation was a "clear violation [both] of the AFL-CIO's position on civil rights and of Title VII of the Civil Rights Act," but it offered organized labor the chance to solve the problem while showing an awareness of the legal possibilities available: "While there are legal remedies available, I write to you first because I am sure your office will diligently prosecute this matter, reflecting the unequivocal position of the AFL-CIO on Civil Rights."[49]

Prior to the mid-1960s, the leaders of black locals often used international union conventions to speak out against discrimination. Following the merger of segregated locals, black union leaders sustained this vocal tradition, and those who were most outspoken were often former leaders of segregated black locals. In the 1970s, black union leaders repeatedly brought up the issue of black representation in the international union. Robert Leeper, a delegate from Virginia, spoke out at the inaugural UPIU convention in 1976: "We, the Black delegates of this convention, are totally dissatisfied in the number of Black representatives." Leeper criticized the fact that the union had only 6 black representatives out of total of 132. He maintained that this lack of representation rendered the union's nondiscrimination posture "meaningless." As did black unionists before him, Leeper prodded the union to live up to its rhetoric of equality. "We can no longer hide under the banner we pledge to be the world's most democratic union," he declared.[50]

Some black union leaders openly criticized the international union for forcing them to go to the federal government to secure racial justice. At the 1976 UPIU convention, James Tyson, an officeholder in the merged local union in Savannah, claimed that the international union was not doing enough to avert Title VII suits. Describing himself as "a true union man," Tyson charged that many black workers had "made allegations to our union" but that UPIU officials had not acted upon them. He argued that black workers wanted to secure racial justice through the union but that the UPIU's lethargy and indifference meant that it would continue to face suits. "We have come a long way," he acknowledged, but "[w]e have not come to the conclusion or to the point where we can sit down as brothers and sisters and deter some of the civil right action. However, had this International Board went to some of our brothers and asked them and said, 'Brothers, with these suits coming within our own body, let's sit down and discuss them.' This hasn't been done. We've been let out to go to the EEOC or whatever ventures that we had to redress ourselves and get justice." "We're going to have some more suits," warned Tyson, "unless this International can reckon with the fact that we want our rights."[51]

At the convention, black union leaders even offered to visit mills where discrimination charges had been filed and to meet with the aggrieved workers, claiming that this would save the international union "thousands and thousands of dollars" in legal costs.[52] At the 1980 convention, Robert Leeper, the chairman of the newly formed Black Caucus in the UPIU, similarly claimed that the union should be more responsive to black workers and thus avoid lawsuits: "Certainly it would be in the best interest of this International Union to clean out its house because we do not enjoy being sued for EEOC charges of discrimination; so let us put our house in order and then we can truthfully say that we are the world's most democratic convention."[53]

"Give All Your Power Away, That's What the Blacks Did": The Merger of Segregated Locals, 1962–1972

The federal government played a central role in bringing about the merger of separate black and white locals in the paper industry. The key moves were made in November 1962, when President Kennedy and Vice President Johnson held a conference with leading figures of the AFL-CIO to discuss civil rights in the labor movement. IBPSPMW president John P. Burke attended the conference, at which one of the major topics of discussion was the merger of segregated local unions. Burke made a pledge not to charter any more segregated locals and to merge all existing locals together. Following the conference, he addressed a letter to all black local unions informing them that they should immediately merge with white locals and return their charters to the international union.[54]

Although the process of merging segregated locals began in 1962, many years passed before all separate locals were eliminated. Indeed, several mills, including Gilman Paper Company, still had separate black and white unions as late as 1970.[55] At International Paper Company in Mobile, one of the two black locals also existed until 1970, and at Georgia Kraft Company in Rome, Georgia, the locals were merged only after a court order in 1972.[56] Merger was also delayed until 1972 at St. Regis Paper Company in Jacksonville, Florida.[57]

Part of the reason for these delays was that many white local unions opposed merging with all-black unions. One of the most notable examples occurred at Scott Paper Company in Mobile. The last president of the black local, William Drakes, related that the members of the black local tried unsuccessfully to merge with the white local but that "Local 423 rejected every proposal made by Local 613 for merger of the two unions. Local 423 was unwilling to consider a merger on any terms." The opposition of white workers to the merger of the local unions was both active and vehement. In October 1970, three members of the black local attempted to attend one of Local 423's meetings but were refused entry. Following this incident, the IBPSPMW placed local 423 under trusteeship until May 24, 1972, at which point blacks were finally admitted to the union.[58]

Several black locals also refused to merge with white unions. Indeed, a 1980 UPIU legal brief asserted that the efforts of the IBPSPMW and UPP to merge separate unions had "been met by the resistance and even defiance of both black and white members."[59] Although opposition came from both blacks and whites, many white union leaders believed that the greatest opposition came from black workers. Wayne Glenn, a former vice president of the IBPSPMW who was responsible for overseeing the merger of many segregated locals in the 1960s, maintained that many black locals were reluctant to merge. "I had more trouble getting the blacks to give their charters up than I did the whites accepting them," he recalled, "because they didn't want to do it, like in Natchez, they hid the charter, they hid it from me. I never did get it. I finally just cancelled it. In Pine Bluff the blacks threatened me with bodily harm and everything else when I went down there to get their charter. . . . Basically, the majority of them did not want to give up their charters."[60]

White workers and union officials sometimes interpreted black opposition to merged unions as signifying black workers' desire to maintain segregation. In fact, most black locals opposed mergers only when they were
carried out in what they felt was a discriminatory fashion. They were keen
to ensure that they were provided with representation within the merged
union and a fair chance for promotion into white jobs.[61] In some cases,
black locals fought long and hard to secure the merger terms that they
wanted, sometimes resorting to legal action if necessary. In 1970, for example, IBPSPMW local 805 in Rome, Georgia, instituted an action in the U.S.
District Court stipulating that it would not merge with its white counterpart
unless certain conditions were met. When the suit was denied, the local
appealed to the U.S. Court of Appeals, ensuring that the merger was not
accomplished until 1972. IBPSPMW local 757 from Jacksonville, Florida, also
strenuously opposed merger, which compelled the international union to
institute legal proceedings in 1972 to enforce it.[62]

As was the case in several locations, the black workers at Georgia Kraft
Company in Rome were not willing to merge unless they received guaranteed representation rights. The local hired a NAACP LDF lawyer, who argued
their case before the U.S. Court of Appeals, demanding a new office in the
merged local that had to be filled by a black, guaranteed representation on all
committees, and the right of "predominantly black woodyard and service
crews to select their own shop stewards."[63] Peter E. Rindskopf, the local's
lawyer, indicated that black workers wanted "a voice in the government of
the merged local, a voice as shop stewards, and a seat at the bargaining
table."[64] Many black workers expressed their opposition to merger in the
case. "We have been working right there side by side for these number of
years," explained Johnnie Pinkard, "and it didn't seem like any other local
was with us, and I couldn't see where it would be worth while to give up
our charter, and go in with another charter, and not know what you are
going into."[65]

The real concern of many African American workers at Georgia Kraft was
progress on the job. They saw little reason to merge and to give up their
union—one of the few forums they had to bring pressure on the company—
if they were not going to be guaranteed access to white lines of progression.
"The line of progression is the only thing we are interested in," explained the
local's president. "That's all I want. . . . The job is what we are interested
in. . . . I still think it would be foolish to merge without any understanding. . . . If we joined this local, what would happen if a job above me
come open?"[66]

Concerns about promotion prospects conditioned the opposition of other black locals to merger. At Hudson Pulp and Paper Company in Palatka, Florida, the black local objected to the specific terms of a merger agreement that they regarded as discriminatory. In *Gilley v. Hudson Pulp and Paper*, the black plaintiffs made it clear that they supported an equitable merger but objected to the terms of a 1966 settlement that contained a side agreement that would protect white jobs. George B. Williams, a former president of the black local, testified that he "went along with the merger but not the thing we had to do to merge." The merger agreement, he asserted, "put all of the whites at the top . . . all of them had to go ahead of the blacks before we could move." Other union members also testified that they were not willing to merge if it meant that they had to "go behind" white workers.[67]

Under pressure to fulfill the commitment it had made in November 1962, the IBPSPMW became increasingly frustrated with locals that refused to merge. In April 1970, for example, IBPSPMW president secretary Joseph P. Tonelli ordered the black local at Georgia Kraft to merge with its white counterpart, warning them that if they did not give up their charter, he would be "compelled" to seize it. In September 1970, Tonelli carried out the threat by invalidating the charter of the black local and telling its members to join the white union.[68] The international union argued that the black local was seeking to gain "special privileges" that were in violation of the Civil Rights Act.[69]

Black locals continued to question why they had to give up their charters in order to merge. They felt that this method of carrying out merger was itself discriminatory because it did not require whites to surrender any power. The attorney for the black local at Georgia Kraft wanted to know in particular why all the pressure was placed upon black unions when white unions were equally segregated: "If the NLRB holds that racially segregated local unions are grounds for revoking the certification of the same as bargaining agents, why have not the certification of the white locals at Georgia Kraft long been revoked?"[70]

In dealing with union mergers, union leaders and black workers often seemed to be speaking at cross-purposes, with both sides blaming each other for holding up a settlement. Most conflict arose because black workers and international union leaders had very different concepts of what a merger entailed. Union leaders conceived of merger as abolishing the black union, but African American leaders viewed it as a chance to merge jobs and advance equal employment opportunity. Not appreciating these concerns, white union leaders often found it difficult to understand why blacks were reluctant to unequivocally surrender their charters.[71]

St. Regis Paper Company in Jacksonville, Florida, was another plant where black workers opposed a merger with an all-white local. The St. Regis case epitomized the frustration of white union officials with black locals who refused to merge. Don Walker, the IBPSPMW representative in charge of St. Regis, testified in 1972 that Local 757 had continually resisted merger attempts: "After many, many meetings, after very much discussion, it became obvious to me that the officers of Local 757 was giving me a snow job, so to speak. I became completely disgusted. . . . I had been told the Federal Government had requested the Company not to negotiate with segregated Local Unions." Clearly frustrated, Walker even tried to repossess the charter and the records of the black local but the officers refused to hand them over.[72]

As was the case for many black locals, records showed that the St. Regis black local did not want to be segregated per se. Indeed, members had repeatedly tried to merge with the white local in the years before the Civil Rights Act. Cuthbert J. Johnson, a trustee and shop steward of the black local, testified that he had approached Don Walker about merging the unions in the past. "I talked to him about merger and suggested merger to him," Johnson related, "and he said at that time he didn't think it would be, that we could do that right now."[73] Black locals wanted to use the merger as a chance to integrate jobs and ensure that black workers would continue to have guaranteed union representation. As the president of the black local explained, his members did not support a merger that left black workers "on the bottom."[74]

As was mentioned earlier, fear of losing representation was a major reason for black opposition to merger. Since black unions were usually smaller than white locals, the international union carried out mergers by revoking the charters of the black unions. At Gilman Paper Company the black local voted not to merge with the white local in 1970, citing fear of losing representation.[75] "I expressed myself as far as saying that things were bad as it was, and if we should merge, then we don't have any representation whatsoever," explained George Jones, a local union member. "In other words, we won't have any blacks in front boosting us."[76]

The same fears were also expressed at many other locations. At the Marathon Southern Corporation in Butler, Alabama, for example, the GSA reported in 1965 that black workers were reluctant to give up their charter because they were "outnumbered." "We would lose what strength we had because we would be absorbed in other locals," declared the workers.[77] At International Paper Company in Mobile, Horace Gill, who held a variety of positions in IBPSPMW black local 412, opposed a merger that would destroy

After the merger of segregated local unions, black representation often decreased. This 1970 picture shows that the newly elected officers for the merged UPP local 189 in Bogalusa, Louisiana, were all white. (Courtesy PACE International Union)

blacks' chance to have representation. "I had request that when we merge that the black would have some kind of representation in the local," he recalled, "because we had to give up all our charter, our shop steward, our officers, everything, we just gave them up. . . . So when we merged we were left high and dry, didn't have no kind of representation." Gill felt that merger left black workers in a worse position than when they had a separate local: "When they integrated the local unions, it did more harm in a sense than it did good because when you just had the black the blacks had their officers in the local. . . . Putting the blacks in the white local, that's just like giving up your house and going to move into somebody else's, give all your power away, that's what the black did, give their power away. . . . They did it the way that they had still the upper hand."[78]

In many other locations, black union leaders resented having to surrender their local union offices without any similar sacrifice from the white locals. For example, Alphonse Williams, a former president of IBPSPMW local 604 in Mobile, recalled that his union opposed merging without guaranteed representation. Williams's opposition confirms that the separate local did provide some degree of autonomy and representation: "The reason we opposed that merger is because under the situation we did have, we did have some representation. . . . The one thing we did have going for us, when one of our men got into it, had problems, we could go represent him, but through this merger without making no provisions for us to have a mouth, so to speak, had to depend on them, our situation wasn't no better." Williams thought that blacks would never get effective representation in a merged union because "we was going to have to take our grievances sometimes to some of the same people what caused our grievances to represent us. . . . They wanted us to merge but under the condition that they still had their feet on you." Local 604 refused to agree to a merger until 1970, when the international union seized the charter, an action that Williams still viewed many years later as arbitrary.[79]

In several mills, union mergers clearly precipitated litigation. Many African American workers felt that when their separate locals had been abolished, they had lost their main forum for bringing pressure to bear upon companies. They often complained that merged unions did not represent black workers properly. In these cases, black workers expressed a sense of loss for their own union, which, unlike the white-dominated union, had stood up for them. As a result, they turned to federal agencies.[80]

In the late 1960s, black workers in many production industries replaced their separate unions with caucus organizations that protested against the racism that they felt was still practiced by management and labor. The most notable black caucuses were concentrated in the automobile industry, the garment industry, and the steel industry. Little is known about caucus activity in the paper industry, but evidence suggests that some black paper workers also formed caucuses, partly to replace the separate unions they felt had been unfairly abolished or "wiped out."[81]

The most notable black caucus organization in the paper industry was the Black Association of Millworkers (BAM), which was formed in 1970 by a group of black workers at Gilman Paper Company in St. Marys, Georgia, in response to the dissolution of their separate local union. As founding member Thomas McGauley recalled, "Our international just deleted our local union so we didn't have any representation at all; they took the charter, so when they took the charter, that left us without anything. . . . That was one of the reasons for organizing BAM. They were the thing that was going to reorganize over the southern states to replace the union and represent the black people. . . . It was a groundroots organization that was getting started up especially where they were taking the charters and black people wasn't getting represented."[82]

The leading figure in the BAM chapter in St. Marys was Elmo Myers, the last president of the black local. Myers described BAM as "a social organization organized at St. Marys to foster equal employment for employees in the mill and the bag plant." He testified that he had deliberately styled BAM as a "social" organization in order to stress its nonviolent stance: "We use the word 'social' because during that time there were a lot of black organizations that were being organized that they were getting a bad name from the public. They were for violence. You know what I mean? So then, we tried to confine this to give it a name such as that, you know, it wouldn't lead to violence, because we wasn't for doing anything violent. It wasn't for demonstrations. We wanted to petition, to write, and complain and sit down and talk with people to try to solve our problems that way. So then we come up with the name of Black Association of Millworkers—BAM."[83]

Myers testified that BAM chapters also existed in many other paper manufacturing centers, including Mobile, Alabama; Panama City, Florida; and Savannah, Georgia, and at several mills in Arkansas and Mississippi. On May 5, 1970, the St. Marys BAM presented their international union representative, Don Walker, with a petition that outlined the goals of the organization. Myers described how the main purpose of the petition was to inform the international union of "the picture of what we, as black employees at Gilman Paper Company, wanted them to negotiate for us in upcoming negotiations."[84]

The BAM petition reflected clearly the confidence and activism of black workers in the paper industry. It called upon the company and the union to abandon "those policies and practices which result in the dimunition of equal opportunity" and instead to adopt "an *Effective* action program" to secure both equal union representation and equal job opportunities. BAM's demands for better union representation included black shop stewards on every shift and black representation on the international union's executive board. The petition also called upon the company to "actively recruit within the Black community until all plants, divisions, departments, job classifications, positions and programs reflect the racial make-up of the labor pool in the hiring area." BAM wanted Gilman to institute training programs and provide scholarships in order to achieve this goal of racial balance. They also demanded that the company abolish all "non–job related" tests.[85]

Neither the company nor the union responded favorably to the petition. Don Walker disliked the racial separatism of BAM and openly rejected its proposals on these grounds. "We would have still had a black organization," he noted. Walker also called the demands "completely unrealistic," particularly objecting to the fact that "this BAM outfit would [have] veto power over a local union." The union refused to recognize BAM, and consequently the organization's proposals were not discussed at the contract negotiations.[86]

BAM turned to the courts, playing a key role in filing the *Myers v. Gilman Paper* case. Elmo Myers testified that BAM contacted the NAACP Legal Defense Fund, who informed them about the litigation that was taking place throughout the southern paper industry. A group of BAM members filed EEOC charges that closely resembled the BAM petition, citing the company for failing to implement an affirmative action program and citing the union for not allowing blacks fair representation. Workers stressed that the unions had been merged in a discriminatory fashion and that they were not willing to see the black local "submerge[d] . . . within a local bargaining unit which has been white and which would be predominantly white." These EEOC charges formed the basis of the *Myers* lawsuit.[87]

At about the same time that BAM was formed, another caucus group emerged at Scott Paper company in Mobile. Here, a group of black workers formed the Black Coalition of Labor in 1969 to "advance blacks' rights." Led by Henry Rembert, a twenty-six-year-old high school graduate, the coalition was concerned that black workers were not being properly informed of their rights under Scott's memorandum of understanding. "We was quite concerned about getting members of the Affected Class to sign waivers," Rembert recalled, "so we wanted to know more about the Affected Class and got a copy of it and began to study it. From this we began to talk to members of the Affected Class to be sure they understood what they were signing." The coalition mimeographed over three hundred copies of the memorandum and held meetings to explain its terms to black workers. Rembert encouraged black workers to enter the white line of progression and helped them prepare for the harassment that they might encounter.[88]

Segregated locals were clearly set up in the paper industry to allow white workers to control the best-paying jobs, and they succeeded in this goal. However, black workers who took part in segregated unions claimed that although they were unable to change segregated job assignments, they were successful at preventing favoritism and arbitrary action within black jobs, one of the principal reasons that the locals were initially organized. This success was partly due to the devotion of countless union officials. Indeed, several African American workers at Gilman Paper Company remembered that their local had a very good record of winning grievances for its members. "I would say at that time we were probably the most effective group in the mill, [Local] 616," recalled Thomas McGauley. "We were successful in grievances, we were very successful in grievances." The difficult task of opening up more jobs proved to be the real stumbling block. As McGauley acknowledged, "Opening up the lines of progression, we were not effective at all in that."[89]

CHAPTER 6
JUST PUNCHING IN AND GOING INTO WORK, YOU WERE SEPARATE
SEGREGATED FACILITIES IN THE SOUTHERN PAPER INDUSTRY, 1945–1970

Until the 1960s, segregated facilities were a central feature of southern society. The "white" and "colored" signs offer one of the best-known and most memorable symbols of the Jim Crow system of race relations that existed across the South from the late nineteenth century until the 1960s. Under this system, African Americans were confined to separate seating areas in public areas such as buses and movie theaters, as well as having to use separate bathrooms and water fountains. It was the obvious injustice of segregated facilities that provoked a great deal of civil rights protest in the 1950s and 1960s, including the Montgomery bus boycott of 1955–56 and the sit-in demonstrations of 1960. The need to break down segregated facilities also figured prominently in the thoughts and writings of major civil rights figures such as the Reverend Martin Luther King Jr.[1]

African Americans who worked in the South's paper mills also had to endure segregated facilities. As in the broader civil rights movement, moreover, the battle to abolish the system of separating black facilities from white was a central part of the struggle for equal rights in the paper industry, both for federal agencies such as the EEOC, the DSA, and the GSA and for black workers themselves. Many black workers indeed deeply resented having to use separate facilities and showed great determination in protesting against them. These protests increased after the passage of the 1964 Civil Rights Act and were usually led by the leaders of black local unions, illustrating again the way that separate locals acted as a forum for wider civil rights protest.

"One Hundred Percent Segregated": Southern Paper Mills before 1964

Prior to the 1960s, facilities in southern paper mills were strictly segregated by race. Black and white workers found that every aspect of their working lives was segregated, from the moment they arrived at the mill to clock in. Separate clock lines for blacks and whites were commonplace, as were separate pay windows. Most mills also had separate entrances into the mill for blacks and whites, separate locker rooms and bathhouses, and a segregated cafeteria. The extent of segregation led many black paper workers to describe their working environment as "totally segregated" or "100 percent segregated."[2]

The Crown-Zellerbach mill in Bogalusa, Louisiana, typified the segregation that existed in southern paper mills. As a 1964 report compiled by CORE described, "All facilities within Crown are segregated: toilets, lunchrooms, time-clocks, lockers, pay-windows—everything. Examples! A Negro walks into a toilet and finds there a plywood partition: one side for him, the other for whites. A Negro goes into the cafeteria [after the whites have been served], buys his lunch and though there are seats and tables not being used takes it to a ramshackle wooden building where he and his color must eat." In the company's new administration building, the report added, black workers also collected their pay at a separate window.[3]

Black workers at Crown recalled vividly how segregation governed every aspect of their working lives. Robert Hicks, who was hired in 1950, remembered,

> Facilities started at the front door, segregated. They had two entrances to the plant. They had a door for whites and they had the "white" over the top of it and they had a door that said "colored." You were going to get fired if you go through that white door. . . . And they had an office where they would pay off . . . they had two windows . . . whites would come to that one, and they'd get paid their check, blacks would come to this one to get their check . . . and the lavatories, toilets were segregated, black and white, and fountains, water-fountains. . . . If you wanted to keep that job and stay there, you'd better not be caught drinking out of that white fountain. If you did, they'd fire you.[4]

Until the mid-1960s, African American workers at IP, the largest paper company in the nation, also found that every aspect of their working lives was segregated. State Stallworth, a tall, lean black man, recalled the working conditions at the company's mill in Moss Point, Mississippi, in the summer of 1954:

When I first got hired at International Paper Company, segregation was just like the lights. They had from the time you went on the company premises, you walked into the gate where you punch your cards, and they had a place there where the whites went through one side and the blacks went through the other side because the pay clocks, they kept the records by race, so you had to go through the black gate to punch your card. And from then on when you went inside the mill they had white water fountains and black water fountains, ain't even got the same water fountains. They had white rest rooms and black rest rooms, they didn't go to the same rest room. You went to the cafeteria, it was one building, but it was a partition in the building, you had the whites on one side and the blacks on the other side.[5]

In most mills, therefore, black paper workers found that their working day started on a segregated basis as they entered the mill and clocked in at a separate place from whites. Most mills placed the time clocks in separate rooms, although in some cases the "colored" time clock was placed outside the building and the white time clock was located inside.[6] Most mills also had a cafeteria that was racially segregated, with black workers usually required to go to inferior facilities at the back of the main cafeteria. At the Albemarle Paper Company in Roanoke Rapids, North Carolina, Joseph Moody described in 1966 how the company's cafeteria was divided by a plywood partition, with the black side being small, crowded, and less well equipped: "On the white side you got nice eating facilities; on [the] colored side you got old stools. You can't hardly get in there, you in a jam and all that kind of stuff. Have tables on the white side; don't have 'em on the colored side." Black workers at Albemarle also had to wait until whites were served before they could order their food.[7]

The cafeteria at Gilman Paper Company in St. Marys, Georgia, was typical of many paper mill dining facilities. Leroy Hamilton, who started working at the mill in 1953, remembered clearly how the segregated cafeteria operated: "We couldn't go in the dining room, we had to go round to the back and go in a door, and there was a little room back there, and they fixed ours and handed it [to] us through a little hole."[8] Similarly, Ervin Humes recalled vividly that at the IP in Georgetown, South Carolina, black workers were not allowed to eat with whites. "Our cafeteria, our eating place, I probably can see it right from here now, its the same building," he stated, sitting in his living room overlooking the mill. He added, "Our orders was completely separated from the whites. They had a big dining room and we had a little dirty back room there, eating place."[9]

In some mills, blacks were not provided with a seating area, so they had to collect their food from the kitchen and return with it to the mill. Where this was the case, black workers usually gave their orders to a coworker who would go and pick up the food for the group. African Americans who worked at Weyerhauser's Plymouth mill in the 1930s and 1940s remembered how they were barred from the company's white-only restaurant. "They had a restaurant in there—once," explained William R. Land. "The blacks couldn't go in. If they got anything, they had to go take it through the window. Whites could go in there and sit down and eat. If the blacks wanted something, a group of one had to take a basket or a wheelbarrow, and go over there and get all the stuff through the window, and they would bring it back."[10] At Hudson Pulp and Paper, black woodyard workers claimed that they were not provided with any eating facilities and had to eat their lunch in the black bathhouse. White workers, however, had a "pretty nice" lunch-room equipped with tables and chairs.[11] Black workers complained that they were not provided other facilities that were given to whites. At Mobile Paperboard in Mobile, Alabama, for example, African American workers recalled that whites were provided shower facilities at the mill but blacks were not.[12]

Many mills also had segregated first aid facilities to treat workers who toiled in an industry with a high rate of workplace accidents.[13] At some mills, paper companies provided dehydrated workers with salt tablets, which were issued in separate dispensers.[14] Some mills also provided a separate annual picnic for black workers.[15] In addition, a small number of companies supported employee clubs that barred blacks from membership. At Georgia Kraft Company in Rome, Georgia, for example, the company ran an employee club with a golf course, a swimming pool, and a bar. As late as 1968, the club excluded blacks from membership. As in other mills, African American workers tried unsuccessfully to integrate the club. A similar club at Union Camp in Savannah also operated on an all-white basis.[16]

In court cases, African American workers often described how companies exerted strong control over their movements within the mills. In *Boles v. Union Camp*, Ulysses Banks, who had worked at the mill since 1950, related that when the city bus brought workers to the plant, blacks had to walk around the bus: "The guards would stop you if you got off the bus and walked right straight through and went across to your station. We had to go around that bus. Whether it's raining, storming, or what, you had to go around that bus. That's humiliation." The bus, moreover, only stopped at the main, whites-only gate; black workers walked to "another gate that only colored went through."[17] Black workers reported that even when the bus came to take workers home from Union Camp, they had to wait until all whites had been taken home before they could board the bus.[18] Several Union Camp workers described the inconvenience of using "colored" facilities, which were often located far away from where they worked. "As far as facilities like restrooms," explained Robert Pluitt, "we had certain restrooms we could go into. We'd have—sometimes we'd be working in an area, we'd have to go a certain distance before we could use the restroom because they have white only and colored only. Water was the same thing."[19]

Legal testimony indicates that African American workers reacted two ways to segregated facilities. On one hand, such facilities were so obviously discriminatory that some workers concluded that complaints against fundamental patterns of job segregation were pointless. If they were not even allowed to share the same facilities, what chance was there of them being afforded equal opportunity in jobs? Weyerhauser worker Sylvester Small, for example, when asked by the company's attorney why he had not complained about being unable to get the skilled job of millwright, answered, "[T]here wouldn't have been no need, because see, you couldn't drink out of the fountain at the time and you couldn't go in the bathroom, so there wasn't a need of filing a complaint against the company on that. . . . There were no need." Thus, segregated facilities clearly helped inculcate in some black workers the futility of racial protest.[20]

On the other hand, many African American workers were especially keen to publicize segregated facilities. In trial testimony and depositions, black workers were usually asked to explain how they felt the company had discriminated against them. Just as civil rights protesters targeted the obvious injustice of segregated facilities, many black paper workers gave descriptions of segregated facilities to illustrate their case. "I've seen a lot of discrimination against black there," claimed one black Weyerhauser worker, "because at one time you could walk through the mill and you could see water fountains—White—wrote on it here. Shower room, locker room—White Only on the door. On another door Colored, and on that fountain over there it would be Colored. We were not allowed to drink out of it."[21] Weyerhauser worker Leroy Griffin was also anxious to let the court know about segregated facilities. "Let me tell you this and then I won't tell you no more," he said at the end of his deposition. "They wouldn't even allow us to drink out of the same spigot they was drinking out of. 'Get you a damn bottle,' Mr Baggett said, 'If I catch you drinking out of there again, I'll fire you.' Now ask them all about that. You ask the whole mill about that. That is the truth."[22]

In interviews conducted in the late 1990s, many retired black workers were eager to describe the injustice of segregated facilities. Ervin Humes, who started working at ip's Georgetown mill in 1943, remembered being shocked by the crudity and severity of the segregation he found in the mill, even though he had grown up in South Carolina: "Drinking fountains, side by side, there's a white, and they was calling us colored then, c-o-l-o-r-e-d, colored. They even paint the black, something on the wall, if a guy [can't read] that you'll know that's black, fountain right side by side, white, black. You had a latrine, you know those old-time latrines, its a long one . . . where three or four guys can go in one time. They had a plyboard . . . four-by-eight, a p[ar]tition in the same latrine, and that plyboard between, colored, white, in the same latrine. That stunned me more than anything else." Even though Humes worked for twenty-five years under such conditions, he explained that he never really accepted them: "I didn't feel good about it. Some guys accepted it, but I never would accept it. . . . My philosophy in life is that I'm no better than you or nobody else any better [than me]. . . . God made all of us, that's my belief. Even if its Rockefeller or the richest man in England, I don't think he is any better than me in God's eyes. I didn't feel good about it, some guys accepted it, but I never would accept it. . . . It grind me to go through that kind of treatment but I had a family and I had to bear it. It was a bitter pill."[23]

The Civil Rights Act and De Facto Segregation

By prohibiting segregated facilities, the 1964 Civil Rights Act decreed major changes, changes that were fiercely resisted by both managers and white workers in the southern paper industry. Many mills, in fact, continued to operate with segregated facilities long after the 1964 Civil Rights Act had been passed. In May 1967, for example, OFCC director Edward C. Sylvester told the American Paper Institute (API) that continued segregation of "eating and sanitary facilities" was one of the most frequent problems his agency had encountered in southern paper mills.[24] Federal agencies repeatedly argued that the industry needed to tackle this problem with a much more "positive approach."[25] A private survey carried out by the API in the summer of 1967 indicated that although most mills had taken down "white" and "colored" signs between 1962 and 1964, there was very little integrated usage across the industry. Of the company officials in thirty mills who were asked to give their "estimated integrated use," only seven reported fully integrated use of locker rooms.[26] In some mills, facilities were still being used on a segregated basis in the 1970s.[27]

Many mills reported that African American workers who used integrated bathrooms after 1964 faced harassment and threats by white workers. At

Union Camp in Savannah, Ed Bartlett, the company's manager of industrial relations, recalled that many black workers complained to the company that they were receiving threats when they used integrated facilities, particularly at night. "They'd hear a voice threatening them bodily harm," he related.[28] Christopher Jenkins, who started working at Westvaco in Charleston, South Carolina, in October 1966, testified that when he went to "a so-called white locker room," a white carpenter "wanted to fight me in the locker room, and in fact he offered to kill me out there just because I went in to the rest room."[29]

At Gilman Paper Company in St. Marys, Georgia, a white worker injured a black worker, Amos Rawls, who was using a formerly whites-only toilet in March 1970. The white worker took advantage of a partition wall that did not reach the ceiling to throw "white liquor," a water solution containing sodium hydioxide that was used in the mill to dissolve wood chips, upon Rawls, leaving him with first- and second-degree burns to his head and scrotum. Following the incident, black workers complained that the company did not do enough to ascertain who was responsible. In 1974, an arbitrator, commenting on the incident, asserted that "the Company manifested what can only be described as an almost total indifference to a shocking event, amounting in the legal sense to condonation."[30]

It is obvious, indeed, that not only did white workers clearly resist facility integration, companies also encouraged this resistance. Across the South, management either directly enforced segregated patterns long after the passage of the Civil Rights Act or acquiesced in white workers' resistance. At International Paper Company in Moss Point, Mississippi, for example, black workers complained in 1967 that they faced "discouragement and admonitions from company officials" when they tried to use previously whites-only facilities. As a result, little progress was made toward facility integration.[31] Many black workers described how supervisors continued to enforce segregation after the Civil Rights Act. Ralph Dallas, who worked at Hudson Pulp and Paper Company in Palatka, Florida, for example, testified that in 1978 a supervisor had told him to use "the Nigger bathroom."[32] At the Olin Mathieson mill in West Monroe, Louisiana, the EEOC found in a 1968 investigation that the company was helping to maintain segregated toilets and lockers. It also reported that the company financially supported a segregated cafeteria, refuting company officials' assertions that this facility was run by workers.[33]

Many companies argued that they were afraid of alienating their white workers if they integrated facilities too quickly. At IP in Moss Point, for example, officials admitted that they had been doing away with segregated facilities in only "a step by step fashion" because they feared white resistance. The company indeed claimed that its gradual plan was the best way of keeping "disagreeable incidents" to a minimum.[34] In some mills, companies' fears of white reactions made them reluctant to integrate facilities at all. At the American Can Company's Naheola plant in Butler, Alabama, a 1965 GSA review found that the maintenance of segregated facilities, together with other violations, constituted a "flagrant violation" of both the Civil Rights Act and Executive Order 10925. The company was threatened with debarment from government contracts unless "immediate remedial action" was taken. American Can managers, however, still dragged their feet, fearing the consequences of facility integration. They told the GSA that "due to long established local customs, and in some instances very strong feeling regarding this issue," managers were hesitant to do away with segregation. In the rural area in which the Naheola plant was located, the company believed that "violence and/or work stoppage" would result from "rapid" facility integration.[35]

Crown-Zellerbach's mills in Bogalusa, Louisiana, illustrate well the way that facility integration was held back both by white workers and by management. In December 1965, the GSA reported that black workers who had used white facilities had been intimidated both by workers and by supervisors. In compliance reviews written in 1965 and 1966, federal agencies repeatedly asserted that facility integration could be accomplished if black workers were willing to venture into the white areas. They tried to encourage this but found black workers understandably afraid. Thus, although rest rooms were integrated by having a door cut into the partition between them, blacks would not go through the doorway, believing that "the first black head that goes through it won't come back."[36] Consequently, de facto segregation persisted.[37]

A good insight into black workers' fears of using integrated facilities is provided by the minutes of the black local at St. Regis Paper Company in Jacksonville, Florida. In 1967 the company integrated the locker room and the minutes show that many black workers were afraid to use lockers on the former whites-only side. Indeed, one speaker, "Brother Jernigan," called for black workers to be "careful how they carry themselves since they had to move to the other lockers."[38] At Albemarle Paper Company, African American workers were similarly reluctant to use the white side of the partitioned cafeteria after a black worker was threatened for sitting there in 1966.[39] As Albemarle worker Joe Moody explained in November 1966, he had not attempted to eat on the white side of the cafeteria "'cause I felt like the [par]tition divides me from the white man. That's the line—they don't want me over there. That's the way I feel." Moody compared the partition to the separate lines of progression that also still existed at Albemarle: "I have not seen a sign 'White only' but they still got that wall divides the colored from the white which is like they got two lines of progression dividing the colored from the white."[40]

Black Protest against Segregated Facilities

Despite the risks involved, some African American workers were determined to confront the atmosphere of fear and intimidation that kept facilities segregated in many mills after 1964. Across the South, indeed, militant workers, usually leaders in the black local unions, personally integrated many facilities.

In many mills, white boycotts were a response to militant black workers who took the initiative and started to use white facilities. A large-scale white boycott at International Paper Company in Mobile was started after Frank Newberry, the president of one of the black locals, personally integrated the cafeteria shortly after the passage of the Civil Rights Act. As white worker Larry Funk recalled, "One of the black activists, his name was Frank Newberry, Frank decided that he would use the white side of the cafeteria. The back entrance was a black entrance, and he came to the front counter and I don't remember whether he was waited on or not, but all the white patrons got up and walked out, and subsequently the cafeteria went out of business because all the whites walked out of the cafeteria and there was not enough blacks to sustain it." As Funk related, the boycott was indeed so damaging that the company was forced to permanently close the cafeteria. In 1997, over thirty-three years after integration, workers at International Paper still had no cafeteria as a result of the original boycott. With African Americans making up no more than a quarter of the company's workforce, they could not provide enough business to keep the cafeteria open.[41]

Alphonse Williams, the former president of one of the black unions at International Paper, also remembered the boycott well. A small, determined man who served as a local union president for over twelve years, Williams remembered how the cafeteria changed from being very busy to almost deserted after Newberry's initiative:

> That cafeteria was over five hundred feet long and about two hundred feet wide, and the whites had the biggest side of it, and sometimes the line would be all the way down side the wall . . . full of them, because they was the majority . . . and I told them when they integrated, I told

them, I said ain't enough of us to make up for them folks. They didn't tear the cafeteria down immediately after we started going but for all practical purposes . . . because over half the folks was buying out there was whites, and when they left, there wasn't enough blacks to make a difference. . . . The whites outnumbered the blacks three and four to one.

Williams, however, felt the company was partly to blame for the success of the boycott because they allowed whites who were boycotting the cafeteria to bring packed lunches into the mill instead.[42]

At Crown-Zellerbach, militant black workers were determined to integrate the bathrooms that remained segregated after 1964. Robert Hicks, a civil rights leader and a leading member of the black union in the box plant, played a key role in this effort. He admitted in retrospect that his actions were risky but claimed that at the time he was deeply committed to civil rights and was determined to integrate facilities: "I said, 'Fellas, I'll tell you what, I think I'm going to take me a white shower today.' And I said, 'All you fellas have been talking about this all the time,' I said, 'now's the day.' And all the blacks didn't come, a lot of the blacks wouldn't even go up there, they wouldn't go in that bathroom . . . there was a lot of fear in them. So we went, about five or six of us went up there." "So I went in there," Hicks continued. "There was three or four whites in there taking a bath, and I went on in there. They stayed in there a few minutes and finally cut the water off and walked on out, and they never did use it no more. Whites never did use the bathroom no more. . . . I left there twenty-five years later, they never did use the bathroom."[43]

At Scott Paper Company in Mobile, black activism also met white resistance, with similar results. The company's cafeteria was integrated by black activists led by local union president Leon Moore. Moore recalled that many African American workers claimed that they did not use the white side of the cafeteria because they did not have enough money. He borrowed three hundred dollars from the company's credit union and distributed it to other black workers so they could no longer use this as an excuse. Moore remembered that most black workers were still unwilling to enter the white side: "Well a large percent of them was reluctant. There was only two of us went in simultaneously, the same afternoon, and we were union leaders at the time. The intent was to ensure that the rank and file would have this opportunity, we wish for you to take advantage. . . . That was a slow process, if memory serves me correctly, it took fifty-six days to get a mass number of blacks to frequent the cafeteria for breakfast, dinner, and supper." According to

Moore, whites reacted to his protest by leaving the cafeteria, with many walking out even though they had "just taken their first bite." As more blacks started to use the cafeteria, whites launched a full-scale boycott.[44] Bobby Radcliff, who started working at Scott in 1962, indeed remembered that tension was "pretty high" when the black union leaders integrated the cafeteria, with most whites responding by bringing their own lunches to the mill.[45]

To Scott's executives, the boycott illustrated the strength of white resistance to facility integration. In *Watkins v. Scott Paper*, James H. Coil, the company's manager of administrative services, related that the company had found "considerable" resistance from its white employees to integration. "We have a cafeteria that runs seven days a week, twenty-four hours a day," he explained, "and when it was integrated, the whites just completely boycotted it and stayed out for over a year, I guess it was over fifteen months before they started coming back." During this time, Scott ran the cafeteria at a "very large economic loss."[46]

In other mills, black union leaders engaged in individual acts of resistance against segregated facilities. At Union Camp, local union president James Tyson drank out of a white watercooler and was reprimanded by the company. "What's the reason for saying who drinks out of it," he asserted, "ain't a health factor, its a color factor, and I wouldn't buy it."[47] Alphonse Williams used similar arguments to protest against the company holding segregated safety meetings. Williams eventually initiated a successful boycott of the meetings, forcing the company to integrate. "We had safety meetings once a month, so we were having segregated safety meetings, that's right," he related. "And I went to them one day and asked them to integrate the meetings. And they told me they'd think about it, and they would let me know. So I told them, 'while you're thinking about it, we ain't going to come, and if you decide that you ain't going to do it, we still ain't coming.' And I tell you what happened. When President John Kennedy was assassinated . . . we was arguing about as simple a thing as safety meetings." In meetings with the company, Williams justified the boycott, which eventually produced the right results. " 'Ain't no black accidents around this mill, and there ain't no white accidents around this mill, its all accidents,' " he told IP executives. "So we didn't go, nobody went, you know what they did about two or three weeks later, they integrated the meeting."[48]

Like company cafeterias, employee clubs often closed rather than integrate. Several paper mills ran all-white recreational clubs in the 1940s and 1950s, which included athletic facilities that were usually supported by company money and were often located on company property. During the 1960s, several of these clubs opted to shut down rather than to accept blacks as members. This was the case at Westvaco in Charleston, South Carolina, where a lily-white employees club voted to disband rather than integrate.[49]

Union Camp in Savannah, Georgia, provides the most striking example of a club that disbanded rather than integrate. Many white workers belonged to the Union Bag Athletic Association (UBAA), a social club on company property that competed in local bowling and baseball leagues. Until the early 1960s, Union Camp's black employees were forbidden from belonging to the UBAA in accordance with Section 14 of the club's bylaws, which restricted membership to whites. A small group of black workers, led by George Sawyer, the president of the black local in the bag mill, however, were determined to integrate the club. The group felt that the club's whites-only rule was particularly unfair because the club was supported by funds from the company's cafeteria, some of which were provided by black workers. In 1962, Sawyer became the first black worker to apply for UBAA membership, and he was refused. The group of black workers then met with the company and persuaded them to stop funding the UBAA. The UBAA was given an ultimatum that it would have to integrate if it continued to receive company funds, but the association's members voted to disband rather than accept black members. The association was dissolved, and the profits were divided among the members.[50]

Company records document the events leading up to the demise of the UBAA. "A secret-ballot vote on a resolution previously passed by the Association's Board of Governors was conducted," wrote company president J. R. Leintz. "The membership was called upon to accept or reject a bylaws change which would have eliminated the limitation of membership to white employees only. We understand the Officers and Board of Governors actively worked for the acceptance and passage of the proposed bylaw change. However, the vote resulted in the rejection of the proposed amendment. . . . The membership subsequently voted to dissolve the corporation with the surrender of its charter to be effective July 31, 1966."[51]

Several African American workers were anxious to use the demise of the UBAA as a chance to build a new club for all workers, regardless of race. Led by Sawyer and by James Tyson, they persuaded the company to fund the building of a new club, the Progressive Recreation Center (PRC). When the PRC opened, however, only black workers used it. Whites refused to join, and their boycott continues today. In 1997, Collis C. Jordan, the center's incumbent manager, was eager to stress that the PRC was open to whites: "Now I want this question clear—we only have Afro-American members, but we are not trying to keep anybody from being a member. If you are an employee of

SEGREGATED FACILITIES

Union Camp, or if you retire from Union Camp, you can be a fully-fledged member." Despite the club's willingness to accept whites, in the late 1990s only blacks used the PRC, a lasting reflection of the continuing racial divide between white and black paper workers.[52]

Federal Pressure and White Boycotts

Despite the resistance that occurred in many mills, in Title VII cases, African American workers across the South testified that facilities were integrated only because of federal pressure. In 1977, for example, Weyerhauser worker Joseph Hooker testified that the company had integrated its facilities following a federal inspection: "The government man come down and told them they had to integrate those bathrooms."[53] At Mobile Paperboard in Mobile, Alabama, African American worker Willie Ford, who worked at the mill between 1947 and 1984, also remembered clearly how the company had integrated facilities after a visit by a federal compliance agency: "See we had different water fountains, different bathrooms, you'd better not be caught in one of them bathrooms, and you had to drink out of spouts from their fountains, you couldn't drink out of the main fountains, and that lasted till that happened. A man come from Washington and told them, 'Well, you've got to take down all these signs, white and black, and have one bathroom, all of them use the bathroom.' And that's the way its been since, when I left there it was like that, all of them use the same bathroom."[54]

The fact that many companies integrated facilities in response to the Civil Rights Act encouraged African American workers to see the act as crucial. At Scott Paper Company, for example, Leon Moore felt that "[t]he Civil Rights Act had a great impact. The bathrooms, for example, there was only a wall that separated the black bathroom if you will from the white. When the act came forth, the wall came down. Fountains were removed with signs saying 'colored' and 'white.'" "Company policies also began to change once the Civil Rights Act was passed," Moore added.[55]

The testimony of company officials also indicates that federal influence was vital in forcing companies to integrate their facilities. Walter Russell Owens, the assistant superintendent of Weyerhauser's Plymouth mill, testified that facilities were integrated after a visit by federal agencies, shortly after the passage of the Civil Rights Act. All lockers and rest rooms had been segregated, Owens explained, but "we changed that after the EEO people started coming in to see us . . . we put up notices then saying the locker room facilities were not segregated. We took down signs over the locker room that said 'BLACK MALE' or 'WHITE MALE.'" Despite these initial changes, it took further intervention by federal agencies to ensure that facilities did not remain segregated by custom.[56]

The agencies responsible for integrating mills, such as the DSA and the GSA, were often relatively unknown, yet they were clearly influential in integrating paper mills across the South. At the Container Corporation of America in Brewton, Alabama, for example, the company's industrial relations manager testified that the company integrated all its rest rooms following several visits by the GSA in 1969.[57] Federal intervention was often very important at small mills, like Container, where company officials were reluctant to confront white workers. Still, as the Container case shows, it often took many years for federal pressure to reach companies. At Carolina Paperboard Corporation in Charlotte, a small mill that employed around one hundred workers, federal judge James B. McMillan found that the company did not eliminate segregated facilities until 1972, "during an investigation by the EEOC."[58]

Companies and federal agencies often clashed with one another over facility integration, with executives annoyed by federal efforts to ensure that facilities were actually used on an integrated basis. At Albemarle Paper Company, for example, the company disapproved of EEOC proposals to assign lockers alphabetically in order to prevent segregated usage. The notice that the company distributed to its workers announcing this change showed clearly that Albemarle was acting reluctantly: "Lockers will be reassigned alphabetically regardless of race beginning in the large locker room and ending in the small locker room. Heretofore, employees have been permitted to select their own locker in either locker room, but the Federal Government does not find this procedure acceptable. Changing clothes is not required so the showers and locker rooms are merely provided as a convenience for those employees who desire to use them."[59] Albemarle's managers claimed that the EEOC's action only exacerbated racial tension in the mill.[60]

Similar disputes took place elsewhere. John VanDillon, International Paper's director of industrial relations in the 1960s, remembered disagreeing with federal officials who wanted to reassign lockers alphabetically in several mills:

At our Natchez mill ... I remember the government people came down and we were over there meeting with them. . . . They said now with respect to the lockers for individual employees, we want you to specifically assign this locker to a black and this to a white, a salt and pepper effect as they said at that time. And that was done. . . . I mean that salt and pepper effect over there in Natchez was a little bit ridiculous in my mind. I mean if you say here's a bank, all in the same room, a bank of lockers here and a bank here, let anybody use whatever one. If there's a vacant one you can assign a black to it or a white to it, didn't make no difference. That was our position. We just felt that this fella was just trying to pour it on. It was a little bit ridiculous to make people rub shoulders.[61]

Like many executives in the industry, VanDillon felt that the federal government actually exacerbated whites' reactions by pushing facility integration too far. In 1972, for example, he testified that the insistence on integrated usage had meant that the company had to build new, integrated bathhouses, which whites refused to use: "We stated that we would assign lockers in the bath house, perhaps, in alphabetical manner. . . . [T]hey came back and said, 'No, that is not good enough.' . . . At the Springhill mill, we spent a hundred and sixty some odd thousand dollars to build new bath houses to accommodate to the number of employees up there. That is pretty much like the money we spent at Natchez to no avail, because none of the whites would use it, after it was finished."[62] Veteran Natchez workers recalled that this boycott was solid and permanent. In 1997, white worker Allen Coley, who had worked at the mill since 1954, remembered that when the federal government pushed the company to remodel facilities, "ninety-eight percent of the whites quit using the bath facilities . . . that lasts up until now. You have very few whites using the bath facilities."[63]

Similar boycotts were reported across the South, particularly when federal agencies insisted on integrated usage. At IP's plant in Georgetown, South Carolina, attempts to insure that both blacks and whites used the company's bathhouse led to a permanent boycott by white workers.[64] At the Container Corporation in Brewton, Alabama, the EEOC found in December 1970 that after the company had integrated the lockers according to GSA guidelines, "most" white workers had responded by clearing out their lockers and never using them again.[65] At Georgia-Pacific in Crossett, Arkansas, the vast majority of whites were still refusing to use the "integrated" shower room more than thirty years after segregated facilities had been abolished.[66] At Continental Can in Port Wentworth, Georgia, white workers also boycotted an integrated bathhouse, and at International Paper Company's mill in Pine Bluff, Arkansas, whites' boycott of an integrated cafeteria led to its closure.[67] At American Can's Naheola plant, where the company had worried so much about the reaction of white workers to facility integration, executives found that when they did integrate their rest rooms after the GSA visit, white workers responded by taking regular trips to the woods surrounding the rural mill.[68] Whites also boycotted other integrated facilities at Naheola.[69]

When federal pressure pushed Crown-Zellerbach to remodel all its facilities on an integrated basis, white workers also reacted with boycotts. Retired black paper mill worker David Johnson remembered the reaction of the white workers well: "They stopped using the bathrooms, you know where you take a shower, they quit taking a shower. We moved in, they moved out." Johnson also recalled seeing white workers "urinating behind a boxcar" rather than use the integrated bathroom.[70] Jack Gentry, a white man who worked in the paper mill from 1950 to 1995, remembered that the white boycott of the bathhouse was permanent: "To my knowledge when I was there no white man ever took a bath in that bathroom again. They just cleaned out their lockers and left."[71]

Many of the white workers at Crown-Zellerbach got together after the mill facilities were integrated and agreed to set up their own facilities rather than use those in the mill. The workers rented a building across the street from the paper mill and built shower and locker facilities there. The facilities were run as a private club, with workers paying six dollars a month to use them. Mervin Taylor, one of the white workers involved in setting up the new facilities, recalled that white workers never used the mill facilities again: "We give that bathroom to the blacks, whites never did go back in there."[72]

In December 1966, the OFCC carried out a detailed compliance review at Crown that pointed to the strength of white workers' opposition to facility integration. Interviews that the agency conducted were especially revealing. "Raymond Haik, white, Box Plant," the OFCC's representative noted, "indicated strongly the resentment of white employees to the integration of the locker room. He volunteered that boycotting the locker room was the moderate approach of the alternatives discussed by white employees." Another white worker, meanwhile, "indicated that white employees would probably never use the locker room as long as Negroes integrated it in the manner now in effect." Some black workers, however, were not concerned by the white boycott because it left them with more room in the locker area.[73]

Black workers also vividly recalled how whites refused to use integrated facilities. At the Weyerhauser mill in Plymouth, North Carolina, white workers abandoned their lockers after integration and refused to go in the former "colored" bathhouse. As black worker Roster Lucas recalled in court testimony, "They rebuilt the bathrooms a little bit. . . . All white and colored could go to the same bathroom. And most of the white people, they went home. Wouldn't even go to the bathroom and take a bath. And so they called our colored bathroom the welfare bathroom, and so they wouldn't go in there. They had lockers in there, and they wouldn't go in there to them."[74] At Mobile Paperboard Company, Willie Ford remembered that many white workers reacted angrily when the company took down "white" and "colored" signs after a federal visit: "Now, some of them said, 'Well I ain't going to use them behind no Niggers, I'm not going to go in there.' They said they'd go down in the woods before they used them. . . . Some of them would go down there now, I'm telling you the truth. Some of those white fellas was shown up mean over there, sure was."[75]

In many ways, the story of facility integration is representative of the integration of the paper industry as a whole. On the one hand, federal intervention was clearly a key force behind what progress was made. The federal government was responsible for doing away with segregated facilities in most mills, and its role was recognized by many paper workers. On the other hand, white resistance severely limited the impact of the federal mandate. The large number of mills that resisted the Civil Rights Act and continued to operate with de facto segregation long after 1964 illustrated the limits of federal power. In the short term, segregation by custom continued in many mills, while in the longer run, permanent boycotts of facilities ensured that even today they are often not used on an integrated basis.

CHAPTER 7
THE JACKSON MEMORANDUM AND THE LIMITS OF FEDERAL INTERVENTION

I n the summer of 1968, the Office of Federal Contract Compliance and International Paper Company announced that they had reached a "memorandum of understanding" that would end racial discrimination at America's largest paper company. The Jackson Memorandum was heralded by the federal government as a significant step forward in fighting historic patterns of employment discrimination. Indeed, Secretary of Labor Willard Wirtz described the agreement as "a significant breakthrough in our national efforts to insure equality of opportunity for all our citizens."[1] Covering more than 14,000 workers in the eleven mills that made up IP's Southern Kraft Division, the Jackson Memorandum was clearly important, yet little is known about the agreement and whether it was successful in fulfilling its ambitious goal of tackling job discrimination.[2]

The Jackson Memorandum was indicative of the close role played by the federal government in the integration of the southern paper industry. In the late 1960s, federal agencies negotiated similar agreements with most other paper companies that operated in the South, playing a pivotal role in pushing companies to tackle discrimination. Using the principles established in *United States v. Local 189* (see Chapter 3), these agencies established a standard of compliance that they sought to apply across the industry. But, although these agreements provided mechanisms to address discrimination, their implementation was left up to companies. In the decade after 1968, ineffective implementation ensured that the Jackson Memorandum, like other agreements modeled upon it, was only partially successful in improving the status of black paper workers. In IP's mills across the South, African American workers who sought promotions into white jobs complained that they faced harassment and a lack of training, which forced them back into traditionally black jobs or pushed them to waive their rights to promotion under the agreement.

The problems that afflicted the Jackson Memorandum were symptomatic of the limits of federal power in integrating the southern paper industry. The records of federal compliance agencies show that across the industry, a number of barriers continued to restrict black promotional opportunities after the Civil Rights Act, especially in smaller firms, where equal employment mandates were often ignored. Job testing, lack of affirmative action, and corporate resistance all ensured that the pace of integration in the southern paper industry was often slow and fraught with problems.

The Slow Pace of Job Integration in the Southern Paper Industry

Although paper companies clearly moved to integrate their workforces in the years after 1961, when the President's Committee on Equal Employment Opportunity was established, progress was often slow and uneven. Throughout the 1970s, lawsuits continued to occur in the industry, highlighting that integration was being thwarted by the legacy of the color of work. At Continental Can in Port Wentworth, Georgia, for example, the court found in a 1976 decision that historic patterns of segregation persisted. From the time the plant opened in 1948 until 1965, black workers were hired only in a separate line of progression in the woodyard. In addition, the vast majority of the jobs in the black line of progression paid less than "all but a few" of the jobs in the white lines of progression. After 1965, this historic pattern proved resistant to change, as black workers claimed that both white workers and company officials were discouraging them from securing jobs that used to be in the white line of progression. In 1976, for example, the court noted the "persistence of the traditional pattern of job segregation" long after the Civil Rights Act. As late as 1972, indeed, economic disparities caused by segregated jobs remained largely intact: 58 percent of white workers, compared to 4 percent of blacks, earned more than $4.00 an hour.[3]

Both the EEOC and federal courts made similar findings in paper mills across the South in the years after 1965. In 1966, for example, the EEOC ruled at Albemarle Paper Company in Roanoke Rapids, North Carolina, that the company was using tests to "perpetuate its historic practices of denying new employment opportunities to Negro applicants and of limiting Negro employees to traditional 'Negro' jobs." The federal agency found that black workers were still excluded from certain departments across the mill: "The lines of progression chart and the employee roster reflect departments that are all white and all Negro. The Negroes are in the lower classifications and

Table 2. Racial Composition of Jobs at Albemarle Paper Company, June 30, 1967

Job	Black	White
Woodyard crane operator	0	9
Woodyard laborer	18	0
Paper machine tender	0	16
Paper machine—back tender	0	12
Paper machine—third hand	0	16
Paper machine—fourth hand	0	16
Paper machine—fifth hand	0	8
Paper machine—sixth hand	0	8
Paper machine—seventh hand	0	4
"A" maintenance employee	0	99

Source: Memorandum Opinion and Order, November 11, 1971, *Moody v. Albemarle Paper*, pp. 6–8.

cannot advance. Experience is not considered."[4] Statistics produced for the *Moody v. Albemarle* case indicate that paper machine jobs, from seventh hand all the way to the top position of machine tender, remained all-white, as did all maintenance jobs, which were some of the highest-paid in the industry.[5] (See Table 2.)

In *Gantlin v. Westvaco*, almost thirteen years later, the EEOC noted that the case involved a large class of black workers who had been subjected to continued racial discrimination: "The facts of this case show a pattern of conscious racial segregation which continued well after the enactment of Title VII with respect to facilities, departments and lines of progression."[6]

A private survey conducted by the American Paper Institute, the main employers' association in the paper industry, also highlighted the slow pace of job integration across the industry. The survey was carried out in July 1967 and was based on responses received from fifty-four mills across the South. Altogether, these mills employed over 57,000 workers, of which just over 12 percent were black. Data produced by the companies showed that black workers were making very slow progress into white lines of progression. At the time of the survey, only 1.6 percent (22) of the 1,418 workers in the paper machine line of progression were African American. The API admitted that "[o]n its face, these results are not very good when compared with assertions made recently by the O.F.C.C. in connection with the inability of Negroes to enter higher lines of progression."[7]

In June 1967, Edward Sylvester, the OFCC director, told the API that there were five equal employment problems his agency frequently encountered in the southern paper industry. Sylvester explained that blacks continued to be locked into the industry's least desirable jobs by "dual progression lines, testing requirements for transfer [or no transfer right at all], and a seniority system which does not afford the Negro employee the normal right to use his length of service as a basis for movement into those more favorable positions which such seniority had entitled non-minority employees." The federal agency also complained that the paper industry had a very poor record in implementing affirmative action programs, finding that in most cases such programs "have not been developed, let alone implemented." Finally, the OFCC noted that segregated facilities remained common across the industry.[8]

The records of federal visits to Crown-Zellerbach's mills in Bogalusa, Louisiana, highlight the prevalence of these problems. In February 1967, for example, Sylvester wrote Crown vice president Francis M. Barnes that the company had "several areas of serious non-compliance with Executive Order 11246." Many of these were the same areas that the OFCC reported elsewhere, including segregated facilities, the "invalid use of testing" and the "discriminatory placement of new hires."[9]

The OFCC repeatedly charged that testing programs were a major obstacle to black progress. Although the agency claimed that black workers were failing the tests in much greater numbers than whites, companies refused to release test scores on a racial basis. Mainly as a result of pressure from the President's Committee on Equal Employment Opportunity, Crown had merged its segregated lines of progression in 1964. In 1963, however, the company had instituted a testing program that kept blacks from taking full advantage of the new job opportunities. Although Crown repeatedly insisted publicly that testing was not discriminatory, the company's private records tell a different story. Data compiled for a six-month period from September 1, 1965, to February 28, 1966, for the entire Bogalusa division showed that only 19.4 percent of blacks, compared to 70.8 percent of whites, passed the company's employment tests.[10]

Evidence indicated that discrimination also continued at Crown in the use of "recall rights" by white workers. In the 1960s, Crown was in the process of reducing employment in its Bogalusa mills through a program of modernization and automation. The company claimed that it needed to undertake "extensive modernization and work force reduction" in order to make the Bogalusa mill "fully competitive."[11] This program led to the creation of separate white and black "extraboards," from which workers without permanent jobs could fill temporary vacancies in the plant, although all jobs were assigned on a racial basis. Workers who had worked in a job and were on the extraboard had claim to permanent openings on that job, in accordance with Crown's occupational seniority system. Thus, since the extraboard was segregated until May 1964, black workers found their path to former white jobs blocked by whites who had prior claims. When the company merged its lines of progression, whites with recall rights were allowed to "leap in" to the progression line using the seniority they had prior to the merger rather than being required to move into the entry job of the newly constituted progression lines. As the OFCC reported in December 1966, this system "limited movement by Negroes up the progression lines since they would be required to wait until the recall rights of all whites in the progression lines had been exhausted." Blacks only had recall rights to the lower jobs in the progression lines because these were the only jobs they had ever held. In addition, in the event of a layoff or cut in production, whites who had leapt into the progression lines could "bump down" through jobs below them. Because the lines had been merged on the basis of existing pay rates, with lower-paid black jobs "tacked on" to the bottom of the white progression lines, whites could now bump through black jobs, while blacks would be bumped back to the extraboard or even "the street."[12]

The OFCC repeatedly maintained that the use of recall rights by whites was a major obstacle to black progress at Crown, an opinion that was shared by African American workers.[13] When federal investigators met with Pedro Mondy, the vice president of one of the black locals, he complained bitterly about the leap-in rights of white workers. The black local's lawyer asserted that his clients were determined to find a solution on recall rights that would provide them with job security.[14]

The OFCC also criticized Crown for not undertaking sufficient affirmative action, claiming that the company was afraid "of disturbing the balance of company-community relations." The company was criticized for not communicating with potential sources of black recruitment and for having "no adequate feed-back system" to measure the effectiveness of its equal employment opportunity efforts.[15]

Across the paper industry, in fact, the records of federal compliance reviews indicate that companies were repeatedly criticized both for not integrating existing black employees fast enough and for failing to recruit enough new African Americans from outside. In April 1968, for example, the GSA cited Kimberly-Clark Paper Company for "insufficient affirmative action in recruitment of minorities and placement in non-traditional job classifications."[16] In a 1967 review of International Paper Company's plant in Camden, Arkansas, the OFCC complained that the paper-making giant continued to maintain "a segregated job structure."[17] In a 1966 investigation, the OFCC also criticized Union Camp in Savannah and threatened sanctions against the company unless it moved at a faster pace to hire more black workers into nontraditional jobs.[18]

Company officials explained their differences with federal agencies by arguing that the government officials did not understand the strength of white resistance to job integration in the South. For example, Ed Bartlett, the manager of industrial relations at the Union Camp mill in Savannah, Georgia, in the 1960s, felt that federal officials wanted to push integration too fast, risking serious white resistance. "Our concern all along was achieving the federal goals, which we agreed with, the goals," he recalled. "Where we had some disagreement with the federal government is how to get there. . . . The problems that we had was the speed, accommodation, we didn't feel in some instances that we were given enough time. We wanted to get this thing done without bloodshed and with the minimum of ill-will and feelings." Bartlett stressed that the threat of serious repercussions was very real. Although the company made every effort to prevent them, he recalled that white workers still made their feelings clear: "There was still some sabotage, shut down some parts of the plant, where they destroyed machinery, just sabotage."[19] Bartlett remembered that the company had some serious disagreements with the government over the pace of integration because they felt that most federal officials did not understand the paper-making process and wanted unqualified blacks placed on jobs that had to be operated by workers with proper training. Bartlett thought that federal officials had no right "coming in here and tell[ing] us how to run the plant."[20]

Federal officials, in turn, became very frustrated with Union Camp, feeling that top management was delaying the integration process. The company was criticized over the slow pace of job integration, with its testing program coming under particularly heavy fire. The OFCC's Gene Heller was unimpressed by the company's response to a federal investigation that had found Union Camp noncompliant. In May 1966, Heller wrote a colleague, "It is indeed a heart-burning thing to see the ingenuity and crackling inventiveness that a contractor can exhibit in an attempt to come out of complying. It's a pity that effort isn't devoted to affirmatively complying. Obviously, they are still fighting us at almost every turn." Heller recommended that sanctions be imposed against the company, preventing it from holding further government contracts "until we know a meaningful affirmative action program is underway at this facility."[21]

Correspondence between Albemarle Paper Company executives and the EEOC reveals the level of management's annoyance with the federal agency.

When the EEOC found "probable cause" that the company had discriminated, company vice president John E. Bryan, in a so-called conciliation meeting, took "vehement exception" to the investigator's report and accused the federal agency of "unethical, irresponsible conduct." The company claimed that the EEOC's proposals to merge lines of progression on the basis of mill seniority, with no tests, were "absurd" and "would not only shut down the mill but would blow it sky high." As at Union Camp, Albemarle executives felt that federal officials were trying to force the pace of integration, putting forward proposals that ignored the qualifications workers needed to run skilled jobs safely and efficiently. Officials from both companies felt that the federal government was trying to apply an abstract principle of black advancement, based on the "rightful place" doctrine, that was impractical and unworkable. "They were not educated in the papermaking process," recalled Bartlett, "and they were trying to impose a principle that just didn't work in every case. We still had the responsibility for safety, we had the responsibility for making a product that was quality at a reasonable price, so that we could get a reasonable return to the stockholder."[22]

The use of employment tests was a constant source of friction between federal agencies and paper industry executives. Many companies responded to being forced to open up their lines of progression by requiring workers to pass tests in order to enter the lines. In general, however, testing was only required if workers wished to change lines of progression. Since white workers had generally been hired in lines that led to better-paying jobs, the new testing policy had little impact on them. International Paper Company introduced testing in 1962 throughout its Southern Kraft Division shortly after it had opened its lines of progression in response to Executive Order 10925. But, as an EEOC investigation of the company's large mill in Natchez, Mississippi, found, the "practical effect" of testing was "to limit upgrading opportunity for Negroes," because most whites did not have to transfer lines in order to progress to higher-paying jobs and therefore did not have to take tests.[23] An agency investigation of the company's Moss Point mill in 1968 came to similar conclusions.[24]

Federal agencies repeatedly insisted that companies abandon testing procedures, arguing that they were blocking black advancement, but many companies took a hard line, denying again and again that their tests were discriminatory.[25] At IP, for example, executives refused to scrap their tests, insisting that they were needed "to assure that we get properly qualified people in our lines of progression."[26] The company claimed that tests actually prevented discrimination and hindered "favoritism." IP managers also argued that unqualified workers often perceived that they were qualified to advance, and it was only by using tests that the company could protect itself against "retarded" employees going into jobs in which they would be "an economic liability to the company." Executives insisted that the lack of blacks in higher-paid jobs reflected their poor qualifications.[27]

Some companies hired industrial psychologists whom they had selected to review the tests to try to prove that their tests were not discriminatory. Companies were reluctant, however, to submit their tests to independent experts or to release the records of test scores. IP's efforts to validate tests did satisfy district court judges in *Stevenson v. International Paper* and *Rogers v. International Paper*, but both of these decisions were overturned by the U.S. Court of Appeals, which criticized the limited statistical samples that the company used.[28]

Across the South, black IP workers charged that these tests operated in a discriminatory fashion. At the company's mill in Mobile, for example, Alphonse Williams thought that the tests were used to prevent blacks from getting promoted into higher-paid jobs. "Most of the [black] people failed the tests," he recalled, "and I didn't agree with it and I knew what they was doing, they wasn't hunting the area of qualification they were hunting an area how to disqualify you."[29] Another IP worker, Horace Gill, believed that tests were used as a way of implementing controlled and token integration. Gill, like many black workers, felt that the company, by keeping test scores secret, would only promote those who it had handpicked: "When they did start opening the lines up, they started giving tests that wouldn't have nothing to do with the job, and they would never let you know what your score was . . . and they would handpick, when they started integrating the line of progression, they would handpick certain people, I called them Uncle Toms. They would handpick them they know they wouldn't cause no trouble and put them there, say they pass the test when they didn't pass it. . . . They would put him there, say we got our line of progression, we got it integrated, got a black there . . . they could say they had one."[30]

The hindering effect of testing was compounded by the operation of seniority systems in the paper industry. Seniority related to many aspects of employment, including layoffs, overtime, and recalls, as well as promotions and transfers to other jobs when there were changes in the size of the workforce. Traditionally, seniority lines in pulp and paper mills tended to be "long and narrow," with workers working their way up a functional line without acquiring skill or seniority rights in another. Thus, within the standard paper machine line of progression, workers advanced from the bottom job of "utility man" to the top job of machine tender. Under this system, if workers in the pulp mill wanted to transfer to the paper mill, they had to start at the lowest job on the paper mill seniority list. Seniority for promotion and layoff would start afresh when such a transfer occurred. Most union contracts stipulated that workers would have to give up their pulp mill seniority if they transferred, which ensured that few transfers of this type actually occurred. Although this occupational seniority system was not discriminatory per se, in the South, "breaks" were inserted into lines of progression that prevented African American workers from progressing to the best jobs. Within the woodyard, where most black workers were employed, blacks were barred from operating the largest and best-paying equipment, restricted instead to laboring and "woodhandling" jobs.[31]

With the passage of civil rights legislation in the 1960s, paper companies began to assign black workers to jobs in formerly white lines. This move did nothing to help African American workers who were still stuck in dead-end lines of progression, however. These workers needed to transfer lines in order to progress, a move that would involve them forfeiting their existing seniority. In many mills, therefore, the seniority system continued to hold black workers in place. "The historical pattern is clear," the court declared in *Myers v. Gilman Paper*. "As systematic discrimination by operation of the jurisdictional job allocation system died away, discrimination by operation of the seniority system rose to take its place."[32]

Again and again, African American paper workers described how loss of seniority effectively prohibited them from transferring to other lines of progression. At Continental Can in Port Wentworth, Georgia, for example, job and line of progression seniority were forfeited under transfer to another line of progression, a system that the court referred to as "identical to that traditionally prevailing in the paper industry."[33] Black workers described the consequences of this system. In 1971, Moses K. Baker explained why he had never sought a transfer: "Well, it wasn't no use, because if a fellow transferred or go to another job, I would lose my seniority over here, plus if that job over there got abolished, I wouldn't have nowhere to go but out the gate. Why sign a transfer and lose your seniority you had? Which I thought was wrong from the beginning."[34] Reedy Thomas testified that he had never tried to get transferred to the maintenance department, even though he felt he could do the work. "You lose your seniority," he explained. "I can't come back to my job with my seniority. So that's what blocks you from trying to get a different position." Other African American workers also testified that supervisors openly discouraged workers who were interested in transferring by telling them it was not worth the "price" of giving up their seniority.[35]

Changing the seniority provisions of union contracts was another thorny issue that often lead to conflict between paper companies and federal agencies. Many companies were concerned that federal efforts to change the seniority system to allow greater promotional opportunities for black workers would endanger the seniority rights that whites had already "earned." At Crown-Zellerbach, where the OFCC and the company engaged in complex negotiations to change the seniority system, both the company and union told the GSA that denying white workers their earned rights would "create a serious risk of labor strife."[36] The issue of earned rights was a constant stumbling block; in December 1965, Crown's personnel manager reported that the company had "basic disagreement" with the federal government over the issue.[37] Federal agencies were particularly determined to break down the mentality that whites had exclusive rights to certain jobs. Noting that the company had continually sought to "protect 'earned rights,'" the EEOC told Crown that "a claim of 'earned right' which categorizes a job as white or Negro is unacceptable."[38]

Although all paper companies disagreed with federal agencies in one respect or another, the pace of integration in the southern paper industry was distinctly uneven. At large companies such as International Paper and Scott, it is clear that real progress was made after 1965, partly because the federal government selected these mills for scrutiny. It was easier for smaller companies to fall through the cracks and to continue discriminatory practices for much longer. In the late 1960s and 1970s, however, a few court cases were prompted by the lack of integration at several small paper companies located in remote areas of the rural South. The most notable involved St. Joe Paper Company in Port St. Joe, Florida, but there were many others, including those at Albemarle Paper Company in Roanoke Rapids, North Carolina, Container Corporation of America in Brewton, Alabama, and Carolina Paperboard near Charlotte.[39]

Kent Spriggs, the civil rights attorney who handled several paper industry cases, felt that larger companies were much more responsive to integration than smaller companies because they had a "national perspective." Spriggs compared the *Watkins v. Scott Paper* and the *Winfield v. St. Joe Paper* cases, both of which he handled, to illustrate this point: "IP and Scott were national companies, Scott's based in Philadelphia. They understood that their southern practices were out of line with what they were doing in the rest of the country, and now that the law had been passed they were going to have to get their act together. . . . They started making some voluntary efforts earlier at a time when St. Joe didn't do anything. . . . IP had ten plants in the South, St. Joe only had one. But, see, IP was getting their act together with less help from outside litigation."[40]

Data from company records does indicate that progress was beginning to be made at large companies, while patterns remained more entrenched at smaller companies. At Scott, for example, the court found in *Watkins* that the company took a number of steps between 1961 and 1963, such as integrating facilities and opening separate lines of progression, that "broke the initial ice and began to give momentum to Scott's program." By 1963, the OFCC and the GSA told Scott that the company was "doing a good job" because it had started to break down job segregation.[41]

Strong disparities remained at companies such as Scott, but progress was clearly being made. This was a far cry from the situation that prevailed at many small paper companies. These companies often simply refused to implement any changes in response to civil rights legislation. By the early 1970s, international union leadership, concerned that they would be sued along with these companies, was pressing management to implement changes to comply with *Local 189*, but the companies continued to refuse. At both Gilman and Albemarle Paper, for example, the UPIU representatives pressed for the seniority system to be changed in accordance with the Jackson Memorandum, but management refused to budge.[42] At many smaller mills, indeed, there was a clear pattern of the international union moving ahead of companies on civil rights by the early 1970s.[43]

Small paper mills located in rural areas received the most damning reviews by federal agencies. In a 1966 review of the American Can Company, which ran a mill in rural Alabama in the small town of Butler, the OFCC heavily criticized the company for noncompliance, calling the conditions at the mill "a flagrant violation of the spirit and intent of the Executive Order (11246) as well as the Civil Rights Act of 1964."[44] The plant hired no black women and maintained segregated facilities after the Civil Rights Act. Only about 6 percent of workers were black, even though the population in the surrounding area was about 50 percent African American. The OFCC concluded that there was "a complete lack of affirmative action" at the mill.[45] In its defense, the company specifically cited the isolated, rural location of the plant as hindering any moves toward equal employment opportunity.[46] The company argued that against this background, whites would strike if job integration occurred too quickly.[47]

The Federal Government and the Jackson Memorandum

It was in response to the continuing obstacles that hindered black progress, particularly the problems caused by testing and the seniority system, that the federal government negotiated the Jackson Memorandum with IP in 1968.

The agreement contained several key provisions that were intended to permanently improve black job opportunities. The central one replaced job seniority with company length of service for determining priority when blacks moved within predominantly white lines of progression. Transfer and advancement qualifications were also amended to assure that they would be no different for blacks than they were for white workers hired at the same time. The agreement also "red circled" black pay rates, assuring that the rates paid blacks who transferred into new lines of progression would be no lower than their current wage rates, regardless of the contract rate for the job into which they transferred.[48]

As early as 1961, Department of Defense officials had made the first moves to provide black workers with equal job opportunities at IP. After Executive Order 10925 had been issued, they visited the paper-making giant and told industrial relations manager John VanDillon that the company was practicing discrimination. As VanDillon admitted, the company began to open up the lines of progression as a result of this visit. He explained that the intervention of the federal government gave the company the authority it felt it needed to integrate and helped it overcome its fears of having to segregate because of "the practicality of labor relations and desires of the union."[49]

Although the federal government had pushed IP to abolish separate lines of progression in 1962, by 1968 it was clear that further federal intervention was needed. Few black workers had transferred into other lines of progression because, as the *New York Times* noted, "many Negro workers found that they suffered financially if they tried to transfer to the formerly white occupations classifications, because they were forced to go to the bottom of the seniority ladder in those classifications."[50]

The court's decision in *United States v. Local 189* was crucial in paving the way for the Jackson agreement. In its March 1968 decision, which was upheld by the Fifth Circuit Court of Appeals on July 29, 1969, the Federal District Court for the Eastern District of Louisiana laid down the principles that were to be the basis of integration in the paper industry. It ruled that a neutral seniority system could be illegal if blacks had historically been restricted to less desirable jobs and if their ability to rectify their status was impeded by the seniority system. Or, in other words, if blacks were still feeling the effects of a prior [even pre–Title VII] discriminatory practice, the law was being violated. It designated as an "affected class" of black workers those hired prior to January 16, 1966, the date when all jobs were opened to blacks. The court ruled that the members of the affected class should be allowed to use their mill, rather than job, seniority, in matters of promotion, demotion, and layoff. This decision meant that the court accepted that members of the affected class could rise to their "rightful place" according to their seniority or to the place where they would have been had they not been discriminated against.[51]

Both civil rights lawyers and paper industry executives saw *Local 189* as a landmark, and the decision was used by both attorneys and the federal government as the compliance standard in subsequent cases. In 1972, UPIU attorney Jim Youngdahl called the *Local 189* case "the key case in the paper industry," adding that "the Crown-Zellerbach Local 189 rule is a rule that now is uniformly applied."[52] Crown-Zellerbach workers themselves felt that the Bogalusa case paved the way for integration in the southern paper industry. David Johnson, a former member of Local 189A, asserted that "after the Bogalusa mills fell in, then all the South just followed the pattern. We were the trial case, the government spent a lot of money on this case."[53]

Between 1968 and 1973, many other paper companies indeed implemented similar agreements. In these years, the DSA and OFCC consistently sought to apply the *Local 189* principles to paper mills across the South. For example, the DSA wrote to Westvaco in Charleston in December 1969 advising that the company would lose government business if it did not follow the *Local 189* ruling: "The standards of compliance . . . with respect to seniority must conform to the principles enunciated by the Court in the Crown Zellerbach decision of 1968."[54]

The OFCC's first target after the *Local 189* decision was International Paper Company. On April 17, 1968, the OFCC presented IP with twelve points that it wanted the company to address in order for it to continue receiving government contracts. In accordance with *Local 189*, two of the new proposals stipulated that black workers should be allowed to use their mill seniority to move into previously white lines of progression and that the pay rates of jobs that blacks transferred into could be no lower than those of the jobs they were leaving. Both company and union representatives from all IP mills in the South were summoned to Jackson, Mississippi, to discuss the OFCC's "Twelve Points."[55]

IP executives, concerned that the government wanted to integrate jobs too quickly, objected to several of these points. Managers claimed that the OFCC's proposals to accelerate black promotions would engender considerable white resistance, asserting that "an attempt to negotiate the changes suggested would generate extreme controversy at each of the Company's Southern mills." The company asserted that the OFCC's broad-based proposals were simply not practical: "Any such broad policy would encourage excessive transfers, be extremely costly and result in chaotic operating conditions."[56]

White union leaders remembered the Jackson meeting as tense. Jesse Whiddon, the southern director of the IBPSPMW, recalled that the federal government's proposals generated "a lot of ill-feeling" among white local union leaders. In fact, he recalled the Jackson conference as being "one of the most sensitive meetings I was ever in." The IBPSPMW leader even arranged for uniformed police to be stationed outside the conference hall in order to forestall potential trouble.[57]

Despite the objections of both the union and the company, the OFCC took a strong stance, threatening to take away government contracts if the twelve points were not agreed to. The OFCC's director, Edward C. Sylvester, told IP that it had two months to implement the twelve points throughout its mills. He told managers that if the company refused, "we will have no alternative but to institute proceedings to impose sanctions, including debarment of the International Paper Company for further contracts and cancellation of contracts now held."[58] Once an informal agreement had been reached, the OFCC repeated this threat.[59]

The OFCC's uncompromising position apparently paid off, since both sides accepted the twelve points with few changes. Those present in Jackson felt that they had little option to disagree. Union representative Chuck Spence, for example, recalled that the union representatives were told in no uncertain terms that they had to follow the federal government's recommendations.[60] Frank Bragg, the president of one of the white local unions at IP's Mobile mill, also remembered the Jackson meeting in a similar light. "If we didn't settle it ourselves," he recalled, "the feds was going to settle it for us."[61]

Black union leaders who were present in Jackson maintained that the threat of removing government business was essential in bringing both the company and white unions to heel. Ervin Humes, a delegate from IP's mill in Georgetown, South Carolina, remembered the Jackson conference clearly:

> When the government call us, call all the mills of International Paper Company down to Jackson, Mississippi, that morning those white boys got up and they denied that blacks are [dis]satisfied. . . . I was a delegate. . . . International Paper Company was sort of hanging on the fence, you know what I mean they was sort of playing it neutral that morning, and when the government said, "Okay, you can continue to do as you doing now in segregating but you will not sell one ounce of paper to the United States government," . . . the company gave up,

company says, "oh no, all we want is good paper, we don't care if its white, black, blue, or green make it," the company succumbed, and that break it down.[62]

Company officials themselves acknowledged that federal intervention was crucial in bringing about the Jackson agreement. Jim Gilliland, IP's current director of employee relations, admitted that the Jackson Memorandum would never have happened without pressure from the federal government: "Judging from some of the furore that we had in administering the Jackson Memo, I think I can safely say that the unions would have never done it on their own, and I seriously doubt we would have either, because it disrupted a lot of things and it upset a lot of people." Gilliland also acknowledged that the threat of losing government business had been very important in securing agreement from both the company and the unions: "Clearly people were made to understand that if IP were debarred from government contracts, a bunch of people would lose their jobs."[63]

The Jackson Memorandum was thus implemented in August 1968 and affected all eleven primary pulp and paper mills from IP's Southern Kraft Division, located in six different states. The agreement was ratified by a two-to-one vote of the rank-and-file union membership in the eleven affected mills. Press coverage also claimed that both unions and the company had consented to the agreement in order to keep government business, pointing out that IP held federal contracts worth "millions" of dollars.[64]

Since International Paper Company was the biggest paper company and a traditional pattern-setter, the Jackson Memorandum was soon copied by other mills across the South. At St. Regis Paper company in Jacksonville, Florida, for example, Henry J. Smith, the company's personnel manager throughout the 1960s, related that the company introduced a memorandum of understanding modeled on the Jackson agreement: "The language mostly was borrowed from International Paper Company's Memorandum of Understanding. There were some variations, but the greater part of that language was just lifted from theirs."[65] In 1971, unions and management at the Container Corporation of America in Brewton, Alabama, also adopted a memorandum agreement that was modeled on the Jackson Memorandum and other major Title VII cases in the industry.[66]

The federal government itself used the Jackson agreement as a model with which to negotiate with other paper companies. Shortly after concluding negotiations with IP, the General Services Administration negotiated a similar agreement with Scott Paper Company. As the court noted in *Watkins v. Scott Paper*, "The 'Jackson Memorandum' was used as a model, because union officials were already familiar with the terms of the agreement and had already agreed to them in conjunction with agreements negotiated at other plants."[67] According to the testimony of Scott's manager of industrial relations in Mobile, the threat of losing lucrative government contracts was again crucial in producing the agreement.[68]

The fact that Scott copied the Jackson Memorandum is important given that the company tried to promote an image of itself as a leader in race relations.[69] In writing his 1969 Wharton School study on the paper industry, Herbert Northrup corresponded closely with Scott's management, and he put forward the view that Scott was an industry "leader" in its placement of black workers into nontraditional positions.[70] Northrup's claims clearly annoyed IP management. John VanDillon, IP's manager of industrial relations, pointed out that IP was the company that had been able to "break the barrier" by signing the Jackson Memorandum. Reacting to Northrup's praise of Scott, VanDillon pointed out that "Scott did not enter a Jackson type agreement until the International Paper Company had done so." He claimed that Northrup had been seduced by Scott's rhetoric and that IP had actually achieved more. "It appears that words speak louder than actions," he wrote in 1973, "for while IP can point to more results apparently than some of these other companies can, they get the credit for *talking a good game*."[71]

VanDillon did have a point. The Jackson Memorandum was clearly a pattern-setting agreement in the paper industry and it was IP that signed it. The effectiveness of Scott's memorandum, as was the case with the Jackson agreement, was hindered by harassment and intimidation that blocked black workers from moving up the lines. In both companies, moreover, these complaints produced similar lawsuits—*Watkins v. Scott Paper* and *Stevenson v. International Paper*.[72]

The Jackson Memorandum: Implementation and Impact

Management, white workers, and African American workers differed greatly in their assessment of how successful the Jackson Memorandum was in opening up job opportunities for black workers. White workers and union leaders usually saw the memorandum as a very significant agreement that was responsible for a great deal of integration in the paper industry. "The Jackson Memorandum changed everything," stated white worker Richard Hathaway. "It was just a brand new look, it just changed the whole way of doing business, of doing things."[73] Whites tended to emphasize the scale of black movement made possible by the agreement. In Moss Point, Mississippi, for example, Elvin King felt that the memorandum provided black workers with a great deal of opportunity: "It gave them total opportunity of anyplace in the mill they wanted to go, and they did, they used it. It brought the segregation to a halt in this part of the country really. . . . It helped the society in this area change to a point that the smaller businesses also followed suit with the Jackson Memorandum because it gave them an avenue. It gave them what they needed to suppress segregation, really. . . . I think the Jackson Memorandum served this whole area."[74]

Paper industry executives also stressed the significance of the agreement. In *Rogers v. International Paper*, IP's lawyer claimed that the Jackson agreement "was heralded in the industry" and was a "tremendous step" toward providing the company's black workers with equal employment opportunities.[75] IP's current director of employee relations, Jim Gilliland, thought that the Jackson Memorandum "was an important agreement everywhere. . . . I think the Jackson Memorandum kind of set the pattern for the redress of past discrimination across the industry as a whole."[76] This positive view was also expressed by many federal officials, especially when the agreement was first announced.[77]

African American workers gave a much more mixed assessment of the Jackson Memorandum, with many complaining that intimidation and harassment prevented them from taking advantage of the agreement's provisions. Courts generally noted that the Jackson Memorandum allowed some black movement but that significant barriers to black progress remained. This mixed assessment is borne out by the historical record, which shows that the agreement facilitated some black movement but fell well short of achieving its full potential.[78]

With the implementation of the agreement, IP's managers claimed that black workers were free to move up the lines of progression. Nevertheless, the company's records from the Mobile mill reveal that the number of black workers who did move under the memorandum was very limited. On September 1, 1972, out of the 218 workers who were eligible to move under the memorandum, the vast majority (153) had refused promotion. Of the sixty-five who had not refused promotion, only sixteen had successfully transferred under the memorandum and were still working in the new line. In the woodyard line, where many blacks worked, twenty-seven out of thirty-nine workers had declined to transfer. In the finishing and shipping department, fifty-six out of seventy-four had not moved.[79]

Black workers claimed that the reasons why so few individuals were promoted under the Jackson Memorandum was because of harassment and intimidation. In *Stevenson v. International Paper*, a class action case brought at the Mobile mill in 1971, the plaintiffs' attorney Morris J. Baller argued that the agreement had been applied in a discriminatory manner. Baller claimed that "the heart" of the black plaintiffs' case was that black workers had been "harassed in attempting to exercise their rights" under the Jackson Memorandum. The agreement was inadequate because "lack of training and harassment made it inadequate."[80]

The plaintiffs argued that blacks who possessed a great deal of mill seniority "became the targets of a concerted campaign of harassment by their white supervisors, or by their white supervisors supported by the white employees. The harassment came in a variety of forms, reprimands, increased and unreasonable workloads, constant surveillance for any mis-step the black employee might make, even veiled threats, to name only a few." Blacks who were not discouraged by these tactics were "unjustly disqualified and demoted" by waiving their rights to further promotions under the agreement. The plaintiffs claimed that these tactics had "enormous success" because "the great majority of affected class employees have, in fact, refused promotions."[81]

African Americans who worked at IP in Mobile in the 1960s agreed with this assessment. Horace Gill, a heavily built man who worked at the mill between 1957 and 1994, described what blacks were typically up against:

When they integrated the jobs, the older blacks, and it was pitiful, the older blacks that didn't have much education and was sort of shy, they harassed them so I would say ninety-five percent of them signed off on the bottom jobs because they were afraid to move up because they would be harassed. For example, if they trained one on a job, you had to be trained by a white, they would show you totally different from what the jobs supposed to be. . . . They would totally harass you, so ninety-five percent of the older blacks and the records would show that they signed off because they couldn't handle it because of the harassment, because they weren't shown proper training.

Gill felt that the Jackson Memorandum helped younger blacks who were able to get promoted, "but the older black was still at a standstill, and all of them retired at a standstill."[82]

In court testimony in *Stevenson*, many black workers had similar complaints. Roosevelt Hurst, who had worked at the mill since 1945, refused a promotion to the utility man job because, having witnessed what had happened to other black workers, he was afraid that he would not receive proper training and would be fired. "I thought if I didn't have the proper training," he testified, "I felt like I shouldn't take the job." When Hurst did try two different traditionally white positions, he complained that whites never accepted him and refused to help him run the jobs. He described what he had experienced as, "you might say[,] resentment. They didn't want me on the job, is the way it seemed to me."[83] Griffin Williams, who had been promoted to a truck driving position, was told by his supervisor that he would have to relinquish the job because white customers "hadn't accepted me as a black man on this truck."[84] Similarly, older black workers who tried to secure jobs on the paper machine testified that they were told by their supervisors that they were "too old" to work on these jobs.[85]

Many older black workers lacked formal educational qualifications, and some white workers clearly took advantage of this by exaggerating the education needed on particular jobs, effectively scaring many into waiving their rights under the Jackson Memorandum. The testimony of woodyard laborer John Taylor epitomized that of many older black workers. A laborer with a fifth-grade education, Taylor transferred to the power plant under the agreement but claimed that a white coworker told him that he "needed at least a high school education to make that job." As was so often the case, the white worker effectively sowed the seeds of doubt in the newly promoted black worker's mind. Taylor told his supervisor that he was unsure whether he could perform the job "because I felt like my education would stop me according to what I had been advised." Taylor's supervisor agreed with the white worker and ensured that Taylor would waive his rights to the job.

Apart from telling black workers that they lacked educational qualifications, whites also simply refused to train black workers when they did get promoted into white jobs. Taylor's testimony also illustrated this problem. When Taylor complained to his foreman that whites were refusing to train him in his new position of "conveyor man," the foreman told him that there were no white workers available to train him. When a white worker was finally assigned to the task, Taylor claimed, he learned little about the job: "He would carry me around in the motor room with the electrician job showing me how much the motors cost. When I would ask him something pertaining to the job I wanted to know he said don't worry about that; that is the operators job. He will take care of that. Don't worry about that. So I didn't get any training with him." Taylor was eventually transferred back to his old job as a result.[86]

The weaknesses of the Jackson Memorandum were clearly exposed by the *Stevenson* case. As the Fifth Circuit Court of Appeals ruled in the case, the memorandum provided "some opportunity" for blacks to advance to their "rightful place," but it was also fraught with "inadequacies."[87] According to the plaintiffs, the Jackson Memorandum "fell far short" of accomplishing its objectives of remedying the effects of past discrimination and of desegregating production jobs. The company had limited the impact of the agreement: "Instead of encouraging affected class members to take advantage of opportunities provided by the Jackson Memorandum," they charged, "the defendants have utilized numerous techniques, some subtler than others, to discourage black advancement to higher jobs and to jobs in departments that are still substantially segregated."[88]

The Jackson Memorandum also had mixed results at other IP mills; it created some new promotional opportunities for black workers, but its impact was also dogged by harassment and white resistance. At the company's mill in Pine Bluff, Arkansas, a large class of African American workers brought a lawsuit in 1971 with complaints similar to those in the *Stevenson* case. The district court, however, dismissed these complaints, ruling that "as a result of the Jackson Memorandum, there has been substantial movement of black employees into the lines of progression. This has not been without some difficulty. However, it has served substantially toward achieving the intended purpose."[89] In a 1975 decision, the U.S. Court of Appeals overruled this finding, ruling that although the Jackson Memorandum had accomplished "some movement," the agreement had not reached its full potential: "No significant movement to rightful places has been realized by former discriminatees."[90]

The less than noteworthy impact of the Jackson Memorandum at Pine Bluff was clearly evident in statistics produced from the company's records. As of November 1971, only 8 blacks held positions in formerly white lines of progression, in a mill employing nearly 1,500 workers and over 100 blacks. Given that no blacks had ever held these jobs before 1968, the Jackson Memorandum had clearly made a start, but historic patterns of discrimination remained striking. African Americans were still overwhelmingly concentrated in the lower-paying jobs. Between February 1969 and November 1971, only 6 percent of black workers, compared to 56 percent of whites, earned more than $4.00 an hour.[91] As the EEOC concluded in a 1978 investigation, the Jackson Memorandum clearly "fell far short of its intended goal."[92]

As did African American workers elsewhere, those at Pine Bluff who did try and transfer under the memorandum also complained about harassment and lack of training. Clance Johnson testified that black workers who transferred into white truck-driving positions received reprimands in an effort to push them off the job. He recalled that he had given up his position of driving a Dumpster because of this: "Everytime that any black, they would start to driving these trucks, they was giving them what you call reprimand . . . why I signed off the Dumpster Driver, it was pressure. They wasn't giving you enough training."[93] Willie Lee Johnson similarly transferred to be a painter but he got "tired" of the harassment he had to put up with and agreed to go back to being a laborer.[94]

Some African American workers were not even aware of the Jackson Memorandum and maintained that the company had not informed them of their rights under it. Typical remarks included, "I don't know nothing about the Jackson Memorandum, so I won't say about the Jackson Memorandum" and "That Jackson Memorandum that they talking around here, I haven't heard anything about it. It just started singing I would say sometime more when this trial started than I heard all of the time I've been working at IP."[95] Many other black workers felt that the company had not implemented the Jackson agreement in good faith.[96] "The job we were at was not run like the Jackson Memorandum said," stated Leonard Marshall.[97]

Many African American workers complained that whites were determined to ensure that they were not aware of their rights under the agreement. Jimmie Hay testified that when the company held meetings to discuss the memorandum with their workers, foremen made blacks "stay over" and work extra, guaranteeing that they missed the meetings.[98] N. A. Thompson testified that white workers were very angry about the Jackson agreement, which caused tension in the mill: "They thought the Memorandum of Understanding was going to upgrade the black into these positions so they were pretty angry with it . . . so we got a lot of name callings and different things like that, we were trying to take their jobs . . . and why we shouldn't come in and be allowed to advance above them."[99]

The Scott Paper Company memorandum suffered from many of the same problems as the Jackson agreement. The paper industry had historically hired blacks primarily for physical labor, and many of the older black workers in the 1960s had a very limited education. African Americans who worked around these laborers emphasized that their lack of education robbed them of the confidence to feel that they could successfully move up the line. As did Horace Gill, Scott worker Bobby Radcliff emphasized that the memorandum primarily helped younger workers: "Older blacks . . . were afraid of the pressure of doing some of the jobs they would have had to do. They were uneducated, most of them that had the seniority, and its easy to put pressure on an uneducated person because they feel just about everything coming on them on account of not being able to cope or comprehend what is happening." These workers, afraid that they would face a lot of pressure if they did advance into higher-paying positions, "made themselves satisfied to stay where they were," leaving the younger generation to take greater advantage of the agreement.[100]

The way that Scott implemented the changes stipulated by its agreement also helps to explain why most African American workers did not take advantage of them. Every black worker was visited by the manager of industrial relations, Edgar Giffen, and the president of the black local, Leon Moore, to have their rights explained to them under Scott's memorandum. Workers were supposed to sign up for jobs that they were interested in and sign a waiver if they did not wish to move. In *Watkins v. Scott Paper*, filed in 1971, a huge class of African American workers complained that they had not had the memorandum explained to them properly and that they had been pushed into signing a waiver. According to attorney Jim Blacksher, the plaintiffs "were not adequately informed of what their rights were or how to proceed to get them."[101]

Kent Spriggs was the plaintiffs' co-counsel in the case, and he maintained that in many of the interviews, workers had been pressured to sign waivers. "In the Scott case," he asserted, "they basically fraudulently got the workers to sign off their rights under the Memorandum of Understanding." Spriggs claimed that most interviews took place on the job, with black workers being asked if they liked their job. Since paper industry jobs were some of the best-paying available jobs, most blacks answered that they liked their job. They then were asked to sign a waiver, often without a full understanding that they were giving up their rights to promotion. As Spriggs put it, blacks signed the waivers "because they were never given quality knowledge of what was going on."[102]

Testimony in the *Watkins* case offered numerous examples of the kind of interviews that Spriggs described. Percy Jones described his 1969 "interview": "When I went in they asked me was I satisfied with my job. And I told them I was. That is all they told me then. They told me, said, 'Sign this piece of paper.' And I signed it." There was no discussion of the requirements or rules of the memorandum.[103] Other workers related that during their interviews they were not aware that they had any other option but to sign a waiver. "I was on the job," explained Jessie King, "and they called me down and I went down to the lunchroom and they asked me if I would sign the waiver sheet. So, I signed it."[104]

The Scott memorandum, like the Jackson Memorandum, excluded maintenance jobs. At the Jackson conference, the delegation of black workers tried to protest this exclusion, but their concerns were brushed aside by the other delegates and by the OFCC, who proposed that maintenance jobs, such as millwright and mechanic, be excluded from their original twelve-point proposal. The OFCC justified this exclusion on the grounds that it was trying to increase black opportunities within the lines of progression and that these

lines had never covered maintenance jobs, which were secured independently and were represented by separate local unions. The unions and the
company also showed little interest in facilitating black entry into maintenance jobs.[105]

The exclusion of maintenance jobs was a major weakness in the agreement because these jobs were the highest-paying and most desirable in the
paper industry. Furthermore, the only transfer that many black workers
were willing to consider was to the maintenance department. The records of
the *Watkins* case highlight that many African American workers wanted to
transfer into maintenance but signed waivers when they were informed that
these jobs were excluded from the agreement. Sykes Bell's attitude was typical: "They asked me did I want to be transferred to a particular job and I told
them there ain't but one that I would be interested in and that's in the
maintenance department."[106]

With little movement occurring under the memorandum of understanding, it was no surprise that many black workers saw it as ineffective. John
Henry White expressed a typical view: "All I know is they were going around
asking to sign it. . . . I never did see anybody get to the jobs they wanted
under that Understanding, though, not that I know about."[107] The feelings
of many Scott workers were expressed by Jesse Washington, who wrote a
letter to the district court about the case. Washington described how the
plant interview caught black workers by surprise: "Now mind you no Blacks
had been given fore warning that Leon Moore and Ed Giffen was going to
seek out Blacks to name three jobs they would like to have, it was a big
surprise." Washington also captured the disappointment of many black
workers when they were informed that maintenance jobs were excluded
from the memorandum: "You tell them that you would like to go into
maintenance, but Ed Griffin [*sic*] tell you you can not go into maintenance
but you can pick any other jobs. Then you feel helpless because Maintenance
is the job most blacks wanted. . . . I turned them down because as I forth
stated I wanted to go into Maintenance." Washington's letter ended with the
plea: "I am asking the Courts is this why I am being punished?"[108]

At other plants that copied the Jackson Memorandum, black workers also
complained that harassment and intimidation hindered their efforts to
move into white jobs. Two years after company officials at Continental Can
in Port Wentworth, Georgia, implemented a "memorandum of understanding" based on the Jackson model, for example, a group of African American
workers complained in a Title VII lawsuit that the agreement had been
ineffective in practice. "Virtually every black employee who broke the barrier into a formerly white job," they maintained, "encountered delay, re-

sistance, hostility, and evasion from Continental Can."[109] Many workers provided examples of harassment in their testimony. Fifty-two-year-old Harry Brown, who worked as a woodyard laborer between 1948 and 1970, shared his story. Brown, aware of the Civil Rights Act, asked to work in the all-white laboratory in 1965. He claimed, however, that his supervisor tried to discourage him by asserting that "it would take a college professor to perform this job." Following this incident, Brown did become the first African American to work in the storeroom. Nevertheless, he asserted white workers subjected him to racial slurs and refused to train him. When he reported these problems to his supervisor, Brown maintained, he was told that he "should have expected some agitation when I got over there."[110] Charles Young, who had worked for the company since 1952, viewed the opportunities available under the company's memorandum agreement, as many blacks did, with some caution: "Most of those jobs, you are intimidate no sooner than you walk into the office."[111]

At Union Camp's mill in Savannah, management and OFCC officials worked out an affirmative action program in 1969 that was modeled on the Jackson agreement. Again, however, black workers turned to litigation because they felt that this agreement was inadequate.[112] Workers complained, in particular, that both company officials and white workers still discouraged them from transferring into white jobs. In typical testimony, Cassius Clinton Reddick related that he had agreed to return to his original job because black machine operators were given much heavier workloads than whites. "The pressure was too severe and it was continuous," he claimed. "It was a continuous thing each week and week after week, so I decided I would just go on back to my job. . . . Every colored man went down there, that's— that's what he had to do. That's why nobody stayed. I think they only got one fellow down there that actually stayed. But they all that went down there, they told them that was the set up . . . that they had to take care of five machines. . . . I don't know of any whites went down there and operate no five machines."[113]

Through important actions such as the Civil Rights Act and the Jackson Memorandum, the federal government provided a nondiscrimination mandate that did produce real change in the southern paper industry. Separate lines of progression were abolished, segregated unions were merged, and white jobs were opened to blacks for the first time. At the same time, however, white workers' and executives' resistance to change was strong and the legacy of discrimination persisted. In the face of determined white opposition, the federal government's solutions for addressing discrimination generally proved to be only partially successful.

CHAPTER 8
LIKE ARMAGEDDON
THE REACTION OF WHITE WORKERS
TO JOB INTEGRATION

The Civil Rights era brought big changes to the lives of the thousands of whites who worked in the South's paper industry in the 1960s and 1970s. Whites had grown used to working in an industry where the best jobs were reserved for them. Separate seniority lines and labor unions locked African Americans into the lowest-paying jobs and provided whites with much greater promotional opportunities than their black co-workers. For most whites who worked in the industry before the 1960s, lines of progression did allow them the opportunity to work their way up to occupy jobs that were some of the best-paid manufacturing positions in the South. Many indeed recognized the benefits they gained from the segregated system that existed until the 1960s. Larry Funk, a white maintenance worker at IP, acknowledged that the high-paying maintenance jobs were reserved exclusively for whites, with no blacks "ever allowed to apply."[1] Chuck Spence, who started working at IP in Mobile in 1953, recognized that blacks "were relegated to all of the low-paying, labor-intensive jobs, physical type jobs. They were also given all of the dirty jobs that nobody else wanted like cleaning the bathrooms and mopping the floors and hauling the garbage out, trash and stuff like that. . . . They done all the sling work, the pick work, but when it come to operating the cranes, the white guys operated the cranes. They couldn't bid on those jobs because they was in the white locals."[2]

For white workers, the civil rights era threatened the very basis of this system, allowing black workers to use their extensive company seniority to bid on previously white jobs outside their all-black departments. By aiming to promote a group of workers on the basis of plant seniority, agreements such as the Jackson Memorandum went against white workers' established concepts of job and department seniority. "The resistance to seniority systems was strong," wrote UPIU president Wayne Glenn. "A worker who had acquired seniority on a particular job, line of progression or department for purposes of future promotion . . . resisted and rejected the concept that a worker from another department could move into a job for which he or she was training and in contact over the years."[3] Whites struggled to adjust to blacks being promoted into traditionally white jobs, and most acknowledged that job integration had been the most memorable and traumatic experience of their working lives.

Moreover, the changes that were occurring in the mills were matched in the outside world, as many other areas of life, including schools and public accommodations, also integrated at the same time. These changes turned the established world of the white worker upside down and led to a difficult period of adjustment. In addition, white paper workers were not protected by class and status; they felt the full impact of these changes.[4] Many struggled to adjust to the speed with which segregation, a system they had been raised under and had taken for granted, was quickly abolished. "It was a big turnaround from what we had been used to," recalled veteran IP worker Billy Culpepper. "The water fountains, that was one of the hardest things that people out there had to accept, being pushed on you just like that, being put to you and when they did all those changes they did them pretty quick. It was a pretty quick thing putting all of that together and then after you're trying to cope with that then they start putting them ahead of you. It was rough being put in that position all at once, and most of the people that I was around at that time was brought up and didn't go to school with them see at that time, hadn't been mingled with them before. That was the biggest crush on us at the time."[5]

"They Didn't Want a Black Man to Operate Nothing out There, Nothing": The Battle for Job Integration

In the 1960s and 1970s, many southern paper mills became a battleground between black and white workers. Agreements that promoted blacks into white jobs on the basis of their company seniority were potentially explosive because they reversed long-standing employment practices. At Container Corporation in Brewton, Alabama, for example, no black person had ever been hired before 1968 except as a woodyard laborer or as a janitor. When the company implemented a memorandum of understanding in 1969, white workers resisted black advancement into nontraditional jobs. In 1974, plaintiffs' attorney J. U. Blacksher indeed reported that there had been "considerable resistance among the majority white membership of Local 888 to the training and advancement of affected class black employees into the previously all-white crane operator job." Blacksher cited the experience of one of the first black workers to be awarded this job to illustrate his complaint. "The white crane operators would not train him until ordered to do so and then only reluctantly and inadequately," he asserted. After this, the company disqualified the black worker from the job. Records from the Container Corporation case also indicated that several white workers sought to use the grievance procedure to protest against black promotions made on the basis of company seniority.[6]

At many locations, white locals openly refused to sign agreements that attempted to allow black workers greater promotional opportunities. At Georgia Kraft Company in Rome, Georgia, for example, a group of African American workers filed EEOC charges in 1970, but when the federal agency drew up a proposed conciliation agreement, both white locals refused to sign it. This refusal forced the case into court.[7] At Scott Paper Company in Mobile, only the black local ratified the company's 1968 memorandum of understanding, which, despite its name, Scott implemented virtually unilaterally. The main white local, IBPSPMW local 423, voted to reject it, and the other white locals never advised the company of their approval.[8] Throughout the region, agreements allowing blacks to be promoted based on their mill seniority were implemented and were very unpopular with white workers. "Here in Mobile and Mississippi, different mills . . . we had problems," recalled international union representative Donald L. Langham. "The white union members fought these decrees, or just resisted, strenuously resisted being forced to integrate."[9]

In Bogalusa, racial tensions were heightened further by the civil rights demonstrations that occurred in the town in 1964–65. Both white and black workers described the atmosphere in the paper mill as very tense, especially when CORE led demonstrations outside the mill in 1964 and 1965. The company even bricked up some of the windows in the mill to stop white workers from throwing missiles at the civil rights pickets.[10] The presence of outside civil rights groups and a large Ku Klux Klan had produced what local civil rights leaders termed "a most explosive situation" in the southern Louisiana town.[11] In May 1965, the BVL, describing Bogalusa as "a lawless city," employed armed guards outside its leaders' homes.[12] For much of 1964 and 1965, whites and blacks were organized into hostile Klan and Deacons of Self-Defense groupings. A CORE report on July 1, 1965, referring to black witnesses in a police brutality case, was typical of many: "Klan called today and threatened to kill any witnesses who returned to the city, and Deacons have been running themselves crazy escorting people in and out of Bogalusa. Tense."[13]

The atmosphere of racial tension inevitably affected job integration in the mill. CORE recorded a large number of incidents in which black workers who transferred into the white lines of progression were harassed and intimidated. In 1965, it noted that three black workers, "all in the 'white line of progression' at Crown-Zellerbach, have been the victims of numerous and continuing harassments, e.g., articles of clothing stolen, lunches stolen, etc. Each has found pinned onto his time card a card reading, 'you have been patronized by a Knight of the Ku Klux Klan.' "[14] Civil rights workers also found themselves attacked by white Crown workers. When CORE worker Bill Yates toured the Crown-Zellerbach plant in 1965, he claimed that a white forklift driver tried to run him over.[15]

As was the case at other plants, individual stories illustrated the resistance faced by black Crown workers who tried to defy the color line. In *United States v. Local 189*, for example, the court detailed the experiences of Anderson Brown and Tom Brown, two black workers who were promoted to operate the electrical overhead cranes, positions that had always been filled by whites. Both men were given little training and told, the court noted, that the job involved "substantial electrical and mechanical hazards which in fact did not exist." Thomas Brown was put on a crane with no brakes and was told by his supervisor "that there is a possibility of getting electrocuted at any time." Anderson Brown had a similar experience. He compared operating the crane without brakes to "driving a shift car without brakes." After two days, both men signed waivers because they were afraid of the crane. "I signed off," explained Anderson Brown, "because I was scared of the thing, because I couldn't stop it." Their action cleared the way for white workers to be promoted around them.[16]

At Crown, many other African American workers who tried to advance into white jobs faced similar harassment and intimidation. L. C. McGee entered the line of progression but quickly returned to his porter's job because white workers threw bolts at him and injured him. McGee's 1966 EEOC charge captured the intensity of white opposition to integration at Crown: "I have been intimidated, cursed, had ironbolts thrown at me, Some of the things such as my locker being burned, my name written on walls saying 'L. C. McGee is a thinking nigger,' hollered at, whooped at, heckled. My supervisors have had these complaints and have done nothing to prevent it. My job is becoming unbearable and dangerous so that I asked for a transfer and it has been denied. I ask that since my union, supervisors and

Crown-Zellerbach had not done anything I ask of you to see if something couldn't be done for my life and livelihood are at stake."[17]

The strength of white opposition to job integration was also illustrated vividly at the beginning of 1968, when the white local union at Crown voted to strike rather than to accept the Justice Department's proposals to amend the seniority system to allow greater opportunities for black workers.[18] Jack Gentry was chairman of the white union at the time, and he recalled how a packed meeting decided to shut the mill down by a unanimous vote: "I was the chairman, and there wasn't a seat in the union hall, they raised the windows and people were standing all outside, and I explained it to them, didn't get one question, unanimous vote." When the votes were tallied, over 98 percent of white workers voted to walk out, an action that was averted by an injunction obtained by the Justice Department.[19]

Crown-Zellerbach workers also recalled that job integration was marked by tension and violence. Several workers remembered that on one occasion white workers hooked up metal weights that they attempted to drop on the black pioneers (or blacks who were the first to take formerly white positions).[20] David Johnson, the former vice president of one of the black locals, recalled that the tension of that time had been so great that he had rarely talked about it: "Bogalusa . . . was a stronghold for the Klan . . . and they was some hard days, and by the way this is the first time I've ever talked about, publicly, about the paper mill as a whole, and I am the last person, black person, that held office in the 'A' local when we merged into the white local. . . . It was tense, it was tense. It was tense so bad that in 1969 I had a major heart attack. It was rough. I'll tell you I had some bad days. I had some days I didn't think I'd ever come out of there alive."[21]

The battles that occurred in Bogalusa were repeated at many other less famous locations, as white workers across the South sought to defend white jobs against black advance. At Hudson Pulp and Paper Company in Palatka, Florida, Lonnie Johnson, who was a qualified welder, faced harassment as he tried to secure a welding job. According to Johnson, one white worker even admitted to him, "Go home tonight and turn white, and you'll get the job."[22] African American workers who were placed on white jobs related that not only were they not properly trained, they were also subjected to racial slurs by whites. Most black workers indeed felt that whites wanted to defend all operating jobs as white and keep blacks confined to laboring. "They didn't want a black man to operate nothing out there, nothing," noted one worker.[23]

At Hudson, as at other paper mills, the main operating job that blacks fought for was the crane operator. In most woodyards, blacks were restricted to working as crane helpers but were forbidden from even sitting on the crane itself. Many African American workers covertly cherished the chance to be a crane operator, and when the Civil Rights Act was implemented in 1965 they seized their chance. Edward Gilley, who worked for over thirty years as a crane helper, was an example: "Ever since I was hired on 12/12/47 and worked up to get on the crane in '48," he maintained, "I just always liked to work around with the crane, and I wanted to be a crane operator. I just wanted to be a crane operator by being there with it."

In 1965, Gilley put in for a transfer to the crane operator's job. He was afraid of white reaction but was determined nonetheless: "I said I don't want to start nothing, no disturbance to tear up the Woodyard, but I want to put in for it." Most whites indeed resisted Gilley's request and were intent on defending the crane as their territory. "The whites had a big disturbance towards me," he explained, "thought I was trying to start something, a big uproar in the Woodyard." According to Gilley, white workers were "getting together to keep the blacks off the crane." The white local union led opposition to Gilley's attempted promotion, and whites wrote racial slurs all over his bid for the job. Gilley testified that he still kept his resolve: " 'Nigger' was wrote all over it, and I thought they was wanting me to start a big stir about it, but I took it to myself and wouldn't even say a word to nobody about it no more, so I just take it and went on. I let it smooth over because I thought they was putting it on for a big issue, so I swallowed and went ahead on." Eventually Gilley secured the crane operator's job, but his white helper refused to assist him. After several months of trying to do both jobs at once, Gilley finally accepted that he would have to go back to his old job as a crane helper: "I thought they was trying to fix up something to fire me, and I wanted to go back and do like I had been doing. I figured the Lord blessed me to go along as far as I did, so I was going to go back. . . . I told them, told the company that I would go back and be the crane helper." Gilley admitted that threatening phone calls to his house had also influenced his decision.[24]

Across the region, black workers found it very difficult to break into the millwright position as well. In most mills, blacks carried tools for the millwrights but were not allowed to do the job itself. When African Americans became millwrights, therefore, it was a big change that was often very unpopular. At Mobile Paperboard Company in Mobile in the mid-1970s, Willie Ford became the first black millwright. A tall, lean man, Ford recalled that he got the job after an inspection by a federal agency. The main inspector talked to Ford and asked him if he wanted a better job than working as a millwright helper. Ford had always thought that he did not have enough education to be a millwright, but the "government man" convinced him to apply, saying that his length of service was the most important factor. Ford claimed that he would never have applied for the job had it not been for the encouragement he received from the federal official: "He put my mind on trying to go higher, yeah. Because I was doubting myself and he said, 'No, you don't have to have all that much education to go higher if you want to get a better job,' and that's what I done. So he gave me a mind to go higher and I did."

Ford had bitter memories of the constant torment he faced from white millwrights, who never accepted him: "The problem I had, they didn't really want me to be a millwright because I was the only black. I had a hard time with them white folks over there, sure did. . . . I couldn't do nothing right. . . . Them fellas rode my back until I left there. . . . See, I was the onliest one that put in for what they called well, I'll tell you what, they said that was a white man's job that I put in for. And I was the only one put in for it, and they were going round there saying, talking, 'A Nigger put in for a white man's job.' . . . 'You don't need that job, its a white man's job' . . . but I put in it for it and I got it." Ford remembered that he was very afraid for much of the time but that his faith kept him going: "You don't feel free when folks are on you like that. . . . I tell you what, I felt so scared I thought some of them would come to my house and try to kill me, that's the way I felt, because they didn't want me to have the job. . . . The good Lord kept me going, and doing the job that I was doing. I done a good job. . . . Now, you talking about a black man beens through it some over there, I went through it. I don't believe there's another millwright went through what I went through and theys all white." Ford eventually retired early because of the problems he encountered at work.[25]

Other African American paper workers remembered that it was a long and difficult battle to break into many of the higher-paying white jobs. Maintenance jobs were excluded from the Jackson Memorandum and other agreements, and obtaining these jobs took a particularly long time. Benjamin Brandon, a worker at Stone Container Corporation in Richmond, Virginia, claimed that white workers fought until the 1980s to ensure that the mill's maintenance shop remained all white.[26] In other mills, African Americans often did not break into maintenance jobs until the 1990s, and even then they complained that white workers often tampered with their equipment or engaged in other forms of sabotage. As Bubba McCall, a black maintenance worker at a mill in Springhill, Louisiana, asserted, the first African American workers needed to be "superoperators" in order to survive.[27]

Many white workers opposed agreements based on *Local 189* because they felt they were being unfairly victimized by them. Whites stressed the amount of progress that blacks were able to make at their expense, viewing integration as a turbulent period during which they were unfairly bumped off their jobs by blacks who used their mill seniority. In mills where the Jackson Memorandum or similar agreements were implemented, black workers cited the continued obstacles that prevented them from being promoted while whites saw themselves as victims of reverse discrimination.

In March 1966, OFCC representatives conducted a number of interviews with white and black workers at Crown-Zellerbach. The difference in perspectives between the two groups was striking. Whereas a black leader claimed that the primary concern of Local 189A "was the lack of opportunity for current Negro employees to be promoted into traditional white progression lines," several white workers maintained that it was whites who were being discriminated against. The OFCC reported that a J. E. King "stated in his opinion that the merger lines were working more favorably to the Negro employees than to the white employees. When asked for an explanation of his statement, he could only say that the Negroes were treated better in Power Plants and that it appeared to him the Negro would eventually advance to the more complex and higher paid positions."[28] Another white worker, Floyd Ruble, could not see any obstacles to promotion that blacks faced.[29]

Across the southern paper industry, the frustration of white workers increased as they looked to their unions to protect their rights but found them apparently powerlessness to stop federally mandated change. Complaint letters first started to appear in the mid-1950s, as disaffected white paper workers began to write to George Meany, the president of the AFL-CIO, to protest organized labor's support of civil rights at the national level. In February 1956, members of a paper makers' union in Rome, Georgia, wrote Meany to "submit to you our protest and profound disappointment in your stand in the segregation issue in the South." The workers "resented" the AFL-CIO's criticism of the Ku Klux Klan and called upon the labor movement to stop funding the NAACP, which, "with every means no matter how foul, is attempting to unseat one of our deepest beliefs and heritages." The workers claimed that the union movement in the South would be "irreparably damaged" if organized labor continued to support civil rights. The letter was signed by sixty-one members of the local.[30]

Faced with such opposition, the AFL-CIO worried that its support of civil rights might cost it valuable members in the South. In 1956, H. L. Mitchell, the president of the National Agricultural Workers' Union, carried out a confidential survey of local unions in Alabama to determine whether they were considering leaving the AFL-CIO over the race issue. In a report titled "The White Citizens Councils v. Southern Trade Unions," Mitchell warned of a "major revolt among southern trade union members against the civil rights policies of AFL-CIO." Mitchell found that the recent riot that had taken place at the University of Alabama after Autherine Lucy attempted to become the first black student was led by union members from nearby rubber, paper, and steel plants.[31] In succeeding years, some paper union members continued to threaten to leave the AFL-CIO because of its support for civil rights. In December 1965, Don Slaiman of the AFL-CIO's Civil Rights Department told a meeting that he had received a resolution from several local unions in the paper industry stating that they were going to withdraw from the AFL-CIO because of funds spent in support of the recent civil rights march from Selma to Montgomery.[32]

Many white local union leaders remembered that their members expected the union to take a much stronger position and uphold segregation. They recalled that union meetings were dominated by discussions of integration and blacks' rights to bid into white jobs. At Union Camp in Savannah, Joe McCullough was recording and corresponding secretary of the largest local union from 1960 to 1994. He remembered that union meetings in the 1960s and 1970s became dominated by attempts to pacify white workers about black advancement: "It affected the union meetings because ninety percent of the union meetings . . . just dealt with civil rights issues, black and white issues. . . . It was a distraction and it caused a lot of hard feelings, it caused a lot of personal feelings, a lot of friends you lost. . . . It caused a lot of heated debate, almost physical debate, it got so bad where you just had to walk away."

As McCullough recalled, white workers' anxieties began after the Supreme Court ruled in the 1954 *Brown v. Board of Education* case that segregated schools were unconstitutional. The *Brown* decision, McCullough explained, made many white workers "as mad as hell," and they carried their opposition to integration into the workplace.[33] After 1969, when Union Camp implemented its affirmative action program, white Union Camp workers were particularly upset by black workers who were able to use their mill seniority to get promoted around white workers. McCullough recalled how most whites viewed this granting of mill seniority to blacks as "reverse discrimination."[34] Many white workers felt that blacks coming into the lines of progression was "like Armageddon," and they looked to the union to stop it. "I used to go to the first couple of meetings where we had membership meetings explaining the affirmative action program," McCullough recalled. "They thought it was the end of the world, they did. They thought it was the end of the world and they thought that the leadership of the union, the local union, was the ones causing it. As long as you've got somebody to blame, you'll feel better."[35]

Minutes from the union meeting that McCullough referred to confirm that the company's affirmative action program led to divisions between the union membership and leadership. When Union Camp presented its affirmative action program to the union members on October 16, 1970, they faced opposition and "long discussions" about the seniority implications of the program. The company made clear, however, that the program was not a subject for negotiation between the company and the union but was an agreement that had been "approved by the federal government."[36] After the company officials had left the meeting, the union committees met on their own and members expressed their disapproval, with many wanting to submit the program to a membership vote. The international union's representatives, however, were reluctant to let union members do this, telling them that the program "has the same power as a federal law, and . . . must become a part of our contract." The meeting eventually adjourned with deadlock between the membership and international union leadership.[37] The union later formally protested to the company that its members would not comply with the affirmative action program.[38]

At International Paper Company in Mobile, the Civil Rights Act and the Jackson Memorandum created serious problems for the white local union leadership. Chuck Spence, a large, forthright man, was president of the white local in the mill during the 1960s. He remembered clearly that integration "created an enormous amount of conflict between the races." "You just don't change people's ways of life overnight," he explained. "We didn't trust them [black workers], they didn't trust us, and the company was standing on the side, and they was just letting us have at each other."[39] Spence also remembered that whites complained continually to him about blacks who used their "superseniority" under the Jackson Memorandum, feeling that they were being unfairly victimized: "There was a lot of mistrust, there was a lot of animosity because the guys that were in the segregated lines, the white guys, said, 'Hey, I didn't put them over there, the company put them over there, so why should they be able to come in here and take my place in the line of progression and go ahead of me on promotions.' . . . The thing that caused the problems was whenever they allowed them to use the superseniority, and they didn't get mad at the black guys, they wanted to whip our

The president of the main white local at IP's Mobile mill in the 1960s, Chuck Spence (second from right, seated), went on to become an international representative with the UPIU in 1972. Here, he is pictured signing a contract at an Alabama mill in September 1974. (Courtesy PACE International Union)

ass." Local union leaders like Spence, however, stressed that they could not help white workers because integration was the federal law and thus could not be violated: "They would tell us, 'Well why don't you go tell them that we're not going to do that.' And we would say, 'Hey, that's the federal government, and you don't tell that damn Yankee government that you're not going to do this because if you do, they going to come down here, and I'm going to jail, and you're going to jail.' "[40]

Frustrated by the reluctance of union leaders to help them, some white workers tried to use the grievance procedure to protest against black advancement. Arnold Brown, an international representative with the UPP and UPIU between 1963 and 1995, remembered that the number of grievances increased a great deal when job integration began: "We didn't have fifteen grievances a year in some of these big paper mills until the problem of integration came, and that's when we went from fifteen to probably a thousand." Whites and blacks both filed grievances challenging "whether some-body else got the job properly," and the complexity of many court decrees added to the problem.[41] In Moss Point, Mississippi, long-serving union officer Elvin King recalled the grievances and that many whites saw the Jackson Memorandum as "reverse discrimination." King added that the agreement "was constantly a subject of grievances."[42]

Many white workers also maintained that the Jackson Memorandum had a very severe psychological impact upon them, describing how the threat of being "bumped" by black workers who used their mill seniority placed a great strain on them. In Mobile, retired white worker Plez Watson claimed that white workers had to cope with increased stress and that some workers had heart attacks or other illnesses as a result. He remembered that blacks being given superseniority under the Jackson Memorandum "hurt and it hurt bad . . . that part to us was devastating. . . . Those things were wrong but the rules give them their rights and you couldn't stop it. . . . That was a devastating thing." "You could say this," Watson continued, "for the white workers it turned our world upside down and caused problems that we never thought existed and we don't think it worked like it should have. Like I said, the white people viewed it as, these people didn't earn the rights to be where they were. They was given special concessions and it was not right or fair for it to be given to them."[43]

Many white workers had bitter memories of the Jackson Memorandum, asserting that their own careers had been slowed down because of the agreement. Like other white workers, Billy Culpepper, who was hired into the Mobile pulp mill in 1957, recognized the discrimination that black workers had traditionally faced but still felt frustrated that his own promotion prospects had suffered because of the Jackson Memorandum: "The biggest problem in the pulp mill is the people that were already there when the blacks started bidding on the jobs, the blacks went around those people. I myself stayed in the digester room seventeen years because every time a job opening would come up, they would get the job and move up. . . . What it did do it took me from age nineteen until I was fifty-nine to get an operator's job. . . . It did bother me them taking my job and you being on a job for years and trying to move up, trying to raise a family, and then you just stay there."[44] Like Culpepper, younger whites who entered the industry from the late 1950s onward argued that they had not been responsible for setting up segregation in the paper industry but felt they were now "paying the price." "My generation was penalized big time," asserted IP worker William Gardner. "The people who actually did the deed, so to speak, they didn't pay, they never have. They put it on somebody else to do."[45]

Unable to express their opposition to civil rights through their union, industrial integration left many white workers with a strong dislike of the federal government, which they blamed for giving unfair advantages to blacks. In many ways, both companies and unions encouraged this belief because they continually blamed the government for integration as a way of deflecting white protest. The alienation that many working-class whites feel from the federal government today can be partly traced to their belief that the government forced integration of the workplace and did so by giving unfair advantages to blacks. For some retired white workers, this alienation remains extremely deap-seated. According to Mervin Taylor, who worked at the Bogalusa mill between 1951 and 1995: "Our government ain't worth a shit, you know that. To be honest with you, the day John F. Kennedy put his name on that integration, that's the day the United States started going down the tubes and it's been going down the tubes ever since then. . . . It kind of got a little bit better when Reagan got in there, but this man we've got today, it started going back down. Everytime you turn the television on, it's black, black, black, black. I used to like to watch football games, baseball games, all that. I don't no more, that's all you see now, black, black, black, black. I don't watch them no more."[46]

Many African American workers also commented on the way that integration left white workers hating the federal government. "The Civil Rights law made them angry," stated Ervin Humes, "and ninety-nine percent of those white boys right now, female too, they hate the federal government, that's one of their main things, because the federal government tries to do right with their citizens, and they hate it, despise it."[47]

Integration in the paper industry also left many white workers with a feeling of powerlessness. They felt that they had no choice but to accept blacks into "their" jobs. "Everybody felt that the change was being controlled from an outside authority that they had no way of dealing with," recalled Frank Bragg. "You will merge these things . . . you figure it out, and if you can't figure it out, we'll figure it out for you. . . . Either you do it voluntarily or we're going to make you do it, the federal government being the ones who are going to make you do it."[48]

The federally mandated integration of the paper industry and the alienation that many white workers felt when black workers were given super-seniority strengthened their support for politicians such as Alabama governor George Wallace, who exploited frustration caused by black gains in the civil rights era. Historians have suggested that support for Wallace was especially strong among union members in Alabama.[49] Interviews with white paper unionists who were active in the labor movement in the 1960s and 1970s provide anecdotal support for this view. "Through this Civil Rights Movement," recalled Plez Watson, "we've had many things flung at us through the law that we didn't like, it shouldn't have happened, but its caused us a lot of heartburns, big time." Wallace was seen as someone that stood against federally mandated integration. "Well everybody supported George Wallace," explained Watson, "he was segregation now, segregation tomorrow, segregation forever. . . . George Wallace, see, he has this great support from organized labor." Chuck Spence felt that as many as "ninety percent" of white paper union members supported Wallace. White paper workers' support for Wallace also led them to overlook the fact that many of his policies did little to help unionized workers.[50]

Ku Klux Klan Was Everywhere

The virulent opposition of many white workers to job integration has led several scholars to suggest links between white union members and violent resistance to civil rights. A recent study, moreover, has pinpointed segregated white locals in the paper industry as being "particularly susceptible to Klan and other right-wing influences," largely because many were located in rural areas of the black-belt South.[51]

In 1965, the paper mill town of Bogalusa, Louisiana, was dubbed "Klantown, USA" by a *Nation* journalist because it was reputed to have "the largest Ku Klux Klan concentration per capita of any community in the South."[52] A congressional investigation into the Ku Klux Klan in Bogalusa suggested that it had strong links with paper mill workers. Albert Laftman Applewhite, who was reputed to be the exalted cyclops of the Bogalusa Klan, was a Crown-Zellerbach worker. Ralph Blumberg, a liberal radio station owner who had spoken out against the Klan, testified to the strength of the organization in Bogalusa when he described how a Klan boycott of his station reduced the number of sponsors from seventy-five a month to just six. Links between the Klan and Crown-Zellerbach workers were also suggested by Klan flyers that were exhibited at congressional hearings on Klan activity conducted by the Committee on Un-American Activities in 1965. Many of these flyers were pro-union, crediting the Klan with defeating hired gunmen sent into to destroy paper unions in the past. "Outsiders have often caused trouble in our city," asserted one flyer distributed at the height of the CORE-led civil rights activities. "A good example of this was when labor unions were forming in Bogalusa. A gang of union busters or hired gunmen were brought into this city to kill those who stood up for the common man.

As a result of such incidents, it is only natural that Bogalusa would be Klannish."[53]

Evidence of substantial Klan influence in the white locals at Crown-Zellerbach is also provided by Jack Gentry, who worked at the mill between 1950 and 1995. Gentry was president of the main white local and was involved in the complex and lengthy negotiations to change the seniority system at Crown when Bogalusa made the national headlines. Although not a Klansman himself, Gentry remembered that the KKK did have influence over the local union: "Some of my officers was in it [the Klan]. . . . And it kind of hurt my feelings that here are people that I'm dealing with every day and trying to represent in the paper mill belong to the Klan and may be reporting on me." Gentry felt that Klan members in the union undermined its credibility and authority in dealing with the federal government: "Can you imagine when you are trying to deal with the EEOC in Washington D.C., and the people that you're traveling with and that you're sitting with belong to the Ku Klux Klan in Bogalusa, where does that put you? You're at a disadvantage right away." Like other Crown workers, Gentry felt that the strength of the Klan in Bogalusa was due primarily to the town's close location to Mississippi, adding that Klansmen from the Magnolia State would come to Bogalusa regularly and recruit members from the paper mill.[54]

Union representatives also recalled that there was a great deal of Klan influence in some of the white locals that they serviced. Arnold Brown, for example, estimated that at Weyerhauser's Plymouth, North Carolina, mill, as many as half the local's members belonged to the Klan, and he remembered that union meetings were often dominated by heated discussions of the 1977 *Garrett v. Weyerhauser* case.[55] Donald L. Langham, the director of UPIU region V, which includes most of the southern states, also acknowledged that he had come across a great deal of Klan influence in paper locals after he became active in the union in the 1950s. "A lot of the locals in the South you had Ku Klux Klan influence in them," he said. "Several of the officers of local unions were members of the Ku Klux Klan or white citizens' councils. . . . Ku Klux Klan was everywhere."[56] In 1991, the UPIU's *Paperworker* also acknowledged that many of its white members had reacted to job integration by turning to the Klan.[57]

"It Took a Long, Long Time": White Workers Adjust to Job Integration

Throughout the 1960s and 1970s, white workers struggled to adapt to job integration. Many were gradually able to adjust by adopting the argument continually stressed by both companies and unions—that integration was the law and could not be avoided. At International Paper Company in Natchez, for example, Allen Coley, who was president of the union in the 1960s and 1970s and was responsible for dealing with white workers' complaints about the Jackson Memorandum, recalled that most white workers "didn't necessarily like it but ninety percent of them, ninety-five percent of them knew it was the law, and knew it was something they had to live by."[58]

Many white workers indeed felt that they had no choice but to accept integration. Nevertheless, adjusting to integration was difficult, especially for men like Mervin Taylor, a Crown-Zellerbach worker who had grown up as an ardent segregationist: "I hated them. Before that integration, man I didn't want to see it come but when they got there there wasn't nothing we could do. If you wanted to stay there, you had to get in with the program or get out. . . . I didn't like it, but there wasn't nothing I could do about it. If the government tells you you've got to do it, you've got to do it."[59] Younger workers entering the industry in the 1970s also reasoned that they had no choice but to accept the Jackson Memorandum, even though it often required them to train blacks who then were promoted around them. William Gardner, a white worker in Mobile hired in the early 1970s, summed up how many reacted: "The first time I ever heard of the Jackson Memorandum I was like, 'Well what in the world is that? What do you mean?' and then I found out what it was and I was like, 'Well you can't fight the government,' so what are you going to do, you carry on. Nothing else to do."[60]

The fact that many whites realized that they had no choice but to accept integration clearly helped to make integration relatively peaceful at most mills. Many local union leaders also deserve credit for working hard to make integration work. At Union Camp, for example, Joe McCullough remembered that local union leaders spent many years educating their members about the need to accept blacks into the lines of progression. They tried to exert a calming influence on their members, again emphasizing that integration was the law and could not be resisted.[61]

Despite these educational efforts, older white workers admitted that it had taken many years for them to personally adjust to integration. IP worker Plez Watson, for example, acknowledged that it was difficult for him to adjust to the changes brought about by the Civil Rights Act after working at a segregated mill since 1941:

Anyway, 1964 brought about a new era for all of us, and really and truly I'm looking back and it was good for the labor movement, and it was good for the country. . . . I know it was, because no man should be denied having the same paid job that he's working on . . . they shouldn't have to sit in the back of a bus or they shouldn't have to sit in the corner of a restaurant, where we had a cafeteria, all those things were wrong, but it took me a lot of years to actually see how wrong it was, to be honest with you, it took a long, long time. . . . It took me a long time to accept some things that should have been accepted right off, but I was raised and I grew up in a neighborhood where there was no blacks.[62]

Both white workers and union leaders viewed integration unanimously as the most significant and most traumatic experience they had had in their working lives. They emphasized that it took many years for divisions to be ironed out, and many claimed that some problems still remained. "It took from 1964 to almost 1980 to get the problems worked out," asserted Chuck Spence. "It was the biggest change. . . . I think the labor unions, it took them a while to get the membership to understand, we didn't make that law . . . it took sixteen years to get it done." Wayne Glenn, who was a vice president of the IBPSPMW in the 1960s and early 1970s before serving as UPIU president between 1978 and 1996, also emphasized the long and difficult journey to integration that he oversaw. "It was just like walking on eggshells all the time," he reflected. "You just had to keep ploughing, that's what I called it. . . . It wasn't an easy time, I can tell you that. . . . I mean threats were a normal occurrence, you just got them."[63]

Although many white workers were clearly opposed to integration, the number who quit the paper industry because of it was small. The main reason for this was that paper industry jobs were some of the best paid in the South and few workers were willing to surrender them. As Russell Hall, who worked as an international union representative throughout the 1960s and 1970s, explained, "They wasn't about to quit their job. . . . They'd threaten you, they'd do all this, but as far as quitting the job, uh-uh, that was not a factor because they were the best jobs around." Hall also felt that white workers knew deep down that it was not the union that was to blame for integration, but the federal government. As a result, few workers actually withdrew from the union. "They would threaten and do all this," he added, "but, again, after they'd done all that threatening, they knew within their own heart that the union was only doing what the law said."[64]

Many white workers admitted that they gave little thought to leaving an industry that offered some of the highest-paying jobs for those without a college education. Billy Culpepper, who felt that his own career was slowed down because of the Jackson Memorandum, nevertheless continued to work at IP. "It was about the best jobs around Mobile at that time," he explained, "and see we had a lot of uneducated people, just finished high school like myself, that there wasn't other jobs that you could get making the money you were making and that's the reason I'm sure that a lot of them stayed with it. More of the young people left and some went back to school when all of that happened, but the rest of us that just had a high school education, this was about the best thing we could get at the time."[65]

Most white workers who did protest against integration did so in ways that did not threaten their own job security. Boycotts of facilities, which were commonplace, did not expose white workers to disciplinary action because they were merely declining to use a facility that was available to them. In some cases, white workers left anonymous notes threatening violence where black workers would see them or tampered with the equipment of black pioneers so that their job performance would be hampered. But companies admitted that it was almost impossible to identify the perpetrators.[66] Very few white workers were willing to risk losing their high-paying jobs over integration.[67]

In some locations workers did withdraw from local unions in protest against the Jackson Memorandum. At International Paper Company's plant in Moss Point, for example, Elvin King remembered that a small group of whites who were "bumped" under the memorandum withdrew from the union: "Basically they saw that as a form of discrimination against whites, and some of those people got out of the union, and they're still out of the union because of that."[68] Other local union leaders also recalled small numbers of white workers who left the local union because they felt that it had acquiesced too much in integrating jobs.[69]

In general, however, very few white workers withdrew from the union on a permanent basis. Joe McCullough related that even in Savannah, where whites protested vehemently to the union about black advancement, few withdrew because these same workers did not want to sacrifice the benefits of union protection. "I think they did a lot of talking," he recalled, "but when the time come, you didn't see a mass exodus of getting out of the union, you didn't see that. They may have been one or two but you didn't say see a mass exodus . . . because they knew, I mean most people knew, that they needed the unions as bad then as they ever did."[70]

"I Felt That the Fellows Were Being Discriminated Against": White Support for Black Activism

Although the integration of the southern paper industry was marked by numerous examples of white resistance, the records also offer glimpses of

JOB INTEGRATION

interracial cooperation and support. Even in mills where patterns of white resistance were striking, some whites were willing to openly stand up and support black efforts to secure equal job opportunities.

Occasionally, African American workers testified about white workers who supported them in their drive for promotion. In some cases, white workers who had worked near blacks and were aware of their ability came to support them, knowing that they could carry out a higher-paid job. At Weyerhauser in Plymouth, black worker Roster Lucas testified in 1977 that he had worked for many years with a white mechanic on the crane and that this mechanic had suggested that Lucas apply to operate the crane, even though this job was seen as a white job at the time. The company refused Lucas the job.[71] Other African American workers provided examples of particular whites who trained them on white jobs and helped them move up the line of progression. At Continental Can in Port Wentworth, Georgia, for example, Charlie Miller remembered a white worker who "had enough guts to tell me how to unload some wood."[72] At Federal Paper Board Company in Riegelwood, North Carolina, Woodrow Daniels was covertly supported in his efforts to become a welder by one supervisor who told him when openings were coming up. "He told me they were going to hire six welders," recalled Daniels. "He said, 'Woodrow, why don't you apply for a job?' He said, 'Don't give me away.'" Daniels did eventually secure a welding position.[73]

Although segregation confined many blacks to unskilled jobs, some black and white workers worked closely together, especially as black laborers often assisted skilled white workers. Black crane helpers, for example, worked in close proximity to white operators, and they sometimes became friends. In other cases, whites realized that if they trained blacks to do their operating job they could use them as cover when they wanted a break. For whatever reasons, on several occasions white workers showed their black coworkers how to perform white jobs. This training was often important in motivating African American workers to protest against discrimination, since they realized that they had the ability to perform white jobs.[74] For example, Edward Cox, a woodyard laborer at Weyerhauser, testified in 1977 that he believed he could hold a higher-paying job because he had already performed an operator's job when the white operator wanted a rest. "I had been going up there carrying the man water," he explained. "And a lot of nights when things were running good, I'd go up there and sit with him, and he would sit back and let me operate it. I didn't tell the foreman that at the time, but I knew I could operate the job."[75]

African American paper workers frequently complained that one of the main obstacles preventing them from securing higher-paying jobs was that they were unable to learn about vacancies. On some occasions, however, workers were able to apply for white jobs because of assistance from a worker in that department. At Gilman Paper Company, for example, David L. Williams wrote that he had applied for a white job because "I was Told about the job opening By a white within the paper machine dept. the white Employee name is Leron McGinn."[76]

Some white workers helped blacks because of their experience serving in the military. Just as military service showed blacks the injustice of segregation, it also transformed the racial attitudes of some whites. At International Paper Company in Moss Point, Mississippi, Elvin King related that serving in the navy in the late 1950s had opened his eyes to the possibility of a world without segregation: "I came out of the navy and came to work here. I saw how it was working everywhere else because I'd never been out of the state of Mississippi until I went in the navy, see, and I saw how it should actually work, and I saw the way they got along. . . . It was the fact that you had no segregation in service and you had it in the South."[77] King recalled that when facilities at Moss Point were integrated, he tried to encourage his black workmates, who had been reluctant to make the first move, to share facilities with him.[78]

In a few cases, individual whites actively supported black workers in their fight against discrimination. For example, white worker William H. Welch's support to the black plaintiffs in *Moody v. Albemarle Paper* was such that, according to the company, he became known as, "a champion of the Black people at the Roanoke Rapids mill."[79] In a 1968 letter to the EEOC, Welch wrote that he supported black workers' efforts to end discrimination because he recognized that they were not treated equally: "I was and have been for some time dismayed at the treatment the colored members of our local have been subjected to and the way they have been treated. I feel they have not been extended the same consideration as other members, in employment and other factors too numerous to mention."[80] Welch supported black workers in their efforts to merge the lines of progression and secure representation on the union's contract negotiating committee. As did many black workers, he argued that some blacks were qualified for jobs in the line of progression because of their extensive work experience in the paper industry: "If these Negroes had worked in this old steam plant for years—some of them since they were sixteen years old—does it not establish itself in a normal person's thinking that perhaps there was some jobs for them in this new line of progression?" Welch argued that older blacks should be allowed to use their mill seniority and should not have younger whites promoted over them.[81] Whites, however, reacted angrily to Welch's efforts to help black workers. As he explained, many of them accused him "of trying to break the union."[82]

In *White v. Carolina Paperboard*, a case brought against a small paper mill in Charlotte, North Carolina, the black plaintiffs were supported by Osborne Rawlins, a white man who worked for the company between 1944 and 1971. Rawlins had started off as a machine tender but had become a shift supervisor by the time he retired in 1971. Testifying in 1975, he openly described the segregation that existed in the mill, relating that virtually all black workers were consigned to working in the "yard crew." Rawlins explained that he wrote to the EEOC on behalf of the black workers: "I felt that the fellows were being discriminated against and I wrote that letter for them. . . . I heard them complain that they couldn't get any other jobs, any better paying jobs."[83]

African American workers also found that there were figures in the labor movement who were willing to help them combat discrimination. The most obvious was Claude Ramsay, the long-serving president of the Mississippi AFL-CIO and a former worker at International Paper Company in Moss Point, Mississippi. Throughout his twenty-six-year tenure as president, Ramsay gave support to the civil rights movement and sought to educate white union members.[84] Sidney Gibson, president of the black IBPSPMW local at International Paper Company in Natchez praised Ramsay's support of black workers' efforts: "Claude Ramsay, he was threatened and everything because he helped blacks. Me and Claude always had a good understanding, we respected each other. He would always do whatever he could to help me get something going." Gibson remembered that Ramsay openly showed his support for black workers by sitting with them at segregated meetings with International Paper Company.[85]

White local union leaders were also sometimes involved in helping African American workers file EEOC charges and bring lawsuits. These leaders often helped black workers for practical purposes, reasoning that they were likely to turn to the federal government to fight discrimination. By aligning with the plaintiffs, white union leaders hoped that they could protect their union from damages and perhaps make the inevitable more palatable. In the 1970s, in particular, there was a growing feeling among UPIU attorneys that working with Title VII plaintiffs would be more productive than trying to fight litigation.[86]

Other white union leaders saw that black workers were being discriminated against and were anxious to use the union's machinery to help them file charges, even if it meant risking their popularity. At the East Texas Pulp and Paper Company in Evadale, Texas, for example, local union leader Boyd

Young helped a group of African American workers bring a Title VII suit in 1973 because he felt that the discrimination they faced "didn't seem right." The suit eventually led to the intervention of the Justice Department, which secured a consent decree that paid $325,000 to the victims of job discrimination.[87] At international union conventions, African American speakers occasionally were also supported by white delegates, especially those from the North.[88] On a few occasions, white union leaders recognized the ability of particular black leaders and tried to secure their promotions in the union.[89]

Regardless of whether white workers opposed or accepted black advancement, there were few who failed to remember the civil rights era and the changes it brought. Across the South, white paper workers described integration as the most memorable and traumatic experience of their working lives. Many claimed that the changes had happened so fast that it took some time before they were able to adjust and begin accepting it. Workers often recalled that the moment this process of adjustment began was when the first black worker was placed on a white job. "I remember the first [black] guy that came into the paper mill," explained Joe McCullough. "It was an oddity, everybody was out there looking at him. . . . It was something very unique, something unusual. The very first people, the first people I always thought was the hardest ones to get through. Then you started to see blacks trickle into your test stations, jobs that they'd never had before, you started to see black patrolmen, black guards, you started to see that. You could actually see this, it was something you could see, you could see that the faces was changing. . . . I'd never seen civil rights movements, I'd never seen this before in my life."[90]

CHAPTER 9
THE ST. JOE SAGA

I n 1938, construction was completed on a paper mill located on a reef in the Gulf of Mexico in Florida. The opening of St. Joe Paper Company was a reflection of the expansion that the American paper industry made into the South in the 1930s. The decade saw the establishment of many major paper mills in the region, including several International Paper Company mills and the huge Union Bag mill in Savannah, Georgia. Much of this expansion took place in northern Florida. Headed by the establishment of a large mill by International Paper Company at Panama City, paper mills arose throughout northern Florida, stretching from St. Regis Paper in Pensacola to several mills in the Jacksonville area.[1]

Although the paper industry has formed an important part of Florida's economy since World War II, little attention has been paid to the labor or social history of Florida's paper mill communities. Florida as a whole has not figured prominently in the recent expansion of southern labor history, and where studies of the state's workers have been carried out, they have usually concentrated on workers in the southern part of the state.[2]

Port St. Joe, a small isolated coastal town along Florida's panhandle, was a paper mill community in an area of the South that has received little historical attention. In the 1970s and 1980s, the town witnessed a major civil rights lawsuit as black workers struggled to overcome the historical legacy of racial discrimination at the mill. *Winfield v. St. Joe Paper Company*, one of the largest and longest lasting cases to occur in the southern paper industry, was based on EEOC charges filed in 1970, but it was not until 1988 that it was settled with a consent decree. Even then, further proceedings continued into the 1990s as the plaintiffs alleged that the company was violating this decree. In 1979, the UPIU's executive board reported that the St. Joe case represented "the most protracted, involved, time-consuming, costly and hard fought of all UPIU cases." UPIU attorney Ben Wyle even dubbed the case "the St. Joe saga" because of the length of time it took to settle.[3]

In many ways, St. Joe Paper Company was not unusual. The district court found that the mill's seniority system was typical of "industry practice." The whole industry had operated on a strictly segregated basis and found it difficult to adapt to federally mandated integration. At large companies such as IP and Scott, harassment and intimidation limited black advancement under the Jackson Memorandum and other similar agreements. Kent Spriggs, the plaintiffs' attorney and an experienced Title VII lawyer, thought that the St. Joe case was "typical" because the whole industry had a common background of recognizable black and white jobs.[4]

The St. Joe Paper Company also typified just how difficult it was to overcome the color of work in smaller paper mills. Indeed, fifteen years after the Civil Rights Act, the vast majority of job assignments at the mill were still following traditional segregated patterns. Other Title VII cases indicate that the strength of white resistance to integration at St. Joe was equal to that in other small paper mills located in rural areas, including the Container Corporation of America in Brewton, Alabama, and the American Can plant in Butler, Alabama.[5]

The records of federal agencies indicate that larger chain companies integrated more quickly and decisively than small companies with mills in isolated southern communities. As Kent Spriggs remembered, large companies such as IP and Scott made some moves after the Civil Rights Act was passed because they had a "national perspective" and realized that their southern practices were out of line with how they operated in the rest of the country. St. Joe, in Spriggs's opinion, failed to make any real changes and remained "at the back of the train of progress in the paper industry." Donald L. Langham, the UPIU representative who serviced Port St. Joe in the 1960s and 1970s, compared the persistence of segregation there to that at other mills: "It wasn't worse, it's just that it existed longer, and it would never have been corrected had it not been for the lawsuit."[6]

While in some ways a typical case, the St. Joe story was also unusual because of the role played by Ed Ball and the Du Pont trust. Shortly after the mill was established, it was purchased by the Alfred I. Du Pont estate. The Du Ponts also owned the only other industries in Port St. Joe—the St. Joseph Telephone and Telegraph Company and the Apalachicola Northern Railroad.[7] The estate was managed by Ed Ball, a powerful entrepreneur who had augmented his fortune by marrying into the Du Pont family. In the 1970s, Ball was widely recognized as one of the most powerful men in Florida. Always eccentric, he lived on the top floor of a hotel in Jacksonville, running a diverse and sprawling business empire. Although Ball was not closely

St. Joe Paper Company, ca. 1970 (Courtesy PACE International Union)

involved in *Winfield* and never testified in the case, he delegated control of the mill to personnel manager John Howard, who adopted a strategy of resistance against what Ball considered federal government "interference" in his business.[8]

Since the paper mill economically dominated Port St. Joe—in 1974, the mill employed nearly 1,000 workers in a town inhabited by fewer than 4,000 people—Ball's resistance had wider consequences for the town and surrounding county.[9] Most Port St. Joe residents felt, as one of them put it, that "St. Joe Paper Company is the town. Whatever they say goes. They run the town."[10] The segregation at St. Joe Paper Company was certainly mirrored in the town of Port St. Joe. The town was completely residentially segregated throughout the 1970s and 1980s, with all blacks living in a ramshackle neighborhood known as North Port St. Joe, located immediately opposite the paper mill. The neighborhood was literally separated by railroad tracks from the white neighborhoods to the east.[11] Port St. Joe's black community lacked political and economic power. There were no black elected officials, and blacks were restricted to menial jobs at the telephone company and the Apalachicola Northern Railroad.[12] Additionally, throughout the 1970s the Port St. Joe area had a strong Klan presence and, in 1972, witnessed a violent and turbulent school integration.[13]

Many African Americans saw the school battle as an extension of the struggle for integration in the mill. "We had problems," remembered R. C. Larry, a black mill worker with children in school in the 1970s.

> You talk about problems. The whole time I was on the paper machine we had to go out there and get our young'uns from out the school, you hear the whistle blow. . . . We had trouble, we had trouble on the job, trouble at the schoolhouse, the same people that mess with you on the job was out there at the schoolhouse. . . . Instead of getting better, it got nastier and nastier. . . . We just fought, every day, you would go and get your children, they were throwing chairs, bricks, knives, guns, everything else. White children. Black too. . . . I know back in them days, when they were integrating the schools, every time they go out there on a raid, they'd get all black and no white, send them to jail. We got, I'm going to use a word you'd better not use in your book, we got shitted all the way round.[14]

Other blacks expressed sadness that school integration had meant that black children had to move to the formerly all-white school, which led to the closure of the black high school. "They didn't want their childrens over here, you see what I'm talking about," reflected Cleveland Bailey. "I don't understand it. But you know, there's one thing about it, people can meet you, smile at you, shake your hand, but that's just a mask, its not in the heart, its not love in the heart."[15]

St. Joe Paper Company and the Color of Work

The persistence of discrimination at St. Joe Paper Company was highlighted well by a district court order issued in June 1979. The court found that "the black employees of St. Joe Paper Company have been the victims of institutionalized discrimination both before and subsequent to the effective date of Title VII," adding that this discrimination expressed itself in "the initial assignment of blacks to the lowliest jobs in the plant." Blacks were locked into these jobs by the "near-total" exclusion of black jobs from a line of progression. "Overt racial discrimination" and "absolute segregation" permeated the mill. In addition, the court found that

> [a]ll job categories were strictly segregated by race. On the whole the jobs held by whites paid more and carried more responsibility than those held by blacks. Black jobs tended to be the most physically demanding, dirty and dangerous at the plant. . . . In the paper mill

discrimination in initial job assignments and segregation of (lines of progression) continued largely unabated following passage of Title VII. . . . The evidence shows, in fact, that . . . even as late as 1976 the overwhelming majority of initial job assignments for black workers were in traditionally black jobs.[16]

The district court's decision in the case, issued in 1985, was a damning indictment of the company. Finding that the company discriminated in its hiring practices, initial job assignments, and transfers, the court ruled that the lines of progression were designed with a discriminatory intent. Between 1968 and 1971, of the 117 blacks hired, only 2 were assigned to "historically white" jobs. As late as 1981, 89 percent of the blacks hired were still placed in traditionally black jobs. The court concluded that "[p]laintiffs' proof on this issue is so strong as to leave room for no other inference but that the Company's initial job assignment practices were based primarily upon racial identity of hirees."[17]

A striking feature of the St. Joe case was that the company offered no real defense or explanation of the persistent and pervasive nature of discrimination. The company official who testified in the case was John Howard, who was personnel manager from 1966 until the early 1990s. Howard's testimony was characterized by evasiveness and an outright refusal to answer many questions. The personnel manager was solely responsible for hiring at St. Joe, and the forms that he used required applicants to give the name of the school they had attended, which allowed them to be racially identified. He maintained, however, that he "would not know" which of the schools in Port St. Joe had been segregated in the past.[18] He responded to many other questions by claiming ignorance.[19] The company's attorneys attempted to mount a systematic defense that stressed the poor qualifications of many black workers and dismissed the plaintiffs' case as "bare assertions." These arguments failed to convince Judge Maurice Paul, however, who noted that some of the evidence the company provided for its defense actually supported the court's conclusion that the company had discriminated.[20]

When the *Winfield* case came to trial in 1977, attorney Kent Spriggs told the court that, until September 1966, "every single job at the plant was a single race job." Indeed, during trial testimony, black workers who were asked by Spriggs to review union contracts from the 1950s were able to mark a "B" by jobs that were solely performed by blacks. M. D. Yon, who went to work at St. Joe in 1942 as a laborer, testified that the mill operated with "Black jobs," which were all "labor." Throughout the mill, these jobs were the lowest-paying and most menial. The 1954 contract, for example, showed that in the woodyard, the only "B" job was laborer, the lowest paid position in the department. "B" laborers received $1.34 an hour, compared to the $2.32 paid to white crane operators. On the paper machine, the only "B" job was laborer, paying $1.34 an hour. All operating jobs were white, and they led to the top position of machine tender, which paid $2.89 an hour.[21]

Other black witnesses described how they were restricted to laboring jobs. Ellis Dunning, for example, who started at the mill when it opened in 1938, explained how the company began operations with "white operators and colored labor," a system maintained by supervisors and white workers, all of whom vigorously defended machine work as "white." Many African American workers complained that they were forbidden from even touching machines unless they were cleaning them. Alphons Mason, who had been working at the mill since 1939, summed up the feelings of many black workers when he declared, "There were two job in St. Joe Paper Company, white job and a black job."[22]

With black workers limited to a small number of laboring jobs that were not in a line of progression, there were few opportunities for promotion. "In 1939, lines of progression was in the contract," explained Howard Garland, who had started working at the mill when it first opened. "But wasn't no black ever set up in the line of progression in 1939 . . . they had lines of progression for the whites, but wasn't no black in the line of progression." Garland added, "In 1939, the black man had to work where he—they tell us. And that was it."[23] This situation changed little over the next twenty years. African American workers indeed claimed that they learned to accept the fact that there were no promotion opportunities available at St. Joe. Alfonso Lewis, who started at the mill in 1957, testified that he had joined the case because he felt it was the only way to secure a promotion. He related that working in a dead-end job "was just a thing that we lived with. I mean, we just understood that the job we were assigned to, there was no moving, you know. . . . It was just an accepted thing."[24]

Black jobs were also more dangerous and dirty than those performed by whites. Those who worked as "broke beaters" were stationed underneath the paper machines, which were operated wholly by whites. These workers picked up reject paper that the machines discarded and put it in a big container, which carried it back to the machine. Adrian Franklin Gantt, who worked as a broke beater for over twenty years, remembered, "We had separate jobs, broke beater was a separate job. The whites worked upstairs and we worked downstairs. . . . Broke beater was the start-up point for the blacks and the ending point in those days." Gantt recalled how black workers had to pick up the hot paper from the machine and run so that it would not burn their hands: "That paper was real hot. We didn't have no gloves, they didn't buy no gloves, you had to pick it up, pick it up and throw it in that container. When it falled, it would be hot . . . you had to run." Because whites literally worked above blacks on the broke beater job, many blacks referred to white work as "working upstairs."[25] Many workers described injuries that they suffered working on black jobs, especially in the woodyard and wood room. Ellis Dunning, for example, suffered a hernia "throwing out oversize logs" and lost three toes working as a crane laborer, which he described as "a dangerous job."[26] Other workers described injuries they received performing the "choke up" job, in which they were responsible for unclogging the chipper feeder when too much wood became jammed in it. This job was described as "very dangerous," and some workers broke fingers and received concussions while performing it.[27]

African American mill workers complained that they lacked defined job assignments and had to obey orders from any white worker. As was typical of many workers, woodyard laborer R. C. Larry recalled that "[e]very white man out there was your bossman, I mean every man out there." Ellis Dunning related that black laborers had to carry out exactly what white operators asked them to do. Like other black workers, Dunning refused a fixed job title because the duties he performed were so varied: "I was named to be the sling man, but I did it all, whatever they wanted you to do. Other words, like children. You tell your child, John, to do this and, Slim, you do that. That's just the way they used us."[28]

Many blacks who came to work at the paper mill related that they quickly learned which jobs they were allowed to hold. In April 1953, Robert Bryant applied for a job at St. Joe after working in an operator's job for a construction company. Bryant, a tall, lean man, recollected:

When I first came to this kind of work, I worked for Florida Asphalt and Paving Company, and I was a heavy equipment operator, that's what I was, I was a professional one. I wind up out there because they had all of that stuff out there. The first day I walked in there, he looked at me, "What do you want, boy?" I said, "I'm looking for a job" "What can you do?" I said, "I'm a heavy equipment operator." "Don't no niggers run nothing like that here." And that was it. He said, "Can you roll salt-cake?" I said, "I don't know, what is rolling saltcake?" He said, "You'll find out." . . . I found out it was putting it in a wheelbarrow and go about one hundred yards over yonder and dump it, just what I do for exercise out there in the yard, really wasn't no mind to it, but it was hard labor work.[29]

Until the 1970s, many African Americans worked in a department that St. Joe termed "General Mills." Black workers, however, knew it as the "bull gang" because of the physical nature of the jobs. Many southern paper mills had bull gangs, and they always included jobs—usually miscellaneous yard jobs that involved a great deal of labor and cleaning—that were assigned to black local unions. Otis Walker worked for many years on the St. Joe bull gang, and he gave a vivid description of the work involved: "Everybody knew it as bull gang . . . because all the work was physical, we had no machines to do the work. Working in hazardous areas, of course digging ditches, cleaning out cascades, cleaning out liquor tanks." Walker compared the bull gang, which was led by black "pushers" who relayed the orders given by white supervisors, to "a form of slavery." He related that the bull gang basically performed jobs throughout the mill that white workers did not want to do, such as cleaning machinery and unloading chemicals. The work was hard and the hours were long: "The Bull Gang have caught the blues at St. Joe Paper Company, and we, oh shuck, we've had to work sixteen hours straight, and I'm talking about not just on the clock man, I'm talking about physical labor, working. We've had situations where we had to sandbag, build dams, or 'they can do it, they're black, they can handle it.' That was the attitude of the supervisor."[30]

One of the main grievances of African American workers was that they had to train whites to operate higher-paying jobs but could not hold these positions themselves. Colbert Bryant testified in 1979 that it took him twenty years to secure his first promotion but that he had trained many whites for jobs from which he was barred. "All these fellows is going around me, these white boys," Bryant testified, "I could learn them the job, but I couldn't ever get it myself." Cleveland Bailey, who worked at the mill for over thirty years, expressed what many black workers thought about inexperienced whites being promoted over blacks: "What I never could understand, how could they hire a man, yes sir I should have understood it, off the streets, and you got blacks working on the job, and he pretty well knows that job. Why they wouldn't allow him the opportunity, a lot of blacks the opportunity, to learn the job, they could hire white and bring them in there, and then he had to learn the job. Well, because I know, the color of their skin, that's what made it all work in."[31]

As in other southern paper mills, facilities at St. Joe were also segregated. M. D. Yon recalled that in the 1940s, "they had all kind of segregation there. They had, when you go in to punch the clock, the white punched in on one side of the fence and the blacks on the other. They had bathrooms on one side of the fence for blacks and whites on the other side of the fence." Many paper mills clung to segregated facilities after 1964, but few mills hung on to them as tenaciously or for as long as St. Joe Paper Company. Indeed, one of the most striking features of the Port St. Joe facility was the way that segregated facilities were rigidly maintained well into the 1970s. In a 1979 order, Judge William Stafford had established that facilities in the mill were still segregated as late as 1978. Until 1972, the company still had black and white signs on most facilities, while segregation in others was maintained "by direct instructions to employees from supervisory personnel." After 1972, the signs were taken down, but "de facto segregation" persisted for six more years.[32]

The case produced some remarkable testimony by African American workers who described the segregation at St. Joe Paper Company. In its December 1995 overview of the case, the court reported, "It began in 1976 as a pattern and practice suit involving widespread racial discrimination at the St. Joe paper mill. The Court vividly recalls evidence showing the following: the wholesale exclusion of blacks from all skilled jobs at the mill; separate drinking fountains; separate eating areas; separate facilities; and rampant use of direct and subtle forms of discrimination. In fact, there were some parts of the mill into which no black had entered."[33]

When the *Winfield* case came to trial in 1977, African American workers testified that many facilities at the mill remained segregated. Black worker Lawrence Martin testified that white and black workers continued to use separate bathrooms. "This side here, make no mistake, is for the whites and this side is for the blacks," he explained as he looked at a picture of the bathrooms. "Both of them are in the same building, but they've got a partition between there." Martin added that blacks and whites used exactly the same facilities as when he started at the mill in 1956. M. D. Yon described how the locker and shower rooms still operated on a segregated basis, and that a white person had "never" taken a shower in the black side in the thirty-five years that he had worked at the mill.[34] The company also tried to use senior black workers to enforce segregated usage of facilities at the mill. Experienced beater operator Capers Allen, for example, related how he was told by his foreman to instruct all newly hired black workers to use the black bathroom. When Allen left the mill in 1974, he claimed that there were "still two bathrooms" and that he had never been told to instruct workers to use any bathroom.[35]

The St. Joe case also vividly highlighted how every aspect of workers' working lives was segregated. The court found that until 1972, "the Company's entrance hallways, time clock areas and clocks, first aid rooms, shower and locker rooms, and restrooms in the lime kiln and broke beater areas were actively segregated by race." Robert Bryant recalled that "they had all kind of segregation there" and described how even first aid facilities remained segregated: "I mean our first aid, one room in the whole first aid . . . but you had to go through a door with 'black' wrote up on it, not black but 'colored.' " "They had a door for white people to go in," he continued, "and a door right beside it for blacks to go in, all of them went right into that one circle, I never understood that to this day." Other black workers recalled that even the numerical code on their time cards identified workers by race: "Every black number began with three. Every white was number one."[36]

African American witnesses also complained that white facilities were invariably better equipped than those for blacks. Adrian Franklin Gantt, who started working at the mill in 1953, described the bathrooms as truly separate and unequal: "They were separated. White had one and we had one. They had one with about four or five stools in it, we had one with one stool over in our end, one stool. One stool, one basin, and one latrine. And the water fountain, we had a little old white cup, leading off from the cooler, and it was about ten feet from the cooler." Furthermore, black workers complained that the "colored" water was never as cold as that provided for whites.[37] The white workers' clock alley contained a phone for whites, but there was no phone for blacks. During bad weather, white workers found shelter in a shack from which black workers were forbidden. One African American worker who sought shelter in the shack claimed that the foreman reprimanded him: "He told me, if he catch me there again, I was going to get some time off."[38]

Many black workers described the humiliation of having to use segregated facilities. Jason Lewis, when questioned about these facilities by the company's attorney Matt Shade, summed up how many other black workers felt: "You wouldn't know how difficult it is to pass by water fountains to get to another water fountain, would you? Well, that's discrimination in my world."[39] Capers Allen described how when the black bathroom was out of order, black workers had to use "the ditch" because they couldn't leave their job for the time it took to go to another black bathroom: "This is another embarrassing word to me now and it was then that you was pinned down at that job where you was compelled to be there at all times, and my mens would use the ditch a lot of times. . . . Because they was pinned down on the job . . . they would use the ditch to keep from—the foreman coming down on us."[40]

St. Joe Paper Company had continued segregation that was outlawed over a decade earlier. In the interim, some black workers had tried to force some integration themselves. Jason Lewis and Robert Wilson tore down a "colored" sign on the bathrooms in 1972. Draughton Bass testified that "[w]e had one old water fountain at the old flume we would use. If we used any other, we was told not to use it," but when he worked on the night shift, he used to drink out of the white fountain when the mill was quiet. "I had to slip in there at night when I was working graveyard and get water," he recalled. "At night, there wouldn't be nobody in there and you could go in and drink without anything said." If discovered, however, black workers who used white facilities faced threats from the company as it stubbornly refused to obey the Civil Rights Act.[41]

Segregated Unionism at St. Joe

Until the 1960s, one of the few avenues of change available to blacks at St. Joe was their segregated local union, IBPSPMW local 379A. Local 379A tried hard to fight discrimination but found its efforts met with determined white resistance. Indeed, testimony in the St. Joe case exposed how white workers and company officials colluded to severely limit the bargaining power of the black local union.

At St. Joe, the separate black local reflected white preference. Although white workers often maintained that blacks preferred separate locals, investigation into the origins of the segregated locals usually disproved this claim. A number of black workers who worked at the mill in the 1930s and 1940s testified that when Local 379 was originally organized in 1938, black workers tried to join but were barred from meetings and had their dues returned to them. Eventually, blacks organized Local 379A in 1946 and requested a separate charter. Howard Garland was one of the African American workers active in organizing the separate union. "We had one union," Garland recalled, "and the whites give the blacks their money back and later on we got—the blacks got them a charter."[42]

Segregated black locals usually lacked bargaining power. Between 1947 and 1951, St. Joe's black local did not even participate in contract negotiations. The local's financial secretary, John Lewis, acknowledged that he never saw a copy of the contract in these years. Lewis remembered that on one occasion he received a letter inviting him to take part in the negotiations but no one ever came by to pick up the black representatives as they waited at the arranged time to attend the negotiations. That was "as close as we got to the negotiations," he commented. Local 379A also lacked an independent grievance procedure in these early years. If blacks had a grievance, they presented it to Local 379: "All we had to do was tell our president. Now, he would go to the white president and they would do what could be done."[43]

By the early 1950s, representatives from the black local did attend the contract negotiations, but their role was strictly circumscribed. They could go in and present their proposals, but they were not allowed to negotiate or argue. Herman Williams, who served as vice president and then president of Local 379A between 1956 and 1959, explained that in the negotiations, "All we did was ask." After their presentation, they were "excused" while the white local's representatives stayed in the room. When negotiations were over, white representatives would report results to the black local. As black officer Howard Garland recalled, "Whenever the union and the company reached a decision, the president of the white local would notify the president of the black local and the black president would call a meeting and tell us what the union done for them." Herman Williams remembered that "[w]e always had to get our main answer from the other—the white local."[44]

Throughout the 1950s, the black local remained largely dependent on the white local to process grievances. Herman Williams testified that supervisors usually denied black requests. Only when blacks secured the help of the white local did the grievances become effective: "We go to our foreman . . . and he would come back and say it's either this or that, take it or leave it, unless we could get something that the white union would take up for us, then we would get some help and probably get a little consideration." Even then, the grievance procedure often failed blacks. When a group of black workers filed a grievance about white workers being hired over blacks regardless of seniority, their efforts were, according to Williams, simply ignored by white local union officials.[45]

Even when black officers took part in negotiations, they had to endure the indignities of segregation. In the 1950s, contract negotiations took place at the company's main office, a building located on the white side of the tracks in Port St. Joe. Howard Garland recalled how black delegates had to leave the building in order to relieve themselves: "It was a place there, but we wasn't allowed to use that. We had to go across to the woods." On another occasion, the black delegates "went over to Mr Thompson's filling station and used the restroom there."[46]

Although denied an equal voice in negotiations, the black local union leaders at St. Joe still tried to open up more jobs for black workers. As was the case across the South, however, these efforts were seldom successful. Herman Williams purposefully used the negotiations to press for more racial justice; in his first negotiations he asked for "a raise and for mill seniority. We were wanting to get a line of progression . . . go right up in the mill like the whites was doing. But they never would grant it to us. We didn't get it." Williams believed that establishing a line of progression was "one of the most basic things we would try to work on, but we could never get anything did about it."[47]

Many former officers of the black local related that the company and white unions refused to engage in a serious debate when blacks demanded better job opportunities. Alfonso Lewis, who took part in several contract negotiations as the local's recording secretary in the early 1960s, remembered, "We had a chance to speak, but it was just to speak and be heard. And there was no cross talk about it or, you know, we don't—we didn't bargain. We just spoke and presented what we had to say."[48]

One of the most effective weapons wielded by the company and the white unions to guard the status quo was fear. Even in the 1960s, Alton Fennell, treasurer of the black local in the mid-1960s, was hesitant to push too hard in negotiations: "Well, at that time, frankly putting it, I was afraid." "We wasn't so afraid of the Union," he continued, "but was afraid of what the Company might do." Fear also constricted the effectiveness of the grievance procedure. Thaddeus Russ, who served as vice president and then president between 1952 and 1968, told the court that many black workers complained to him about discrimination on the job. Only a minority, however, were willing to file grievances because most feared being "hard-timed on the job by the foreman."[49]

These fears are central to understanding why black workers turned to the courts to fight discrimination. Many African American workers increasingly thought that the separate union could never effectively achieve racial justice because union representatives were themselves workers who could lose their jobs if they "pushed too hard." Hence, an outside agency had to help them if any advances were to be made. As Lamar Speights, a black worker in the lawsuit, explained, "That union would never do nothing, the men worked out there, they're scared they might lose their jobs, you need somebody out of the mill."[50] Another plaintiff similarly stated that the black union leaders "didn't have no kind of power. They're scared they're going to lose their jobs, see they're a plant man just like I was. There wasn't nothing they could do. You could file a grievance all day long, ain't nothing going to be done about it."[51]

The Origins of the *Winfield* Case

Although St. Joe Paper Company made few changes when the Civil Rights Act was passed in 1964, the act clearly marked the beginning of the end for segregation at the mill. As in other locations, African American workers were aware of the act's passage and were no longer willing to tolerate discrimination. In court testimony, Thaddeus Russ, the long-serving president of the black local union, described the start of this change. Russ related that he used the act's passage to propose to the head of the white local that the lines of progression be integrated. "I went to the white fellows there," he explained, "and told them that I thought after the Civil Rights Bill had passed I thought it would be a good time for us to try to start integrating these lines, the jobs." Russ continued to press for black jobs to be placed in the lines of progression in the years immediately after the Civil Rights Act, but he made little progress.[52]

When it became clear to many African American workers that the union was ineffective in tackling discrimination, they began to make the first moves toward fighting for their rights through the courts. In 1968, a group of black workers, led by Thaddeus Russ and Sam Bryant, contacted Theodore Bowyers, a Panama City attorney and a participating member of the NAACP Legal Defense Fund. Bowyers had become somewhat renowned for helping Florida workers file charges with the Equal Employment Opportunity Commission. Bryant, a laborer at the mill since 1946, obtained Bowyer's name from the NAACP, of which he was a member. Bowyers came to Port St. Joe and talked with the workers in the back of a local store. The group signed a charge of discrimination, which was sent to the EEOC and eventually became the lawsuit.[53]

By filing EEOC charges, however, workers were not abandoning efforts to end discrimination through the union. In 1968, following pressure from the international union, the black and white locals merged to form an integrated union. After this merger, many black workers turned to the grievance procedure to process racial discrimination complaints, especially complaints of racist language used by supervisors against black workers. In 1970, for example, African American worker Willie James Jenkins filed a grievance because his supervisor had told him that his work area "looks like a Negro whorehouse." In April 1975, a group of black woodyard workers complained that "we are grieved—Woodyard supervision is discriminating against employees with regard to race, creed and color." And in February 1977, Otis Walker filed a grievance regarding the racist language the woodyard superintendent used.[54]

St. Joe Paper Company refused to address such grievances, in most cases simply denying that discrimination took place. After they failed to secure results through the grievance procedure, black workers took up their cases with the EEOC. Willie James Jenkins filed EEOC charges detailing the same complaint as his grievance, but he also addressed many other areas in which he felt black workers were being unfairly treated. Indeed, as did other workers, Jenkins said that he had complained to the union "without success" and

Thaddeus Russ, president of Local 379A in the 1960s. Russ was one of the workers who filed EEOC charges in 1968 that precipitated the *Winfield* case. (Courtesy PACE International Union)

feared that he would lose his job if he pressed too hard.[55] As was the case in paper mills across the South, black workers turned to federal agencies only after they had tried to work through the union. "Well, the union was handling this," explained Clyde Garland, "so they could never get any agreements with the company, so I went to see a lawyer."[56]

While the grievance procedure was clearly ineffective, black workers soon discovered that the EEOC was no panacea either. Many indeed became disillusioned with the slow pace at which the agency moved. The frustration of many black workers who filed EEOC charges was captured by Robert Williams, who wrote to the agency to follow up on his charge in 1976: "I am writing you to find out what was your findings on my charge against St. Joe Paper Company. . . . We have facts and evidence so what are we waiting on[?] I realize you have a backlog of cases, but if you don't get some of these cases settle you are going to always have a backlog. You are in authority and my hands are not tied so let's turn the green light on."[57]

Leaders of the merged union also played an important role in encouraging workers to file EEOC charges. Although the union risked being sued in any lawsuit, it helped black workers file EEOC charges and helped ensure that these charges would lead to a class action lawsuit. In particular, the union took up black workers' demands for a nondiscriminatory seniority system. By the early 1970s, litigation across the South had led the UPIU to press for all contracts to conform to federal nondiscrimination guidelines. The union at St. Joe tried repeatedly to implement a nondiscriminatory seniority system, proposing in 1975 that the contract be changed so that black workers could use their mill seniority. This proposal, along with other nondiscriminatory provisions, was rejected by the company.[58]

Following the company's unwillingness to implement a nondiscriminatory contract, UPIU international representative Donald L. Langham and local union president Charles Davis, both whites, flew to the EEOC in Miami and filed charges on behalf of St. Joe's black workers. As Langham testified, charges alleged "general discrimination" against the company, which had "failed to negotiate in good faith" to implement a nondiscriminatory contract. The charges were filed in the name of the racially merged Local 379 on November 24, 1975, claiming that the company discriminated "against the Black members of Local 379 because of their race."[59]

Hoping to resolve the case, EEOC representative Jimmy Mack arrived in Port St. Joe in the summer of 1976 to negotiate a settlement that would avoid litigation. He traveled around the town trying to persuade black workers to sign waivers in return for a cash settlement. Langham, meanwhile, was advising them against signing. Before a packed union meeting on July 29, 1976, the union representative encouraged black workers "to please not sign now because it would mean only a few dollars to each individual and would release the company, by signing a waiver, of all liabilities." Four black St. Joe workers—Sam Bryant, James Winfield, Willie Jenkins, and Clyde E. Garland—took Langham's advice, traveled to Tallahassee shortly after the union meeting, and met with NAACP Legal Defense Fund attorney Kent Spriggs. By late 1976, Spriggs filed the original *Winfield* lawsuit. Two years later, the federal court upheld the plaintiffs' claim that the EEOC settlement had been fraudulent, clearing the way for the class action suit to be expanded considerably.[60]

The four workers who filed the original lawsuit emphasized that their motives were to end discrimination at the mill and provide black workers with better promotion opportunities. As Clyde Garland put it, "We went to see Mr. Spriggs because we all had been discriminated against . . . we got together to come and see what we could do about it. . . . I had so much discrimination, so we were trying to see could we stop some of it." Garland continued, "What we wanted to accomplish was to see that most of the black peoples that was working at the mill would have the same opportunity as the white person had. This was the main purpose." In addition, the plaintiffs emphasized their attempts to file grievances through the merged union and the lack of results.[61]

The *Winfield* lawsuit elicited few responses from St. Joe Paper Company. Racial discrimination continued to be rife at the mill long after the case began. In 1984, at a nonjury trial dealing specifically with black workers' complaints of continuing discrimination at St. Joe Paper Company, black witnesses testified how they endured discrimination during the 1960s and 1970s. Kent Spriggs outlined how African American workers were disciplined more often than whites, receiving a disproportionate amount of reprimands and terminations. The main complaint of discrimination, however, concerned job assignments. Black workers continued to be hired into traditionally black jobs. In 1969, the paper machinist position, the central operating job in the industry, remained a white position. Not until 1972 was the first black hired on the paper machine. The broke beater job, historically a black position, remained so until 1977. There was, as Spriggs put it, "a continuing pattern of discrimination in initial job assignment." Data from the company's own records confirmed Sprigg's assertion.[62]

To further substantiate his claim, Spriggs employed Dr. David W. Rasmussen, an economics professor from Florida State University, to analyze company data from the years between 1968 and 1983. When Rasmussen was asked at the nonjury trial whether "massive discrimination" continued at St. Joe, he replied, "Yes. I certainly would reach that conclusion." He described how historic perceptions of black and white work had proven to be very difficult for the company to overcome. "From '74 forward blacks have systematically been assigned to jobs that were historically black," Rasmussen concluded. "Blacks generally are assigned to black jobs in the 1974 to '81 period, even though they may be integrated, in the sense that some blacks are in those jobs. The data is very clear on this point." Indeed, many of the craft jobs, such as welder and machinist, were still lily-white in 1977, and patterns of segregation remained striking. Between 1968 and 1977, for example, only 5 blacks were assigned to the paper machine, compared to 158 whites. Rasmussen also testified that black jobs continued to receive lower wages than white jobs, adding that pay differentials were something that "jumped out at me."[63]

As at other paper mills, black workers who did break into white jobs often faced particular opposition from white workers and supervisors. David J. Lewis, the first black worker ever to apply for a job at St. Joe's bleach plant, described how he was unable to become permanent because the white operator refused to train him. Lewis felt that if he had been white, he would have stayed in the bleach plant. African Americans who secured jobs on the paper machine in the 1970s often faced similar problems, complaining that they were taken off jobs because white workers refused to train them or sabotaged their work.[64]

R. C. Larry was the first black hired on the paper machine, and his experiences highlight white opposition to blacks working in this central production area. Larry had been hired as a woodyard laborer in 1967, but five years later he moved to the paper machine. A lively, talkative man, Larry vividly recalled the hostility he encountered:

I was the first black on the paper machine. It was hell up there, you talk about people giving you a hard time. Man, they made you do everything, wouldn't hardly show you nothing. You had to learn on your own. It was dangerous up there too, talking about dangerous. It was hard, dangerous, they ride you all the time. . . . Laying on your back, all the time. You couldn't do nothing to satisfy them, you couldn't do nothing to suit them, everything you did was wrong, and they wouldn't show you, wouldn't take time to show you nothing, you just had to find out on your own. They were making it hard for me because I was the first one, first black that ever went on the paper machine.

Larry also recalled how "if you get under a lot of pressure, you can't think right, because you scared you going to make a mistake. That's what they were doing to me on the paper machine."

Tragically, Larry's experience on the paper machine ended when a drunk white coworker failed to stop the machine and Larry's arm was severed. Yet, Larry remained philosophical about the ordeal: "See I was working with a man when I got my arm cut off, man out there drunk, when I got my arm cut off, it isn't supposed to happen, but it did. . . . You can't put it back on, it ain't going to grow back. . . . It was just a human error, if you drunk, you don't know what's going on, it was on a Saturday morning . . . this man was on there, he just had the machine running too fast, and instead of him cutting it off, he went the other way. . . . It's one of those things, you just have to live with it."[65]

As late as 1984, when the nonjury trial took place, many black workers were still hired in the woodyard, the traditional black area of work. The testimony of Howard Garland Jr. captured just how little had changed on the woodyard. Garland was the son of one of the most senior *Winfield* plaintiffs and had started working on the woodyard in 1967: "The white workers were assigned on the wood yard to work and to operate the cranes, the front end loaders. . . . [D]uring that time I think the crane operator was making around 4 dollar per hour. And we were only making 2.27 per hour." He testified that he had never applied for one of the jobs that the whites held "because that was a no no," adding, "When you was black you went to the wood yard. You already knew your qualifications and you knew what you were there to do. We knew you were not going to operate the crane, you know you are not going to operate the front end loader. You were going to do whatever the supervisor tell you to do, other than be an operator. That was completely out of the question."[66]

Another central area of discrimination was the application of disciplinary rules. African American workers repeatedly claimed that they were reprimanded and fired more often than white workers; the company's records supported their assertion. Between 1967 and 1977, blacks made up around 22 percent of the mill's hourly workforce, yet they received 41 percent of the reprimands. Many African American workers claimed that they still lived in fear of being discharged, which limited their willingness to challenge discriminatory practices. This fear of being fired never went away at St. Joe, and it was responsible for holding blacks in a tenuous position at the mill.[67]

Black workers' complaints that they were unfairly disciplined were captured in the testimony of Cleveland Bailey. Bailey, who had worked at the mill since 1956, testified that he was awarded a white assistant crane operators job in 1976. He related that he had never received a reprimand during the twenty years he had worked as a laborer but that this changed once he was assigned a white job. His reprimand occurred after he dented one of the company's cranes. Bailey claimed that whites who had damaged the company's equipment were never reprimanded. "No, I wouldn't have received it [a reprimand] if I had been white," he explained. "I know other fellows have torn up equipment from the ground to the sky, and to my knowledge nothing—I haven't heard anybody say they got any reprimand."[68] In 1997, Bailey continued to question the company's disciplinary policy as he had done in his court testimony fourteen years earlier, maintaining that the company often promoted whites who had "torn up" company equipment.[69]

Many African American workers complained of racist treatment from supervisors. They related that foremen put far more pressure on black workers and "rode" them a lot more. "Most white guys, you know, they did primarily what they wanted to do in the labor gang," explained Fred L. Brown. "Nobody put any pressure on them at all. . . . You would be working along side of a guy, you know, and the foreman would hardly of said anything to him, but he stayed on your case most of the time." Brown claimed that supervisors came looking for black workers when they went on breaks.[70] African American workers also complained that supervisors graded their job performance unfairly. B. T. Lowery, who started working at the mill in 1974, complained that "the blacks was getting poor grades and when they were doing better work. And the whites were getting excellent and good when they wasn't doing that satisfactory work." These poor evaluations were used as a basis for discharging black workers or preventing them from securing promotions.[71]

African American workers also complained that well into the 1980s supervisors and white operators regularly used racist slurs. For example, Daniel Sims, who started working at the mill in 1975, testified, "This name calling, you know . . . you usually get that around on the job. . . . They call you coon or lightening, something like that."[72] Some even claimed that the only way to secure a good working relationship with a supervisor was to adopt a deferential attitude and deliberately understate qualifications.[73] This feeling that it was necessary to downplay qualifications was commonplace among blacks hired in the paper industry before the 1960s, yet testimony showed that it persisted into the 1970s at St. Joe. Mark Anthony Williams related that when he applied for a job at the mill in 1972, he deliberately underperformed on the test given him because he was afraid that the company might not hire him otherwise: "I know white peoples you know, they want to help black people think they are good. . . . I didn't want to try to score or for him to think I was trying to be more than I was. So deliberately I missed some of the answers." Although he had experience as a brick mason, Williams had flunked the test "in order to give the impression that I was just another dumb black. Because I figured that would also aid in my getting and keeping the job." Williams maintained that his eventual promotion to the paper machine in 1975 was due to the fact that he had let his supervisor use racial epithets and tell racist jokes: "He had a thing about telling what you call

Nigger jokes, you know. And he would always ask about black women, and tell you about the size of black penis and stuff like this. . . . In order for me to progress, or to stay at the mill, I had to try to go along with whatever he said. You know, to keep the job. . . . Mr Gilliard came to me one day and told me that he was going to get me a job on the paper machine, because I was a very good worker. And he like me. Really, that was a kind of good feeling to me, because I figured I had accomplished something by letting him say what he had to say, and doing my job to my best ability."[74]

Although *Winfield v. St. Joe Paper* initially was settled in 1988 by a consent decree that granted black workers greater promotion rights into formerly white jobs, legal maneuverings were still necessary into the 1990s. Plaintiffs contended that the company violated the provisions of the original decree because many of the black transfers that did take place "were aborted by a new round of racist behavior." They asserted that black workers in the historically white electrical department, in particular, received inadequate training and were harassed by company officials. Not until 1997 was the case finally settled when the U.S. Court of Appeals rejected the plaintiffs' appeal for further relief.[75]

As in many communities where black workers had engaged in litigation, there was a big divergence in how plaintiffs felt about the outcome of the case. Many African American workers saw the lawsuit as a watershed, believing the case had finally forced the company to make some improvements. According to Adrian Franklin Gantt, "They didn't do nothing until the lawsuit, until they filed a lawsuit." Other workers remained angry, however, thinking that the company had escaped largely unpunished. "We lost years of wages because of discrimination," Otis Walker fumed, "we were just totally shafted by the company and, as far as I'm concerned, the judicial system."[76]

The *Winfield* case certainly demonstrated that Title VII litigation was no easy solution to deep-rooted employment discrimination. Moreover, if companies chose to resist change, Title VII litigation could become protracted, unsatisfactory, and messy. Many workers indeed felt that litigation failed to alter fundamental patterns of segregation in Port St. Joe. In the late 1990s, residential areas of town were still strictly segregated by railroad tracks, and this seemed unlikely to change. Employment opportunities clearly had improved little at the mill, with blacks entering white jobs in small numbers. Within the small paper mill town, moreover, the prevailing feeling was that very little had changed. When asked what Port St. Joe was like in the 1950s and 1960s, for example, Cleveland Bailey exclaimed, "Just like it is now. They over there and we over here."[77]

CONCLUSION

In February 1991, *The Paperworker* marked Black History Month with a special issue titled "Integrating the Paper Industry." The issue highlighted the fact that until the 1960s the paper industry across the South had been characterized by the strict segregation of jobs and local unions. For a generation of young unionists, this history was almost unknown. As the UPIU journal explained, "It may come as a surprise to young trade unionists that race relations in the labor movement have changed considerably over the past thirty years. In the 1950s and 1960s, local unions in the rural South were segregated into Negro and white, the mill facilities and job lines were strictly segregated, and some paper workers turned to the Ku Klux Klan and other racist groups to fend off the movement of Blacks toward equal social and economic opportunity." Pointing out important milestones in the industry's integration, such as the *Local 189* case and the Jackson Memorandum, *The Paperworker* added that "the paper industry became the hot battleground on civil rights cases because it had always employed large numbers of blacks."[1]

This study has attempted to explore the important but largely neglected story of segregation in the paper industry. Using a large body of rich legal records, it emphasizes that the historic segregation of jobs and local unions made the struggle for civil rights in the southern paper industry particularly difficult. Whites fiercely resisted black advance into traditionally white jobs, and the first black workers to succeed faced hostility, harassment, and intimidation from both workers and supervisors. The color of work, indeed, continued to assert itself long after the Civil Rights Act of 1964 became law.[2]

In a recent study, Alan Draper has pointed out that little research has been conducted to determine whether black unionists tried to use unions as a forum for advancing civil rights.[3] This study shows how far African American workers were willing to go with their unions to protest against discrimination. Across the southern paper industry, segregated black locals were active in protesting against unequal treatment and fought especially hard to open up more jobs for African American workers. This activism, moreover, occurred over a long period of time and continued despite repeated rebuffs. It is clear that segregated unions did give blacks the space to voice their demands. Not hindered by whites, African American workers united to put forward proposals to merge lines of progression and end job segregation.

This activism did not mean that segregated locals were not inherently discriminatory, because they were. They helped to codify discrimination, locking black workers into a small number of low-paying jobs. Black local unions were usually outnumbered by white unions and thus lacked the power to effect meaningful change. In fact, the inability of separate locals to change fundamental racial patterns pushed black workers to turn to federal agencies after many years of trying to seek remedies through the union. Separate locals were something of a paradox, giving black workers a voice but locking them into a system that made it all but impossible for this voice to be effective.

Across the South, African American paper workers increasingly turned to litigation when the 1964 Civil Rights Act provided them with a vehicle to bring class action suits that could tackle historic practices of discrimination. In general, many of those who brought Title VII suits had tried for many years to remedy these problems through the union and the grievance procedure. Repeated failures led them to turn to the federal government once it provided them with an effective redress. But, even after suits had been filed, black workers tried again and again to remedy discrimination through the union. Black workers in the paper industry appear to have worked through the union structure more than those in the steel industry, an industry that also experienced a great deal of Title VII litigation. In fact, in the steel industry, union leaders repeatedly complained that black workers ignored the union and went straight to the EEOC.[4]

To date, historians have concentrated most of their attention on the protests that led up to the Civil Rights Act and have viewed the act as the peak of the civil rights movement.[5] Rather than ending the civil rights movement, however, the act stimulated a new era of protest in southern industry. The act did mark the end of protests for equal access to public facilities but it stimulated a new round of activism for many southern workers.[6] For black paper workers, the act was crucial in that it gave them the means to challenge segregation in a way that had not been possible previously. The Civil Rights Act may have led to the close of the heroic period of activism that historians have covered so well, but it did not mean an end to activism per se.

This activism was only partially successful in pushing the paper industry toward equal employment opportunity. In fact, the Civil Rights Act was far more effective as a weapon of protest than as a weapon of change. The act was very important in providing the machinery for black workers to fight discrimination but much less effective at compelling companies to abandon discriminatory practices. Moreover, the continuity of black protest after 1964 reflected the slow pace of integration in many paper plants and the persistence of historic discriminatory practices.

Thus, although the federal government was central to the integration of the paper industry, this study also points to the weaknesses and limitations of federal intervention. The federal government's attempt to end job discrimination at IP, America's biggest paper company, for example, met only partial success. Harassment by white workers and supervisors ensured that only a minority of blacks took advantage of the opportunities offered by the 1968 Jackson Memorandum. At the same time, the memorandum clearly did not go far enough in doing away with job segregation, especially since it excluded maintenance jobs, the very jobs that were most prized by whites. The federal government also decreed the end of segregated facilities in paper mills, but white workers again resisted the mandate. With the acquiescence of supervisors, they maintained de facto segregation in many mills and boycotted facilities when federal agencies insisted that they be integrated. The messy legal struggle that took place at St. Joe Paper Company also illustrates the ineffectiveness of Title VII litigation in dealing with companies that ignored federal nondiscrimination mandates.

Many of the central features of the battle to integrate the southern paper industry reflect those of the wider southern civil rights struggle. For example, a number of studies note the importance of World War II veterans to the civil rights movement. Black World War II veterans, having fought in a worldwide struggle for freedom, returned to the South determined to protest against segregation, and they played a leading role in early civil rights protests.[7]

There is evidence from other industries that segregated local unions often provided a platform from which to fight discrimination. Black workers often filed complaints under the name of a segregated local, which acted as an organizing tool that helped bring workers together. In the tobacco industry, for example, separate locals existed in several southern locations and were active in protesting against segregated facilities and job segregation. At the Liggett and Myers plant in Durham, a segregated local of the Tobacco Workers' International Union (TWIU) filed a number of complaints with the President's Committee on Equal Employment Opportunity. In October

1961, the local charged the company with discrimination in employment opportunities and in maintaining segregated facilities. On November 20, 1963, and October 19 and 24, 1964, the local asserted in additional complaints that black workers were frozen in "low paying, menial jobs."[8] At the American Tobacco Company in Reidsville, North Carolina, the segregated black TWIU local engaged CORE activist and lawyer Floyd McKissick to help its members file a variety of charges with federal agencies in the 1960s.[9] The local also gave funding to the local branch of the NAACP, and its long-serving president was also the president of this branch. McKissick himself regularly addressed the local's meetings and urged members to let company officials "know we have been treated unfair." Black TWIU locals also filed charges with federal agencies claiming that automation in the tobacco industry was having a discriminatory impact.[10]

The fact that black paper workers sometimes fought to maintain segregated locals after 1964 confirms the work of other scholars who have recently pointed out that African American workers in the South did not automatically oppose segregated unions. Robin Kelley, for example, has pointed out that southern black workers in general, as those in the paper industry, did not oppose segregated locals if they were able to secure effective representation.[11] Similarly, Bruce Nelson has shown in his recent study of longshoremen in New Orleans that black workers were more concerned with having a union that could give them effective workplace representation than whether or not it was segregated.[12] Other industries also offer many examples of cases in which segregated black locals resisted merger after the Civil Rights Act.[13] There was, for example, opposition to the merger of segregated locals in the railroad industry.[14] As in the paper industry, in some cases black locals brought lawsuits in an effort to prevent their international union from canceling their charter and forcing a merger. One notable case was brought by a black local of the American Federation of Musicians, which was still resisting merger in 1971.[15]

Black paper workers' opposition to the merger of segregated local unions also has some parallels with the story of school integration in the South. In both cases, blacks fought integration when it was carried out in a discriminatory manner, especially when "integration" meant the destruction of black institutions and black autonomy. Several historical studies have shown that blacks opposed school integration when it meant that black schools would be closed and black teachers would be fired. In Hyde County, North Carolina, for example, blacks carried out a sustained boycott in 1968–69 in protest against a desegregation plan that required the closure of two historically black schools. As was the case in the paper industry, blacks questioned why desegregation had to be a "one-way street" that required black institutions to disband and to give up their autonomy and independence. Some African Americans also came to oppose busing where it meant that black schools would be shut down and black children would be moved to integrate white schools.[16]

The experiences of the first black workers who entered white jobs were also similar to those of the first black students who entered formerly white schools. Indeed, unfriendly white students can be compared to the hostile white workers that often harassed and insulted black workers in paper mills. In many communities, paper workers remembered that school integration was occurring at the same time as plant integration, which added to the tremendous adjustments that white workers were required to make. For example, union representative Arnold Brown recalled that in Plymouth, North Carolina, "they integrated the schools as well, and that was still eating at the whites and that carried over into the mill."[17] Many white paper workers looked to their unions to fight for their interests and to oppose integration, an understandable reaction in an industry that had always unionized on a segregated basis. The fact that many whites looked to their unions to uphold their interests as whites also supports the conclusions made by scholars about the racial attitudes of white workers in other industries.[18]

The way that passage of the Civil Rights Act encouraged black protest in the paper industry was also reflected in many different industries. Across the South, African American workers were aware of Title VII and were eager to use it to challenge historic patterns of discrimination. The records of civil rights agencies often reflected this. At a lumber mill in Madison Parish, Louisiana, for example, CORE workers reported in July 1965 that black mill workers were anxious to learn how to file a lawsuit under Title VII.[19] A few days later, CORE noted that the lumber workers were determined to test Title VII, which had been in effect for eight days. "The labor situation here is tense among workers at the lumber mill," wrote one CORE worker. "Last Thurs we met with them. Mon. they are to start testing discrimination in pay checks, restrooms, and drinking fountains."[20]

Rather than defusing black militancy, the Civil Rights Act clearly played a great role in encouraging it. Presidents Kennedy and Johnson had hoped that the Civil Rights Act would get blacks "off the streets and into the courts" by providing legal remedies to fight discrimination. In fact, as Adam Fairclough has noted, the effect of the act "was to get blacks into the courts *and* into the streets." Emboldened by the fact that the federal government had moved so decisively against segregation, blacks in many locations were keen to actively test compliance with the Civil Rights Act. In Bogalusa, for exam-

Although black entry into operating jobs in the southern paper industry was often resisted by whites in the 1960s and 1970s, by the early 1990s many blacks had moved into operating positions, as this 1991 picture of black powerhouse worker indicates. (Courtesy PACE International Union)

ple, African Americans repeatedly tested the compliance of local restaurants and other public facilities with the Civil Rights Act during 1964–65. Similarly, during the SNCC-led "Freedom Summer" project of 1964, SNCC leaders wanted to concentrate on voter registration but found themselves in conflict with local activists who were determined to integrate facilities and test the mandate of the Civil Rights Act. As was the case so often in the paper industry, moreover, these activists were led by military veterans, in this case two local brothers, Silas and Jake McGhee, whose military experience made them determined to eradicate discrimination in Mississippi. As Sally Belfrage described in her account of Freedom Summer: "It was the policy of the Summer Project to limit its activities this side of the Civil Rights Act, and not to engage in testing the law or desegregating public facilities. . . . There were people in Greenwood, however, particularly young admirers of Silas McGhee, who were quite unmoved by the idea of registering voters. The bill had been passed, and they wanted to see it work." Local blacks, led by the McGhee brothers, braved white violence in an attempt to integrate the movie theater in Greenwood.[21]

The important role played by the federal government in the struggle for civil rights in the paper industry also confirms the central importance of

Automation has meant that modern-day jobs in the paper industry are very different from the physical tasks performed by the first generation of African American paper workers in the 1940s and 1950s. Here, Samson Ervin monitors quality control at Boise Cascade's Jackson, Alabama, mill in 1992.
(Courtesy PACE International Union)

federal intervention in changing the hiring practices of southern industries as a whole. As in the textile and tobacco industries, it was only after the 1964 Civil Rights Act and other federal intervention that traditional discriminatory practices began to be changed. The Civil Rights Act was crucial because it provided a mechanism for both the federal government and black activists to bring pressure on companies. Although historians have often treated the civil rights movement and the integration of southern industry as two separate phenomenon, they were actually closely linked. The integration of southern industries such as the paper industry was only made possible by the civil rights activism of African American workers and local civil rights leaders who were determined to make Title VII a reality. The litigation that they brought was crucial in pushing the industry to abandon discriminatory practices. These activists admitted that they could have achieved little without the federal mandate provided by Title VII and that before the Civil Rights Act passed, they were "scuffling."[22]

The Civil Rights Act has clearly enabled African Americans to move into higher-paying jobs in the paper industry. In 1998, for example, African Americans comprised 25.3 percent of workers in the UPIU's main southern region, a considerable increase from the 15 percent in the 1960s, when blacks

Although much progress has been made, more traditional job assignments also persist. Here, black mechanic helper Joe Clemons is pictured with mechanic Carl White at Boise Cascade's Jackson, Alabama, paper mill in 1992.
(Courtesy PACE International Union)

were still confined to laboring positions.[23] Blacks now hold many paper machine jobs, prompting complaints from some white workers that the machines do not run as well as when they were operated by whites.[24]

Since the 1960s, however, mechanization and automation have taken some of the shine off the progress that African Americans have been able to make in the southern paper industry. As in other industries, it is somewhat ironic that the desegregation of the southern paper industry has occurred at a time of declining employment opportunities. The laboring jobs in which blacks had traditionally been placed were the jobs that were most easily replaced by mechanization.[25] In court cases, black workers themselves sometimes related how their traditional jobs were being phased out by modernization.[26] In many paper mill towns, black gains occurred against a backdrop of declining employment opportunities. In Bogalusa, for example, black workers advanced into many higher-paying positions in the 1980s and 1990s and Robert Hicks himself became a supervisor. At the same time, with the mill employing less than half as many workers, by the late 1980s Bogalusa had lost over one quarter of its 1960 population.[27] Similarly, in the paper-making center of Mobile, by the late 1990s the industry employed less than half the number of workers that it had at the time of the Jackson Memorandum a generation earlier.[28]

While reducing employment, however, automation has helped the paper industry to survive, and in the late 1990s it continues to be a major American industry. The industry has not suffered the kind of catastrophic decline that has afflicted manufacturing industries such as textiles and steel. Still located predominantly in small towns, paper mills continue to dominate the economic life of scores of small southern communities. Contrary to some predictions, the industry has benefited from the information revolution, with the spread of computers and other electronic reporting devices increasing the world's demand for paper. In this context, the abolition of separate lines of progression and other discriminatory practices in the 1960s and 1970s was very important, enabling the current generation of African American workers to have a much better opportunity of securing high-paying jobs in an industry that continues to offer some of the best-paying manufacturing work in the South.[29] Looking back on their working lives, the former leaders of black local unions unanimously emphasize that opportunities for African Americans in the industry have improved, but they stress that this progress occurred only because they fought for it. "A lot of the young fellas that came behind us, they don't realize how rough it was to get that road paved," George Sawyer reflected as he sat in the kitchen of his Savannah home. "And even now, even now in 1997, there's still some bumpy spots. It's still not all smooth sailing. . . . What we have gained, we've fought for it. It wasn't anything handed to us on a silver platter. We fought for all the gains we received."[30]

NOTES

Abbreviations

COREP   Congress of Racial Equality Papers (microfilm), Cambridge University Library, Cambridge, England
CRDP   AFL-CIO Civil Rights Department Papers, George Meany Memorial Archives, Silver Spring, Md.
NYT   New York Times
UPIUP   United Paperworkers' International Union Papers, Paper, Allied-Industrial, Chemical, and Energy Workers' International Union, Nashville, Tenn.
UPPP   United Papermakers and Paperworkers Papers, Paper, Allied-Industrial, Chemical, and Energy Workers' International Union, Nashville, Tenn.
WSP   Wharton School's Industrial Research Unit Papers, The University Archives and Records Center, University of Pennsylvania, Philadelphia, Pa.

Introduction

1. Deposition of Henry Armistead, May 19, 1977, *Garrett v. Weyerhauser*, pp. 10, 11, 12, 14.

2. Northrup, "Negro in the Paper Industry," pp. 31, 53.

3. Amended Pre-Trial Order, January 10, 1973, *Watkins v. Scott Paper*, p. 1.

4. The large number of studies that have appeared on textile workers in the last fifteen years include Hall et al., *Like a Family*; Hodges, *New Deal Labor Policy*; Flamming, *Creating the Modern South*; Salmond, *Gastonia 1929*; Carlton, *Mill and Town in South Carolina*; Newby, *Plain Folk in the New South*; Minchin, *What Do We Need a Union For?*; Leiter et al., *Hanging by a Thread*; Simon, *Fabric of Defeat*; and Clark, *Like Night and Day*. On longshore workers, see Arnesen, *Waterfront Workers*; Nelson, "Class and Race"; and Nelson, *Workers on the Waterfront*. As evidence of the recent upsurge in southern labor history, see especially Zieger, ed., *Organized Labor in the Twentieth-Century South*, and Zieger, ed., *Southern Labor in Transition*. For an important recent work, see Stein, *Running Steel, Running America*.

5. To the best of the author's knowledge, historical scholarship on the paper industry is limited to Northrup, "Negro in the Paper Industry," and Robert Zieger's *Rebuilding the Pulp and Paper Workers' Union*, a monograph on the growth of the IBPSPMW in the 1930s. See also Kaufman, "Emergence and Growth of a Nonunion Sector," a recent article that explores the recent growth of the nonunion sector in the paper industry from an industrial relations perspective.

6. Leading examples of this school include Honey, *Southern Labor and Black Civil Rights*; Korstad, "Daybreak of Freedom"; Korstad and Lichtenstein, "Opportunities Found and Lost"; Goldfield, *Decline of Organized Labor*, esp. pp. 231–45; Halpern, "Interracial Unionism in the Southwest"; and Letwin, "Interracial Unionism." For an overview of this argument, see Draper, *Conflict of Interests*, pp. 9–13, and Halpern, "Organised Labour."

7. Draper, *Conflict of Interests*, pp. 11–12; Honey, *Southern Labor and Black Civil Rights*; Honey, "Labor and Civil Rights in the South"; Korstad, "Daybreak of Freedom"; Korstad and Lichtenstein, "Opportunities Found and Lost"; Goldfield, *Decline of Organized Labor*, esp. pp. 231–45; Honey, "Labor, the Left, and Civil Rights in the South"; Honey, "Labour Leadership and Civil Rights in the South"; Halpern, "Interracial Unionism in the Southwest".

8. Draper, *Conflict of Interests*, p. 7.

9. Boyd Young interview.

10. Nathan, *Jobs and Civil Rights*, pp. 13–16.

11. Norrell, "One Thing We Did Right," pp. 65–75; Woodward, *Burden of Southern History*; Carson et al., eds., *Eyes on the Prize*; Williams, *Eyes on the Prize*.

12. EEOC Decision, April 11, 1968, *Miller v. International Paper*, pp. 2–3.

13. Boyd Young interview.

Chapter One

1. Deposition of Samuel H. Moore, February 6, 1978, *Garrett v. Weyerhauser*, pp. 5–6. For another similar example, see Trial Testimony of Anthony Jackson, May 14–15, 1980, *Myers v. Gilman Paper*, pp. 40–43.

2. Complaint, June 15, 1972, *Gantlin v. Westvaco*, p. 14.

3. James Tyson interview.

4. Promotion still depended on the worker having the skill and ability to perform the job.

5. Findings of Fact and Conclusions of Law, February 18, 1981, *Myers v. Gilman Paper*, pp. 12, 13.

6. Alphonse Williams interview.

7. Testimony of James Farmer, July 26, 1963, Senate Subcommittee, *Bills Relating to Equal Employment Opportunities*, pp. 217–18.

8. Testimony of B. Tartt Bell, January 15, 1962, House Subcommittee, *Proposed Federal Legislation to Prohibit Discrimination in Employment*, p. 762.

9. Testimony of Herbert Hill, January 15, 1962, ibid., p. 719.

10. Testimony of Leslie Dunbar, August 2, 1963, Senate Subcommittee, *Bills Relating to Equal Employment Opportunities*, p. 457.

11. As Hill explained, "'Thus, a Negro worker with 20 years seniority in a southern steel mill, papermaking factory, tobacco manufacturing plant or oil refinery, may be 'promoted' only from 'toilet attendant' to 'sweeper'" (Testimony of Herbert Hill, January 15, 1962, House Subcommittee, *Proposed Federal Legislation to Prohibit Discrimination in Employment*, p. 721).

12. Testimony of A. Philip Randolph, January 17, 1962, ibid., p. 851. For more information on Randolph, see Anderson, *A. Philip Randolph*.

13. In 1960, for example, Wilkins urged IBPSPMW president John P. Burke to eliminate discrimination, claiming, "Investigation of complaints received from our members in several states . . . indicate a pattern of segregated affiliated local unions

throughout the South" (Roy Wilkins to John P. Burke, April 19, 1960, Folder 74, Box 19, CRDP).

14. Testimony of Herbert Hill, January 15, 1962, House Subcommittee, *Proposed Federal Legislation to Prohibit Discrimination in Employment*, p. 721.

15. David R. Jones, "NAACP Aide Says Unions Are Stalling on Desegregation," *NYT*, June 30, 1966, p. 23.

16. Roy Wilkins, for example, claimed in 1963 that employment discrimination "is one of the principal reasons for the protest demonstrations which are taking place today in all parts of the Nation." He added, "Although the affronts in public accommodation are most abrasive to the spirit, the deeper hurt, the one that ramifies into all other areas of living, is economic deprivation and discrimination" (Testimony of Roy Wilkins, July 26, 1963, Senate Subcommittee, *Bills Relating to Equal Employment Opportunities*, pp. 196, 197).

17. Testimony of James Farmer, July 26, 1963, ibid., pp. 217, 219.

18. Northrup, "Negro in the Paper Industry," pp. 11, 14–15, 17.

19. Boyd Young interview.

20. Zieger, *Rebuilding the Pulp and Paper Workers' Union*, p. 15.

21. "Interview with Mr L. A. Combs, Vice President, Container Corp. of America," September 27, 1968, Folder 16, Box 45, and Continental Can Interview, December 14–15, 1970, Folder 17, Box 45, WSP.

22. Northrup, "Negro in the Paper Industry," p. 4; Plaintiffs' Trial Memorandum, August 8, 1972, *Rogers v. International Paper*, pp. 3–5.

23. Northrup, "Negro in the Paper Industry," p. 5.

24. "Reasonable Workforce Analysis," February 17, 1998, data provided by UPIU President's Office (copy in author's possession).

25. Northrup, "Negro in the Paper Industry," pp. 20–21, 34.

26. Kaufman, "Emergence and Growth," pp. 298–99; Eaton and Kriesky, "Collective Bargaining in the Paper Industry," pp. 30–31.

27. "Interview with John Bryan," March 10, 1966, Folder 16, Box 46, WSP.

28. Northrup, "Negro in the Paper Industry," pp. 22–25.

29. Howard Bardwell interview.

30. Northrup, "Negro in the Paper Industry," pp. 9–10; EEO-1 Reports, December 21, 1968, Folder 34, Box 45, WSP.

31. Northrup, "Negro in the Paper Industry," pp. 9–11; Kent Spriggs interview; "Defendant Union Camp Exhibit U-21," n.d., *Boles v. Union Camp*.

32. Northrup, "Negro in the Paper Industry," pp. 95–104.

33. "Defendant Union Camp Exhibit U-15," September 12, 1973, *Boles v. Union Camp*; "Submission of Affidavit in Support of Motion to Dismiss," July 22, 1972, ibid., pp. 3–4. The company was originally called Union Bag, but, following a merger with Camp Manufacturing Company in 1956, the name was changed to Union Bag–Camp Paper Corporation. In 1966, the company's name became simply Union Camp Corporation. Details of the company's history can be found in "Defendant Union Camp Corporation's First Request for Admissions," May 5, 1975, ibid. Details of the name changes are on p. 4.

34. Zieger, *Rebuilding the Pulp and Paper Workers' Union*, p. 143; R. B. Shackelford, *People and Paper*.

35. *Stevenson v. International Paper*, 516 F. 2d 103 at 107.

36. "Report of Investigation, Union Bag–Camp Paper Corporation Savannah, Georgia," June 26, 1963, Folder 15, Box 46, WSP, p. 3.

37. *Watkins v. Scott Paper*, 530 F. 2d 1159 at 1165.

38. Trial Testimony of James H. Coil, January 29, 1973, ibid., pp. 1252, 1277.

39. Ibid., 530 F. 2d 1159 at 1165.

40. EEOC Decision, May 7, 1969, Exhibit 3, *Gantlin v. Westvaco*, p. 4.

41. "Summary and Analysis of Annual Income Averaged by Race," Exhibit A, *White v. Carolina Paperboard*; Plaintiffs' Post-Trial Memorandum, March 5, 1975, ibid., p. 3.

42. Pay disparities were particularly noticeable within departments of the Mobile mill. In the woodyard, for example, there were only five white workers and forty-one blacks, but the whites earned $4.72 an hour and the blacks, $3.62. On the company's six paper machines, whites earned $4.33 and blacks, $3.45. See "Average Hourly Rates by Department and Race," December 31, 1971, Plaintiffs' Exhibit 3, *Stevenson v. International Paper*.

43. Deposition of Elmer Melvin Levitt, April 11, 1978, *Garrett v. Weyerhauser*, pp. 18, 22.

44. "Statement of Uncontested Facts," October 24, 1972, *Suggs v. Container Corporation*; Deposition of Arthur Larson, November 21, 1972, ibid., pp. 30, 43, quotation on p. 30.

45. Deposition of Walter Russell Owens, October 24, 1977, *Garrett v. Weyerhauser*, pp. 68, 107, 169. Similarly, W. M. Sloan, the labor relations manager at Georgia Kraft Company in Rome, Georgia, testified in 1970 that until 1964 the company maintained black and white jobs: "We only hired Negroes for jobs open in certain lines of progression and whites for openings in other lines." Transfers between lines were not permitted (Transcript of Proceedings, January 8–9, 1970, *Long v. Georgia Kraft*, p. 34).

46. Trial Testimony of William J. McCanless, February 7, 1972, *Rogers v. International Paper*, p. 180.

47. Trial Testimony of John F. VanDillon, February 11, 1972, ibid., p. 1328. John Love, the senior vice president of industrial relations at Gilman Paper Company in St. Marys, Georgia, similarly admitted, "If you looked at the structure of the workforce in any paper company at this time, in 1960, in any mill, there were certain jobs that were filled by black employees and there were certain jobs that were filled by white employees" (John Love interview).

48. Deposition of Arthur Larson, November 21, 1972, *Suggs v. Container Corporation*, p. 32; Trial Testimony of William J. McCanless, February 7, 1972, *Rogers v. International Paper*, pp. 179–80.

49. Deposition of Kirkwood F. Adams, December 13–15, 1967, *Moody v. Albemarle Paper*, p. 67.

50. Jim Gilliland interview.

51. John F. VanDillon interview.

52. Ibid.

53. Ed Bartlett interview.

54. "Moss Point Mill," n.d., Folder 37, Box 45, WSP.

55. Deposition of Elmer Melvin Levitt, April 11, 1978, *Garrett v. Weyerhauser*, p. 7; John Love interview.

56. John Love interview. In his interview, Love repeated essentially the same argument that he had used when he had testified in *Myers* in 1980. In this testimony, he had asserted that Gilman had segregated "[b]ecause of the custom—the industrial

custom and the social custom of that time" (testimony of John Love, Transcript of Non-Jury Trial, *Myers v. Gilman Paper*, p. 156).

57. Deposition of Marvin Waters, October 27, 1977, *Garrett v. Weyerhauser*, p. 82.

58. Northrup, "Negro in the Paper Industry," pp. 40–44; "UPIU's Memorandum in Support of Motion for Reconsideration," February 12, 1981, *Miller v. Continental Can*, p. 4. Kent Spriggs, an attorney who handled class action Title VII cases in the South, explained how northern paper mills differed from those in the South:

> One of the things that used to be found was you could compare the assignment of jobs where the workforce was all white, like in Maine or in Washington, the state of Washington, where they had, you know, same company, and they didn't have a separate line of progression in the woodyard because there weren't any black people, so they had to integrate the black-assigned duties, in quotes, into the white, because everybody was white. . . . The beginner whites did the bad jobs. You worked your way into the good jobs. But in the South you had the luxury of permanently assigning the terrible jobs, like chipper feeder, to black people. But that was one of the things that was fun was that you could take a single company and show how they organized where there was only one race in the workforce, in Maine, Washington, places like that, show how they organized the plant there, and then compare it to what was going on in the South. . . . Because in Maine they didn't have any choice, you had to use white people for everything, there weren't any black people." (Kent Spriggs interview)

59. Deposition of Lee M. Baggett, October 4, 1972, *Miller v. Continental Can*, p. 12.

60. Deposition of Marvin Waters, October 27, 1977, *Garrett v. Weyerhauser*, p. 83.

61. Trial Testimony of Nicholas C. Vrataric, March 20, 1968, *United States v. Local 189*, p. 219.

62. Proposed Findings of Fact and Conclusions of Law, n.d., *Moody v. Albemarle Paper*, p. 12.

63. Pretrial Memorandum [Companies' Brief], July 16, 1971, ibid., pp. 6, 14.

64. Affidavit of Claude Adams, December 8, 1978, *Miller v. Continental Can*, pp. 3–4.

65. Memorandum, December 11, 1967, Folder 8, Box 45, WSP, pp. 4–5.

66. Pretrial Memorandum [Company's Brief], July 16, 1971, *Moody v. Albemarle Paper*, p. 13.

67. John F. VanDillon interview.

68. Ed Bartlett interview.

69. John F. VanDillon interview.

70. "100 Years of Challenge and Progress: The United Paperworkers' International Union," UPIUP.

71. Trial Testimony of John VanDillon, March 30, 1973, *Stevenson v. International Paper*, pp. 1762–67; Plaintiffs' Trial Memorandum, August 8, 1972, *Rogers v. International Paper*, pp. 3–4.

72. EEOC Brief, September 11, 1978, *Rogers v. International Paper*.

73. See, for example, Sidney Gibson interview; Arnold Brown interview.

74. GSA Compliance Review, November 24, 1965, Folder 11, Box 45, WSP, p. 11.

75. Arnold Brown interview; Nathaniel Reed interview.

76. Deposition of Charles Gordon, January 22, 1975, *Boles v. Union Camp*, p. 13.

77. Complaint, Civil Number 66-242, *Mondy v. Crown-Zellerbach*, p. 4.

78. Findings of Fact and Conclusions of Law, *Myers v. Gilman Paper*, p. 10; Plaintiffs' Proposed Findings of Fact and Conclusions of Law, June 22, 1980, ibid., p. 14.

79. Wayne Glenn interview.

80. Ervin Humes interview.

81. Deposition of Willie Holder, January 24, 1975, *Boles v. Union Camp*, pp. 4–5.

82. Deposition of John Bonner, January 24, 1975, ibid., p. 15.

83. At Albemarle Paper Company in Roanoke Rapids, North Carolina, for example, several African American workers were moved off operating jobs that they had filled during the war. See, for example, Deposition of Lonnie Lee, January 18, 1968, *Moody v. Albemarle Paper*, pp. 381–83, and Deposition of W. H. Mason, January 17, 1968, ibid., pp. 585–94.

84. For an exploration of the wartime racial climate in Mobile and the progress that African Americans are able to make in the shipyards, see Nelson, "Organized Labor."

85. Trial Testimony of Louis Robinson, September 5, 1972, *Stevenson v. International Paper*, p. 1585.

86. Trial Testimony of Jessie Stevenson, September 5, 1972, ibid., p. 1639.

87. Trial Testimony of Sykes Bell, January 29, 1973, *Watkins v. Scott Paper*, pp. 636–49, quote on p. 649.

88. Trial Testimony of Horace Crenshaw, January 29, 1973, ibid., pp. 677, 678.

89. Trial Testimony of Griffin Williams, September 5, 1972, *Stevenson v. International Paper*, pp. 1663–72, quote on p. 1670.

90. These leaders are profiled in detail in Chapter 4.

91. Julius Gerard interview.

Chapter Two

1. Sidney Gibson interview.

2. State Stallworth interview.

3. Deposition of Lester Williams, January 22, 1975, *Boles v. Union Camp*, pp. 20–21.

4. Deposition of Arthur Kilroy, January 21, 1975, ibid., pp. 16, 18.

5. Deposition of Edward Cox, May 20, 1977, *Garrett v. Weyerhauser*, pp. 34–35.

6. Willie Ford interview.

7. Trial Testimony of N. A. Thompson, February 9, 1972, *Rogers v. International Paper*, p. 695. For other examples of similar testimony, see Trial Testimony of Lee Jewell Randle, March 20, 1972, ibid., p. 1198; Deposition of Elmorn Hurse, January 23, 1975, *Boles v. Union Camp*, pp. 7–8; and Deposition of Charles H. Boles, June 30, 1971, *Boles v. Union Camp*, p. 7.

8. Sidney Gibson interview.

9. Trial Testimony of Claude Adams, August 21, 1973–September 20, 1973, *Miller v. Continental Can*, p. 1728.

10. Leon Moore interview.

11. In numerous court cases, African American men described how they were hired to pull wood by many of the paper companies that started operations in the region in the 1930s and 1940s. At Albemarle Paper Company in Roanoke Rapids, North Carolina, Lonnie Lee began working in the woodyard in 1937. He related that "when I first come to the company we have this eight foot wood handled by hand" (Deposition of Lonnie Lee, January 18, 1968, *Moody v. Albemarle Paper*, p. 379).

12. Deposition of Dennis Cox, February 6, 1978, *Garrett v. Weyerhauser*, pp. 6–7, 17.

13. Nathaniel Reed interview.

14. Deposition of Tarlton Small, February 6, 1978, *Garrett v. Weyerhauser*, p. 8.

15. At International Paper Company in Pine Bluff, Arkansas, for example, the company attempted to rename the "Bull Gang" as "General Yard Maintenance" in the mid-1960s. "Bull Gang" continued to be a term used by both black and white workers alike, however. See trial testimony of George H. Denton, February 9, 1972, *Rogers v. International Paper*, p. 570.

16. Plez Watson interview.

17. Alphonse Williams interview.

18. Bobby Radcliff interview. In court testimony, black workers indeed described how they were hired to perform a broad variety of laboring tasks in the paper industry. At Albemarle Paper Company in Roanoke Rapids, for example, many young African American men were hired by the company to load the coal boilers that powered the paper mill. The job involved shoveling coal by hand and tipping it directly into the hot boilers. William Townes, hired in 1937, described the job that he performed for thirty years: "Well, they started me then to rolling coal in the boiler room, right in the coal shoot . . . you had to put board down to if you loaded up it would hold about two hundred pounds of coal. . . . [A]ll of it was operated by colored. . . . [I]t sure was hard work and sweat" (Deposition of William Townes, January 18, 1968, *Moody v. Albemarle Paper*, pp. 421–22, 454).

19. Deposition of James Fields, July 1, 1971, *Boles v. Union Camp*, p. 12.

20. Trial Testimony of Moses K. Baker, August 21–September 20, 1973, *Miller v. Continental Can*, pp. 31, 44.

21. Deposition of Willie L. Jernigan, October 20, 1971, *Roberts v. St. Regis Paper*, pp. 1–12, quotations on pp. 9–10, 11, 12.

22. Deposition of Gurvies L. Bryant, May 17, 1977, *Garrett v. Weyerhauser*, pp. 5–6; Deposition of Leroy Griffin, February 6, 1978, ibid., p. 5.

23. Deposition of Emanuel Small, February 8, 1978, ibid., pp. 5, 6.

24. Deposition of Gurvies L. Bryant, May 17, 1977, ibid., pp. 6, 7.

25. Deposition of Arthur Kilroy, January 21, 1975, *Boles v. Union Camp*, p. 18.

26. Deposition of Leroy Griffin, February 6, 1978, *Garrett v. Weyerhauser*, p.6.

27. Deposition of Charlie Miller, June 9, 1971, *Miller v. Continental Can*, pp. 4, 5.

28. Deposition of Joe P. Moody, November 9, 1966, *Moody v. Albemarle Paper*, p. 7.

29. Sammie J. Hatcher interview.

30. Nathaniel Reed interview.

31. Complaint, June 9, 1967, *Miller v. International Paper*, pp. 6–7; State Stallworth interview; Alphonse Williams interview; Lamar Speights interview.

32. Humes explained: "Say if I get an injury on the job and I couldn't perform my main duty, I'm black. Ninety percent of the time, or ninety-five percent of the time, if I couldn't perform my duty, I would stay on. Okay, if a white got hurt on the job and couldn't perform his duty they had what they called a lighter duty, watchman, they put him on the watchman force, right. He had that saviour. . . . That was something to keep him going, at least he wouldn't be at the gate, but most blacks, until they breaked down those lines, that's how we were being treated" (Ervin Humes interview).

33. Complaint, June 15, 1972, *Gantlin v. Westvaco*, p. 10.

34. "Our Complaints," Plaintiffs' Exhibit D, *Moody v. Albemarle Paper*.

35. Joe P. Moody to David Mills, February 5, 1966, ibid.; Deposition of Joseph P. Moody, November 9, 1966, ibid., pp. 32, 33.

36. "Our Complaints," Exhibit D, ibid.

37. Willie Ford interview.

38. Collis C. Jordan interview.

39. Leon Moore interview.

40. Transcript of Class Certification Hearing, September 22–October 10, 1980, *Gilley v. Hudson Pulp and Paper*, p. 77.

41. Deposition of Leroy Griffin, February 6, 1978, *Garrett v. Weyerhauser*, pp. 7, 8, 25.

42. Complaint, June 15, 1972, *Gantlin v. Westvaco*, p. 15.

43. Deposition of Arthur Kilroy, January 21, 1975, *Boles v. Union Camp*, p. 14.

44. Deposition of James Tyson, June 30, 1971, ibid., pp. 33, 34, 35.

45. Trial Testimony of Booker T. Williams, March 24, 1972, *Rogers v. International Paper*, pp. 2177–81, quotations on p. 2178.

46. Claim Form of Luther Walker, December 9, 1981, *Myers v. Gilman Paper*. Similarly, Leotis L. Parrish described how black workers were unable to get white jobs: "You was made to believe that these jobs were not for black" (Claim form of Leotis L. Parrish, December 9, 1981, ibid.).

47. Claim Form of Sam E. Fuller, December 9, 1981, ibid.

48. Claim Form of Nathaniel Joseph, December 2, 1981, ibid.

49. Claim Form of Roosevelt Dawson, December 2, 1981, ibid.

50. Claim Form of Elvridge Lawrence, December 2, 1980, ibid.

51. Claim Form of Robert Hill, December 2, 1981, ibid.

52. Claim Form of John G. Eaddy, December 9, 1981, ibid.

53. Claim Form of Rufus Dawson, January 6, 1982, ibid.

54. Claim Form of Harvey Jordan, December 2, 1981, ibid.

55. Claim Form of Nathaniel McGauley, December 2, 1981, ibid.

56. Claim Form of Johnny L. Stafford, December 2, 1981, ibid.

57. Until the 1960s, most paper companies in the South did not hire black women. Most jobs filled by blacks in the paper industry, such as those in the woodyard and the digester operations, were considered male jobs, partly because of the physical strength requirements discussed above. Women were employed in noncorrugated converting plants, as well as in clerical jobs in primary paper mills, but they were exclusively white. Opening up these jobs to black women was demanded by black male workers in some locations, especially in Bogalusa, as is discussed further in Chapter 4. See Northrup, "Negro in the Paper Industry," pp. 21–22.

58. Sammie J. Hatcher interview.

59. Willie Ford interview.

60. Collis C. Jordan interview.

61. Claim Form of George E. Smith, June 11, 1974, *Gantlin v. Westvaco*.

62. Claim Form of David L. Williams, December 9, 1981, *Myers v. Gilman Paper*.

63. Trial Testimony of Moses K. Baker, August 21–September 20, 1973, *Miller v. Continental Can*, p. 80. In other cases, many African American workers complained that lack of job posting prevented them from finding out about the availability of better-paying jobs. Robert Pluitt testified that at Union Camp, "[t]he job in the line of progression would come open, but we wouldn't get the job. See, in the department, what we were asking, when a job come available in a line of progression, could

it be posted on the bulletin board, which it doesn't happen" (Deposition of Robert Pluitt, January 21, 1975, *Boles v. Union Camp*, p. 12).

64. Ervin Humes interview.

65. Bobby Radcliff interview.

66. Sidney Gibson interview.

67. Willie Ford interview.

68. Under further questioning, however, a clearly embarrassed Randle added, "He told me, 'I don't need any of you so-and-soing Niggers, because I can hire me three white boys and put in the place of one of you Niggers and run this job just the same' " (Trial Testimony of Lee Jewell Randle, March 20, 1972, *Rogers v. International Paper*, pp. 1211–12). For similar testimony, see also Testimony of Anthony Jackson, Transcript of Non-Jury Trial, May 14–15, 1980, *Myers v. Gilman Paper*, p. 105.

69. Deposition of James Hardy, January 22, 1975, *Boles v. Union Camp*, pp. 7–8. Other black Union Camp workers made similar complaints. See, for example, Deposition of Charles H. Boles, June 30, 1971, ibid., pp. 14–15.

70. Many white paper workers remembered how jobs were strictly segregated, acknowledging that blacks faced a great deal of discrimination. Arnold Brown, for example, who worked at West Virginia Pulp and Paper Company in Covington, Virginia, before becoming a UPP representative in the South, also acknowledged in retrospect the discrimination that blacks faced: "Any dirty job, it was their job, and they basically worked on the woodyard. . . . They had five-foot wood coming in and they took a wood hook and throwed it. . . . They did hire them in on those laboring jobs and then they couldn't go anywhere from there" (Arnold Brown interview).

71. Frank Bragg interview. Frank Arant, a worker at Scott Paper Company between 1947 and 1980, similarly related, "All the service and laboring jobs were held by black people, and they all belonged to the same local. . . . The whites had the better jobs and the blacks had the labor jobs. . . . In the South white people wanted white people separated from black people almost 100 percent" (Frank Arant interview).

72. The complaint that even summer workers were segregated was also heard from workers at other mills. At the Union Camp mill in Savannah, for example, black workers also complained about the fact that even students were segregated when they worked at the mill. In an EEOC charge filed in 1969, they claimed that black students "are placed in 'Negro' positions, while all of the white students so employed are placed in 'white' positions" (EEOC Charge of Discrimination, January 24, 1979, Folder 83, Box 17, CRDP).

73. Donald L. Langham interview.

Chapter Three

1. Remarks of Kent Spriggs at trial, November 30, 1977, *Winfield v. St. Joe Paper*, p. 305.

2. Warren Woods to William E. Pollard, February 19, 1970, Folder 86, Box 17, CRDP.

3. Deposition of Christopher Jenkins, June 6–7, 1973, *Gantlin v. Westvaco*, p. 85.

4. John Defee interview.

5. For the historical emphasis on the 1954–65 framework, see Williams, *Eyes on the Prize*; Fairclough, "Historians and the Civil Rights Movement," p. 387; Norrell, "One Thing We Did Right," pp. 65–75; Woodward, *Burden of Southern History*; and Garrow, *Bearing the Cross*.

6. The committee was created under Executive Order 10925, which required equal employment opportunity within federal agencies and in all firms holding government contracts.

7. Union Camp asserted that aptitude tests were necessary in order to ensure that workers possessed the intelligence and mechanical ability to perform skilled jobs safely. Black workers, however, repeatedly complained about the tests. Japan Holmes, who took a test to enter a line of progression, claimed that the test "did not have any bearings on the job I applied for," adding, "I feel that I passed the test but because of my race I was discriminated against." Refuting the relevance of a test, another worker asked whether "the fact that I had worked there sixteen years play[ed] any part in my being considered for a promotion." In another typical complaint, Edward Slay complained about segregated unions: "Because of my race and color I am segregated in an all Negro local of the Brotherhood of Pulp, Sulphite and Paper Mill Workers, AFL-CIO. This union furthermore has negotiated separate racial seniority lines in the union contract which limits my employment opportunities." See Complaint Form of Japan Holmes, April 11, 1963, Folder 81, Box 19, and Complaint Form of Edward Slay, April 11, 1963, Folder 81, Box 19, CRDP. See also Complaint Form of James Tyson, April 2, 1963, ibid.

8. Warren Woods to Donald L. Hollowell, February 19, 1970, Folder 86, Box 17, CRDP.

9. EEOC Charge of Discrimination, June 23, 1966, Folder 88, Box 17, CRDP.

10. EEOC Charges of Charlie Miller et al., May 4, 1971, Folder 84, Box 19, CRDP.

11. Charge of Discrimination, January 24, 1969, Folder 83, Box 17, CRDP.

12. For an excellent discussion of the litigation that occurred in the steel industry, see Stein, *Running Steel, Running America*, esp. pp. 89–120, 147–68.

13. Michael Hamilton interview.

14. See, for example, EEOC Charge of Elwood Johnson, Willie J. Bradley, Henry Hill, and Arthur Mitchell, February 17, 1966, Folder 85, Box 17, CRDP. A typical group of charges filed by black workers at International Paper Company in Natchez, Mississippi, in 1967, for example, singled out the structure of separate lines of progression and segregated jobs. "International Paper Company maintains dual lines of progression that exclude Negroes from higher job classifications and newly hired whites are allowed to move into higher classifications," wrote Natchez worker John H. Scott (EEOC Charge of Discrimination Forms of John H. Scott et al., August 2, 1967, Folder 86, Box 19, CRDP). For an example of EEOC support, see EEOC Decision, March 31, 1966, Folder 86, Box 19, CRDP.

15. Herbert Hill Memo, December 4, 1958, and Herbert Hill to Charles S. Zimmerman, July 20, 1960, Folder 84, Box 17, CRDP.

16. Thus, in 1979, UPIU attorney Ben Wyle reported to the union's Executive Board that "one of the elements upon which the NAACP Legal Defense Fund hopes to build its case against the UPIU is that the Paperworkers maintained separate black and white locals in the South" ("Significant Legal Developments Report to UPIU Executive Board," August 1, 1979, UPIUP [Legal Files]).

17. C. Gerald Fraser, "Tactics Planned on Job Bias Fight," *NYT*, July 20, 1968, p. 17.

18. Hill, "Equal Employment Opportunity Commission," pp. 45–46.

19. Testimony of Jack Greenberg, October 6, 1971, Senate Subcommittee, *Equal Employment Opportunities Enforcement Act of 1971*, p. 248. For the Legal Defense Fund's activism in enforcing Title VII, see Stein, *Running Steel, Running America*, p. 91.

20. William Robinson of the LDF described how the fund had moved to make Title VII effective, adding, "The cases handled by the legal defense fund represent a substantial portion of all cases involving racial discrimination and employment now pending under the act" (Testimony of William Robinson, December 1, 1969, House Subcommittee, *Bills to Promote Equal Employment Opportunities for American Workers*, p. 92).

21. 282 F. Supp. 39 (E.D. La. 1968); 301 F. Supp. 906 (E.D. La. 1969); 416 F. Supp. 980 (5th Cir. 1969). For details of the Jackson Memorandum and its impact on the industry, see Chapter 7.

22. "Pending UPIU Litigation as of January 15, 1982," p. 1, and "Report to the International Executive Board, United Paperworkers' International Union," February 4–8, 1985, UPIUP.

23. 352 F. Supp. 230 (S.D. Ala. 1972); 516 F. 2d 103 (5th Cir. 1975); 510 F. 2d 1340 (8th Cir. 1975).

24. 1971 WL 10781 (E.D.N.C. 1971); 474 F. 2d 134 (4th Cir. 1973); 422 U.S. 405 (1975).

25. *Miller v. Continental Can*, 1976 WL 614 (S.D. Ga. 1976). The district court's decision did not prove to be the end of the case. In 1977, the Supreme Court issued a decision in *International Brotherhood of Teamsters v. United States* that reversed a line of cases upon which the plaintiffs in *Miller v. Continental Can Company* relied to support their case. The *Miller* case was then reopened by an order dated December 28, 1979, for reconsideration in the light of the *Teamsters* case. In an opinion dated January 30, 1981, the district court held that there was insufficient evidence to establish discrimination among clerical and salaried employees. However, the court did find that the seniority system was perpetuating discrimination and therefore violated Title VII (431 U.S. 324 [1977]; 544 F. Supp. 210). For an overview of the *Teamsters* decision and its implications for Title VII litigation, see Stein, *Running Steel, Running America*, pp. 181–83.

26. *Boles v. Union Camp*, 57 F.R.D. 46 (S.D. Ga. 1972).

27. 392 F. Supp. 413 (S.D. Ga. 1975); 544 F. 2d 837 (5th Cir. 1977); "1977 Updated Paper Industry Civil Rights Memorandum of Law," January 14, 1977, "Pending UPIU Litigation as of January 15, 1982," and "A Report to the Executive Board of the United Paperworkers' International Union," February 1983, UPIUP. Like *Miller*, the *Myers* case was also reopened in the light of the Supreme Court case *United States v. Teamsters*. Because of this decision, the Fifth Circuit vacated its opinion and remanded the case to the district court to determine whether plaintiffs could "proceed on other theories, whether new findings of fact could be made, and whether plaintiffs should be allowed to present additional evidence relevant to the issues raised in the complaint." After an evidentiary trial held on May 14–15, 1980, the district court found that job differences were due to intentional racial discrimination and therefore violated Title VII (431 U.S. 324 [1977]; 556 F. 2d 758 [5th Cir. 1977]; 1981 WL 141 [S.D. Ga. 1981]; 527 F. Supp. 647 [S.D. Ga. 1981]).

28. Minutes of the International Executive Board Meeting of the United Paperworkers' International Union, February 7–10, 1983, UPIUP; Report of the International Executive Board to the 1st UPIU Convention, October 11, 1976, UPIUP, p. 58.

29. Leonard Appel to Main Hurdman, January 5, 1982, UPIUP, p. 3.

30. Peter Schuck and Harrison Wellford, "Democracy and the Good Life in a Company Town: The Case of St. Mary's, Georgia," *Harper's Magazine* 244 (May 1972): 57, 59.

31. Claim Form of Robert Edwards, December 9, 1981, *Myers v. Gilman Paper*.

32. Claim Form of Albert Lee Price, December 2, 1981, ibid.

33. Claim Form of Rossie Massey, December 2, 1981, ibid. For some of the other workers who mentioned World War II as a justification for their belief that they were qualified to fill higher-paying jobs, see Claim Form of Alton Maynor, December 2, 1981, ibid., and Claim Form of Jeff W. Brewton, December 31, 1981, ibid.

34. EEOC Charge Form of Lionel Smith, October 16, 1969, ibid.

35. Deposition of Samuel Roberson, May 18, 1977, *Garrett v. Weyerhauser*, pp. 15, 22.

36. Deposition of Linell Long, September 5, 1968, *Long v. Georgia Kraft*, pp. 74–75.

37. Deposition of William D. Gee, May 19, 1977, *Garrett v. Weyerhauser*, p. 13.

38. The integration of the armed forces began in 1948 under President Truman and continued until the end of the Korean War (Chafe, *Unfinished Journey*, p. 91).

39. Herman Robinson interview.

40. Claim Form of Roosevelt Dawson, December 9, 1981, *Myers v. Gilman Paper*.

41. Proof of Claim Form of I. Watson Sr., August 1, 1973, *Gantlin v. Westvaco*; Proof of Claim Form of O. L. Sparkman, July 24, 1973, ibid.

42. Deposition of W. H. Mason, January 16–18, 1968, *Moody v. Albemarle Paper*, p. 594.

43. Ibid., pp. 606–7.

44. Claim Form of Wordie Hubbard, December 9, 1981, *Myers v. Gilman Paper*.

45. Claim Form of Alfred Bryant, December 3, 1981, ibid.

46. See, for example, Claim Form of Thomas C. Myers, December 2, 1981, ibid. Morgan Myers, who listed a large number of jobs that he felt qualified for, illustrated how workers often cited both their military experience and their practical skills: "I was a maintenance clerk in the army. I built my own house in the 1950's. I have good mechanical and electrical abilities. Had mechanic course in army" (Claim Form of Morgan Myers, December 3, 1981, ibid.). Harvey Jordan's claim form in the *Gilman* case was typical of several others: "Built my own home in 1956–57, worked with Tidewater Construction as a carpenter helper for 5 or 6 years, before coming to Gilman. Worked as cement finisher with Tidewater Construction. Any type of skilled labor that I have attempted, I have been able to perform successfully" (Claim Form of Harvey Jordan, December 2, 1981, ibid.). Lawrence Campbell captured the variety of skills that many black workers had acquired outside the paper industry, including lumber work: "Loaded pulp wood trucks for a pulp mill, ran a log loader for a saw mill, I do yard work using a tractor, and I have always enjoyed working with mechanical tools. Any job that I have been given, I have always been able to perform satisfactorily. I can do some plumbing work, also" (Claim Form of Lawrence Campbell, November 2, 1981, ibid.).

47. African American workers often held second jobs as painters or mechanics, or they farmed "on the side." Luther Walker, for example, wrote that he was taking part in the case because, "I farm, built my own house and do some plumbing work on the side. I have always tried to better myself and learn new skills. Any task or job that I have been given, I have been able to perform, and feel that if I had been given the same opportunities as white employees, I would have been able to handle the jobs" (Claim Form of Luther Walker, December 3, 1981, ibid.).

48. Claim Form of Robert L. Jordan Sr., December 5, 1981, ibid.

49. Claim Form of Herbert Myers, December 9, 1981, ibid.

50. Claim Form of Warren Mitchell, December 2, 1981, ibid.

51. Claim Form of George Edwards, December 3, 1981, ibid.

52. Claim Form of Ferris Everett, December 3, 1981, ibid.

53. Proof of Claim Form of John B. Neal, July 20, 1973, *Gantlin v. Westvaco*.

54. Trial Testimony of Wilbert Brown, January 29, 1973, *Watkins v. Scott Paper*, p. 556.

55. Trial Testimony of Edgar Giffen, January 29, 1973, ibid., p. 61.

56. Deposition of Arthur Kilroy, January 21, 1975, *Boles v. Union Camp*, p. 12. In another case, Scott worker Joseph Gordon wanted to be promoted to the job of chip bin attendant but was disqualified because the job required a high school education. "I been working there twenty-one years and I have been operating it since I have been in there," he testified in 1973. "When they used to bring a new man in there they would tell me to take him in there and show him how to do the job, until he learned it" (Trial Testimony of Joseph Gordon, January 29, 1973, *Watkins v. Scott Paper*, p. 587). For other examples of similar experiences, see Affidavit of Linell Long, September 5, 1968, *Long v. Georgia Kraft*; Deposition of Linell Long, September 5, 1968, ibid., p. 47; Deposition of Joe L. McElroy, September 5, 1968, ibid., pp. 13–14.

57. Tommie Lee Harris, for example, tried to get a variety of white jobs but was told by his supervisor that he was not qualified. The support of family members was crucial to Harris, who was eventually awarded the job he wanted. As Harris related, "My wife, Willie Ruth Harris[,] and my brother, Alphonso Harris. . . . They thought I should keep trying, which I did and eventually I got an Equipment Operator Job in 1974 or 1975" (Claim Form of Tommie Joe Harris, December 9, 1981, *Myers v. Gilman Paper*).

58. Claim Forms of Hessie Mattox and Earnest Baker, December 9, 1981, ibid. Similarly, Leroy Hamilton noted on his claim form, "I mentioned this to my wife Pauline Hamilton, many times from 1953 (when I came to work) until 1970 (when the white and black locals merged) and she asked, 'As smart as you are why can't you get the better jobs?' " (Claim form of Leroy Hamilton, December 9, 1981, ibid.).

59. Claim Form of Calvin P. Wilson, January 5, 1982, ibid. The Westvaco claim forms also illustrated the persistent desire of workers to overcome discrimination. Despite being given few opportunities for promotion, these workers had also retained a deep-seated belief that they were worth more than the menial jobs the company had given them. "I don't have much education," W. B. Lee wrote in a typical claim, "but I am willing to be taught anything to help me better my condition." Another Westvaco worker wrote that he was willing to do "anything in order to better my condition. I have asked about every available opening in order to elevate myself from the Bottom status" (Claim Form of William Rivers, September 14, 1973, *Gantlin v. Westvaco*; Claim Form of W. B. Lee, August 13, 1973, ibid.; Claim Form of Willis Gantlin, July 6, 1973, ibid.).

60. Deposition of Samuel H. Moore, February 6, 1978, *Garrett v. Weyerhauser*, p. 11.

61. Deposition of John Bonner, January 24, 1975, *Boles v. Union Camp*, pp. 14–15.

62. Deposition of Joe L. McElroy, September 5, 1968, *Long v. Georgia Kraft*, p. 25.

63. Deposition of Gurvies L. Bryant, May 17, 1977, *Garrett v. Weyerhauser*, p. 27. Many other black plaintiffs gave similar testimony. In *Boles v. Union Camp*, for example, John Bonner indicated that he supported the case because "I think it's a lot of things been did to me wrong. Not only me, all the blacks up there" (Deposition of John Bonner, January 24, 1975, *Boles v. Union Camp*, p. 8).

64. Deposition of William D. Gee, May 19, 1977, *Garrett v. Weyerhauser*, p. 26.

65. Testimony of George B. Williams before the Hearing on Class Certification, July 28–29, 1980, *Gilley v. Hudson Pulp and Paper*, p. 142.

66. Deposition of Johnnie Pinkard, September 5, 1968, *Long v. Georgia Kraft*, p. 35. At International Paper Company in Pine Bluff, Arkansas, black plaintiff George H. Denton similarly testified, "[M]y intention is not to do away with anybody's job, but I think that I have a rightful place in the line myself" (Trial Testimony of George H. Denton, February 9, 1972, *Rogers v. International Paper*, p. 648).

67. Deposition of Tony Neal Jr., October 19, 1971, *Roberts v. St. Regis Paper*, pp. 126, 129.

68. Deposition of Theodore Daniel, November 9, 1966, *Moody v. Albemarle Paper*, p. 87.

69. Other Albemarle workers also testified that they were aware of the passage of the 1964 Civil Rights Act and expected it to lead to much better job opportunities for them. Ernest Garner testified: "I felt like, well I felt like in 1964 when the Civil Rights Law had passed, I definitely thought someone on the yard would get a good promotion, but nobody didn't get one" (Deposition of Ernest Garner, January 11, 1968, *Moody v. Albemarle Paper*, p. 483). Across the South, black paper workers saw the Civil Rights Act as the chance to get a better job. At Scott Paper Company in Mobile, Henry Pope had worked in an all-black cleaning job for over a year, but in 1965 he walked over to the personnel department and told the company that he wanted to enter a white line of progression. "Well, what happened after the Civil Rights Bill passed," he explained, "I had been in clean-up about a year—maybe a year and a half—I was just tired of being on the broom, really, and I was qualified for something better than that. . . . I figured I'd try myself, and I was determined" (Trial Testimony of Henry F. Pope, January 29, 1973, *Watkins v. Scott Paper*, p. 1049).

70. Claim Form of Oscar E. Morris, December 2, 1981, *Myers v. Gilman Paper*.

71. Deposition of George Postell, January 23, 1975, *Boles v. Union Camp*, pp. 5–6.

72. Claim Form of Johnnie L. Robinson, December 9, 1981, *Myers v. Gilman Paper*.

73. Thomas McGauley interview.

74. Jesse L. Armistead to Leroy Ange, July 28, 1965; Armistead to Ange, April 23, 1965; Armistead to C. Hutchinson, July 28, 1965, all in *Garrett v. Weyerhauser*.

75. GSA Compliance Review, November 24, 1965, Folder 11, Box 45, WSP.

76. William E. Pollard to Henry Segal, November 23, 1965, Folder 72, Box 19, CRDP; EEOC Decision for International Paper Company in Natchez, May 29, 1969, Folder 86, Box 19, CRDP; Complaint, n.d., *Maddox v. Gulf States Paper*, p. 4; EEOC Complaint Forms of Elwood Johnson, Willie J. Bradley, Theodore Daniels, Joe P. Moody, Henry Hill, and Arthur Mitchell, February 17, 1966, Folder 85, Box 17, CRDP.

77. George L. Holland to Gentlemen, January 28, 1966; "Charge of Discrimination," September 17, 1965, both in Folder 59, Box 19, CRDP.

78. Alphonse Williams interview.

79. Testimony of George B. Williams before the Hearing on Class Certification, July 28–29, 1980, *Gilley v. Hudson Pulp and Paper*, p. 144. In court testimony, Williams also described his reasons for filing suit: "Well, in my thinking, the way I feel about it, we put in the lawsuit because the company held us back so many years, wouldn't give us no jobs, and we put in the lawsuit to get the back pay and better jobs for black people" (ibid., p. 134).

80. Robert Hicks interview.

81. Fairclough, *Race and Democracy*, p. 378.

82. Handwritten statement by Robert Hicks, February 28, 1965, Part 2, Reel 6, COREP.

83. "Report from Gale Jenkins on Bogalusa situation," May 19, 1965, Part 2, Reel 6, COREP.

84. Transcript of Trial, July 17–August 15, 1974, *Gantlin v. Westvaco*, pp. 1290–91.

85. Deposition of Charles Munn Jr., March 19, 1979, *Munn v. Federal Paper Board*, p. 79.

86. Leroy Hamilton interview.

87. "Interview with L. D. Tullock, Bowater Paper Company, Calhoun, Tennessee, February 1, 1967," Folder 15, Box 45, WSP.

88. Ed Bartlett interview.

89. Affidavit of E. J. Bartlett, July 22, 1972, *Boles v. Union Camp*, p. 3, 6.

90. "Outline for Meetings with Employees," August 24, 1965, *Hill v. Crown-Zellerbach*.

91. "Outline for R. R. Ferguson for Employee Meetings," December 3, 1965, ibid.

92. "Outline for R. R. Ferguson for Employee Meetings," December 23, 1965, ibid.

93. "Union Meeting with Union Camp Corporation," September 1, 1967, Exhibit 13, *Boles v. Union Camp*.

94. The wide differences between black and white views on job integration are explored further in Chapter 7.

95. Elvin King interview.

96. Frank Bragg interview.

97. Leroy Hamilton interview.

98. Willie Ford interview.

99. At Weyerhauser in Plymouth, North Carolina, for example, veteran black worker Joseph Hooker, who had worked at the mill since 1940, testified that "the first black I remember seeing working to the Paper Machine was along, I think it was '65, directly after the Civil Rights Bill was passed in '64 by President Johnson for fair employment" (Deposition of Joseph Hooker, October 25, 1977, *Garrett v. Weyerhauser*, p. 14). Similarly, veteran Weyerhauser worker Edward Cox told the court in 1977, "I was denied privilege to move from the time that I went into the mill to clean on up until the Federal Government come in with this, saying that you had to give the black man a chance to move" (Deposition of Edward Cox, May 20, 1977, ibid., p. 17).

100. Deposition of Ulysses Banks, June 30, 1971, *Boles v. Union Camp*, p. 51.

101. Claim Form of Wilbert D. Sibley, December 1, 1981, *Myers v. Gilman Paper*. Union Camp's Cleve Williams similarly testified in 1975 how he had secured a promotion into a formerly white job: "I got the job in approximately 1969 by filing a complaint with the Equal Job Opportunity out of Atlanta" (Deposition of Cleve Williams Jnr., January 23, 1975, *Boles v. Union Camp*, p. 14).

102. Claim Form of N. E. Foreman, December 5, 1981, *Myers v. Gilman Paper*.

103. Chuck Spence interview.

104. Wayne Glenn interview.

105. For example, Arnold Brown, an international union representative who worked in the South between 1957 and 1995, felt that companies would never have integrated without the Civil Rights Act. He declared in 1997, "Look, they used blacks as long as they could use them until the Civil Rights Act was passed. To get the blacks using their back instead of their mind" (Arnold Brown interview).

106. Michael Hamilton interview.

107. Deposition of Edward Earl Benson Jr., November 22, 1977, *Garrett v. Weyerhauser*, p. 28.

108. R. M. Hendricks to Charles E. Smith, November 25, 1969, filed as Exhibit 85, *Gantlin v. Westvaco*.

109. Transcript of Trial Testimony of James How, August 21–September 20, 1973, *Miller v. Continental Can*, pp. 1861–62. Lee M. Baggett, a supervisor at Continental Can, testified that management frequently discussed civil rights litigation at this time: "Title VII cases and charges of discrimination in the southern paper industry at this time were quite frequent, and we had a lot of conversations about the general subject." The company introduced mill seniority for an affected class because of their awareness of other Title VII cases, including the *Crown-Zellerbach* case, which Baggett described as "one of the more obvious." See Trial Testimony of Lee M. Baggett, August 21–September 20, 1973, ibid., pp. 1702, 1704.

110. At several International Paper Company mills, for example, the AFL-CIO's files recorded that federal officials had successfully settled several charges filed by black workers: "8/29/68 an agreement has been reached between the union and the International Paper Company eliminating separate lines of progression based on race. This was accomplished thru the efforts of OFCC. Recommend closing" (Present Status Form, December 20, 1968, Folder 74, Box 19, CRDP). For evidence that federal pressure led directly to the integration of facilities, see, for example, Deposition of Walter Russell Owens, October 24, 1977, *Garrett v. Weyerhauser*, pp. 37–38. For both the importance of government policy and complaints of its inconsistency and lack of overall strategy, see Northrup, "Negro in the Paper Industry," esp. pp. 117–19.

111. "Settlement Agreement," June 3, 1970, Folder 81, Box 17, CRDP.

112. EEOC Decision, January 11, 1966, and Conciliation Agreement, August 30, 1967, Folder 59, Box 19, CRDP.

113. Report of the International Executive Board to the Fourth Constitutional Convention, United Papermakers and Paperworkers, October 3, 1966, and Report of the International Executive Board to the Fifth Constitutional Convention, United Papermakers and Paperworkers, August 18, 1969, Box 2, UPPP.

114. Report of the International Executive Board to the Sixth Constitutional Convention, United Papermakers and Paperworkers, August 7, 1972, Box 2, UPPP, p. 15.

115. Ben Wyle to Wayne E. Glenn, February 2, 1988, UPIUP (Legal Files). The statement "This is another Title VII class action case claiming discrimination against blacks" became commonplace in union correspondence. See "Minutes of Executive Board Sessions," January 24–28, 1977, Folder 11, UPIUP, pp. 85, 98–99.

116. *The Paperworker* 1, no. 8 (May 2, 1973): 1, 5.

117. Joseph P. Tonelli to All International Officers, April 24, 1975, filed as Defendant Union's Exhibit 16, *Winfield v. St. Joe Paper*.

118. Joseph P. Tonelli to All Members of the International Executive Board and to All International Representatives, May 12, 1975, filed as Defendant Union's Exhibit 17, ibid.

119. Deposition of Don B. Walker, January 13, 1972, *Roberts v. St. Regis Paper*, pp. 27, 29.

Chapter Four

1. *Pulp, Sulphite, and Paper Mill Workers' Journal*, March–April 1950, p. 29.

2. Very little research has been done on how segregated unions were set up and

operated in the paper industry. The last decade has witnessed an "emerging revision" of scholarship on black workers in general in the twentieth-century South, but the paper industry has been largely neglected by this writing. Because existing scholarship has focused largely on industries in which unions had integrated locals, its conclusions need to take into account the paper industry, which was unique in having segregated locals across the region. For examples of this scholarship, see Korstad, "Daybreak of Freedom"; Honey, *Southern Labor and Black Civil Rights*; Halpern, *Down on the Killing Floor*; and Halpern, "The CIO and the Limits of Labor-Based Civil Rights Activism." For an overview of the recent literature on black workers in the South, see Halpern, "Organized Labour," and Draper, *Conflict of Interests*, pp. 9–14. For the growth of southern labor history in general in the last decade, see Zieger, ed., *Organized Labor in the Twentieth Century South*; Zieger, ed., *Southern Labor in Transition*. In addition to concentrating on unions that operated in industries with large black participation, much of the recent scholarship has concentrated on textile workers, an industry in which blacks were almost totally excluded from the workforce before the 1960s. See, for example, Hall et al., *Like a Family*; Flamming, *Creating the Modern South*; Hodges, *New Deal Labor Policy*; Carlton, *Mill and Town*; and Newby, *Plain Folk*.

3. Chuck Spence interview.

4. List of separate locals in Folder 56, Box 19, CRDP; Jesse Whiddon interview; Wayne Glenn interview.

5. Homer Humble, "The Colored Worker of the South," *Pulp, Sulphite, and Paper Mill Workers' Journal*, July–August 1942, pp. 5–6.

6. Zieger, *Rebuilding the Pulp and Paper Workers' Union*, p. 116.

7. "Extracts from the Recommendation that the Petition of the SKWOC [CIO] to the NLRB be denied," Folder 36, Box 45, WSP.

8. Deposition of Joseph Hooker, October 25, 1977, *Garrett v. Weyerhauser*, pp. 5–9.

9. Transcript of Class Certification Hearing, September 22–October 10, 1980, *Gilley v. Hudson Pulp and Paper*, p. 268; Alphonse Williams interview.

10. Plaintiff's Pre-Trial Brief, May 17, 1972, *Watkins v. Scott Paper*, pp. 1–2.

11. Order, October 19, 1981, *Gantlin v. Westvaco*, p. 6.

12. Sidney Gibson interview.

13. Nathaniel Reed interview.

14. Howard Bardwell interview.

15. Roy Wilkins to John P. Burke, April 19, 1960, Folder 74, Box 19, CRDP.

16. Minutes of June 27, 1960, "Minutes of the Executive Board Sessions, held at Albany, New York, June 27 thru June 30, 1960," Box 1, UPPP, p. 24.

17. Warren F. Cunningham to Eugene Thomas, July 19, 1965, and GSA Compliance Review, November 24, 1965, Folder 11, Box 45, WSP.

18. Memorandum Opinion, December 18, 1973, *Rogers v. International Paper*, p. 9.

19. Wayne E. Glenn Affidavit, September 16, 1980, *Miller v. Continental Can*, pp. 16–18.

20. Russell Hall interview.

21. Chuck Spence interview.

22. Deposition of James C. Green, October 19, 1971, *Roberts v. St. Regis Paper*, p. 7.

23. Horace Gill interview.

24. Deposition of Willis L. Gantlin, July 18, 1973, *Gantlin v. Westvaco*, pp. 132–33.

25. Trial Testimony of Willis L. Gantlin, July 17–August 15, 1974, ibid., p. 1481.

26. Trial Testimony of Willis L. Gantlin, July 17–August 15, 1974, ibid., pp. 1481–82; Plaintiff's Exhibit 9, ibid.

27. Trial Testimony of Willis L. Gantlin, July 17–August 15, 1974, ibid., pp. 1483–86, quote on p. 1486.

28. Plaintiff's Exhibit 11, ibid.

29. Trial Testimony of Willis L. Gantlin, July 17–August 15, 1974, ibid., p. 1498; Plaintiff's Exhibits 14 and 18, ibid.

30. Transcript of trial, July 17, 1980, ibid., p. 69.

31. Deposition of Charles Jenkins, June 6–7, 1973, ibid., p. 148.

32. Deposition of James Tyson, June 30, 1971, *Boles v. Union Camp*, p. 36.

33. Herbert Hill to James Tyson, March 11, 1959, Sawyer Papers, private collection held by George Sawyer.

34. James Tyson interview.

35. Complaint Form, April 2, 1963, Folder 81, Box 19, CRDP.

36. George Sawyer, "My Years With Union Camp Corporation," January 31, 1987, Sawyer Papers; George Sawyer interview.

37. George Sawyer to John P. Burke, July 25, 1959, and George Sawyer and Aaron Davis to John P. Burke, August 8, 1962, Sawyer Papers.

38. *Report of the Proceedings of the Twenty-third Convention of the International Brotherhood of Pulp, Sulphite, and Paper Mill Workers*, October 5–10, 1953, pp. 94–95; *Report of the Proceedings of the Third Constitutional Convention of the United Papermakers and Paperworkers*, September 9–14, 1963, pp. 254–55.

39. *Report of the Proceedings of the Twenty-fifth Convention of the International Brotherhood of Pulp, Sulphite, and Paper Mill Workers*, August 31–September 5, 1959, pp. 100–101.

40. Ibid., pp. 103, 104.

41. *Report of the Proceedings of the Twenty-sixth Convention of the International Brotherhood of Pulp, Sulphite, and Paper Mill Workers*, September 10–16, 1962, p. 390.

42. Trial Testimony of Lee Jewell Randle, March 20, 1972, *Rogers v. International Paper*, pp. 1201–5.

43. Ray Robinson to EEOC, September 17, 1965, and George L. Holland to Olin Mathieson, January 28, 1966, Folder 59, Box 19, CRDP.

44. Deposition of Joe L. McElroy, September 5, 1968, *Long v. Georgia Kraft*, pp. 14–15.

45. State Stallworth interview.

46. "J. F. Kimble Local 613 International Brotherhood of Pulp, Sulphite, and Paper Mill Workers' Local Program," filed as Exhibit 14, *Watkins v. Scott Paper*.

47. Trial Testimony of Elijah Watkins, January 29, 1973, *Watkins v. Scott Paper*, pp. 241, 243, 244–45.

48. Trial Testimony of Willie Brown, January 29, 1973, ibid., p. 408.

49. Sidney Gibson interview.

50. EEOC Charge of Discrimination, June 22, 1969, Folder 90, Box 17, CRDP.

51. Sidney Gibson interview.

52. State Stallworth interview.

53. Letter of Discrimination by Samuel B. Sutton, President of Local 943 et al., May 28, 1967, and "EEOC Files Suit under New Enforcement Power," May 11, 1972, Folder 16, Box 45, WSP.

54. Cobb, *Selling of the South*, p. 119; Minchin, *Hiring the Black Worker*, pp. 163–66.

55. Trial Testimony of Lee Jewell Randle, March 20, 1972, *Rogers v. International Paper*, p. 1203.

56. The activism of black local union leaders against segregated facilities is detailed in Chapter 6.

57. Jonnie L. Robinson and Hayman B. Brown to John P. Burke, June 17, 1963, Plaintiffs Exhibit 16, *Myers v. Gilman Paper*; Deposition of Elmo Myers, January 28, 1974, ibid., p. 123.

58. Quote from Minutes of Eastport Local 757 for September 11, 1963, *Roberts v. St. Regis Paper*. See also Minutes of Eastport Local 757 for March 29, 1965, ibid.

59. Minutes of Eastport Local 757 for November 2, 1966, ibid.

60. Ibid., June 19, 1968.

61. Ibid., March 29, 1965.

62. George Sawyer interview; Sidney Gibson interview.

63. Willis Gantlin interview.

64. George Sawyer interview.

65. Sidney Gibson interview.

66. Robert Hicks interview. For details about the organization of the DDJ, see Fairclough, *Race and Democracy*, pp. 342–43.

67. Hicks declared in June 1966: "The Deacons are growing. A surprising number of people aren't turning the other cheek any more. Maybe violence is the only way to awaken people's conscience, but I hope not" (Nicholas von Hoffman, "A 'Come-On,' Said Bogalusa Man," *Washington Post*, June 3, 1966, p. A4, clipping in Folder 69, Box 19, CRDP).

68. Sidney Gibson interview.

69. John Defee interview.

70. David Johnson interview.

71. Sidney Gibson interview.

72. King often expressed largely the same point as Gibson. In 1964, for example, he asked, "Of what advantage is it to the Negro to establish that he can be served in integrated restaurants or accommodated in integrated hotels, if he is bound to the kind of financial servitude which will not allow him to take a vacation or even take his wife out to dinner?" (King quoted in Charles J. Levy, "Scripto on Strike: The Race-Wage Picket Line," *Nation*, January 11, 1965, pp. 31–32, quote on p. 32). For the way that King repeatedly stressed the importance of economic issues after 1965, see Washington, ed., *Testament of Hope*, pp. 555–633, and Garrow, *Bearing the Cross*, pp. 527–624.

73. Alphonse Williams, for example, felt that job integration was much more important than the integration of facilities: "To me that wasn't a major problem. I'm not saying now that it shouldn't have been, but what was hurting us was money, we was channeled onto jobs that didn't pay nothing." Williams remembered telling the company about the damage caused by economic discrimination:

> You just don't have no idea of how much damage you have [caused] by the practice of discrimination, you don't know how much damage you have done to me and my people, here's the damage you've done . . . you kept our income at the lowest possible minimum . . . and if you can't make but a little bitty money, you can't have but a low standard of living. . . . My daddy, so to speak, he couldn't go up because you discriminated against him, therefore he couldn't

educate me, and here years later I then come along, I'm working and I've got children, I can't help them, do nothing for them because of the standard of living that I'm under, that's the way I'm denying them." (Alphonse Williams interview)

74. Gene Roberts, "CORE Maps Drive in Bogalusa, LA," *NYT*, July 5, 1965, pp. 1, 4. For a detailed account of the civil rights movement in Bogalusa, see Fairclough, *Race and Democracy*, pp. 344–80.

75. "Crown-Zellerbach in Bogalusa," March 31, 1964, Part 2, Reel 6, COREP.

76. "Summer Parish Scouting Report: Washington Parish," Spring–Summer 1964, Part 2, Reel 6, COREP.

77. Vera Rony, "Bogalusa: The Economics of Tragedy," Part 3, Series C, Reel 15, COREP.

78. Robert Hicks interview.

79. Wats Line Report, April 7, 1965, Part 2, Reel 6, COREP.

80. Washington Parish Report, July 20, 1965, Part 2, Reel 6, COREP.

81. "Additions to Bogalusa Intimidations List," March 29, 1965, Part 2, Reel 6, COREP.

82. "Summary of Incidents in Bogalusa, Louisiana," April 7–9, 1965, Part 2, Reel 6, COREP.

83. Complaint, Civil Action 66-242, *Mondy v. Crown-Zellerbach*, p. 4.

84. Steve Miller to Shirley, February 12, 1965, Part 2, Reel 6, COREP.

85. "624 Demands July 65," and Jeremiah S. Gutman to Don Slamin, July 23, 1965, Folder 69, Box 19, CRDP.

86. Jeremiah S. Gutman to Don Slaiman, July 20, 1965, Folder 69, Box 19, CRDP.

87. Bogalusa Voters' League, "Memorandum of Position on Employment at Crown-Zellerbach's Bogalusa Plants," July 15, 1965, Folder 69, Box 19, CRDP.

88. Ibid.

89. Ibid.

90. Gene Roberts, "CORE Maps Drive in Bogalusa, LA," *NYT*, July 5, 1965, p. 4.

91. Bogalusa Voters' League, "Memorandum of Position on Employment at Crown-Zellerbach's Bogalusa Plants," July 15, 1965, Folder 69, Box 19, CRDP.

92. "Armed Force Protects Negroes in Rights March Through Louisiana," *NYT*, August 19, 1967, pp. 1, 12.

93. "Louisiana March Nears Its Climax," *NYT*, August 20, 1967, p. 40.

94. "15 Whites Attack Louisiana Negroes On Rights March," *NYT*, August 16, 1967, p. 25; "Attack by Whites on March Halted," *NYT*, August 17, 1967, p. 25; "Guard to Protect Louisiana Negroes," *NYT*, August 18, 1967, p. 17; "Armed Force Protects Negroes in Rights March Through Louisiana," *NYT*, August 19, 1967, p. 1.

95. "Louisiana March Nears Its Climax," *NYT*, August 20, 1967, p. 40. For an overview of the emergence of "Black Power," see Chafe, *Unfinished Journey*, pp. 302–20; Garrow, *Bearing the Cross*, pp. 481–89, 496–97, 532–34; and Fairclough, *To Redeem the Soul*, pp. 309–31.

96. Fairclough, *Race and Democracy*, p. 413; "Rap Brown Seized on an Arms Charge by Federal Agents," *NYT*, August 19, 1967, p. 1.

97. Chafe, *Civilities and Civil Rights*; Chafe, *Unfinished Journey*, p. 165; Morris, *Origins of the Civil Rights Movement*.

Chapter Five

1. Draper, *Conflict of Interests*, p. 7.
2. Wayne E. Glenn Affidavit, September 16, 1980, *Miller v. Continental Can*, p. 18.
3. Deposition of Charles Munn Jr., March 19, 1979, *Munn v. Federal Paper Board Company*, pp. 30, 32, 34.
4. Arnold Brown interview.
5. "Employer Information Report EEO-1," December 21, 1968, Folder 34, Box 45, WSP.
6. Alphonse Williams interview.
7. Leroy Hamilton interview.
8. Thomas McGauley interview.
9. Howard Bardwell interview.
10. Thomas McGauley interview.
11. See, for example, Ervin Humes interview.
12. Leon Moore interview.
13. Deposition of Tarlton Small, February 6, 1978, *Garrett v. Weyerhauser*, pp. 11, 25.
14. Deposition of Sylvester Small, February 7, 1978, ibid., p. 25.
15. Ray Robinson to EEOC, September 17, 1965, and George L. Holland to Olin Mathieson, January 28, 1966, Folder 59, Box 19, CRDP.
16. Nathaniel Reed interview.
17. "Interviews," June 12, 1967, Folder 30, Box 45, WSP.
18. Robert Hicks interview.
19. David Johnson interview.
20. OFCC Compliance Review, December 13–16, 1966, Folder 24, Box 45, WSP, p. 21.
21. Willie Ford interview.
22. James Tyson interview.
23. Deposition of Charles Jenkins, June 6, 1973, *Gantlin v. Westvaco*, p. 151. Similar views were also expressed by many other workers. See, for example, Howard Bardwell interview.
24. Claim Form of George E. Jones, December 9, 1981, *Myers v. Gilman Paper*. Similarly, at Weyerhauser, Albert Small, who had worked at the mill since 1942, testified that some black workers wanted to move up the line of progression in the engineering department but could not because they could not transfer locals: "See, where we were, we couldn't move up unless we transferred in a different local, and they said they couldn't do it" (Deposition of Albert Small, February 7, 1978, *Garrett v. Weyerhauser*, pp. 22–23).
25. Gilman Paper Company was a classic example of the way that segregated locals controlled segregated jobs and prohibited black workers from crossing the color line. Leroy Hamilton, who wanted to work as a recovery operator, described how his supervisor refused him the job: "It was made plain to me when I was hired, and each time I asked, that this job was not available to a member of my union, the black local no. 616. . . . I was aware of this policy of dividing jobs according to race, but asked Mr. Austin about it anyway" (Claim Form of Leroy Hamilton, December 9, 1981, ibid.). Lonnie B. Mitchell similarly wrote, "I asked my Pres. why I could not get a job as crane operator, Receiving clerk or Lime Kiln operator and he told me that our local union did not cover those jobs" (Claim Form of Lonnie B. Mitchell, December 2, 1981, ibid.).

26. George Sawyer interview.

27. Horace Gill interview.

28. Ibid.

29. Alphonse Williams interview.

30. Complaint, Civil Action 66-242, *Mondy v. Crown-Zellerbach*, pp. 4–7; L. C. Dawson to 'Gentlemen', December 7, 1967, ibid.

31. James Tyson interview.

32. Deposition of Willis Gantlin, July 18, 1973, *Gantlin v. Westvaco*, p. 141; Trial Testimony of Willis Gantlin, July 17–August 15, 1972, ibid., p. 1498.

33. State Stallworth interview.

34. Howard Bardwell interview; Herman Robinson interview.

35. Nathaniel Reed interview.

36. Deposition of Harry L. Brown, June 9, 1971, *Miller v. Continental Can*, pp. 76–77.

37. Trial Testimony of Charlie Miller, August 21, 1973–September 20, 1973, ibid., p. 373.

38. Deposition of Moses K. Baker, June 10, 1971, ibid., p. 49. For similar testimony, see Trial Testimony of Moses K. Baker, August 21, 1973–September 20, 1973, ibid., p. 70.

39. Deposition of Charlie Miller, August 3, 1971, ibid., p. 15.

40. Deposition of John Basnight, February 7, 1978, *Garrett v. Weyerhauser*, pp. 36–37.

41. As John Basnight explained, workers filed a lawsuit after concluding that the grievance procedure "just couldn't get it done" (ibid., p. 13).

42. Deposition of Morris Garrett, May 17, 1977, ibid., pp. 7–37, quotation on p. 37; EEOC Charge of Discrimination of Morris Lee Garrett, January 10, 1974, ibid.

43. Deposition of William E. Gibbs, May 19, 1977, ibid., pp. 17–18.

44. Plaintiffs' Proposed Findings of Fact and Conclusions of Law, August 5, 1971, *Moody v. Albemarle Paper*, p. 1.

45. "Presented to the Albemarle Paper Company, January 11, 1966," ibid.; "Our Complaints: To the Albemarle Paper Company," n.d., Exhibit D, ibid.

46. "Our Complaints: To the Albemarle Paper Company," n.d., Exhibit D, ibid.

47. Deposition of Theodore Daniels, November 9, 1966, ibid, p. 80; Proposed Findings of Fact and Conclusions of Law, n.d., ibid, p. 12.

48. This pattern was well illustrated by the experiences of James B. Crowell, who was president of IBPSPMW Local 953, a black union at the American Can Company, which was located in the Alabama countryside near Butler. Crowell described to a GSA official in 1965 how he had repeatedly complained to the company about racial discrimination in the lines of progression. In 1965, Crowell told the company that it should change immediately "because if a complaint is filed, it won't come as a surprise" (GSA Compliance Review, November 24, 1965, Folder 11, Box 45, WSP, pp. 6–11).

49. Harvey Johnson to Elmer T. Kehrer, September 10, 1965, Folder 56, Box 19, CRDP.

50. *Report of the Proceedings of the First Convention of the United Paperworkers' International Union*, October 11–15, 1976, p. 263.

51. Ibid., p. 262.

52. Ibid., p. 265.

53. *Report of the Proceedings of the Second Constitutional Convention of the United Paperworkers' International Union,* August 25–29, 1980, p. 293.

54. John P. Burke to President and Secretary, February 21, 1963, filed as UPIU Exhibit 8B, *Boles v. Union Camp;* Jesse Whiddon interview.

55. Proposed Findings of Fact and Conclusions of Law, May 12, 1980, *Myers v. Gilman Paper,* p. 7.

56. Alphonse Williams interview.

57. Proposed Findings of Fact and Conclusions of Law, May 12, 1980, *Myers v. Gilman Paper,* pp. 22–23.

58. J. U. Blacksher to William B. Hand, September 15, 1972, and Affidavit of William Drakes, September 22, 1972, *Watkins v. Scott Paper.*

59. Proposed Findings of Fact and Conclusions of Law, May 12, 1980, *Myers v. Gilman Paper,* p. 23.

60. Wayne Glenn interview.

61. Proposed Findings of Fact and Conclusions of Law, March 12, 1980, *Myers v. Gilman Paper,* p. 22.

62. Ibid., pp. 22–23.

63. Decision of the United States Court of Appeals for the Fifth Circuit, January 28, 1972, *Long v. Georgia Kraft,* p. 5.

64. Brief in Support of Motion for Further Relief, September 24, 1970, ibid., p. 2.

65. Deposition of Johnnie Pinkard, September 5, 1968, ibid., p. 22.

66. Deposition of Linell Long, September 5, 1968, ibid., pp. 62, 63–64.

67. Plaintiffs' Memorandum in Support of Class Certification, December 1, 1980, *Gilley v. Hudson Pulp and Paper,* pp. 11–12; Testimony of George B. Williams before the Hearing on Class Certification, July 28–29, 1980, ibid., pp. 137–38.

68. Joseph P. Tonelli to Jayson McElroy, August 28, 1970, *Long v. Georgia Kraft;* Tonelli to McElroy, April 15, 1970, ibid.; Jesse W. Whiddon to R. A. Rock, September 8, 1970, ibid.

69. Memorandum of Law in Opposition, October 29, 1970, ibid., p. 6.

70. Plaintiffs' Response to Memorandum of International Unions in Opposition, November 5, 1970, ibid., p. 3.

71. Wayne E. Glenn to Glenn P. Clasen, October 25, 1967, Folder 86, Box 19, CRDP.

72. Deposition of Don B. Walker, January 13, 1972, *Roberts v. St. Regis Paper,* p. 29.

73. Deposition of Cuthbert J. Johnson, January 13, 1972, ibid., p. 10.

74. Local's Minutes quoted in the Deposition of Fred Roberts, January 13, 1972, ibid., pp. 16, 25–26, 66, 69, quote on p. 66.

75. Deposition of Elmo Myers, January 24, 1974, *Myers v. Gilman Paper,* pp. 83–87.

76. Deposition of George Jones, January 28, 1974, ibid., p. 9.

77. GSA Compliance Review, November 24, 1965, Folder 11, Box 45, WSP.

78. Horace Gill interview.

79. Alphonse Williams interview.

80. African American workers' complaints that unions failed to represent them certainly increased after separate locals had been merged. In many lawsuits, workers complained that the unwillingness of predominantly white locals to handle discrimination grievances forced them to turn to federal agencies. In *Garrett v. Weyerhauser,* for example, black plaintiffs testified that they had filed the lawsuit because the merged union refused to fight discriminatory pay rates (Deposition of John Basnight, February 7, 1978, *Garrett v. Weyerhauser,* pp. 13, 15; Deposition of Tarlton

Small, February 6, 1978, ibid., pp. 13–14. See also Deposition of Christopher Jenkins, June 6–7, 1973, *Gantlin v. Westvaco*, pp. 35–38, 43, 56, 68).

81. For an overview of black caucus activity, see Hill, "Black Labor."

82. Thomas McGauley interview.

83. Trial Testimony of Elmo Myers, December 2–5, 1974, *Myers v. Gilman Paper*, pp. 244, 273–74.

84. Ibid., p. 247.

85. "Petition," Plaintiffs' Exhibit 20, May 5, 1970, ibid.

86. Trial Testimony of Don B. Walker, December 2–5, 1974, ibid., pp. 515–16, 541.

87. "Charge of Discrimination," Plaintiffs' Exhibit 35, n.d., ibid.

88. "Plaintiff's Statement of the Testimony of Witness Henry Rembert," Exhibit C, *Watkins v. Scott Paper*; Testimony of Henry Rembert, January 31, 1973, ibid., pp. 2–3.

89. Thomas McGauley interview; Testimony of Anthony Jackson before the Non-Jury Trial, May 14–15, 1980, *Myers v. Gilman Paper*, p. 100; *Pulp, Sulphite, and Paper Mill Workers' Journal*, March–April 1949, p. 26, March–April 1950, p. 29.

Chapter Six

1. Carson et al., eds., *Eyes on the Prize*, pp. 44–60, 120–22; Washington, ed., *Testament of Hope*, pp. 99–106, 117–25, 217–20. For the importance of segregated facilities in major civil rights protests, see Chafe, *Civilities and Civil Rights*; Chafe, *Unfinished Journey*, pp. 161–76; Thornton, "Challenge and Response"; White, " 'Nixon Was the One' "; and Corley, "Quest for Racial Harmony."

2. Herman Robinson interview; Transcript of Proceedings, August 21, 1973–September 20, 1973, *Miller v. Continental Can*, pp. 1730–32; Frank Bragg interview.

3. "Crown-Zellerbach in Bogalusa," March 31, 1964, Part 2, Reel 6, COREP.

4. Robert Hicks interview.

5. State Stallworth interview.

6. "Excerpts of Testimony before the Honorable Susan H. Black," September 24, 1980, *Gilley v. Hudson Pulp and Paper*, p. 224.

7. Deposition of Joseph P. Moody, November 9, 1966, *Moody v. Albemarle Paper*, pp. 56–57.

8. Leroy Hamilton interview.

9. Ervin Humes interview.

10. Deposition of William R. Land, May 18, 1977, *Garrett v. Weyerhauser*, pp. 23–24.

11. Transcript of Class Certification Hearing, September 22–October 10, 1980, *Gilley v. Hudson Pulp and Paper*, p. 264.

12. Willie Ford interview.

13. Black worker Ervin Humes recalled that the first aid facilities at the George-town, South Carolina, mill were segregated: "Okay, in the first aid, you know when you get an injury, they had these, you know you had your chair you go to sit in for the nurse to attend you. They had our chair painted black" (Ervin Humes interview).

14. John Defee interview.

15. "Black Paperworkers: Laying Down Those Jim Crow Chains," *The Paperworker* 19, no. 2 (February 1991): 10.

16. Deposition of Linell Long, September 5, 1968, *Long v. Georgia Kraft*, pp. 29–30, 87–90; George Sawyer interview.

17. Deposition of Ulysses Banks, June 30, 1971, *Boles v. Union Camp*, pp. 40, 42.

18. Deposition of Robert Pluitt, January 21, 1975, ibid., pp. 8–9; Collis C. Jordan interview.

19. Deposition of Robert Pluitt, January 21, 1975, *Boles v. Union Camp*, p. 8.

20. Deposition of Sylvester Small, February 7, 1978, *Garrett v. Weyerhauser*, pp. 29–30.

21. Deposition of William R. Land, May 18, 1977, ibid., p. 23.

22. Deposition of Leroy Griffin, February 6, 1978, ibid., p. 26.

23. Ervin Humes interview.

24. Thomas D. Finney Jr. to William Gittens, May 10, 1967, Folder 12, Box 45, WSP.

25. M. F. Maney to E. J. McMahon, June 20, 1967, ibid.

26. "Preliminary Results of A.P.I. Equal Employment Survey," September 21, 1967, ibid.

27. Plaintiff's Post-Trial Memorandum, March 5, 1975, *White v. Carolina Paperboard*, p. 5.

28. Ed Bartlett interview.

29. Deposition of Christopher Jenkins, June 6–7, 1973, *Gantlin v. Westvaco*, pp. 26–27.

30. Thomas McGauley interview; Gerald Roberts interview; 61 LA 416–21, quote on p. 418.

31. "Charge of Discrimination," May 12, 1967, *Miller v. International Paper*, p. 2; EEOC Decision, April 11, 1968, Folder 82, Box 17, CRDP, p. 6.

32. Hearing on Class Certification, July 28–29, 1980, *Gilley v. Hudson Pulp and Paper*, p. 274.

33. In its description of the bathrooms, the EEOC noted: "Negroes were crowded into a small area with facilities inferior to those of white employees, and locker assignments were made according to race. Respondent firm went to considerable expense to isolate a small area of this almost brand-new facility with a 'locker wall' which separated Negroes from whites." With regard to the cafeteria, the report described how "the cafeteria is run on a co-op basis by only white employees and receives its operating funds from vending machines throughout Respondent's plant. Negroes eat in an area about one-third the size of the white area on the other side of a dividing wall. Furthermore, the land on which the cafeteria is constructed was donated by Respondent. The evidence clearly indicates that the discriminatory cafeteria policy has the blessings and support of Respondent Company" (EEOC Decision, May 10, 1968, Folder 82, Box 19, CRDP).

34. "Moss Point Mill," n.d., Folder 37, Box 45, WSP.

35. General Services Administration Synopsis Sheet, November 24, 1965; General Services Administration Nondiscrimination Survey of Government Contractor, July 19, 1965; and William H. Brewster to Ellsworth M. Pell, January 21, 1965, Folder 11, Box 45, WSP.

36. Fairclough, *Race and Democracy*, p. 350; Compliance Review, March 1–March 4, 1966, Folder 24, Box 45, WSP.

37. Winn I. Newman to Frankin D. Roosevelt, December 16, 1965, Folder 26, Box 45, WSP.

38. Minutes of Eastport Local 757 for November 15, 1967, *Roberts v. St. Regis*.

39. EEOC Decision, February 27, 1967, filed as Appendix B, *Moody v. Albemarle Paper*.

40. Deposition of Joseph P. Moody, November 9, 1966, ibid., pp. 44–45.

41. Larry Funk interview; Horace Gill interview.

42. Alphonse Williams interview.

43. Robert Hicks interview.

44. Leon Moore interview.

45. Bobby Radcliff interview.

46. Trial Testimony of James H. Coil, January 29, 1973, *Watkins v. Scott Paper*, pp. 1272–73.

47. James Tyson interview.

48. Alphonse Williams interview.

49. Willis Gantlin interview.

50. George Sawyer interview; Ed Bartlett interview.

51. J. R. Lientz to G. P. Clark, July 8, 1966, Folder 15, Box 46, WSP.

52. Collis C. Jordan interview.

53. Deposition of Joseph Hooker, October 25, 1977, *Garrett v. Weyerhauser*, p. 26. Other Weyerhauser workers gave similar testimony. Roster Lucas, for example, also testified that facilities had been integrated after a federal inspection: "I think the Federal Government kind of walked in a little bit, and little changes were made then. . . . [T]hey rebuilt the bathrooms a little bit. And we could go to the bathroom. All white and colored could go to the same bathroom" (Deposition of Roster Lucas, May 18, 1977, ibid., p. 13).

54. Willie Ford interview.

55. Leon Moore interview.

56. Deposition of Walter Russell Owens, October 24, 1977, *Garrett v. Weyerhauser*, pp. 37–38.

57. Deposition of Dixon D. Adams, December 13, 1972, *Suggs v. Container Corporation*, pp. 28–29.

58. Findings of Fact and Conclusions of Law, September 15, 1975, *White v. Carolina Paperboard*, p. 6.

59. Paul M. Thompson to Kenneth F. Holbert, April 27, 1967, and K. F. Adams to "All Employees of the Roanoke Rapids Division," April 24, 1967, Folder 8, Box 45, WSP.

60. John E. Bryan Jr. to F. D. Gottwald Jr. et al., May 8, 1967, ibid.

61. John F. VanDillon interview.

62. Deposition of John VanDillon, April 26, 1972, *Stevenson v. International Paper*, pp. 46–47.

63. Allen Coley interview.

64. Richard Hathaway interview.

65. EEOC Director's Findings of Fact, December 7, 1970, *Suggs v. Container Corporation*, pp. 12–13.

66. Nathaniel Reed interview.

67. International union representative John Defee recalled events in Pine Bluff clearly:

I serviced Pine Bluff, Arkansas. . . . In Pine Bluff, Arkansas, they had one of the finest cafeterias you ever saw, I mean it was really a very nice, well-run cafeteria. So the orders came down to integrate that cafeteria, and the white locals went into a spasm, you know, but the law was the law and the company abided by it. They were going to integrate that thing and they found themselves with threats and everything else, so the company then just closed down that cafeteria and the next time I was up there, these guys were sitting on the floor in front of these vending machines, eating out of these coin-operated vending machines. (John Defee interview; Transcript of Trial Testimony of Claude Adams, August 21–September 20, 1973, *Miller v. Continental Can*, pp. 1736–43.)

68. Neil Maxwell, "Same Old South: Small Towns Yielding Little to Integration Despite Federal Laws," *Wall Street Journal*, August 14, 1968, clipping in Folder 11, Box 45, WSP.

69. Union representative Wayne Glenn clearly remembers the fierce resistance of whites in Naheola to integrated facilities: "Naheola, they had separate bathrooms, separate drinking fountains, and I told them they had to integrate, had to have one cafeteria, one bathroom, you wouldn't believe what that created, yeah, I got castigated by that one pretty good too. Well I just did it, I just told them this is the way it's got to go, you can't have it separate, and I had more fights with the union people than I did the company about it. The company knew what the law was by then. Well, what happened I think, most of the whites they just quit changing clothes" (Wayne Glenn interview).

70. David Johnson interview.

71. Jack Gentry interview.

72. Mervin Taylor interview.

73. OFCC Compliance Review, December 13–16, 1966, Folder 24, Box 45, WSP, p. 15.

74. Deposition of Roster Lucas, May 18, 1977, *Garrett v. Weyerhauser*, p. 13.

75. Willie Ford interview.

Chapter Seven

1. "3 Unions, Paper Firm Enter Landmark Collective Bargaining Agreement to Increase Negro Job Opportunities," Labor Press Service, August 12, 1968, Folder 74, Box 19, CRDP.

2. EEO-1 Data, "Consolidated Report," dated 1965, Folder 34, Box 45, WSP. Northrup's "Negro in the Paper Industry" does give limited coverage to the Jackson Memorandum, but because this study was published shortly after the agreement was implemented, it does not explore the long-term impact of the agreement. See Northrup, "Negro in the Paper Industry," pp. 104–6.

3. Findings of Fact, August 18, 1976, *Miller v. Continental Can*, pp. 6, 12, 28, quotations on pp. 6, 12.

4. Decision, February 17, 1966, *Dunlap et al. v. Albemarle Paper*, copy in Folder 85, Box 17, CRDP, pp. 4–5; EEOC Decision, September 7, 1966, *Daniels et al. v. Albemarle Paper*, copy in Folder 85, Box 17, CRDP, pp. 8, 14.

5. Memorandum Opinion and Order, November 11, 1971, *Moody v. Albemarle Paper*, pp. 6–8. Paper machine jobs were grouped in a line of progression in which an employee started at seventh hand and worked his way up to sixth hand and so on until he reached the top job of machine tender. See Northrup, "Negro in the Paper Industry," p. 41.

6. "Motion and Brief on Liability Issues by the Equal Employment Opportunity Commission as Amicus Curiae," January 29, 1979, *Gantlin v. Westvaco*, pp. 1, 15.

7. "Preliminary Results of A.P.I. Equal Employment Survey," September 21, 1967, Folder 12, Box 45, WSP.

8. William B. Gittens to "Members, American Paper Institute, Inc. Industrial Relations Committee," June 15, 1967, ibid.

9. Edward C. Sylvester to Francis M. Barnes, January 10, 1966, Folder 22, Box 45, WSP.

10. Northrup, "Negro in the Paper Industry," p. 98; Inter-Office Communication from John Skov to R. R. Ferguson, March 11, 1966, Folder 29, ibid.

11. Crown-Zellerbach statement, July 30, 1965, Folder 21, ibid.

12. OFCC Compliance Review, December 13–16, 1966, Folder 24, ibid.; Northrup, "Negro in the Paper Industry," pp. 98–99.

13. OFCC-GSA Compliance Review, February 28–March 4, 1966, Folder 24, Box 45, WSP, p. 8.

14. Interviews with Revius Ortique and Pedro Mondy, February 28 and March 1, 1966, Folder 24, Box 45, WSP.

15. Synopsis of investigation, February 28–March 4, 1966, ibid.

16. George W. Dorsey to John R. Kimberly, April 17, 1968, and "Equal Employment Opportunity Joint Compliance Review of the Kimberly-Clark Company Coosa Pines, Alabama," April 24, 1968, Folder 8, Box 46, WSP.

17. Robert R. Hobson to Girard P. Clark, December 13, 1966, and Compliance Review written by J. C. O'Keefe, January 12, 1967, Folder 33, Box 45, WSP.

18. Charles Ed Clark to Union Bag-Camp Paper, March 25, 1966, Folder 15, Box 46, WSP.

19. Ed Bartlett interview.

20. Ibid.

21. Gene Heller to G. P. Clark, March 1, 1966, Folder 15, Box 46, WSP.

22. "Report on Conciliation Meeting with the EEOC at Roanoke Rapids," April 5, 1967, Folder 8, Box 45, WSP; Ed Bartlett interview.

23. EEOC Decision, May 26, 1969, Folder 86, Box 19, CRDP, p. 6.

24. EEOC Decision, April 11, 1968, Folder 82, Box 17, CRDP, pp. 2–3; Northrup, "Negro in the Paper Industry," pp. 51, 57.

25. "Commission Finds 4 Tests Given by Southern Paper Company Discriminate," January 6, 1967, Folder 11, Box 46, WSP.

26. Compliance Review by J. C. O'Keefe, January 12, 1967, Folder 33, Box 45, WSP.

27. "Moss Point Mill," n.d., Folder 37, ibid. IP executives argued: "The Company must point out that the educational deficiencies of many of its Negro employees and applicants will continue to impose serious limitations on their qualifications for skilled maintenance work. The increasingly complex mechanical work craftsmen must perform is making basic education and mechanical comprehension requirements even more necessary than they were when the test standards were first set up" ("For Discussion with Office of Federal Contract Compliance," n.d., Folder 35, ibid., p. 4).

28. 516 F. 2d 115, 116; 510 F. 2d 1347–1349.

29. Alphonse Williams interview.

30. Horace Gill interview. Other African American workers also viewed the tests as a ruse. At International Paper Company in Natchez, Mississippi, for example, Sidney Gibson remembered that all tests were graded with a pencil, asserting that this gave the company a free hand to disqualifying blacks: "We got an executive order [10925] . . . that was in 1961. . . . They were giving you IQ tests for promotions after we got that order, and they passed who they wanted to because they graded it all with a lead pencil, so they could change the answers when they get ready. . . . That was a way

of keeping you, saying, 'Well, you didn't pass the tests.'" At Natchez, only two blacks were said to have passed the tests, "and that's all we had, and the rest of us didn't qualify" (Sidney Gibson interview).

31. These points are explained in greater detail in Northrup, "Negro in the Paper Industry," pp. 40–44.

32. Findings of Fact and Conclusions of Law, February 18, 1981, *Myers v. Gilman Paper*, p. 13.

33. Findings of Fact, May 1976, *Miller v. Continental Can*, p. 10.

34. Deposition of Moses K. Baker, June 10, 1971, ibid., pp. 30–31. For similar testimony, see also Trial Testimony of Moses K. Baker, August 21–September 20, 1973, ibid., p. 70.

35. Deposition of Reedy Thomas, June 10, 1971, ibid., pp. 30–31; Trial Testimony of Ed Young, August 21–September 20, 1973, ibid., p. 328.

36. R. R. Ferguson et al. to William H. Brewster, October 18, 1965, *Hill v. Crown-Zellerbach*.

37. "Outline for R. R. Ferguson for Employee Meetings," December 3, 1965, ibid.

38. Herman Edelsberg to R. C. Nelson, December 9, 1965, ibid.

39. Kent Spriggs interview.

40. Ibid.

41. Findings of Fact and Conclusions of Law, August 23, 1973, *Watkins v. Scott Paper*, pp. 16, 20.

42. Proposed Findings of Fact and Conclusions of Law, May 12, 1980, *Myers v. Gilman Paper*, pp. 12–14.

43. At Albemarle Paper Company, for example, the international union also proposed changes to eradicate discrimination that were resisted by the company. See Proposed Findings of Fact and Conclusions of Law, n.d., *Moody v. Albemarle Paper*, p. 12.

44. William H. Brewster to Ellsworth M. Pell, January 21, 1966, Folder 11, Box 45, WSP.

45. Case Summary, Naheola Plant, Butler, Alabama, of the American Can Company, January 20, 1966, ibid.

46. The plant was located in what the OFCC itself described as "essentially a rural area, dedicated historically to farming, lumbering and pulpwood production. It is a segment of the Deep South in its total context, with a history of tenant farming and extreme social stratification as between white and non-white" (Warren F. Cunningham to Eugene Thomas, July 19, 1965, ibid., p. 1).

47. "Synopsis Sheet," November 24, 1965, Folder 11, Box 45, WSP.

48. "3 Unions, Paper Firm Enter Landmark Collective Bargaining Agreement to Increase Negro Job Opportunities," Labor Press Service, August 12, 1968, Folder 74, Box 19, CRDP. Red circling applied up to a ceiling of $3.00 an hour, causing complaints from some black workers who earned more than this. See Plaintiffs' Pre-Trial Statement of Facts, August 2, 1972, *Stevenson v. International Paper*, p. 6.

49. Deposition of John VanDillon, April 26, 1972, *Stevenson v. International Paper*, pp. 30, 31.

50. Eileen Shanahan, "International Paper Pact Ends Job Discrimination," *NYT*, August 6, 1968, clipping in Folder 35, Box 45, WSP.

51. Findings of Fact and Conclusions of Law, August 27, 1973, *Watkins v. Scott Paper*, pp. 20–21. For an excellent overview of the Crown-Zellerbach case, see Northrup, "Negro in the Paper Industry," pp. 95–104.

52. Trial remarks of Jim Youngdahl, February 7, 1972, *Rogers v. International Paper*, pp. 24, 25.

53. David Johnson interview.

54. G. S. Young to R. M. Hendricks, December 16, 1969, filed as Exhibit 7, *Gantlin v. Westvaco*; M. R. Shafer to T. Paul Keuchenius, April 3, 1970, filed as Exhibit 89, ibid.

55. "For Discussion Purposes Only," and Edward C. Sylvester to Ralph W. Kittle, May 20, 1968, Folder 35, Box 45, WSP.

56. "For Discussion with Office of Federal Contract Compliance," n.d., ibid., p. 6.

57. Jesse Whiddon interview.

58. Edward C. Sylvester to Ralph W. Kittle, May 20, 1968, Folder 35, Box 45, WSP.

59. Ward McCreedy to Ralph W. Kittle, June 28, 1968, ibid.

60. Chuck Spence interview.

61. Frank Bragg interview.

62. Ervin Humes interview.

63. Jim Gilliland interview.

64. "3 Unions, Paper Firm Enter Landmark Collective Bargaining Agreement to Increase Negro Job Opportunities," Labor Press Service, August 12, 1968, Folder 74, Box 19, CRDP.

65. Deposition of Henry J. Smith, January 24, 1972, *Roberts v. St. Regis Paper*, p. 21.

66. Joint Pretrial Document, October 24, 1972, *Suggs v. Container Corporation*, pp. 4–5.

67. Findings of Fact and Conclusions of Law, August 23, 1979, *Watkins v. Scott Paper*, p. 21.

68. Trial Testimony of Edgar Giffen, January 29, 1973, ibid., pp. 85–91.

69. "Summary of Affirmative Action," June 11, 1968, Folder 13, Box 46, WSP.

70. Northrup claimed, "Scott has moved steadily forward as a leader in minority integration in the industry" ("Negro in the Paper Industry," p. 110).

71. F. J. VanDillon to J. J. Reid, July 8, 1969, Folder 30, Box 45, WSP.

72. Bobby Radcliff interview.

73. Richard Hathaway interview.

74. Elvin King interview.

75. "Opening Statement of Defendant I. P.," February 7, 1972, *Rogers v. International Paper*, p. 30.

76. Jim Gilliland interview.

77. Eileen Shanahan, "International Paper Pact Ends Job Discrimination," *NYT*, August 6, 1968, clipping in Folder 35, Box 45, WSP.

78. Herman Robinson interview; Sidney Gibson interview; Horace Gill interview.

79. "Current Status Re-Cap of Affected Class Employees," September 1, 1972, filed as Exhibit 28, *Stevenson v. International Paper*. For an insight into the lack of movement under the Jackson Memorandum, see also Trial Testimony of Charles F. Perkins, March 30, 1973, ibid., pp. 1975–2064.

80. Transcript of Trial Testimony, September 5, 1972, ibid., pp. 739, 750.

81. Plaintiffs' Pre-Trial Statement of Facts, August 2, 1972, ibid., p. 10.

82. Horace Gill interview.

83. Trial Testimony of Roosevelt Hurst, September 5, 1972, *Stevenson v. International Paper*, pp. 1121–22, 1127.

84. Trial Testimony of Griffin Williams, September 5, 1972, ibid., p. 1676.

85. Trial Testimony of Ira Burks, September 5, 1972, ibid., p. 2074.

86. Trial Testimony of John Taylor, September 5, 1972, ibid., pp. 1558–59, 1560–61.

87. Copy of Fifth Circuit Court of Appeals Decision, July 16, 1975, ibid., p. 6521.

88. Plaintiffs' Pre-Trial Statement of Facts, August 2, 1972, ibid., pp. 5, 9.

89. Memorandum Opinion, December 10, 1973, *Rogers v. International Paper*, p. 18.

90. U.S. Court of Appeals for the Eighth Circuit Decision, January 7, 1975, ibid., p. 31.

91. Trial Testimony of Martin Mador, February 8, 1972, ibid., pp. 309–10, 376.

92. EEOC Decision, September 11, 1978, ibid., p. 19.

93. Trial Testimony of Clance Johnson, March 24, 1972, ibid., pp. 2193–94.

94. Trial Testimony of Willie Lee Johnson, March 24, 1972, ibid., pp. 2144–47, quotation on p. 2147.

95. Trial Testimony of Leonard Marshall, February 11, 1972, ibid., p. 1072; Trial Testimony of Clance Johnson, March 24, 1972, ibid., p. 2195.

96. Clifton Fair, for example, claimed that the memorandum had not been implemented where he worked: "It would have worked, but it haven't been in effect out there. Not on the Wood Yard, I'll say it like this, it hasn't been in effect on the Wood Yard" (Trial Testimony of Clifton Fair, February 10, 1972, ibid., p. 798).

97. Trial Testimony of Leonard Marshall, February 11, 1972, ibid., p. 1092.

98. Trial Testimony of Jimmie Hay, February 10, 1972, ibid., p. 865.

99. Trial Testimony of N. A. Thompson, February 9, 1972, ibid., p. 769.

100. Bobby Radcliff interview.

101. Trial Remarks of Jim Blacksher, January 29, 1973, *Watkins v. Scott Paper*, p. 231.

102. Kent Spriggs interview.

103. Trial Testimony of Percy Jones, January 29, 1973, *Watkins v. Scott Paper*, p. 923.

104. Trial Testimony of Jesse King, January 29, 1973, ibid., p. 325.

105. Trial Testimony of Horace Gill, September 5, 1972, *Stevenson v. International Paper*, pp. 471–73, 538; Chuck Spence interview.

106. Trial Testimony of Wilbert Brown, January 29, 1973, *Watkins v. Scott Paper*, p. 554; Trial Testimony of Sykes Bell, January 29, 1973, ibid., p. 643. Testimony in other cases also indicates that many blacks wanted to enter maintenance and saw these jobs as the most prized in the industry. See, for example, Deposition of John Bonner, January 24, 1975, *Boles v. Union Camp*, p. 17, and Deposition of Elmorn Hurse, January 23, 1975, ibid., p. 10.

107. Trial Testimony of John Henry White, January 29, 1973, *Watkins v. Scott Paper*, p. 305.

108. Jesse Washington to William J. O' Connor, December 21, 1978, ibid.

109. Post-Trial Memorandum for Plaintiffs, May 21, 1974, *Miller v. Continental Can*, pp. 15–20, 54, quote on p. 54.

110. Trial Testimony of Harry L. Brown, August 21–September 20, 1973, ibid., pp. 672–85, quotes on pp. 683 and 680.

111. Trial Testimony of Charles Young, August 21–September 20, 1973, ibid., pp. 245–90, quote on p. 288.

112. "Submission of Affidavit in Support of Motion to Dismiss," July 22, 1972, *Boles v. Union Camp*, pp. 21, 25–26; Deposition of Charles H. Boles, June 30, 1971, ibid., p. 4.

113. Deposition of Cassius Clinton Reddick, January 23, 1975, ibid., pp. 13–14, 15. For similar complaints from other African American Union Camp workers, see Deposition of Edward Davis, January 23, 1975, ibid., p. 14; Deposition of George Postell, January 23, 1975, ibid., p. 11; and Deposition of Elmorn Hurse, January 23, 1975, ibid., pp. 12–13.

Chapter Eight

1. Larry Funk interview.

2. Chuck Spence interview.

3. Affidavit of Wayne E. Glenn, September 16, 1980, *Miller v. Continental Can*, p. 29.

4. For the way that working-class whites often bore the costs of integration, see Bartley, *New South*, pp. 421, 466.

5. Billy Culpepper interview.

6. Joint Pre-Trial Document, October 24, 1972, *Suggs v. Container Corporation*; J. U. Blacksher to Virgil Pittman, January 8, 1975, ibid.; Robert C. Steele and Hurston Barnes to Benjamin Wyle, June 27, 1974, ibid.

7. Findings of Fact and Conclusions of Law, March 2, 1970, *Long v. Georgia Kraft*, pp. 1–3.

8. Trial transcript, January 29, 1973, *Watkins v. Scott Paper*, p. 121; Findings of Fact and Conclusions of Law, August 27, 1973, ibid., pp. 22–23.

9. Donald L. Langham interview.

10. Jack Gentry interview.

11. "Text of Telegram to Gov. McKeithen," April 16, 1965, Part 2, Reel 6, COREP.

12. "Summary of Incidents: Bogalusa, Louisiana," January 28–July 1, 1965, ibid.; Robert Hicks interview.

13. "Statement Bogalusa Voters and Civic League," May 25, 1965, and Wats Line Report, July 1, 1965, Part 2, Reel 6, COREP.

14. "Additions to Bogalusa Intimidations List," February 28–March 30, 1965, ibid.

15. "Bogalusa, Louisiana, Incident Summary: January 25–February 21, 1965," ibid.

16. Memorandum Opinion and Findings of Fact and Conclusions of Law, June 27, 1969, *Local 189 v. United States*, p. 15; Trial Testimony of Thomas Brown and Anderson Brown, May 1, 1968, ibid., pp. 94, 141–142.

17. "Memorandum of Position on Employment at Crown-Zellerbach's Bogalusa Plants," July 15, 1965, and EEOC Charge of Discrimination, January 25, 1966, Folder 69, Box 19, CRDP.

18. Joseph A. Loftus, "Step to Cut Bias May Cause Strike," *NYT*, January 31, 1968, p. 18; "White Union Is Prohibited from Striking Paper Mill," *NYT*, February 1, 1968, p. 20; G. S. Day et al. to T. I. Meehan, January 17, 1968, and David Johnson et al. to John M. Defee, January 18, 1968, filed as Exhibits 21 and 22, *Mondy v. Crown-Zellerbach*.

19. Jack Gentry interview; Northrup, "Negro in the Paper Industry," p. 101; Tom Roy Averette to Editor, January 22, 1968, "Local 189" folder, UPIUP.

20. Robert Hicks interview; Albert Walker interview; Mervin Taylor interview.

21. David Johnson interview.

22. Transcript of Class Certification Hearing, September 22–October 10, 1980, *Gilley v. Hudson Pulp and Paper*, p. 182.

23. Testimony of George B. Williams before the Hearing on Class Certification, July 28–29, 1980, ibid., p. 163.

24. Transcript of Class Certification Hearing, September 22–October 10, 1980, ibid., pp. 679–721, quotations on pp. 688, 692, 702, 714, 720.

25. Willie Ford interview.

26. Benjamin Brandon interview.

27. Bubba McCall interview.

28. Interviews with Revius Ortique and J. E. King, February 28 and March 4, 1966, Folder 24, Box 45, WSP.

29. Interview with Floyd Ruble, March 4, 1966, ibid.

30. Warren W. Bowdoin et al. to George Meany, February 24, 1956, Folder 40, Box 4, CRDP. For an example of another letter from a paper union official expressing concern about organized labor's support of civil rights, see Jack W. Gager to George Meany, February 17, 1956, ibid.

31. H. L. Mitchell, "The White Citizens Councils vs. Southern Trade Unions," March 12, 1956, Folder 42, Box 4, CRDP.

32. Minutes of Meeting, November 10, 1965, Folder 56, Box 19, CRDP.

33. Joe McCullough interview.

34. Ibid. White workers in other locations often felt the same way. See, for example, Albert Walker interview.

35. Joe McCullough interview.

36. "Union Meeting with Union Camp Corporation," October 16, 1970, Exhibit 14A, *Boles v. Union Camp*.

37. "Minutes of the union committees, after the meeting with the company, and without the presents [*sic*] of any company officials," ibid.

38. "Submission of Affidavit in Support of Motion to Dismiss," July 22, 1972, *Boles v. Union Camp*, p. 25.

39. Chuck Spence interview.

40. Ibid.

41. Arnold Brown interview.

42. Elvin King interview. Similarly, Chuck Spence remembered that a lot of the animosity at Mobile was expressed "through the grievance procedure and arbitration process" (Chuck Spence interview).

43. Plez Watson interview.

44. Billy Culpepper interview.

45. William Gardner interview.

46. Mervin Taylor interview.

47. Ervin Humes interview.

48. Frank Bragg interview. Similarly, Plez Watson felt that "[w]e never did hate them for being black, we just hated what was happening to us because the federal government come in and said you have got to do these things whether you believe its right or good, bad or indifferent, its got to be" (Plez Watson interview). Mobile worker Larry Funk believed that white workers felt that they had no choice but to accept integration, which they viewed as "something that was being done to them by the government" (Larry Funk interview).

49. Norrell, "Labor Trouble."

50. Plez Watson interview; Chuck Spence interview; Billy Culpepper interview; Norrell, "Labor Trouble," p. 263. For detailed insight into Wallace's political career, including his relationship with organized labor, see Carter, *Politics of Rage*, esp. pp. 350–51, 432.

51. Norrell, "Labor Trouble"; quote from Draper, *Conflict of Interests*, p. 164.

52. Paul Good, "Klantown, USA," *The Nation*, February 1, 1965, pp. 110–13, quote on p. 110.

53. House Committee, *Activities of Ku Klux Klan Organizations in the United States*, pp. 2415–30, 2547–49, quotation on p. 2430.

54. Jack Gentry interview. International union representative John Defee also

recalled that many white union members in Bogalusa belonged to the Klan. See John Defee interview.

55. Arnold Brown interview.

56. Donald L. Langham interview.

57. The special issue of the *Paperworker* noted, "In the 1950s and 1960s, local unions in the rural South were segregated into Negro and white, the mill facilities and job lines were strictly segregated, and some paperworkers turned to the Ku Klux Klan and other racist groups to fend off the movement of Blacks toward equal social and economic opportunity" (*The Paperworker* 19, no. 2 [February 1991]: 9, 11). Black workers themselves often claimed that many white workers belonged to the Klan. Sidney Gibson, former president of the black local at the IP mill in Natchez, Mississippi, recalled that Klan influence was great among IP's white workforce, maintaining that "seventy percent of IP employees was Ku Klux Klan, everything that wasn't black." See EEOC Charge of Discrimination of Sidney Gibson, May 18, 1968, Folder 90, Box 17, CRDP, and Sidney Gibson interview.

58. Allen Coley interview.

59. Mervin Taylor interview.

60. William Gardner interview.

61. Joe McCullough interview.

62. Plez Watson interview.

63. Chuck Spence interview; Wayne Glenn interview. Plez Watson viewed integration as "the most traumatic, terrible ordeal for the union to have to deal with. . . . It has really put us to the task and caused us to suffer black eyes when we were not guilty of any of the things that the people thought we were" (Plez Watson interview).

64. Russell Hall interview.

65. Billy Culpepper interview.

66. Ed Bartlett, the industrial relations manager at Union Camp in Savannah, remembered that when facilities at the mill were integrated, blacks faced anonymous threats, especially in restrooms, but the company was unable to catch any of the workers who made the threats. See Ed Bartlett interview.

67. White union leaders like Arnold Brown, an international union representative in the South between 1957 and 1995, were unanimous on this point. "[Paper mill jobs] were the best-paying jobs in town. Oh no, [paper mill workers] didn't give up anything" (Arnold Brown interview).

68. Elvin King interview.

69. For example, long-serving local union officer William Gardner recalled that at IP's mill in Mobile, a small number of white workers "got out of the union" because of the Jackson Memorandum (William Gardner interview).

70. Joe McCullough interview.

71. Deposition of Roster Lucas, May 18, 1977, *Garrett v. Weyerhauser*, p. 9.

72. Claim Form of Hessie Mattox, December 9, 1981, *Myers v. Gilman Paper*; Deposition of Charlie Miller, June 9, 1971, *Miller v. Continental Can*, p. 46.

73. Deposition of Woodrow Daniels, March 19, 1979, *Daniels v. Federal Paper Board*, p. 24.

74. Gilman Paper Company worker Hessie Mattox wrote on his claim form: "I worked as a helper under a crane operator and felt that since I saw the job performed on a day to day basis, as well as having been shown how to operate the crane by one of the operators, I could have done that job, if given the same opportunity and training

as was given to whites" (Claim Form of Hessie Mattox, December 3, 1981, *Myers v. Gilman Paper*; Willie Ford interview; Collis C. Jordan interview).

75. Deposition of Edward Cox, May 20, 1977, *Garrett v. Weyerhauser*, p. 18.

76. Claim Form of David L. Williams, December 9, 1981, *Myers v. Gilman Paper*.

77. Elvin King interview.

78. Ibid.

79. Pretrial Memorandum, July 16, 1971, *Moody v. Albemarle Paper*, p. 6.

80. William H. Welch to the Equal Employment Opportunity Commission, June 8, 1968, ibid.

81. Deposition of William H. Welch, May 21, 1969, ibid., pp. 18, 23, 24–26, quotation on p. 24.

82. Ibid., p. 73.

83. Court Reporter's Transcript of Proceedings, February 24, 1975, *White v. Carolina Paperboard*, pp. 24, 35.

84. For excellent discussions of Ramsay's career, see Draper, *Conflict of Interest*, pp. 122–60, and McElvaine, "Claude Ramsay."

85. Sidney Gibson interview.

86. Michael Hamilton interview.

87. Justice Department Press Release, February 8, 1974, Folder 14, Box 45, WSP.

88. For examples of support from white delegates, see *Report of the Proceedings of the Twenty-sixth Convention of the International Brotherhood of Pulp, Sulphite, and Paper Mill Workers*, September 10–16, 1962, p. 369, and *Report of the Proceedings of the Twenty-fifth Convention of the International Brotherhood of Pulp, Sulphite, and Paper Mill Workers*, August 31–September 5, 1959, p. 101.

89. David O. DuBose and P. H. Riggs to IBPSPMW Executive Board, September 27, 1971, Tyson Papers, Savannah, Ga.

90. Joe McCullough interview.

Chapter Nine

1. "Golden Anniversary Celebration, Gulf County, Florida, June 6–14, 1975," booklet held at Port St. Joe Public Library, p. 33; Zieger, *Rebuilding the Pulp and Paper Workers' Union*, pp. 142–43.

2. Hahamovitch, "Standing Idly By"; Lichtenstein, " 'Scientific Unionism' "; Wilkens, "Gender, Race, Work Culture."

3. Michael Hamilton to Lynn Agee, December 21, 1995; Ben Wyle to Wayne E. Glenn, February 2, 1988; and "Significant Legal Developments," Report to UPIU Executive Board, August 1, 1979, UPIUP (Legal Files). In 1982, a union document noted the seriousness of the union's concern over the *Winfield* case: "The Paperworkers are Defendants in *Winfield v. St. Joe Paper*. The exposure in this case is overwhelming. This racially discriminatory system is going to cost us a lot of bucks" (Kent Spriggs to Lynn Agee, November 9, 1982, ibid.).

4. Memorandum Opinion, June 25, 1979, *Winfield v. St. Joe Paper*, p. 37; Kent Spriggs interview.

5. Kent Spriggs interview. For the resistance to integration at the two locations mentioned, see Chapters 6 and 7.

6. Kent Spriggs interview; Donald L. Langham interview.

7. "Golden Anniversary Celebration, Gulf County, Florida," June 6–14, 1975, booklet held at Port St. Joe Public Library, p. 33.

8. Kent Spriggs said of Ed Ball: "I think most people would agree that in the seventies Ed Ball was the most powerful man in the state of Florida" (Kent Spriggs interview). Ball was reputed to have an intense dislike of outside interference in his business operations, especially from the federal government, and this helps explain the company's strategy of resistance throughout the lawsuit. See Arnold Brown interview and Donald L. Langham interview.

9. "Golden Anniversary Celebration, Gulf County, Florida," June 6–14, 1975, booklet held at Port St. Joe Public Library, p. 33.

10. R. C. Larry interview.

11. Attorney Kent Spriggs recalled the segregation he saw in Port St. Joe when he started to visit the town in the 1970s: "Every single black lived in one compact and configurous neighborhood, and it was 100 percent racially segregated, and the racial segregation was literally divided by railroad tracks. In the States we have a term called 'the other side of the tracks'; this was literally true here. North Port St. Joe, where all the blacks lived, is on one side of the railroad tracks, and the rest of the town, which was 100 percent white, was on the other side of the railroad tracks" (Kent Spriggs interview).

12. Ibid.

13. Donald L. Langham interview; Kent Spriggs interview; R. C. Larry interview; Cleveland Bailey interview.

14. R. C. Larry interview.

15. Cleveland Bailey interview.

16. Memorandum Opinion, June 25, 1979, *Winfield v. St. Joe Paper*, pp. 38, 42, 57.

17. Findings of Fact and Conclusions of Law, August 5, 1985, ibid., pp. 11–20, 23.

18. Transcript of Non-Jury Trial, February 14, 1984, ibid., p. 38.

19. Transcript of Non-Jury Trial, July 20, 1978, ibid., pp. 32–44.

20. Findings of Fact and Conclusions of Law, August 5, 1985, ibid., copy in UPIUP (Legal Files), p. 29; Brief of Defendant St. Joe Paper Company, December 21, 1984, *Winfield v. St. Joe Paper*, pp. 14, 48–49, 51, 70, 75.

21. Trial Testimony of M. D. Yon, December 1, 1977, *Winfield v. St. Joe Paper*, pp. 100–120; Opening Remarks of Kent Spriggs before the Non-Jury Trial, February 13, 1984, ibid., p. 24; Plaintiffs' Exhibit 3, July 26, 1954, ibid.

22. Trial Testimony of Ellis Dunning, December 2, 1977, ibid. p. 76; Affidavit of Willie James Jenkins, February 12, 1974, ibid.; Trial Testimony of Alphons Mason, December 2, 1977, ibid., p. 203.

23. Trial Testimony of Howard Garland, December 1, 1977, ibid., pp. 218, 219, 220.

24. Deposition of Alfonso Lewis, October 24, 1979, ibid., p. 15.

25. Adrian Franklin Gantt interview; Deposition of Jason Lewis, November 9, 1983, *Winfield v. St. Joe Paper*, p. 4.

26. Trial Testimony of Ellis Dunning, December 2, 1977, *Winfield v. St. Joe Paper*, pp. 77, 79.

27. Plaintiffs' Proposed Findings of Fact and Conclusions of Law, October 16, 1978, ibid., pp. 11–12.

28. R. C. Larry interview; Trial Testimony of Ellis Dunning, December 2, 1977, *Winfield v. St. Joe Paper*, pp. 78–79.

29. Robert Bryant interview.

30. Otis Walker interview.

31. Deposition of Colbert Bryant, October 25, 1979, *Winfield v. St. Joe Paper*, p. 5; Cleveland Bailey interview.

32. M. D. Yon interview; Order, August 22, 1979, *Winfield v. St. Joe Paper*, pp. 5–6.

33. Findings of Fact and Conclusions of Law, December 18, 1995, *Winfield v. St. Joe Paper*, p. 44.

34. Trial Testimony of Lawrence Martin, November 30, 1977, ibid., pp. 8–19, quotation on p. 15; Trial Testimony of M. D. Yon, December 1, 1977, ibid., pp. 121–25, quotation on p. 125.

35. Trial Testimony of Capers Allen, December 2, 1977, ibid., pp. 99–102, quotation on p. 101.

36. Findings of Fact and Conclusions of Law, December 18, 1995, ibid., p. 44; Robert Bryant interview; R. C. Larry interview.

37. Adrian Franklin Gantt interview; R. C. Larry interview.

38. Trial Testimony of Draughton Bass, November 30, 1977, *Winfield v. St. Joe Paper*, p. 52.

39. Deposition of Jason Lewis, November 9, 1983, ibid., p. 19.

40. Trial Testimony of Capers Allen, December 2, 1977, ibid., p. 101.

41. Deposition of Jason Lewis, November 9, 1983, ibid., pp. 7–8; Trial Testimony of Draughton Bass, November 30, 1977, ibid., pp. 50, 53.

42. Trial Testimony of Howard Garland, December 1, 1977, ibid., p. 201. Other African American workers gave similar testimony. John Lewis, for example, recalled, "We all wanted to be in one union, so we thought, and we joined 379. I can't recall the time, it might have been three weeks or a month or so, but they returned us our money" (Trial Testimony of John Lewis, December 2, 1977, ibid., pp. 109–10).

43. Trial Testimony of John Lewis, December 1, 1977, ibid., pp. 178, 183.

44. Trial Testimony of Howard Garland, December 1, 1977, ibid., pp. 209–10; Trial Testimony of Herman Williams, December 1, 1977, ibid., p. 249.

45. Trial Testimony of Herman Williams, December 1, 1977, ibid., pp. 251–52.

46. Trial Testimony of Howard Garland, December 1, 1977, ibid., pp. 210–11; Trial comments of Kent Spriggs, November 30, 1977, ibid., p. 221.

47. Trial Testimony of Herman Williams, December 1, 1977, ibid., pp. 248–49, 260.

48. Deposition of Alfonso Lewis, October 24, 1979, ibid., p. 42.

49. Alton Fennell, in Plaintiffs' Proposed Findings of Fact and Conclusions of Law, October 16, 1978, ibid., pp. 29–30; Trial Testimony of Thaddeus Russ, May 16, 1978, ibid., pp. 42–43.

50. Lamar Speights interview.

51. R. C. Larry interview.

52. Trial Testimony of Thaddeus Russ, May 16, 1978, *Winfield v. St. Joe Paper*, pp. 47–55, quote on p. 47.

53. "Charge of Discrimination," June 1968, ibid.

54. Willie James Jenkins, "Grievance No. 210," February 13, 1970; "Request for Adjustment of Grievance" (Local 379), April 28, 1975; and Otis Walker, "Request for Adjustment of Grievance," February 11, 1977, all in ibid.

55. EEOC Charge of Discrimination of Willie James Jenkins, July 22, 1972; Affidavit of Willie James Jenkins, February 12, 1974; Otis Walker, "Request for Adjustment of Grievance," February 11, 1977; "Request for Adjustment of Grievance" (Local 379), April 28, 1975; Willie James Jenkins, "Grievance No. 210," February 13, 1970; and C. E. Garland, "Request for Adjustment of Grievance," June 19, 1975, all in ibid.

56. Testimony of Clyde E. Garland before the Non-Jury Trial, February 16, 1984, ibid., p. 21.

57. Robert J. Williams to United States Equal Employment Commission, February 11, 1976, ibid.

58. Trial Testimony of Donald L. Langham, July 20, 1978, ibid., pp. 120–46.

59. Ibid., pp. 139–40; EEOC Charge of Discrimination of UPIU Local 379, November 24, 1975, *Winfield v. St. Joe Paper*.

60. Minutes of Local 379 Meeting, July 29, 1976, *Winfield v. St. Joe Paper*, p. 1; Kent Spriggs interview.

61. Testimony of Clyde E. Garland before the Non-Jury Trial, February 16, 1984, *Winfield v. St. Joe Paper Company*, pp. 24, 26; Testimony of James Winfield before the Non-Jury Trial, February 16, 1984, ibid., p. 121.

62. Opening Statement of Kent Spriggs before the Non-Jury Trial, February 13, 1984, ibid., pp. 17–27, 30–31, quotation on p. 27; Plaintiffs' Exhibit 4, ibid.

63. Testimony of David W. Rasmussen before the Non-Jury Trial, February 15, 1984, ibid., pp. 37, 83, 88; Plaintiffs' Exhibits 4, 5(a) and 5(b), ibid.

64. Testimony of David J. Lewis, February 17, 1984, ibid., pp. 77–80; Testimony of Thomas Sims, February 15, 1984, ibid., pp. 194–205.

65. R. C. Larry interview.

66. Testimony of Howard Garland Jr. before the Non-Jury Trial, February 14, 1984, *Winfield v. St. Joe Paper*, pp. 155–56.

67. Opening Statement of Kent Spriggs before the Non-Jury Trial, February 13, 1984, ibid., pp. 30–31; Deposition of A. D. Fennell, December 1, 1983, ibid., p. 4.

68. Testimony of Cleveland Bailey before the Non-Jury Trial, February 13, 1984, ibid., pp. 98, 100.

69. Cleveland Bailey interview.

70. Testimony of Fred L. Brown before the Non-Jury Trial, February 21, 1984, *Winfield v. St. Joe Paper*, p. 23. Several other workers claimed that blacks were treated far more harshly by supervision than whites were. See, for example, Testimony of B. T. Lowery before the Non-Jury Trial, February 20, 1984, ibid., pp. 38–45.

71. Testimony of B. T. Lowery before the Non-Jury Trial, February 20, 1984, ibid., pp. 59–60.

72. Testimony of Daniel Sims before the Non-Jury Trial, February 20, 1984, ibid., p. 16.

73. Testimony of Mark Anthony Williams before the Non-Jury Trial, February 20, 1984, ibid., pp. 169–219, quotation on p. 207; Testimony of Daniel Sims before the Non-Jury Trial, February 20, 1984, ibid., pp. 16, 22–23.

74. Testimony of Mark Anthony Williams before the Non-Jury Trial, February 20, 1984, ibid., pp. 169, 171, 178, 180, 218.

75. "Motion for Further Relief for Violation of the Consent Decree," July 31, 1992, UPIUP (Legal Files); Kent Spriggs interview; Mark Brooks to Robert Sugarman, September 29, 1989, UPIUP (Legal Files).

76. Adrian Franklin Gantt interview; Otis Walker interview.

77. Cleveland Bailey interview.

Conclusion

1. *The Paperworker* 19, no. 2 (February 1991): 9, 11.

2. Final Investigation Report, August 12, 1966, Folder 85, Box 17, CRDP, p. 4.

3. Draper, *Conflict of Interests*, p. 7.

4. Nelson, "CIO Meant One Thing," pp. 134–38.

5. Carson et al., eds., *Eyes on the Prize*, pp. 160–62; Norrell, "One Thing We Did Right," pp. 65–66.

6. For the way that the 1964 Civil Rights Act also stimulated protest by African American workers in the southern textile industry, see Minchin, "Black Activism."

7. Fairclough, "Historians and the Civil Rights Movement," pp. 388–89; Sitkoff, "Racial Militancy and Interracial Violence"; Wynn, *Afro-American and the Second World War*; Finkle, *Forum for Protest*.

8. "In the Matter of Local 208 of the Tobacco Workers International Union and Locals 176 and 177 of the Tobacco Workers International Union and Liggett and Myers Tobacco Company, Durham, North Carolina," April 8, 1966, Part 3, Series C, Reel 29, COREP, pp. 7–8.

9. Trial Testimony of Floyd B. McKissick, March 2, 1981, *Russell v. American Tobacco*, pp. 49–54.

10. As McKissick urged the local at one meeting, "[T]he big thing in the ATC is automation. He said dont stop working, you must fight hard, Pres. Griggs and the 3 Negro locals have all filed complaint before the presidents committee" (Minutes of Local 191 Meetings, May 18, 1963, May 4, 1963, July 20, 1963, *Russell v. American Tobacco*).

11. Kelley (*Race Rebels*, p. 26) notes, "Contrary to popular belief, black workers did not always resist segregated local unions. Indeed, in some instances African American workers preferred segregated locals—as long as they maintained control over their own finances and played a leading role in the larger decision-making process."

12. Nelson, "Class and Race in the Crescent City," pp. 40–45.

13. This was especially notable in the longshore industry, where separate locals helped black workers to maintain some control of the hiring process. In *United States v. International Longshoremen's Association* (1970), a case brought against segregated locals in Baltimore, several black longshoremen testified that they were opposed to the merger of their locals. See 319 F. Supp 737 at 742.

14. At Jacksonville Terminal Company in Jacksonville, Florida, for example, the U.S. Court of Appeals noted in *United States v. Jacksonville Terminal Company* (1971) that there was "no evidence" that black members of a segregated Brotherhood of Maintenance of Way Employees (BMWE) local had attempted to merge with the white local. Indeed, the black local had "recently voted against merger" with its white counterpart. The court found that separate locals existed in the railroad industry on a voluntary basis (451 F. 2d 418 at 435, 436).

15. In 1971, A. F. of M. local 274 brought a suit in an attempt to prevent the international union from implementing its March 31, 1971, order to cancel the local's charter. Local 274 was a black local chartered in 1935 that had around 500 members. A larger white union, Local 77, had over 5,000 members. The A. F. of M. had been trying to eliminate segregated locals since 1954, when it had dual unions at thirty-eight locations across the United States. In negotiating efforts conducted between 1965 and 1970, however, a majority of Local 274's membership repeatedly voted not to merge. As the court reported, the local was determined not to give up its charter: "Local 274's President Adams testified that the merger will not benefit the members of 274. He stated that the members consistently voted against merger because they would lose the prestige, reputation and goodwill in the community that over thirty years of meritorious effort have brought them. He expressed concern over the loss of control of their own affairs, the loss of their meetinghouse and the clubhouse liquor license, and opined that the reserved offices would not necessarily assure them a

meaningful voice in the control of the merged locals." Adams also claimed that the merger would destroy "black leadership," adding, "This has been the history of the black in this system. They would get so far; and then the laws of somebody would set them back again." The court, however, ruled that segregated locals were a violation of the 1964 Civil Rights Act and ordered a merger (329 F. Supp. 1226 at 1228, 1230, 1232).

16. Cecelski, *Along Freedom Road*, pp. 7–8, 10, 15; Fairclough, *Race and Democracy*, pp. 386, 446–61; Pride and Woodard, *Burden of Busing*, pp. 169–70, 192–95.

17. Arnold Brown interview.

18. Roediger, *Wages of Whiteness*; Arnesen, " 'Like Banquo's Ghost' "; "Lucy Case Splits Alabama Unions," *NYT*, February 26, 1956, p. 46.

19. CORE reports captured the mood of the lumber workers. One report noted that on the day that Title VII became effective, workers were asking: "Procedure— who do you file suit with? How long does it take? Is suit also filed with the Attorney General?" See Wats Line Report, July 2, 1965, Part 2, Reel 5, COREP.

20. Wats Line Report, July 2, 1965, July 10, 1965, July 15, 1965, Part 2, Reel 5, COREP.

21. Fairclough, *Race and Democracy*, p. 378; Sally Belfrage quoted in Carson et al., eds., *Eyes on the Prize*, p. 181. For a compelling story of another black community that mobilized after the Civil Rights Act, see Greene, *Praying for Sheetrock*.

22. Howard Bardwell interview; State Stallworth interview. For the importance of federal intervention in the tobacco industry, see Northrup, "Negro in the Tobacco Industry." On the integration of the southern textile industry, see Minchin, *Hiring the Black Worker*.

23. "Reasonable Workforce Analysis," February 17, 1998, data supplied by the UPIU's president's office (copy in author's possession).

24. Mervin Taylor interview; Chuck Spence interview.

25. *The Paperworker* 19, no. 2 (February 1991): 11.

26. Horace Crenshaw, for example, described in 1973 how the Scott Paper Company eliminated the traditionally black position he held. Consequently, Crenshaw lost all his seniority when he was forced to leave the mill and was rehired at Scott after a year's absence. See Trial Testimony of Horace Crenshaw, January 29, 1973, *Watkins v. Scott Paper*, pp. 673–74.

27. Mervin Taylor interview; Fairclough, *Race and Democracy*, p. 377.

28. Chuck Spence interview.

29. Eaton and Kriesky, "Collective Bargaining," p. 28.

30. George Sawyer interview.

BIBLIOGRAPHY

Manuscripts

Cambridge, England
  Cambridge University Library
    Congress of Racial Equality Papers (microfilm)
East Point, Georgia
  Federal Records Center, East Point, Georgia
    United States District Court Records (RG 21)
    Legal Cases listed in alphabetical order by company name:
    Joseph P. Moody et al. v. Albemarle Paper Company
      United States District Court for the Eastern District of North Carolina, 1966
    Willie White et al. v. Carolina Paperboard Company
      United States District Court for the Western District of North Carolina, 1973
    William Henry Suggs v. Container Corporation of America
      United States District Court for the Southern District of Alabama, 1972
    Charlie Miller et al. v. Continental Can Company
      United States District Court for the Southern District of Georgia, 1971
    Charles Munn, Jr. v. Federal Paper Board Company
      United States District Court for the Eastern District of North Carolina, 1978.
    Linell Long et al. v. Georgia Kraft Company
      United States District Court for the Northern District of Georgia, 1969
    Elmo V. Myers et al. v. Gilman Paper Company
      United States District Court for the Southern District of Georgia, 1972
    John D. Maddox et al. v. Gulf States Paper Corporation
      United States District Court for the Northern District of Alabama, 1969
    Edward Gilley et al. v. Hudson Pulp and Paper Company
      United States District Court for the Middle District of Florida, 1976
    James P. Miller et al. v. International Paper Company
      United States District Court for the Southern District of Mississippi, 1967
    Jesse Stevenson et al. v. International Paper Company
      United States District Court for the Southern District of Alabama, 1971
    Elijah Watkins et al. v. Scott Paper Company
      United States District Court for the Southern District of Alabama, 1971
    James Winfield et al. v. St. Joe Paper Company
      United States District Court for the Northern District of Florida, 1976
    Fred Roberts et al. v. St. Regis Paper Company
      United States District Court for the Middle District of Florida, 1970
    Charles H. Boles et al. v. Union Camp Corporation
      United States District Court for the Southern District of Georgia, 1969

Willis Gantlin et al. v. West Virginia Pulp and Paper Company [Westvaco]
    United States District Court for the District of South Carolina, 1972
Morris Garrett et al. v. Weyerhauser Corporation
    United States District Court for the Eastern District of North Carolina, 1977
Fort Worth, Texas
    Federal Records Center, Fort Worth
    United States District Court Records [RG 21]
    Robert Hicks et al. v. Crown-Zellerbach Corporation
    United States District Court for the Eastern District of Louisiana, 1966
    Anthony Hill et al. v. Crown-Zellerbach Corporation
    United States District Court for the Eastern District of Louisiana, 1967
    Pedro Mondy et al. v. Crown-Zellerbach Corporation
    United States District Court for the Eastern District of Louisiana, 1966
    Henry Lee Rogers et al. v. International Paper Company
    United States District Court for the Eastern District of Arkansas, 1971
    United States of America v. Local 189, United Papermakers and Paperworkers
    United States District Court for the Eastern District of Louisiana, 1968
Nashville, Tennessee
    Paper, Allied-Industrial, Chemical, and Energy Workers' International Union
    (PACE)
    United Paperworkers' International Union Papers
    United Papermakers and Paperworkers Papers
    International Brotherhood of Pulp, Sulphite, and Paper Mill Workers Papers
Philadelphia, Pennsylvania
    The University Archives and Records Center, University of Pennsylvania
    Wharton School's Industrial Research Unit Papers
Savannah, Georgia
    James Tyson Papers, in personal possession of James Tyson
Silver Spring, Maryland
    George Meany Memorial Archives
    AFL-CIO Civil Rights Department Papers

Author's Interviews

Gail Amonett, October 14, 1997, Moss Point, Miss.
Frank Arant, July 21, 1997, Mobile, Ala.
Cleveland Bailey, July 24, 1997, Port St. Joe, Fla.
Howard Bardwell, July 8, 1998, Moss Point, Miss.
Ed Bartlett, October 2, 1997, Savannah, Ga.
Frank Bragg, July 15, 1997, Nashville, Tenn.
Benjamin Brandon, July 15, 1997, Nashville, Tenn.
Arnold Brown, September 25, 1997, Callaghan, Va.
Robert Bryant, July 23, 1997, Port St. Joe, Fla.
Sam Bryant, July 23, 1997, Port St. Joe, Fla.
Allen Coley, October 13, 1997, Natchez, Miss.
Billy Culpepper, July 19, 1999, Mobile, Ala.
John Defee, August 11, 1997, Fort Worth, Tex.
Willie Ford, October 10, 1997, Mobile, Ala.

Larry Funk, July 21, 1997, Mobile, Ala.
Willis Gantlin, October 1, 1997, Charleston, S.C.
Adrian Franklin Gantt, July 23, 1997, Port St. Joe, Fla.
William Gardner, July 19, 1999, Mobile, Ala.
Jack Gentry, July 22, 1997, Poplarville, Miss.
Julius Gerard, October 1, 1997, Charleston, S.C.
Sidney Gibson, October 13, 1997, Natchez, Miss.
Horace Gill, July 22, 1997, Mobile, Ala.
Jim Gilliland, October 10, 1997, Mobile, Ala.
Wayne Glenn, July 18, 1997, Nashville, Tenn.
Russell Hall, August 4, 1997, Pensacola, Fla.
Leroy Hamilton, July 25, 1997, Woodbine, Ga.
Michael Hamilton, July 17, 1997, Nashville, Tenn.
Sammie J. Hatcher, October 10, 1997, Mobile, Ala.
Richard Hathaway, September 30, 1997, Georgetown, S.C.
James Hayes, July 15, 1997, Nashville, Tenn.
Robert Hicks, July 22, 1997, Bogalusa, La.
Ervin Humes, October 1, 1997, Georgetown, S.C.
David Johnson, July 22, 1997, Bogalusa, La.
Collis C. Jordan, October 4, 1997, Savannah, Ga.
Elvin King, October 14, 1997, Moss Point, Miss.
Donald L. Langham, October 10, 1997, Mobile, Ala.
R. C. Larry, July 23, 1997, Port St. Joe, Fla.
Raymond Laston, July 16, 1997, Nashville, Tenn.
John Love, July 15, 1998, St. Marys, Ga.
Bubba McCall, July 15, 1997, Nashville, Tenn.
Joe McCullough, October 3, 1997, Savannah, Ga.
Thomas McGauley, July 27, 1997, St. Marys, Ga.
Leon Moore, August 4, 1997, Mobile, Ala.
Bobby Radcliff, October 10, 1997, Satsuma, Ala.
Nathaniel Reed, July 7, 1998, Crossett, Ark.
Gerald Roberts, July 15, 1998, St. Marys, Ga.
Herman Robinson, October 14, 1997, Moss Point, Miss.
George Sawyer, October 4, 1997, Savannah, Ga.
Lamar Speights, July 23, 1997, Port St. Joe, Fla.
Chuck Spence, July 17, 1997, Nashville, Tenn.
Kent Spriggs, July 20, 1997, Tallahassee, Fla.
State Stallworth, July 8, 1998, Moss Point, Miss.
Mervin Taylor, July 20, 1999, Bogalusa, La.
James Tyson, October 3, 1997, Savannah, Ga.
John F. VanDillon, August 4, 1997, Mobile, Ala.
Albert Walker, July 20, 1999, Ocean Springs, Miss.
Otis Walker, July 24, 1997, Apalachicola, Fla.
Plez Watson, July 19, 1997, Mobile, Ala.
Jesse Whiddon, July 21, 1997, Mobile, Ala.
Alphonse Williams, July 21, 1997, Mobile, Ala.
M. D. Yon, July 24, 1997, Wewahitchka, Fla.
Boyd Young, July 18, 1997, Nashville, Tenn.

Convention Proceedings

International Brotherhood of Pulp, Sulphite, and Paper Mill Workers Convention
Proceedings
United Papermakers and Paperworkers Convention Proceedings
United Paperworkers' International Union Convention Proceedings

Government Documents

U.S. Congress. House. Committee on Un-American Activities, *Activities of Ku Klux Klan Organizations in the United States: Hearings before the Committee on Un-American Activities*, 89th Cong., 1st sess., October 19, 20, 21, 22, and 25, 1965.
——. General Subcommittee on Labor of the Committee on Education and Labor, *Bills to Promote Equal Employment Opportunities for American Workers: Hearings before the General Subcommittee on Labor of the Committee on Education and Labor*, 91st Cong., 1st and 2nd sess., 1970.
——. Special Subcommittee on Labor of the Committee on Education and Labor, *Proposed Federal Legislation to Prohibit Discrimination in Employment in Certain Cases because of Race, Religion, Color, National Origin, Ancestry, or Sex: Hearings before the Special Subcommittee on Labor of the Committee on Education and Labor*, 87th Cong., 2nd sess., 1962.
U.S. Congress, Senate. Subcommittee on Employment and Manpower of the Committee on Labor and Public Welfare, *Bills Relating to Equal Employment Opportunities: Hearings before the Subcommittee on Employment and Manpower of the Committee on Labor and Public Welfare*, 88th Cong., 1st sess., 1963.
——. Subcommittee on Labor of the Committee on Labor and Public Welfare, *Equal Employment Opportunities Enforcement Act of 1971: Hearings before the Subcommittee on Labor of the committee on Labor and Public Welfare*, 92nd Cong., 1st sess., 1971.

Newspapers/Magazines

Harper's Magazine
Nation
New York Times
The Paperworker
Washington Post

Books, Articles, and Dissertations

Anderson, Jervis. *A. Philip Randolph: A Biographical Portrait*. New York: Harcourt Brace Jovanovich, 1973.
Arnesen, Eric. " 'Like Banquo's Ghost, It Will Not Down': The Race Question and the American Railroad Brotherhoods, 1880–1920." *American Historical Review* 99, no. 5 (December 1994): 1601–33.
——. *Waterfront Workers of New Orleans: Race, Class, and Politics, 1863–1923*. New York: Oxford University Press, 1991.
Bartley, Numan V. *The New South, 1945–1980: The Story of the South's Modernization*. Baton Rouge: Louisiana State University Press, 1995.

Carlton, David L. *Mill and Town in South Carolina, 1880–1920*. Baton Rouge: Louisiana State University Press, 1982.

Carson, Clayborne, et al., eds. *The Eyes on the Prize Civil Rights Reader: Documents, Speeches, and Firsthand Accounts From the Black Freedom Struggle, 1954–1990*. New York: Penguin Books, 1991.

Carter, Dan T. *The Politics of Rage: George Wallace, the Origins of the New Conservatism, and the Transformation of American Politics*. New York: Simon and Schuster, 1995.

Cecelski, David S. *Along Freedom Road: Hyde County, North Carolina, and the Fate of Black Schools in the South*. Chapel Hill: University of North Carolina Press, 1994.

Chafe, William H. *Civilities and Civil Rights: Greensboro, North Carolina and the Black Struggle for Freedom*. New York: Oxford University Press, 1980.

——. "The End of One Struggle, the Beginning of Another." In *The Civil Rights Movement in America*, edited by Charles W. Eagles, pp. 127–48. Jackson: University Press of Mississippi, 1986.

——. *The Unfinished Journey: America Since World War II*. 3rd ed. New York: Oxford University Press, 1995.

Clark, Daniel J. *Like Night and Day: Unionization in a Southern Mill Town*. Chapel Hill: University of North Carolina Press, 1997.

Cobb, James C. *The Selling of the South: The Southern Crusade for Industrial Development, 1936–1980*. Baton Rouge: Louisiana State University Press, 1982.

Colburn, David R. *Racial Change and Community Crisis: St. Augustine, Florida, 1877–1980*. New York: Columbia University Press, 1985.

Corley, Robert G. "The Quest for Racial Harmony: Race Relations in Birmingham, Alabama, 1947–1963." Ph.D. diss., University of Virginia, 1979.

Douglas, Davison M. *Reading, Writing, and Race: The Desegregation of the Charlotte Schools*. Chapel Hill: University of North Carolina Press, 1995.

Draper, Alan. *Conflict of Interests: Organized Labor and the Civil Rights Movement in the South, 1954–1968*. Ithaca: ILR Press, 1994.

Eaton, Adrienne, and Kriesky, Jill. "Collective Bargaining in the Paper Industry: Developments Since 1979." In *Contemporary Collective Bargaining in the Private Sector*, edited by Paula Voos, pp. 25–62. Madison, Wisc.: Industrial Relations Research Association, 1994.

Fairclough, Adam. "Historians and the Civil Rights Movement." *Journal of American Studies* 24, no. 3 (December 1990): 387–98.

——. *Race and Democracy: The Civil Rights Struggle in Louisiana, 1915–1972*. Athens: University of Georgia Press, 1995.

——. *To Redeem the Soul of America: The Southern Christian Leadership Conference and Martin Luther King, Jr.* Athens: University of Georgia Press, 1987.

Fink, Gary M. *The Fulton Bag and Cotton Mills Strike of 1914–1915: Espionage, Labor Conflict, and New South Industrial Relations*. Ithaca: ILR Press, 1993.

Finkle, Lee. *Forum for Protest: The Black Press during World War II*. Rutherford, N.J.: Fairleigh Dickinson University Press, 1975.

Flamming, Douglas. *Creating the Modern South: Millhands and Managers in Dalton, Georgia, 1884–1984*. Chapel Hill: University of North Carolina Press, 1992.

Garrow, David. *Bearing the Cross: Martin Luther King, Jr., and the Southern Christian Leadership Conference*. New York: Morrow, 1986.

Goldfield, David R. *Black, White, and Southern: Race Relations and Southern Culture 1940 to the Present*. Baton Rouge: Louisiana State University Press, 1990.

Goldfield, Michael. *The Decline of Organized Labor in the United States*. Chicago: The University of Chicago Press, 1987.

Graham, Hugh Davis. *The Civil Rights Era: Origins and Development of National Policy, 1960–1972*. New York: Oxford University Press, 1990.

Greenberg, Stanley B. *Race and State in Capitalist Development: Comparative Perspectives*. New Haven: Yale University Press, 1980.

Greene, Melissa Fay. *Praying for Sheetrock: A Work of Nonfiction*. London: Secker and Warburg, 1992.

Hahamovitch, Cindy. "Standing Idly By: 'Organized' Farmworkers in South Florida during the Depression and World War II." In *Southern Labor in Transition, 1940–1995*, edited by Robert H. Zieger, pp. 15–36. Knoxville: University of Tennessee Press, 1997.

Hall, Jacquelyn Dowd. "Disorderly Women: Gender and Labor Militancy in the Appalachian South." *Journal of American History* 73 (September 1986): 354–82.

Hall, Jacquelyn Dowd, James Leloudis, Robert Korstad, Mary Murphy, Lu Ann Jones, and Christopher B. Daly. *Like a Family: The Making of a Southern Cotton Mill World*. Chapel Hill: University of North Carolina Press, 1987.

Halpern, Rick. "The CIO and the Limits of Labor-Based Civil Rights Activism: The Case of Louisiana's Sugar Workers, 1947–1966." In *Southern Labor in Transition, 1940–1995*, edited by Robert H. Zieger, pp. 86–112. Knoxville: University of Tennessee Press, 1997.

———. *Down on the Killing Floor: Black and White Workers in Chicago's Packinghouses, 1904–1954*. Urbana: University of Illinois Press, 1997.

———. "Interracial Unionism in the Southwest: Fort Worth's Packinghouse Workers, 1937–1954." In *Organized Labor in the Twentieth-Century South*, edited by Robert H. Zieger, pp. 158–82. Knoxville: University of Tennessee Press, 1991.

———. "Organised Labour, Black Workers and the Twentieth-Century South: The Emerging Revision." *Social History* 19, no. 3 (October 1994): 359–83.

Hill, Herbert. "Black Labor, the NLRB, and the Developing Law of Equal Employment Opportunity." *Labor Law Journal* (April 1975): 207–23.

———. "The Equal Employment Opportunity Commission: Twenty Years Later." *Journal of Intergroup Relations* 11, no. 4 (Winter 1983): 45–72.

Hodges, James A. "J. P. Stevens and the Union: Struggle for the South." In *Race, Class, and Community in Southern Labor History*, edited by Gary M. Fink and Merl E. Reed, pp. 53–64. Tuscaloosa: University of Alabama Press, 1994.

———. *New Deal Labor Policy and the Southern Cotton Textile Industry, 1933–1941*. Knoxville: University of Tennessee Press, 1986.

Honey, Michael K. "Labor and Civil Rights in the South: The Industrial Labor Movement and Black Workers in Memphis, 1929–1945." Ph.D. diss., Northern Illinois University, 1987.

———. "Labor, the Left, and Civil Rights in the South: Memphis during the CIO Era, 1937–1955." In *Anti-Communism: The Politics of Manipulation*, edited by Judith Joel and Gerald M. Erickson, pp. 57–85. Minneapolis: MEP Publications, 1987.

———. "Labour Leadership and Civil Rights in the South: A Case Study of the CIO in Memphis, 1935–1955." *Studies in History and Politics* 6 (1986): 97–121.

———. *Southern Labor and Black Civil Rights: Organizing Memphis Workers*. Urbana: University of Illinois Press, 1993.

Kaufman, Bruce E. "The Emergence and Growth of a Nonunion Sector in the Southern Paper Industry." In *Southern Labor in Transition, 1940–1995*, edited by Robert H. Zieger, pp. 295–329. Knoxville: University of Tennessee Press, 1997.

Kelley, Robin D. G. *Race Rebels: Culture, Politics, and the Black Working Class*. New York: The Free Press, 1994.

Korstad, Robert. "Daybreak of Freedom: Tobacco Workers and the CIO, Winston-Salem, North Carolina, 1943–1950." Ph.D. diss., University of North Carolina, 1987.

Korstad, Robert, and Nelson Lichtenstein. "Opportunities Found and Lost: Labor, Radicals, and the Early Civil Rights Movement." *Journal of American History* 75 (December 1988): 786–811.

Leiter, Jeffrey, Michael D. Schulman, and Rhonda Zingraff, eds. *Hanging by a Thread: Social Change in Southern Textiles*. Ithaca: ILR Press, 1991.

Letwin, Daniel. "Interracial Unionism, Gender, and 'Social Equality' in the Alabama Coalfields, 1878–1908." *Journal of Southern History* 61, no. 3 (August 1995): 519–54.

Lichtenstein, Alex. "'Scientific Unionism' and the 'Negro Question': Communists and the Transport Workers' Union in Miami, 1944–1949." In *Southern Labor in Transition, 1940–1995*, edited by Robert H. Zieger, pp. 58–85. Knoxville: University of Tennessee Press, 1997.

McElvaine, Robert S. "Claude Ramsay, Organized Labor, and the Civil Rights Movement in Mississippi, 1959–1966." In *Southern Workers and Their Unions, 1880–1975*, edited by Merl E. Reed, Leslie S. Hough, and Gary M. Fink, pp. 109–37. Westport, Conn.: Greenwood Press, 1981.

Minchin, Timothy J. "Black Activism, the 1964 Civil Rights Act, and the Racial Integration of the Southern Textile Industry." *Journal of Southern History* 65, no. 4 (November 1999): 809–44.

———. *Hiring the Black Worker: The Racial Integration of the Southern Textile Industry, 1960–1980*. Chapel Hill: University of North Carolina Press, 1999.

———. *What Do We Need a Union For? The TWUA in the South, 1945–1955*. Chapel Hill: University of North Carolina Press, 1997.

Morris, Aldon D. *The Origins of the Civil Rights Movement: Black Communities Organizing for Change*. New York: Free Press, 1984.

Nathan, Richard P. *Jobs and Civil Rights: The Role of the Federal Government in Promoting Equal Opportunity in Employment and Training*. Washington, D.C.: U.S. Commission on Civil Rights/Brookings Institute, 1969.

Nelson, Bruce. "'CIO Meant One Thing for the Whites and Another Thing for Us': Steelworkers and Civil Rights, 1936–1974." In *Southern Labor in Transition, 1940–1995*, edited by Robert H. Zieger, pp. 113–45. Knoxville: University of Tennessee Press, 1997.

———. "Class and Race in the Crescent City." In *The CIO's Left-Led Unions*, edited by Steven Rosswurm, pp. 19–45. New Brunswick: Rutgers University Press, 1992.

———. "Organized Labor and the Struggle for Black Equality in Mobile." *Journal of American History* 80, no. 3 (December 1993): 952–88.

———. *Workers on the Waterfront: Seamen, Longshoremen, and Unionism in the 1930s*. Urbana: University of Illinois Press, 1988.

Newby, I. A. *Plain Folk in the New South: Social Change and Cultural Persistence, 1880–1915*. Baton Rouge: Louisiana State University Press, 1989.

Norrell, Robert J. "Labor Trouble: George Wallace and Union Politics in Alabama."

In *Organized Labor in the Twentieth-Century South*, edited by Robert H. Zieger, pp. 250–72. Knoxville: University of Tennessee Press, 1991.

———. "One Thing We Did Right: Reflections on the Movement." In *New Directions in Civil Rights Studies*, edited by Armstead L. Robinson and Patricia Sullivan, pp. 65–80. Charlottesville: University Press of Virginia, 1991.

———. *Reaping the Whirlwind: The Civil Rights Movement in Tuskegee*. New York: Alfred A. Knopf, 1985.

Northrup, Herbert R. "The Negro in the Paper Industry." In *Negro Employment in Southern Industry: A Study of Racial Policies in Five Industries*, part 1, edited by Herbert R. Northrup, Richard L. Rowan, Darold T. Barnum, and John C. Howard. Philadelphia: Industrial Research Unit, Wharton School of Finance and Commerce, University of Pennsylvania, 1970.

———. "The Negro in the Tobacco Industry." In *Negro Employment in Southern Industry: A Study of Racial Policies in Five Industries*, part 3, edited by Herbert R. Northrup, Richard L. Rowan, Darold T. Barnum, John C. Howard. Philadelphia: Industrial Research Unit, Wharton School of Finance and Commerce, University of Pennsylvania, 1970.

Pride, Richard A., and Woodard, J. David. *The Burden of Busing: The Politics of Desegregation in Nashville, Tennessee*. Knoxville: University of Tennessee Press, 1985.

Roediger, David R. *The Wages of Whiteness: Race and the Making of the American Working Class*. New York: Verso, 1991.

Salmond, John A. *Gastonia 1929: The Story of the Loray Mill Strike*. Chapel Hill: University of North Carolina Press, 1995.

Shackelford, R. B. *People and Paper: A History of Scott-Mobile, 1939–1989*. Daphne, Ala.: New Providence Trading Company, 1989.

Simon, Bryant. *A Fabric of Defeat: The Politics of South Carolina Millhands in State and Nation*. Chapel Hill: University of North Carolina Press, 1998.

Sitkoff, Narvard. "Racial Militancy and Interracial Violence in the Second World War." *Journal of American History* 58, no. 3 (December 1971): 661–81.

Stein, Judith. *Running Steel, Running America: Race, Economic Policy, and the Decline of Liberalism*. Chapel Hill: University of North Carolina Press, 1998.

Thornton, Mills. "Challenge and Response in the Montgomery Bus Boycott of 1955–1956." *Alabama Review* 33 (July 1980): 163–235.

Ward, Brian, and Tony Badger, eds. *The Making of Martin Luther King and the Civil Rights Movement*. Washington Square, N.Y.: New York University Press, 1996.

Washington, James M., ed. *A Testament of Hope: The Essential Writings and Speeches of Martin Luther King, Jr.* San Francisco: Harper Collins, 1986.

White, John. " 'Nixon *Was* the One': Edgar Daniel Nixon, the MIA and the Montgomery Bus Boycott." In *The Making of Martin Luther King and the Civil Rights Movement*, edited by Brian Ward and Tony Badger, pp. 45–63. Washington Square, N.Y.: New York University Press, 1996.

Wilkens, Mark. "Gender, Race, Work Culture, and the Building of the Fire Fighters Union in Tampa, Florida, 1943–1985." In *Southern Labor in Transition, 1940–1995*, edited by Robert H. Zieger, pp. 176–204. Knoxville: University of Tennessee Press, 1997.

Williams, Juan. *Eyes on the Prize: America's Civil Rights Years, 1954–1965*. New York: Viking Penguin, 1987.

Woodward, C. Vann. *The Burden of Southern History*. Baton Rouge: Louisiana University Press, 1968.

Wright, Gavin. "Economic Consequences of the Southern Protest Movement." In *New Directions in Civil Rights Studies*, edited by Armstead L. Robinson and Patricia Sullivan, pp. 175–83. Charlottesville: University Press of Virginia, 1991.

Wynn, Neil A. *The Afro-American and the Second World War*. New York: Holmes and Meier, 1976.

Zieger, Robert H. *Rebuilding the Pulp and Paper Workers' Union, 1933–1941*. Knoxville: University of Tennessee Press, 1984.

Zieger, Robert H., ed. *Organized Labor in the Twentieth-Century South*. Knoxville: University of Tennessee Press, 1991.

———. *Southern Labor in Transition, 1940–1995*. Knoxville: University of Tennessee Press, 1997.

INDEX

local unions at, 76–77, 102; integration at, 107, 135

Crowell, James, 27, 63, 238 (n. 48)

Crown-Zellerbach Company, 14–15, 28; litigation against, 52–53, 63–64, 151; integration at, 65–66, 91, 166–67; segregated local unions at, 74, 94–97, 103, 105–6; target of civil rights demonstrations, 93–97; job testing at, 95, 142; attitudes of white workers toward integration at, 103, 136, 166–67, 170, 175, 178; segregated facilities at, 122, 128; black struggle for integrated facilities at, 130; criticized by federal agencies, 142–43, 147–48; Ku Klux Klan at, 176–77

Culpepper, Billy, 164, 174

Dallas, Ralph, 127

Danger: black exposure to, 40–41, 190–91, 202

Daniel, Theodore, 62

Daniels, Woodrow, 181

Davis, Charles, 200

Dawson, Roosevelt, 44, 57

Dawson, Rufus, 44

Deacons for Defense and Justice (DDJ), 91–92, 165–66

Defee, John, 50, 92, 242–43 (n. 67), 249–50 (n. 54)

Defense Supply Agency (DSA), 16, 121, 134

Denton, George H., 230 (n. 66)

Discrimination: in southern industry, 9–11; racial statistics and, 17–19, 140–41, 201–2, 220 (n. 42)

Drakes, William, 112

Draper, Alan, 3, 207

Dunbar, Leslie, 9

Dunning, Ellis, 190, 191

Durham, N.C., 209–10

Eaddy, John, 44

East Texas Pulp and Paper Company, 183–84

Edwards, George, 58–59

Edwards, Robert, 55

Equal Employment Opportunity Commission (EEOC), 3, 10, 17, 26; charges filed with, 49–50, 51, 54, 56, 81–82, 88, 106, 111, 118–19, 165, 166, 182, 183, 185, 198–99, 225 (n. 72); and enforcement of 1964 Civil Rights Act, 66, 69, 89, 102, 121, 127, 134, 140, 145, 158, 231 (n. 101). See also Civil Rights Act of 1964

Everett, Ferris, 59

Executive Order 10925, 80, 128, 145, 150

Executive Order 11246, 66, 142

Fair, Clifton, 247 (n. 96)

Fairclough, Adam, 64, 211, 236 (nn. 74, 95)

Farmer, James, 11, 95

Farming: background of black workers in, 38–40, 228 (n. 47)

Federal government: role in integrating the southern paper industry, 4–5, 65–71, 105–7, 121, 133–35, 153, 162, 168–69, 173, 175, 212–13, 231 (n. 99), 232 (n. 110), 242 (n. 53); limitations of federal power, 135–37, 139–40, 162, 209, 232 (n. 110); white workers' dislike of, 175–76

Federal Paper Board Company, 51, 64, 100, 181

Fennell, Alton, 197

Fields, James, 37–38

Florida: paper industry in, 185

Ford, Willie, 34, 41, 45, 133, 137, 168–69

Foreman, N. E., 68

Freedom Summer, 212. See also Student Non-Violent Co-Ordinating Committee

Fuller, Sam, 43

Funk, Larry, 129, 163

Gaillard, Alphonse, 7

Gantlin, Willis, 80–82, 90, 99, 106

Gantlin v. Westvaco, 7, 40, 141; origins of case, 64, 80–82, 106

Gantt, Adrian Franklin, 190–91, 194, 205

Gardner, William, 174, 250 (n. 69)

Garland, Clyde, 199, 200, 201

Garland, Howard, Jr., 203

Garland, Howard, Sr., 190, 195, 196

Garment industry, 117

Garner, Ernest, 230 (n. 69)

Garrett, Morris, 108

Garrett v. Weyerhauser Corporation, 18, 108–9, 177, 238 (n. 41); case summary, 54; complaints of black plaintiffs in, 55–56, 60–61, 239–40 (n. 80); testimony in, 75, 101–2, 108–9

Garrow, David, 236 (n. 95)

Gee, William G., 56, 61

General Services Administration (GSA), 69, 88, 121, 128, 134, 148, 153

Gentry, Jack, 104, 136, 167, 177

Georgetown, S.C.: International Paper Company mill in, 15, 29, 40, 46, 125–26, 135

Georgia Kraft Company, 56, 86, 112, 113, 114, 124, 165, 220 (n. 45)

Georgia-Pacific Company, 135

Gerard, Julius, 31

Gibbs, William E., 108–9

Gibson, Sidney, 33, 35, 46, 250 (n. 57); as leader of black workers, 76, 88–89, 90, 91, 92–93, 183; on job testing, 244–45 (n. 30)

Giffen, Edgar, 160, 161

Gill, Horace, 79, 115–16, 146, 156, 159

Gilley, Edward, 168

Gilley v. Hudson Pulp and Paper, 114; testimony in, 167–68

Gilliland, Jim, 20, 153, 155

Gilman Paper Company, 21, 28, 43–44, 45, 182, 220–21 (n. 56); litigation against, 53–54, 227 (n. 27); complaints of black workers at, 54–55, 57–60, 62–63, 224 (n. 46), 229 (n. 57), 250–51 (n. 74); segregated local unions at, 62–63, 89, 101, 104, 112, 119, 237 (n. 25); integration at, 67, 68; merger of local unions at, 115; and Black Association of Millworkers, 117–19; segregated facilities at, 123; violence at, 127; and seniority at, 147, 149

Glenn, Wayne, 28, 68, 78, 79, 99, 112, 164, 179, 243 (n. 69)

Gordon, Charles, 27–28, 84

Gordon, Joseph, 229 (n. 56)

Green, James C., 79

Greenberg, Jack, 52

Greenwood, Miss., 212

Grievance procedure: black efforts to use, 86, 107–9, 198–99, 238 (n. 41), 249 (n. 42); and white use of, 165, 173–74, 249 (n. 42)

Griffin, Isiah, 42

Griffin, Leroy, 39, 42, 125

Gutman, Jeremiah S., 96

Hall, Russell, 78, 179

Hamilton, Leroy, 67, 101, 123, 229 (n. 58), 237 (n. 25)

Hamilton, Michael, 51–52, 68

Hardy, James, 47

Harper's Magazine, 55

Harris, Tommie Lee, 229 (n. 57)

Hatcher, Sammie J., 39–40, 44–45

Hathaway, Richard, 154

Hay, Jimmie, 159

Heller, Gene, 144

Hicks, Robert, 63–64, 91, 94–95, 103, 122, 130, 214, 235 (n. 67)

Hicks v. Crown-Zellerbach, 63–64, 94–95

Hill, Herbert, 9, 10, 218 (n. 11), 240 (n. 81)

Hodge, La., 110

Holder, Willie, 29

Holmes, Japan, 226 (n. 7)

Hooker, Joseph, 75, 133, 231 (n. 99)

How, James, 68, 232

Howard, John, 187, 189

Hubbard, Wordie, 58

Hudson Pulp and Paper Company, 41–42, 61; litigation against, 63, 114, 230 (n. 79); segregated local unions at, 75–76, 114; segregated facilities at, 124, 127; white opposition to integration at, 167–68

Humble, Homer, 74

Humes, Ervin, 29, 40, 46, 123, 125–26, 175, 240 (n. 13)

Hurst, Roosevelt, 156–57

International Association of Machinists, 26

International Brotherhood of Electrical Workers, 26

International Brotherhood of Paper Makers (IBPM), 25

International Brotherhood of Pulp, Sul-

183–84, 200; and Jackson Memorandum, 152; opposition to integration, 164–65, 167, 168, 170–74, 179; and Ku Klux Klan activity, 176–77; loss of membership, 180. *See also* International Brotherhood of Pulp, Sulphite, and Paper Mill Workers; United Papermakers and Paperworkers; United Paperworkers' International Union
Land, William R., 124
Langham, Donald L., 47, 165, 177, 186, 200
Larry, R. C., 188, 191, 202–3
Larson, Arthur, 18
Lee, Lonnie, 222 (n. 11)
Lee, W. B., 229 (n. 59)
Leeper, Robert, 110–11
Leintz, J. R., 66, 132
Levitt, Elmer Melvin, 18
Lewis, Alfonso, 190, 197
Lewis, David J., 202
Lewis, Jason, 194–95
Lewis, John, 195, 253 (n. 42)
Liggett and Myers Company, 209–10
Lines of progression: defined, 8–9, 243 (n. 5); company officials and, 19, 20; union leaders and, 28; black workers' complaints and, 51–52, 63, 109–10, 113, 119, 128–29, 226 (n. 14), 238 (n. 48); merger of, 69, 70, 150, 162, 182, 215, 232 (n. 110); discriminatory effects of, 140–42, 189–90; white workers' views of, 163–64, 170
Litigation: importance of, 2, 3–4, 51–53, 67, 186, 197, 208, 232 (n. 109); major cases, 50–54; limitations of, 185–86, 205, 209
Long, Linell, 56
Long v. Georgia Kraft Company, 56
Longshore industry, 255 (n. 13)
Love, John, 21, 220–21 (nn. 47, 56)
Lowery, B. T., 204
Lucas, Roster, 136–37, 181, 242 (n. 53)
Lumber industry, 211, 256 (n. 19)
Lynch, Lincoln, 97

McCall, Bubba, 169
McCanless, William J., 18, 19
McCauley, Nathaniel, 44

McCullough, Joe, 171–72, 178, 180, 184
McElroy, Joe L., 86
McGauley, Thomas, 63, 101, 117, 119
McGee, L. C., 166–67
McGhee, Jake, 212
McGhee, Silas, 212
Mack, Jimmy, 200
McKeithen, John, 97
McKissick, Floyd, 210, 255 (n. 10)
McMillan, James B., 134
Maintenance jobs: black exclusion from, 12, 160–61, 163, 168–69, 209, 247 (n. 106)
Male workers: dominance of paper industry, 13, 44–45, 224 (n. 57)
Marathon Corporation, 27, 115
March on Washington (1963), 10
Marshall, Leonard, 159
Martin, Lawrence, 193
Mason, Alphons, 190
Mason, W. H., 57
Massey, Rossie, 55
Meany, George, 170
Military service, 182; role in encouraging black protest, 55–57, 90–91, 228 (n. 46); integration of, 228 (n. 38)
Miller, Charlie, 39, 108, 181
Miller v. Continental Can, 19, 78, 108, 227 (n. 25); case summary, 53
Mitchell, H. L., 171
Mitchell, Lonnie, 237 (n. 25)
Mitchell, Warren, 58
Mobile, Ala., 69, 85, 165; International Paper Company plant, 8, 18, 37, 47, 63, 75, 78, 79, 115–16, 155–58, 163, 172–73; development of paper industry in, 14, 15; Scott Paper Company plant, 17, 36, 76, 88, 101, 112, 119, 130–31, 159–61; World War II in, 29–30, 222 (n. 84); Mobile Paperboard Company plant, 34–35, 41, 45, 124, 133, 137, 168–69; Non-Partisan Voters' League, 87; and decline of paper industry, 214–15. *See also* International Paper Company; Mobile Paperboard Company; Scott Paper Company
Mobile Paperboard Company, 34–35, 39–40, 41; segregated facilities at, 124; integration of facilities at, 133, 137

Mondy, Pedro, 94, 104, 143
Montgomery Bus Boycott, 121
Moody, Joe P., 39, 123, 128–29
Moody v. Albemarle Paper Company, 39,
182–83; company's arguments in, 23;
plaintiffs' complaints in, 40–41, 57;
case summary, 53; origins of, 109–10
Moore, Leon, 35, 41, 101, 130–31, 133, 160,
161
Moore, Samuel H., 7, 60
Morris, Oscar E., 62
Moss Point, Miss.: International Paper
Company mill in, 5, 21, 33, 56, 63, 66–
67, 77, 106–7, 122, 127–28, 154–55, 174,
180, 182
Munn, Charles, 64, 100
Munn v. Federal Paper Board, 64
Myers, Elmo, 117–18
Myers, Herbert, 58
Myers, Morgan, 228 (n. 46)
Myers v. Gilman Paper Company, 43, 44;
case summary, 54, 227 (n. 27); com-
plaints of black plaintiffs in, 54–55,
57–60, 62–63, 118–19, 228 (n. 46), 229
(nn. 57, 58); court decision in, 147

Natchez, Miss.: International Paper
Company mill in, 33, 35, 76, 88–89,
91, 92, 112, 135, 145
Nation, 176
National Agricultural Workers' Union,
171
National Association for the Advance-
ment of Colored People (NAACP), 9,
10, 170, 210; assistance to black
workers, 52, 77, 106–7, 108, 198, 201;
black workers' complaints to, 82, 87–
88
NAACP Legal Defense Fund: assistance
to black workers, 52, 87–88, 106, 113,
118, 198, 201, 226 (n. 16), 227 (n. 20)
National Labor Relations Board
(NLRB), 26
Neal, John B., 59
Neal, Tony, 62
Negro American Labor Council, 10
Nelson, Bruce, 210, 222 (n. 84)
Newberry, Frank, 129
New York Times, 10, 96, 97, 150

Nonviolence: questioned by black paperworkers, 91–92, 97
Northrup, Herbert, 65, 102–3, 154, 232
(n. 110), 243 (n. 2)

Office of Federal Contract Compliance
(OFCC), 4, 53, 103, 136, 162, 170; black
workers' complaints to, 64, 88; and
enforcement of nondiscrimination,
68–69, 232 (n. 110); negotiates Jackson Memorandum, 139, 151–52; crit-
icisms of paper companies, 141–44,
147–48, 149
Oil, Chemical, and Atomic Workers' International Union, 26
Olin-Mathieson Paper Company:
EEOC charges at, 63, 69, 85–86, 102;
segregated facilities at, 127, 241 (n. 33)
Owens, Walter Russell, 18, 133–34, 232
(n. 110)

Palatka, Fla., 41, 61, 63, 127, 167
Panama City, Fla., 73
Paper, Allied-Industrial, Chemical, and
Energy Workers' International Union
(PACE), 15, 16, 17, 27, 79, 81, 86; cre-
ation of, 26
Paperworker, The, 177, 207, 250 (n. 57)
Parish, Leotis L., 224
Paul, Maurice, 189
Perkins, Charles F., 246 (n. 79)
Peters, Otha, 96
Pine Bluff, Ark.: International Paper
Company mill in, 18, 19, 26, 35, 43, 47,
78, 85, 89, 112, 135, 158–59, 242–43
(n. 67)
Pinkard, Johnnie, 113
Pluitt, Robert, 125
Plymouth, N.C.: Weyerhauser Corpora-
tion mill in, 1, 7, 18, 21–22, 42, 54, 75,
124, 133, 136; school integration in, 211
Pope, Henry, 230 (n. 69)
Port St. Joe, Fla., 3, 74, 185–205 passim;
economic structure of, 185–87; segre-
gation in, 187–88, 196, 205, 252 (n. 11)
Port Wentworth, Ga.: Continental Can
mill in, 19, 23, 35, 38, 39, 45–46, 51, 79,
85, 108, 140, 147, 161, 181
Postell, George, 62

complaints about, 84; white workers complain to, 173–74

United Paperworkers of America (UPA), 25

United Paperworkers International Union (UPIU), 5, 13, 22, 28, 177; creation of, 26; impact of Civil Rights Act on, 50, 54, 69–70, 185, 200, 226 (n. 16), 232 (n. 115); black members complain to, 110–11; white members complain to, 173–74

United States v. Local 189, 14–15, 207; case summary, 52–53; impact of ruling, 70, 139, 149, 150–51, 170; testimony in, 166–67

VanDillon, John F., 18, 20, 25, 134–35, 150, 154

Vietnam War, 90

Violence: incidents of, 91, 127, 144, 167, 180; company fears of, 127–28, 144, 149

Walker, Don, 70, 115, 118

Walker, Luther, 43

Walker, Otis, 192, 198, 205

Walker, W. D., 103

Wallace, George, 175–76, 249 (n. 50)

Waters, Marvin, 21, 22

Watkins v. Scott Paper Company, 17, 30, 131, 148, 153–54; case summary, 160; testimony in, 160–61, 229 (n. 56)

Watson, I., 57

Watson, Plez, 37, 174, 176, 249 (n. 48), 250 (n. 63)

Welch, William H., 182–83

West Monroe, La., 63, 69, 127

West Virginia Pulp and Paper Company (Westvaco), 7, 17–18, 31, 42, 50, 225 (n. 70); black workers' complaints against, 57, 59, 64, 229 (n. 59); segregated local unions at, 76, 80–82, 104, 106; litigation against, 106; employee club at, 131–32; EEOC findings at, 141; changes in seniority at, 151

Weyerhauser Corporation, 14: black employment at before 1964, 1, 18, 34, 36, 37, 38–39, 42; litigation against, 54,

55–56, 108–9; complaints of black workers at, 55–56, 61, 63; impact of 1964 Civil Rights Act on, 68, 133–34, 231 (n. 99); segregated local unions at, 75, 102, 237 (n. 24); segregated facilities at, 124, 125; integration of facilities at, 133–34, 242 (n. 53); reaction of white workers to integration at, 136–37, 177, 181; Ku Klux Klan at, 177

Wharton School (University of Pennsylvania), 65, 102–3, 154

Whiddon, Jesse, 152

White, Carl, 214

White, John Henry, 161

White v. Carolina Paperboard, 183

White workers, 42, 248 (n. 4); boycotts of integrated facilities, 129–33, 135–37; views on integration, 4, 47, 66–67, 85, 101, 163–84 passim, 249 (n. 48), 250 (nn. 67, 68); support for black workers, 180–84

Wilkins, Roy, 10, 77, 218–19 (n. 13), 219 (n. 16)

Williams, Alphonse, 8–9, 37, 63, 100, 105, 116–17, 129–30, 131, 146, 235–36 (n. 73)

Williams, Booker T., 43

Williams, Cleve, 231 (n. 101)

Williams, David L., 45, 182

Williams, George B., 61, 63, 114, 230 (n. 79)

Williams, Griffin, 30, 157

Williams, Herman, 196–97

Williams, Mark Anthony, 204–5

Wilson, Calvin P., 60

Wilson, Robert, 194–95

Winfield, James, 200

Winfield v. St. Joe Paper, 148, 185–205 passim; case summary, 185; testimony in, 189–205; origins of case, 197–201; settlement of, 205

Wirtz, Willard, 139

Women workers: lack of in paper industry, 13, 44, 149, 224 (n. 57); efforts to increase numbers of, 61, 89, 96–97, 149, 224 (n. 57)

Woods, Warren, 50

World War II: impact on southern paper industry, 28–30, 222 (n. 83); role in encouraging black protest, 55–57, 83, 90–91, 209, 228 (n. 33)

Wright, Gail, 82

Wyle, Ben, 185, 226 (n. 16)

Yates, Bill, 166

Yon, M. D., 189, 192, 193

Young, A. Z., 94; leads Bogalusa march, 97–98

Young, Boyd, 5, 11–12, 183–84

Young, Charles, 162

Youngdahl, Jim, 151

Zieger, Robert, 75, 217 (n. 5)